James G. Williams

Girardians

AF628496

Beiträge zur mimetischen Theorie

Religion – Gewalt – Kommunikation – Weltordnung

herausgegeben von

Herwig Büchele (Universität Innsbruck),
Stanisław Budzik (Tarnow/Polen),
Bernhard Dieckmann (Katholisch-Theologisches Seminar Marburg),
Wilhelm Guggenberger (Universität Innsbruck),
Michael Kirwan (University of London),
Erich Kitzmüller (Graz),
Gerhard Larcher (Universität Graz),
Ralf Miggelbrink (Universität Essen),
Józef Niewiadomski (Universität Innsbruck),
Eckhard Nordhofen (Frankfurt),
Wolfgang Palaver (Universität Innsbruck),
Raymund Schwager † (Universität Innsbruck),
Roman Siebenrock (Universität Innsbruck),
João J. Vila-Chã (Universidade Católica Portuguesa)

Band 32

LIT

James G. Williams

Girardians

The Colloquium
on Violence and Religion,
1990 – 2010

LIT

The printing of the book was supported by:
Colloquium on Violence & Religion
Imitatio

IMITATIO

Bibliographic information published by the Deutsche Nationalbibliothek
The Deutsche Nationalbibliothek lists this publication in the Deutsche Nationalbibliografie; detailed bibliographic data are available in the Internet at http://dnb.d-nb.de.

ISBN 978-3-643-90281-8

A catalogue record for this book is available from the British Library

©LIT VERLAG GmbH & Co. KG Wien,
Zweigniederlassung Zürich 2012
Klosbachstr. 107
CH-8032 Zürich
Tel. +41 (0) 44-251 75 05
Fax +41 (0) 44-251 75 06
e-Mail: zuerich@lit-verlag.ch
http://www.lit-verlag.ch

LIT VERLAG Dr. W. Hopf
Berlin 2012
Fresnostr. 2
D-48159 Münster
Tel. +49 (0) 2 51-620 320
Fax +49 (0) 2 51-23 19 72
e-Mail: lit@lit-verlag.de
http://www.lit-verlag.de

Distribution:
In Germany: LIT Verlag Fresnostr. 2, D-48159 Münster
Tel. +49 (0) 2 51-620 32 22, Fax +49 (0) 2 51-922 60 99, e-mail: vertrieb@lit-verlag.de

In Austria: Medienlogistik Pichler-ÖBZ, e-mail: mlo@medien-logistik.at

In Switzerland: B + M Buch- und Medienvertrieb, e-mail: order@buch-medien.ch

In the UK: Global Book Marketing, e-mail: mo@centralbooks.com

In North America: International Specialized Book Services, e-mail: orders@isbs.com

Contents

Acknowledgments

This book is both an expression of gratitude and, I hope, a contribution to the ongoing work of the Colloquium on Violence and Religion and to any future readers and scholars who wish to know more or write about René Girard and the mimetic theory. It is an expression of gratitude to Girard and his work and to many colleagues in the Colloquium who have been my friends and teachers in so many facets and ramifications of Girard's mimetic theory. It is intended as a contribution in bringing together a historical overview of a twenty year period in which the reader may find a view of an intellectual and spiritual phenomenon centered in the work and humble, brilliant charisma of one of the greatest thinkers of the twentieth century, a view that might otherwise be lost in time, scattered sources, and the passing of various aging persons who are important in the total picture.

For encouragement and financial support I am grateful to the Board of Directors of the Colloquium on Violence and Religion and to Imitatio, a branch of the philanthropic enterprises of Peter Thiel that is devoted to furthering the mimetic theory in various avenues of research and publication.

I would like to dedicate this book both to René and Martha Girard and to my beloved wife Yvonne and our children, grandchildren, and great-grandchildren: Katherine, Michael, and Shanah Gail; Shanah Lynn, Michael, Jr., Alia, †Kadeem, and Nyasa; Amber, Jacob, Gabrielle, Tiara, and Terrence.

Preface

In presenting this book, I put before you, the reader, a history of which I am and have been a part. For me it is a great privilege to write this account and to participate in it even as I write. It is a great privilege because the person and work of René Girard is so powerful and inspiring, and scarcely less so are the personalities, work, and general ambiance of so many friends and colleagues in the Colloquium on Violence and Religion (COV&R). COV&R was started at Stanford University in 1990 by a small group of scholars who were seriously engaged with Girard's thought and wanted to do research, hold discussions, and perpetuate the insights of his mimetic theory in a more organized way. There will be more on this in chapters 1 and 2. I had a major role in those beginnings and its early development, so I am not a disinterested historian. That does not mean that all "objectivity" is lacking in the history related here. Within a certain frame of reference, which is sketched out in what follows, I have attempted to be fair and judicious, which entails avoiding ad hominem discourse without overlooking problems and flaws in some events, procedures, and policies. Yet my final goal has been to show how great are both the mimetic theory and the person who brought it to the light of day and how valuable are both the work and the friendships and collegial relations that the formation of COV&R has produced.

Concerning René Girard the man, the question that loomed larger and larger in my mind as I advanced in this project was not only how to present the sweep of his thinking about human origins, the human condition, human relations, and the biblical witness to revelation, but also how to honor him in an appropriate manner without engaging in inappropriate adulation.

Girard is eighty-seven years old at this writing. Although in good health for his age, he is no longer able to participate in intellectual endeavors with the vigor and acuteness of mind he displayed in earlier years. Therefore, we Girardians are in the process of coming to grips with his passing from the scene. One of the goals of this account is to contribute to preserving his legacy, so that the present and future generations will have an instructive source on the man and his work—a source of fact, of inspiration, and of renewal. Indeed, though this book is a history of COV&R in form and content, I have intended it simultaneously as a primer on Girard's mimetic theory and its ramifications, not only as he has presented them, but as they extend out into the world through his friends and colleagues, who gather about him in this fellowship and whose common desire is to know and express the truth of the human condition.

The telling of the story and the organization of material in this history is basically chronological. I made the decision at the very start to proceed year by year, with occasional doubling back to the past or anticipating the future from a given standpoint in this history.

A guiding principle has been to focus on what is centrally important for understanding the mimetic theory and the identity of COV&R. It was thus necessary to keep in my mind and before the reader two subjects, which are obviously interrelated: the theme and content of the respective annual meetings and the many persons who have made COV&R real in the world. Regarding the annual meetings, I decided at the very beginning of this project that an overview of each and every annual conference would have to be given. The annual meetings are absolutely necessary for the ongoing life of an organization like the Colloquium. As for other events and matters of interest (for example, some items of business, whether from the advisory board or the annual business meeting; semiannual meetings with the American Academy of Religion; publishing projects; related organizations), they have been included as I have had personal knowledge or informants or as I have been able to find printed or Internet sources. Although sometimes an arduous process, the whole project has been for me a wonderful review, resulting in new information and new insights along the way.

In order to ferret out and highlight central elements of the discussions in the annual conferences, I have begun with the theme of each symposium and examined the keynote and other important presentations related to the theme. As the membership and attendance increased through the years, these presentations keyed to the theme became plenary sessions. My own notes and recollections were sometimes helpful, but it was necessary to resort to various sources. Interviews of a number of colleagues were very important, but I also took advantage of written sources such as the *Bulletin of COV&R*, papers published in our journal *Contagion*, and annual conference websites (not always still available).[1] I have also made use of online videos in recent years, and papers and other kinds of information that colleagues have kindly sent to me. I have had to make decisions as to which of these to include in the history, because if I wrote about all of them it would make the book much too long.

As for papers given in parallel sessions or workshops, it has simply been necessary to pick out a few that in my view were particularly significant. I realize that there have been many excellent shorter papers in the parallel sessions, but it would have been impossible to review and report on a significant number of them.

What colleagues have written and said is the second subject that must be elucidated in order to describe COV&R's identity. The consequence of this attention to what colleagues have written and said is that this book is really, to define it precisely, a history of the mimetic theory as construed and represented through COV&R and through the very existence of COV&R itself. It is not just that we think and talk and write about a certain subject; at the heart of those activities is the need not simply of a professional organization, but more profoundly of an intellectual and spiritual fellowship. The work and personal charisma of René Girard is the necessary condition of this fellowship, this association of friends and sympathizers, but the sufficient condition as we proceed into the future is the continual cultivation and elaboration of the mimetic theory, with all its ramifications.

What COV&R is and is about could not be stated without taking into account certain personalities, especially those in the period of beginnings. Therefore, in chapters 1 and 2 René Girard and Raymund Schwager loom large and are of crucial importance. There will be much to tell about Schwager, especially in the second chapter. The three founders, Robert Hamerton-Kelly, Charles Mabee, and I, had a significant role. Among other virtues that are manifest in Hamerton-Kelly and Mabee as persons and scholars, two of the most prominent are the cardinal virtue of courage and the theological virtue of hope. They were ready to imagine and do a new thing that they envisioned as worthy of their efforts. As for me, I will appear often enough in this story as an agent apart from my role as narrator. The reader will therefore learn something about me, for good or for ill, in the course of the narration.

For special recognition, I have selected sixteen persons who have made a distinguished contribution to COV&R. In some instances they have been steady at the helm for the better part of the Colloquium's history, or in other cases for the entire period. Still others have had a well-nigh indispensable role during critical periods of the organization's history. At the end of chapters 1 through 5 I have included a brief biographical summary of the work and contribution of these notable colleagues. They are Ann Astell, Gil Bailie, Cesáreo Bandera, Diana Culbertson, Robert Daly, Sandor Goodhart, Robert Hamerton-Kelly, William Johnsen, Charles Mabee, Andrew McKenna, Józef Niewiadomski, Wolfgang Palaver, Martha Reineke, Raymund Schwager, Julia Shinnick, and Theophus Smith. There is, of course, so much about Girard himself in the narrative that there was no need to add a separate biographical note.

As intimated in the opening paragraph, in the course of this account I have not hesitated to give my own evaluations of the Colloquium as an organization and a scholarly enterprise, and sometimes I propose a diagnosis and corrective course. The brief concluding chapter is entirely devoted to this sort of evaluation and proposal for the future. These sections of the book are offered for whatever they may be worth in the years to come. I recognize that readers may disagree at points or discern questions and issues that I have not seen or have neglected. But in any event, here is a manual that can serve as a point of departure for consideration and discussion.

CHAPTER ONE

In the Beginning

April in Strasbourg

It was a beautiful day in April 1985, in Strasbourg. I was there for a few weeks during an academic leave to give a couple of lectures to the theological faculties of the University of Strasbourg and to visit friends both there and across the Rhine River in Germany. This was my third visit to Strasbourg, so I had already become familiar with the city and the region of Alsace. In 1974–1975 my family and I lived there for almost a year while I taught in Syracuse University's international studies program in Strasbourg. I had also returned on my own in the early months of 1980 to do research for a book and to revitalize my French.

On that sunny day in April I was in a bookshop browsing when my eyes fell upon a book that caught my attention. It was *La violence et le sacré* (Violence and the Sacred) by René Girard. I don't recall whether up until a day or two before I had ever heard of Girard. But that changed in a brief conversation after I presented a lecture to the biblical professors of the Catholic and Protestant theological faculties. The topic of my lecture was patterns in the narratives of enemy brothers in the book of Genesis (Cain and Abel, Jacob and Esau, Joseph and his brothers; also Isaac and Ishmael to some extent). This was a subject well known to biblical scholars, theologians, and many others. What had received little or no attention, as far as I could learn, was the relation of these narrative texts to certain legal passages concerning the offering of sacrifice, that is, the mandates to offer to God not only first fruits of the field and firstlings of the cattle and flocks, but also the firstborn sons. There are many passages that are quite clear about this. According to Numbers 3:40–51 the firstborn sons may each be ransomed by a Levite who is given over to duty to the Lord, and when the number of Levites is exceeded, then each son is ransomed by a money offering. One statute in the book of Exodus is absolute, making no provision for ransoming the first born: "You shall give me the first-born of your sons" (Exodus 22:28). I construed the text as really saying what it appeared to say: you shall slay the first born of your sons to offer as sacrifices to the God of Israel.

Now in the stories of the brothers in Genesis the younger brother always prevails over the older. The exception to this was Cain and Abel; in that account Cain, the older, murders Abel precisely because the offering of Abel, the younger, was acceptable to the Lord and Cain's was not. A curse is laid upon Cain, who becomes the builder of the first city. Otherwise, the pattern holds, and my studies led me to the conclusion that the younger or earlier displacing the older was a structural factor in other biblical accounts beyond the brother stories. My question at the end of that lecture to my Strasbourg colleagues was this: Is there any connection of thought or worldview between the enemy brother accounts in which the older son loses and is superseded by the younger son and the sacrificial codes and commands where the firstborn son is to be offered to the God of Israel? My sense was that I had hit upon something important, but I confessed openly that I did not know how to proceed further.

In a private conversation after the lecture one of the Catholic scholars, Raymond Kuntzmann, told me, "You should read René Girard." Kuntzmann had drawn upon Girard's work, including *Violence and the Sacred,* for the research that earned him the State Doctorate in France and was published under the title *Le symbolisme des jumeaux au Proche Orient ancien* (The Symbolism of Twins in the Ancient Near East).

I had not gone into the bookstore with the intention of finding *La violence et le sacré* or any book by Girard, although what Kuntzmann told me was certainly fresh in my mind. So coming so quickly upon one of his books struck me as good luck, or even as providential. I felt it was something meant to be. I began reading it immediately and had completed three or four chapters before returning home from France. I found it engrossing and believed that I understood it well. However, my impression was that he favored ritual sacrifice, at least of animal victims. Eventually I learned that I was not the first reader to understand his position that way. It was only later, when I read further in the English translation that I found out that he radically criticized sacrifice. Actually, I was partly correct in my first impression, for since the time of forming his full theory of religion and culture Girard has always held that the sacrifice of one victim is preferable to the chaos that prevails without sacrificial ritual. Sacrifice, in his thought, is rooted in the primordial, unreflective attempts of the emerging human race to control the chaos of violence.[1] The sacrifice of victims and the origins of human culture go together, hand in glove. To explicate this fundamental point in Girard, as well to indicate how most of us who launched the new scholarly society understood the mimetic theory, an overview of Girard's work and thought in the formative period of his distinctive research will be sketched later in this chapter.

By Way of the Jesus Seminar and BINAC

Back home, the adventure continued. I continued to read *Violence and the Sacred*, and in the next year or so I went on to other books Girard had written, most notably *Things Hidden since the Foundation of the World* and *The Scapegoat*. Girard's work, his anthropology of religion and culture, began slowly to enter into my own thinking and my approach to teaching graduate and undergraduate courses, as well as my research and writing and my perspective on human relations. In my search for intellectual and religious meaning I had gone through a structural phase in the 1970s, but I found it to be a dead end as a source of meaning beyond a kind of intellectual play. I had then turned to a literary approach involving a close reading of texts and viewing texts and narratives as worlds of language in their own right, without reference to actual events outside the text. During this phase I wrote a book stemming from this literary approach: *Those Who Ponder Proverbs: Aphoristic Thinking and Biblical Literature* (1981). A second book was literary, but in it I was beginning to move in a more theological direction: *Women Recounted: Narrative Thinking and the God of Israel* (1982). In a third book I combined literary concerns with a much a greater appreciation of historical meaning: *Gospel Against Parable: Mark's Language of Mystery* (1985). About the time this last book was published I spent three weeks in Strasbourg and made the presentation on enemy brothers and the sacrifice of the first born to the Strasbourg biblical faculties, as recounted at the beginning of this chapter.

Later that year, in the fall of 1985, I became a member of the Jesus Seminar. Robert Funk, who was an outstanding New Testament scholar, an academic entrepreneur, and a person known for his outbursts of temper, founded the Jesus Seminar. I was invited to join on the recommendation of Leo Perdue. Perdue, who eventually became the dean of Brite Divinity School at Texas

Christian University, was an Old Testament scholar specializing in biblical wisdom literature. He suggested my name because he liked my book, *Those Who Ponder Proverbs,* which included the parables and sayings of Jesus in its scope.

The project of the Jesus Seminar was to "come clean," from Funk's point of view, about Jesus and early Christianity. The purpose that drove the seminar, which met twice a year, was to disclose to the public what biblical scholars who were trained in the various forms of historical and literary criticism had been thinking and saying for years. To that end the fellows of the seminar discussed and voted on the sayings of Jesus as recorded in the canonical Gospels and in the noncanonical sources. (Narrative material in the Gospels and post–New Testament sources were taken up in later years.) Votes were held, with colored tokens, at the end of the presentations and discussions of the various parables and other saying materials. There were four categories: Jesus probably said this or something like it (red); he possibly said it (pink); it's unlikely he said it (gray); it's certain that he did not say it (black). A lot of the sayings were "blackballed"!

It dawned on me almost from the beginning that Funk's deep-seated motivation—and inner rage, it seemed to me—was directed against fundamentalist Christianity, and indeed, he wished to undercut any form of Christian orthodoxy, fundamentalist or not. That came home to me in a painful way at the second meeting of the seminar I attended, at the University of Redlands in California in March 1986. I was on the program with a paper in which I argued that even parables and other sayings of Jesus that the early tradition had supplemented or revised were valuable in their own right and should not be discounted or viewed as "inauthentic." There is authenticity in the Jesus tradition as represented in the Gospels even if we do not have the exact words of Jesus.[2] There is, as Girard has said, a certain intelligence, an inspired understanding, that shines through the Gospels, and the source of that is Jesus himself.

When I arrived in Redlands I found that Funk had pulled me from the program without informing me. And the reason soon became clear. He did not want me to have any kind of spotlight because there were reporters and writers there from various newspapers, and at least one journalist from a national magazine and one television reporter from a public broadcasting station in Los Angeles. The latter two interviewed me. Although I was not permitted to present my paper, Funk's intention to divert attention from me was partially foiled, as the papers had already circulated prior to the meeting and were listed in the printed program. The journalists talked to me because I was a voice of dissent from the approach of the Jesus Seminar. The Jesus Seminar received a lot of media attention beginning with that meeting and continued to do so through the rest of the decade. It became notorious in many Christian circles after the meeting in Atlanta in 1988 when newspapers across the nation ran articles headlining that Jesus Seminar scholars had debunked the Lord's Prayer (Matthew 6:9–13; Luke 11:2–4).

Needless to say, I fell out of favor with Funk. I continued attending the meetings of the Seminar for another year and a half, but it was more and more apparent that I was a persona non grata in the Jesus Seminar group. However, other opportunities opened up under the umbrella of Funk's organization, the Westar Institute, located in Sonoma, California. Funk's plan was to start various seminars besides the Jesus Seminar, which would meet, join in shared research and discussion, and publish their results through one of his other enterprises, the Polebridge Press. One of the other groups did sociological research on Christian origins and there was eventually another that engaged in literary criticism of the Bible. The group of which I became a member was formed at the meeting of the Jesus Seminar at Notre Dame in the fall of 1986. As I remember the discussion that took place, Funk, and Werner Kelber, who led the initial discussion, had in mind the formation of a group that would analyze biblical narratives and bring their results to bear on ethical questions. It would have been a literary approach to biblical texts. He also seemed to have in mind a study of American mythology—the cowboy/outlaw hero, for example—and how cultural myths affected biblical interpretation. However, the majority of the group that gathered there adopted his approach only in part, and that may be why a more literary group was later started in the Westar Institute.

Charles Mabee was chosen to chair the new group. I had met Mabee at the annual convention of the American Academy of Religion /Society of Biblical Literature in Chicago in 1984 while we were both waiting in the hotel lobby to meet someone for dinner. That person for whom he was waiting happened to be Darrel Fasching, one of my former Syracuse University graduate students. Mabee and I struck up a conversation and we stayed in contact after that. When I became a member of the Westar Institute through the Jesus Seminar, I recommended him for membership, so he came to the meeting at Notre Dame. He quickly moved into a leadership position as we discussed the new seminar, and with him those present decided to move in the direction of studying and writing on the relation of biblical hermeneutics to American culture. That is, how does the American cultural setting affect the way the Bible is viewed and interpreted and how could and does the Bible serve as a source of criticism of American culture? The name we gave to the new ongoing seminar was Bible, Narrative, and American Culture, or BINAC. This concept of the group was close in some respects to Funk's, but was different in its generally positive view of the biblical tradition and its negative evaluation of mythology.[3]

I have a very dim memory of the first meeting of BINAC, in conjunction with the Jesus Seminar and the Social Foundations of Christianity Seminar, in the spring of 1987. We were groping for a relevant topic that we could all agree on and use to move forward in our research and discussions. Nothing definitive resulted from that meeting. Meanwhile, I became more and more immersed in reading and thinking about Girard's work, so that summer I recommended that Mabee begins reading Girard and thinking about making his particular form of cultural anthropology the center of our efforts. Mabee took up my suggestion and by the end of the summer he was enthusiastic about looking to Girard as our central point of reference in perspective and methodology. At the next meeting in St. Paul, Minnesota, in the fall of 1987, I made a presentation on Girard and there was considerable input from Robert Hamerton-Kelly on the basics of Girard's mimetic theory.

Hamerton-Kelly's connection with the Westar Institute began with participation in the Jesus Seminar, which had its first meeting in the spring of 1985. In one of the sessions of the first conference I attended, in fall 1985, he mentioned Girard's name. I don't remember the Gospel text under discussion, but he said something to the effect that the seminar members should consider what Girard had to say that was relevant to understanding the text. At the dinner gathering that evening I sought out Hamerton-Kelly, introduced myself, and asked him about his comment in the discussion. I found out that he was Dean of the Chapel at Stanford University. (He resigned that position in 1986 and became a Fellow of the Center for International Security and Arms Control at Stanford.) He was a good friend of René Girard, having known him since Girard arrived at Stanford in 1981 from Johns Hopkins University.[4] He would be instrumental in arranging for me to meet Girard, and through him we were able to have Girard with us for discussions during the spring meetings of BINAC in 1988, 1989, and 1990.

After the meeting of the Westar seminars at Willamette University in Salem, Oregon, in the spring of 1987 I traveled down to Stanford. Kelly had made a reservation for me at a university guesthouse, and the next day he introduced me to Girard over lunch in the Faculty Club. My first impression of him was of a gentle, kindly, somewhat shy man. The three of us had a polite conversation, nothing particularly remarkable. From my standpoint it was basically a meeting to get acquainted, and I was pleased to have that opportunity. However, even though I had read his work for two years, it still had not fully dawned on me just how pioneering, how revolutionary, Girard's work was, and of course I had no intimation of his future impact on the world of thought, as reflected in the formation of COV&R and other groups and in his election to the French Academy in 2005.

After that lunch conversation at Stanford I was one of the participants with him at the spring meetings of BINAC in 1988 and 1989.[5] At some point late one afternoon or in the evening of the meeting in March 1988, members of the BINAC seminar met in a small room to decide on the direction in which we would go. Whether this was at Funk's command or due to our own sense of the need for direction, neither Mabee nor I can remember. In any case, it was immediately clear to most of us that we had two choices: to go in the direction of Funk or in the direction of Girard. We—at least the leading voices—chose Girard. I had limited correspondence with him and perhaps a couple of telephone conversations. Our friendship didn't begin to emerge until I went to Stanford on an academic leave in the winter quarter (January–March) of 1990. It was during the period of my leave that the Colloquium on Violence and Religion (COV&R) was founded.

But before turning to the beginning of COV&R, I will say a little more about BINAC and give an initial overview of Girard's mimetic theory. BINAC's sessions were not totally devoted to the understanding and application of Girard's thought. Not all of the participants were committed to a long-term research and writing project based on his work. Funk's objectives for each of the Westar seminars included publishing the results of its work as expeditiously as possible. Some of our BINAC papers were published as articles in the Westar journal, *Forum*. *Forum* 5.1 (1989) included four articles by members of our seminar. However, it is telling that mine was the only one of the four that discussed Girard's work. The assimilation and presentation of Girard in some book form moved slowly, much too slowly for Funk. Eventually the work of our seminar resulted in an anthology, *Curing Violence*, edited by Mark Wallace and Theophus Smith, which appeared in 1994.

But by autumn 1989 it had become clear that Funk would terminate BINAC in the not too distant future. Girard came from Stanford to our meetings in Sonoma in the spring, 1988–1989, as already mentioned. We devoted one day each year to conversations with him. In 1989 he gave a plenary address to all the Westar people who were present. However, Funk was not pleased at all about his presence, apparently viewing him as an interloper. And indeed he was, in the sense that he represented an approach to the Bible and Christianity that was diametrically opposed to Funk's designs. I did not help matters when I introduced Girard at the plenary session. I stated that Girard's hermeneutics would turn out to have a greater influence on biblical studies than that of Rudolf Bultmann, the great German New Testament scholar. There was an audible gasp from the audience when I said it. It was a strategic mistake on my part. It came across as a grandiose statement. I believe it is true, but it was inappropriate in that situation and I think that the way I said it was like throwing down the gauntlet. It was a large room, with perhaps eighty or ninety persons present. The chairs were set along three of the four walls rather than a conventional arrangement of seating in front of the speaker. In retrospect it seemed like throwing René to the wolves, or to a pit of lions. But he calmly strode down from the podium and handled the situation with composure, although the questions posed after his talk were generally unfriendly.

In the fall of 1989, Charles Mabee and I had a couple of conversations about the future of BINAC. In a telephone conversation he suggested that it was time to start a group devoted to Girard's thought, which would be independent of Westar. I immediately agreed. The whole process began as simply as that. We both knew that the days of BINAC were numbered. Mabee expected Funk to discontinue the group after the next meeting early in March in Sonoma. We both saw the resources and implications of Girard's work as so rich and potentially attractive to many scholars, as well as to intellectually alert psychologists, clergy, and others, that it could be the point of departure for a collegial group on into the indefinite future. Though it was a crisis period for BINAC, it was a propitious time to launch a new organization. I was about to take a semester's academic leave from Syracuse University. Girard had agreed to accept me at Stanford as a fellow in his Interdisciplinary Research Program, which was supported by Andrew Mellon funds for five years. By that time, sometime in November as I recall, my wife and I had already made plans to drive across the country to Palo Alto and rent an apartment there while I undertook research, writing, and conversations at Stanford. Mabee and I knew that Hamerton-Kelly would support the plan and would be a good resource person.

So the next step was for me to talk to Girard himself and find out whether he would agree to this idea of starting a new group. I telephoned him soon after my conversation with Mabee, and he readily agreed to our proposal. We could invite some scholars, most of whom would be on the way to the Westar seminars in March, to come to Stanford for a day.[6] Girard would draw from his Mellon funds to cover their lodging and meals while there. We would see what we could get started. Thus the idea for COV&R was born, although we did not have a name for it yet. So the death of BINAC led to the birth of COV&R.

But before turning to focus on this new professional society, I will give an overview of the work of Girard in his formative scholarly period, which established in turn a basic corpus of reference for so many avenues of research and application in the years to come. It was this body of work that became the point of reference for BINAC and served as the background presupposed in the origin of COV&R. It should be pointed out that I consider this overview a fair summation of what those of us in BINAC who initially got the new organization started understood his thinking to encompass and entail.[7] I will comment on this further at the end of the next section.

René Girard and the Mimetic Scapegoat Theory

Girard's initial work in history would not seem to have prepared him for the pattern of thought that would eventually drive his career. He grew up in Avignon, a storied locale of French Catholic culture. He entered the Ecole des Chartres in Paris in 1943 when he was nineteen going on twenty years old, and he completed his work there with a thesis on *La vie privée à Avignon dans la seconde moitié du XVe siècle* (Private Life in Avignon in the Second Half of the Fifteenth Century). He traveled to the United States in 1947 on a fellowship to study at Indiana University. He had intended to stay for only a year, or perhaps two, but he continued on to get his Ph.D. in history in 1950. His doctoral dissertation was titled "American Opinion of France, 1940–1943." Not long after obtaining his doctorate he married a young American woman from Indiana who had been one of his students in French, Martha McCullough. She became his wife in 1951. Her support and warmth and intellectual acuity enhanced Girard's life and work, qualities that are apparent to all who know her. Indeed, his accomplishments would have been very much more difficult without her at his side.

Something crucial for his career happened during his years as a graduate student at Indiana: he was asked to teach some courses in French literature, which he continued to do as a faculty member after receiving his doctorate. As he taught courses on French novelists of the nineteenth and twentieth centuries he became excited about the insight into human interaction that he found there. It was then that he began to conceive his concept of mimetic desire. His earlier interest in cultural modes, fashions, and opinions certainly fed into this concept, but it was his engagement with the great novelists, his reflection on the relations of their main characters vis-à-vis his own personal experiences and observations, that led eventually to the thesis he argued in *Mensonge romantique, verité romanesque* (Romantic Lie, Novelistic Truth) published in 1961. (It appeared in English as *Deceit, Desire, and the Novel* in 1966.) In it he analyzed the work of Cervantes, Stendhal, Flaubert, Proust, and Dostoyevsky in terms of mimetic desire.

What is mimetic desire? It is the desire—the wishing, the longing—by which a person unconsciously imitates a model. It may take the form of "coveting," which is prohibited in the Tenth Commandment in Exodus 20 and Deuteronomy 5, that is, reaching out aggressively to acquire the object of desire as one imitates the model. It is not an instinct. It is not programmed into us, so it does not work like instincts in other creatures. It is a potential of the human being: the developing self, mind and body, of the infant coming into the world. Normally this new being is ready to become activated and initiated into a world that she knows by means of mimesis or mimetic desire. The child is initially completely dependent on her models, the mediators of her world or reality, and even as she grows up and becomes an adult this mimesis will continue to operate more or less dependently on models, although individuals vary greatly in the extent to which they exercise personal creativity and gain insight into this dynamic by which human existence takes form.

What Girard describes as the work of mimetic desire is not good or bad in itself. It simply is a fact of being human. It is true that in a theological sense it is good as part of creation, as the means by which humans can relate to the world and to their divine origins. However, it is a dynamic possibility that can be actualized in various ways. People familiar with his thought will often speak of "good mimesis" or "bad mimesis." This is understandable, but a distinction must be made between the working of mimesis itself, on the one hand, and the model and the object of desire, on the other hand. The working of mimesis has to be evaluated on the basis of the model and the object of desire that the subject learns to seek from her imitation of the model. Mimesis as such may be considered good or beneficial as a possibility of the created order, but in its actuality everything depends on the kind of model and object of desire and, concomitantly, the kind of relation of subject to model and object. So desiring to have what given models desire is necessary for becoming "humanized" or acculturated, for entering into the human world, for living, loving, working, and playing with others. It is clear, however, that it can and does lead to conflict and violence. How does this occur?

There is an inherent element of uncertainty and instability in the life of all humans. Human evolution led to the development of a complex self with a large and highly complicated brain that is only loosely related to instinct in the sense that animals have instincts. So we must cope with memories of experiences, our own and those of ancestors, and we have to anticipate future events while we are continually adjusting to and interacting with a world. All of this takes place initially and basically through the imitation of models that mediate the world as we know it. One may counter that we choose our models, but that is true only as we grow older and even then only on the basis of a long and deep background of education or formation that is mimetic at its foundations. What happens in many instances is that if our desire to be like a model is sufficiently intense, if we identify with a model in the sense of deriving identity from the model, our desire to have what the model has or to be what the model is can take a form that leads us to become *rivals* of our models. Conflict then emerges between the person and his model. Another possibility is that we compete with one another as imitators of the same model, but at the same time we imitate our rivals even as we compete with them. This rivalrous situation happens time and again in personal, social, and political life among individuals, groups, cultures, and nations.

Although Girard has never rushed to demonstrate the relevance of his mimetic concept to modern cultural patterns and trends, it is obvious from even a superficial survey of what is around us in society and culture that it clarifies a great many phenomena, for example, those figures whom the modern media put before us as heroes and role models—not to speak of fashion models. These models that are the stuff of entertainment and advertising suggest what their admirers should desire.

In the late 1950s until about 1970 Girard extended his concept of the work of mimesis in human beings, and the major influences on his thinking were two: his Christian conversion and the effect of further research. Here I will comment on his major books through the publication of *The Scapegoat.* His published articles are important too, and often these essays anticipated further developments of his thought. But the early books serve as major markers of the evolution of his thinking.

While writing his first book, *Deceit, Desire, and the Novel,*[8] he experienced a conversion, a kind of "literary" or "intellectual" conversion. He had been raised as a Roman Catholic, yet he dropped away from the church in adolescence, and later as an adult he viewed himself as an agnostic until his midthirties. But as he worked on his book about the five great novelists, he came more and more to perceive the truth of Christianity in its Gospel foundations.[9] He later experienced a more dramatic, "existential" conversion occasioned by a health problem and his recovery from it.[10]

The reading of *Deceit, Desire, and the Novel* introduced us not only to the great novelists that composed the texts that were so revelatory for Girard, it was for some of us in BINAC a first quite important brush with Friedrich Nietzsche. In the first chapter Girard points out that Nietzsche acknowledged a debt to Stendahl in understanding that "the romantic state of mind is pervaded by *ressentiment*.[11] It was intriguing, but personally I did not grasp the significance of this at first. It was only when a few of us in BINAC were driving Girard home from Sonoma after his first visit to a meeting of the Westar Institute in 1988 that it began to come home to me, and I think to the others in the car. We were having a spirited discussion of the mimetic theory that turned early on to Nietzsche and his notion of *ressentiment*, the sublimated wish for violent vengeance that obsesses those caught up in mimetic rivalry with others who are considered their equals. Nietzsche saw this as the result of Christianity's influence on Western culture; he himself longed for a return to the violence of those who were noble. As Girard has noted, Nietzsche's insight concerning the influence of Christianity is correct, but the German philosopher's conclusion that *ressentiment* is the *source* of Jesus' message and the Christian religion is wrong. It was in that discussion, which lasted the hour or more from Sonoma to Stanford, that I first began to develop a real grasp of what modernity is.

Turning to the Gospels, the entire New Testament, and the rest of the Bible had a long-term effect on Girard's thought and, of course, his entire life-orientation. He began to reflect on Jesus as innocent victim and his crucifixion. But this was also strengthened and extended through reading in other sources. He read extensively in Frazer and other anthropologists and ethnologists such as Tyler and Robertson-Smith. As he studied primitive religions with the mimetic concept in mind he began to see that mimesis typically led to collective violence against a single victim. As he read the great Greek tragedians he became more and more convinced of their power and relevance, particularly Sophocles' Oedipus cycle and Euripides with his stunning exposure of mimetic violence in *The Bacchae*. An idea began to emerge and became more and more convincing to his mind: it was from the scapegoat victim that human culture began to emerge. Or one could say, from the scapegoat victim culture and *religion* began to emerge, there being no distinction between the two in primitive and archaic societies and hardly any in traditional societies.

He also found intriguing Freud's hypothesis of the primitive murder of the father by the horde of brothers in *Totem and Taboo*. In the French original of *Deceit, Desire, and the Novel* he did not mention Freud. However, in the English edition, published five years later, he added a footnote on Freud indicating that "One of the tasks facing criticism is the establishment of a genuine dialogue with Freud."[12] At that point he had yet to arrive at a criticism of Freud's Oedipus triangle, which he would do in chapter 7 of *La violence et le sacré* (*Violence and the Sacred*), which appeared in 1972. So in this variety of reading and reflection he extended the mimetic concept, showing that the tensions, conflicts, and violence that inevitably resulted from mimetic desire brought about a tendency in human relations and human civilization that he described as a "mechanism" because it does its work without human awareness of what lies behind it. This is the "scapegoat mechanism."

Girard published two books in the 1970s that, along with *Deceit, Desire, and the Novel,* formed the foundation of everything he has thought and written in subsequent years, although he has modified some views along the way and delved into new fields of study. These are *La violence et le sacré,* just mentioned, and *Des choses cachées depuis la fondation du monde* (*Things Hidden since the Foundation of the World*). In the former book he laid out his complete thesis concerning the scapegoat mechanism that stems from mimetic desire and a multitude of accusations and conflicts that snowball into convergence upon a victim.[13] The victim is blamed for disorder, for whatever chaos or malady that plagues the community. Rituals of sacrifice and rituals of scapegoating are advanced forms of the primordial lynching and spontaneous scapegoating that led to a period of relief, albeit tenuous and often short-lived, from the accumulation of rivalries and conflict that could explode into mass violence. Myth and ritual represent a double transference: the transfer of blame and guilt onto a victim, who may well be a substitute for someone else who could be blamed for misfortune (in many cases, for the entire group or community), but then also the transfer of credit, of honor and glory to the victim, because it is felt that the power of the victim as sacrifice results in solidarity and peace for the community. This must be stressed: *violence directed against the victim creates community anew.* But this community is bought at the tremendous price, the heavy mortgage, of the scapegoat mechanism.

Myth and ritual thus contribute to the generation of the gods. Those who are viewed as weak and vulnerable are blamed for societal misfortune, but they often come to be seen as powerful deities because of the peace that their execution brings about. There is also a connection between scapegoating and kingship. Girard theorizes that the victim was potentially so powerful that if there was a delay in her execution, more and more people in the community were attracted to her. This sacral power and authority stem from being viewed as the cause of the community's ills, yet its members anticipate that the victim's immolation will cure its ills. The victim thus frequently gathered support as leader of the group, and this was the seed of the institution of monarchy. There are many known instances of the sacrificial execution of a king or a queen. Since the monarch is at the center of the community, he or she bears the burden of blame when things go wrong.[14] The monarch "passes out of society, so to speak, by the roof, just as the *pharmakos* [person chosen to be the scapegoat] passes out through the cellar."[15]

As is well known, Freud speculated in his book *Totem and Taboo* that in some primordial setting a horde of brothers who were competing for the women of the group and greater power murdered the father-leader of the band. This murder was the source of their bonding and the understanding that they would not do the same to one another. The guilt that they internalized because of that deed was repressed, and for that reason it became even more powerful in their unconscious, returning in many forms through taboos, superstitions, and the illusions of religion, both in individual lives and in collective traditions. Girard was impressed with Freud's speculation, although his own conclusion was that desire is not necessarily fixed in an obsessive way on the father figure as mediator and rival. Desire, as he conceives it, is a kind of force field that may take any number of objects depending on the significant others that are mediators of what is important in the subject's world. This point touches on the "Oedipus complex," Freud's theory of the innate character of desire for the parent of the opposite sex.

Before continuing on the Oedipus complex I would like to pause for a moment to say that Freud's postulation of a primordial murder is the most important part of Girard's encounter with Freud. The problem of violence stands first and foremost for him, existentially and intellectually. This is the fundamental problem of human relations, human community, and human society. Thus Girard points the reader to the *rival brothers* rather than to the father in Freud's theory. It is they who are in competition and conflict over power, prestige, and property—in the case of Freud's scenario, over the women of the clan—who must set prohibitions and develop rituals and myths enabling them to avoid the chaos and loss of life that violence entails. However, what is it that leads to this chaos of violence? This is where Girard's critique of the Oedipus complex is so important, for from the standpoint of the mimetic theory it simply leads us astray in trying to understand and renounce our violence. In Girard's engagement with Freud his critique of the Oedipus complex ranks second in importance only to the primordial murder with which culture begins.

As Girard notes in chapter 7 of *Violence and the Sacred,* Freud seems initially attracted to conceiving desire as mimetic, but he is ambivalent in that he also speaks of the desirability of objects as though there is some innate drive to become attached to them. In the first book dealing with the Oedipus complex, *Group Psychology and the Analysis of the Ego,* Freud speaks of the identification of the son with the father, which is mimetic, that is, the father is the model, the mediator of the child's world. Yet at the same time Freud points to an innate libidinous attraction of the son to the mother. This conflicting duality appears also in the second book, *The Ego and the Id,* although the Oedipus complex as the innate desire for the mother and rivalry with the father has become more entrenched in his thinking. He thus explained the conflict as due to a purely cathectic desire for the mother (cathexis being an investment in an object of desire that is innate and invested with emotion). He glimpsed the importance of mimesis, but abandoned it in favor of his libidinal or sexual theory.

It was in reading this chapter of *Violence and the Sacred* that Girard's work really came alive for me. I had read a lot in Freud during my seminary days, and I thought I had some understanding of Freudian theory, yet I didn't connect with it. But Girard's critique of Freud resonated with me. I had some sense of Freud's basic concepts, such as wish fulfillment, the Oedipus complex, the incest taboo, and so on, but they did not illuminate anything I examined in my own experience or academic training.

In most families with a father and mother both present, the father typically has a mediatory function for sons and likewise the mother for daughters. But it doesn't necessarily work out that way. Girard's point is that desire has a more general field of play; it is not by "nature" or "innately" attached to any particular object. Its objects depend on relationships with the other, with other humans who play a mediatory role in one's life. To understand the place of desire in Girard's thinking it is necessary to see that it is basically *mimetic and triangular.* It is always desire according to the desire of another who is imitated, so there is always a kind of triangle in any relationship: one desires the object of desire of one's model. There is always an interplay of subject—model—object. In what he calls "deviated" or "metaphysical" desire, the subject effectively forgets about the object of desire and becomes fixed on the model in such a way that the model is a kind of god, possessing something akin to supernatural power. As stated before, one of the main points about mimetic desire is that it is not bad in itself; it is good in the sense that it is necessary for human relationships and to become humanly engaged with one's environment. It is just that it can become demonic or pathological when the model does not set a pattern that inspires and encourages a loving and just interaction with others, but instead is a mediator who consumes one's being. This phenomenon is the source of the "double" whom Dostoyevsky wrote about with such profound insight in *The Double*. It is probably a huge factor in schizophrenia and many acts of violence, including murder, in which the perpetrators subconsciously feel that they must sever themselves violently from the all-powerful model. Furthermore, the inversion of homicide in the form of suicide, self-murder, typically stems from the same phenomenon of this pathological form of mimetic desire. Yet at the same time mimetic desire under the influence of a liberating model who does not invite or encourage mimetic rivalry is the source of charity and justice in the world. There we come to the subject of religion, which I will discuss shortly.

Another interpreter who was important for Girard's thinking as it developed in the 1960s was Claude Lévi-Strauss, whose work he also discusses in *Violence and the Sacred*. It turned out that Lévi-Strauss influenced his methodology in reading texts, but Girard rejected his basic premises and conclusions concerning myth and culture. First of all, he acknowledged that Lévi-Strauss was right about the importance of myth, and he found very useful his analysis of the linguistic polarities in myth, especially with respect to the mythic treatment of twins and enemy brothers. Mythical thought reflects the birth of differential thought among human beings, that is, the establishment of differences in language and culture that enable humans to make comparisons and contrasts that are necessary to meaning and stability in cultural life. But Lévi-Strauss shows no interest in ritual, which is prior to myth and thus even more important for comprehending primitive cultures. For Girard ritual represents the sacrificial gestures that stem from the violence occurring at the very foundations of culture. This signals the most noteworthy deficiency in Straussian anthropology: it fails to get behind the linguistic expression of differential thought to real referents, and at the center of the real referents is the violent expulsion of the victim and the victim's revalorization as beneficial to the community.

What Girard was trying to construct was basically worked out when he published *Violence and the Sacred*, but the most important part of his thought, which included the centrality of the Incarnation and Passion of Christ, was not published until later. Of all of Girard's major works *Things Hidden since the Foundation of the World* would have to be rated as the most significant in indicating both the scope of his thinking and his view of the Bible, particularly the Gospel witness to Christ. These texts testify to the antidote for violence, namely the consenting scapegoat.[16] At the center of this volume he offers the culminating stage of his basic theory, the part entitled "The Judaeo-Christian Scriptures." The volume is a kind of triptych divided into three "books": the first book is devoted to "Fundamental Anthropology" and the third is named "Interdividual Psychology." These two parts recapitulate and extend his thinking that began to take form some twenty years before. However, the discussion of the Bible is the central element, and there the key chapter is "A Non-Sacrificial Reading of the Gospel Texts." The format of the work is a lengthy conversation with two French psychiatrists who are collaborators: Jean-Michel Oughourlian and Guy Lefort. Many of Girard's writings stem from the context of dialogues and interviews.

As Girard himself has indicated, the central theme of this book, reflecting the third stage of his basic theory, is the revelatory power of the Passion of Jesus, understood in the context of the whole Bible, the Judeo-Christian Scriptures.[17] The first stage was the concept of mimetic desire, worked out in *Deceit, Desire, and the Novel.* The second was the discovery of the scapegoat mechanism, treated at length in *Violence and the Sacred.* In *Things Hidden* he arrives at the Gospel witness to the Passion of Christ and makes known his Christian faith for the first time in a book-length work.[18]

He acknowledges structural parallels between the Gospels and archaic myth and religion, such as the persecution of someone considered at fault, "guilty" of crimes that undermine the social order. Moreover, Christianity holds that the victim is divine, similar to the divinization of the victim in ancient myth. However, the differences between the two could not be greater. In the myths it is the crowds who speak, their point of view dominates, but in the Gospels it is a tiny minority who give witness against the illusory charges of the persecutors. The Christian texts give account of the actual innocence of the victim, his suffering and death, and they affirm the action of the one true God in raising him from the dead. The Gospels do not condemn the victim, which they would do if they were myth—but neither do they condemn the lynchers. Whatever the traces of anger and condemnation one may find toward those who persecuted Jesus, these texts nevertheless give the astonishing testimony that Jesus himself does not ask God the Father to take vengeance upon them and he even asks the Father to forgive them (Luke 23:34).

The revelation of God in the Passion of Christ, which is confirmed in his resurrection, is the real basis of the rehabilitation of scapegoats. Girard calls it "the most extraordinary and fruitful adventure of all humanity."[19] In the Bible "God is present wherever this [scapegoat] mechanism is prevented from functioning."[20] And the revelation of the scapegoat mechanism is not simply a disclosure of the *fact* of the mechanism, but *why* it occurs. The reason goes back to mimesis: our normal way of learning and communicating, which comes about in its fundamental aspects at the level of unconscious imitation of others, can easily lead to *contagion* in a crowd, and crowds frequently turn into mobs. This process occurs also in societies as a whole, but not as rapidly as in a crowd gathered in one place. From the persecution of Jews in the Middle Ages through the accusations of witchcraft in the sixteenth and seventeenth centuries to modern lynchings of African-Americans in the United States and the Dreyfus affair in France—these and many other examples can be given concerning the phenomenon of mimetic contagion erupting in violence. The Gospels expose this mimetic contagion at the culmination of a long history of coming to the knowledge of God to which the Bible gives witness. The Bible and the Gospels "subvert the universal illusion and found a new era in human history."[21]

So this revelation is not simply the unveiling of an important piece of knowledge. It is the definitive moment that will eventually transform all things. It is the primary justification of the doctrine of the Trinity, for the revealing of God as Father, Son, and Holy Spirit is nothing other than the revelation that God is love. Girard says that the subversive revelation of founding violence is of a piece with the Christian interpretation of the biblical God, which "is inseparable from the willing victim. What justifies the Trinitarian concept of God lies precisely there."[22]

The Gospels, in keeping with Jesus' teaching in parables, testify to "things hidden since the foundation of the world" (Matthew 13:35). They are the primary textual witness to the revelation of the basis of culture in the scapegoat mechanism and the way of deliverance into the kingdom of God through participating in the crucifixion and resurrection of Jesus. It is the imitation of Christ that will move us beyond scandal, beyond the *skandalon* or stumbling block of the model-obstacle. Scandal is whatever attracts us to the extent it offends us. It is the outcome of mimetic rivalry that issues in resentment, conflict, and violence between individuals, groups, and nations.[23] It is the source of indignation and retribution, which in turn leads only to the refueling of rivalry. The source of salvation offered by God is therefore the faith in Christ that takes form in the world as nonviolent imitation of him. Violent mimesis leads only to death, to the tomb. For the imitator of Christ, the stone to the tomb is rolled back. As Girard says toward the end of *Things Hidden,* when the women come to the tomb of Jesus, "nothing that they were expecting is to be found; there is no obstacle and no dead body any more" (Mark 16:1–4).[24]

The fourth work to be highlighted here is *The Scapegoat*. Appearing in French in 1982 as *Le Bouc Emissaire,* it came out in English in 1985. It includes some beautiful and powerful readings of certain biblical texts, and in this respect it continues the project begun with *Things Hidden*. It includes also a noteworthy discussion of certain myths. However, in *The Scapegoat* Girard presents two really new things in extending the mimetic theory. One is the further reflection on the empirical phenomena that can be found and verified in myth. There are two aspects of this reinforcement of the mimetic scapegoat theory: (1) the empirical or historical referents in myth, and (2) the stereotypes of persecution.

Myth is both a perspective and a narrative form that camouflages its origins. This means that acts of scapegoating are not made explicit. Therefore, it is futile to search for a *theme* of scapegoating, for scapegoating is not scapegoating in the mind of persecutors. Cultural and religious patterns are presented in symbols, stories of gods, heroes, foundations of social order, and so forth, and much if not all of this seems fantastic and incredible to modern critical thinking. However, Girard argues that there are two factual referents at the generative level of myth. One is a social or cultural *crisis* and the other is collective violence directed against a victim—or victims—who is blamed, due to stereotypes of persecution, for the crisis. In primitive and archaic societies these victims are also credited with the peace and harmony that comes about when they are sacrificed. This is the human origin of the "gods."

Girard demonstrates this in chapter 1 of *The Scapegoat*. There he takes a fourteenth-century text by Guillaume de Machaut, *Judgment of the King of Navarre,* as a test case for actual historical referents in myth. In this work the poet ascribes the bubonic plague that struck France to the work of the malicious, avaricious Jews, who were hanged, burned, drowned, and beheaded for poisoning rivers and fountains throughout the country. Any historian reading this text will readily discern mythical elements in it, but no one can doubt that the plague caused a severe social crisis and that the Jews were actually killed as scapegoats for the alleged crime, not only of the murder of individuals, but of crippling the whole order of society. The allegedly guilty Jews are not divinized because the Christian culture was "mixed," having stemmed from a confluence of Christian revelation and tradition and its long pagan roots. It still often reverted to its archaic past, and so could be sacrificial and persecutory, but it had nonetheless moved beyond the stage of divinizing victims. However, a certain "demonization" of its victims could still occur and would continue as a possibility in certain circumstances even up to our own day.

The other aspect of solidifying the mimetic theory in a social scientific sense at the empirical level was the identification of stereotypes of persecution, the subject of chapter 2 in *The Scapegoat.* This is a kind of "grammar" of persecution. First, there is a crisis in which cultural distinctions or differentiations are threatened. This could be rank in a social hierarchy of classes, gender differences, difference between native and foreigner, and so on. In the nineteenth and twentieth centuries the distinction between a putatively native or superior race and a foreign, inferior race became the camouflage for the loss of other distinctions and led to "ethnic cleansing" and genocide. In this respect the Holocaust of the Jews in Europe is definitive for understanding the true nature of apocalypse in history ancient and modern: when all differences are erased human beings turn upon scapegoats in their mimetic fury. The second stereotype of persecution is accusation against individuals or members of a group. The accusation, in keeping with the first stereotype, is of a particular kind: it is that of committing a crime particularly dangerous to the maintenance of social distinctions. In ancient times the two basic crimes of this type were parricide and incest, both of which Oedipus is alleged to have committed in Sophocles' *Oedipus Rex.* In modern times there are many varieties of such accusations, ranging from miscegenation to treasonous acts against a nation-state. The third stereotype in this grammar of persecution is that of bearing the sign or mark of someone to blame, which amounts to being different in an unacceptable way in a given system of cultural differences. One can be readily marked as a potential victim if one is a foreigner or of a different race, or has a physical handicap, or does not fall within accepted sex and gender categories, or holds a status extremely low in the social order or a status extremely high. Those who have low or marginal status are weak and have little ability to retaliate. Those of extremely high status, such as monarchs, dictators, and to some extent even elected leaders in republican democracies, are vulnerable to the whims and scrutiny of the masses.

The second new development in the mimetic scapegoat theory that Girard presented in this book was his meditation on the work of the Holy Spirit, particularly as attested in the Gospel of John. He had ended *Things Hidden* by quoting Ezekiel 37:1–10, Ezekiel's vision of the life-giving Spirit of God, who would resurrect dead Israel. But in the last chapter of *The Scapegoat,* "History and the Paraclete," he offers a commentary on the Holy Spirit in John 14–16. He states, "The passages in John's Gospel devoted to the *Paraclete* gather together all the themes of this book."[25] The Paraclete is the advocate, the One "called to be for or beside" the prisoner, the victim of violence.[26] As Christ was the Paraclete while on earth as a historical being, so the Spirit continues his work against violence, against the false gods of this world—against Satan, who is the personification of accusation and unjust persecution.

Here I will pause to indicate some things that most of us in BINAC *did not* know in the early years, but which only became clear later, particularly with the publication of Girard's last two major books, *Evolution and Conversion* and *Battling to the End.* For one thing, we had no knowledge of Girard's struggle, his *agon,* in working out the mimetic theory and writing *Violence and the Sacred.* None of us had any inkling at the time of his reading of the German poet Hölderlin and his identification with the poet's struggle and decision to withdraw from the world. He says in *Battling to the End* that he began reading him no later than 1967.[27] "For me, discovering Hölderlin was a turning point. I read him during the most hyperactive period of my life I have known, at the end of the 1960s, when I alternated between elation and depression in the face of what I was trying to construct."[28] Whether or not he himself was ever clinically manic-depressive, the chapter on Hölderlin certainly suggests that he experienced a self-identification with Hölderlin's condition. "He passes through the hell of bipolarity, the never-ending-come-and-go of mimetic desire that makes us feel like we are everything when the 'god is near,' and like nothing when the god moves away."[29] What difference knowledge of Girard's personal experience would have made to us, I am not sure. I do think that we have to go through a kind of initiation process, though not formal or ritualized, and which may take many years, to appropriate the mimetic theory and integrate it intellectually and existentially.

Nor would we learn until much later the extent of Girard's debt to Charles Darwin, both as a model for scientific research and for the main contours of his theory of evolution. Girard refers to him only in passing in *Violence and the Sacred* and *Things Hidden,* and not at all in *The Scapegoat.* However, all the chapters in *Evolution and Conversion* are headed with an epigraph from Darwin's works. As he tells his interlocutors, his process of reasoning in formulating the mimetic theory was, as Darwin expressed it regarding his theory of evolution, "one long argument from the beginning to the end."[30] Indeed, Girard began reading Darwin as an adolescent. In an interview published in *Le Monde* (October 2, 2009) he says that already in his youth he read Darwin and was impressed with his work.

Girard construes human evolution as very complex, but his way of interpreting it via the mimetic theory is clear and elegant. In fact, one could say that the mimetic theory *is* a theory of evolution as applied to the origins of culture. To get a good sense of it in short order we need to see that three phenomena stand out for him: mimetic crisis, sacrifice, and conversion. In discussing Terrence Deacon's book, *The Symbolic Species,* he states that Deacon's concept of the emergence of "counter-intuitive" symbolic structures would be best explained by positing a crisis of mimetic violence that ended in a scapegoat resolution.[31] Prohibition stemming from sacrifice is the doorway to hominization. Everything that "Terrence Deacon says in his book . . . would become much more convincing if primitive modalities of the scapegoat mechanism were postulated."[32] Conversion to awareness and opposition to this sacrificial drive of the scapegoat mechanism—which is to say, awareness and opposition to the true meaning of the rule of Satan—is the next major state of the evolutionary process, which comes about through the Christian revelation.

As for the apocalyptic dimension of the Christian message, it was clear early on that it had a role in Girard's interpretation of the New Testament Gospels. However, in *Things Hidden* he turns to apocalypse only in a brief discussion of apocalypse and parable.[33] It is well known to those who have followed Girard's work that he views the Gospel of Matthew's version of the parable of the murderous tenants of the vineyard as of capital importance because in Matthew—unlike the same parable in Mark and Luke—Jesus asks, "When therefore the owner of the vineyard comes, what will he do to those tenants?" The auditors answer, "He will put those wretches to a miserable death, and let out the vineyard to other tenants who will give him the fruits in their seasons" (Matthew 21:40–41). In other words, Jesus does not ascribe violence to God, it is his audience that does this.[34] Yet it was only in the first decade of the twenty-first century that the full extent of Girard's apocalyptic theme was publicly expressed. There is a brief segment on "the apocalyptic feeling" in the last chapter of *Evolution and Conversion.* Indeed, in the early part of that chapter he makes a comment indicating that the apocalypse is looming as the end point of humanity's present evolutionary course and the end of history of we know it:

> Any great Christian experience is apocalyptic because what one realizes is that after the decomposition of the sacrificial order there is nothing standing between ourselves and our possible destruction. How this will materialize, I don't really know.[35]

However, the theme of apocalypse permeates his most recent book, *Battling to the End.* He says so straightway in the introduction, at the end of the first paragraph: "This is an apocalyptic book."[36] Apocalypse or apocalyptic thought is the recurring topic in every chapter. Girard holds that history is accelerating and contemporary economies and political entities are rushing to mimetic extremes. He envisions apocalypse in this crisis, which will result in undifferentiation of all cultural forms, institutions, and relations: either the undifferentiation of chaos and violence or the undifferentiation of the kingdom of God. I cannot develop this further here, but there will be a long discussion of *Battling to the End* and Girard's apocalyptic vision in chapter 5.

So even apart from what we were yet to learn in the "school of Girard's mimetic scapegoat theory," we already knew in the years leading up to 1990 that his was a distinctive body of work.[37] Those of us who started COV&R were convinced that Girard's interpretation of this tradition could spark a way out of the religious and cultural morass of the late twentieth century and offered a foothold for the rehabilitation of the biblical heritage. One way to sum it up is by referring once more to Girard's own summary of the three great moments of discovery in his thought and research.[38] The first moment was the discovery of mimetic desire and rivalry, which he found to account for so much, far beyond the literature he studied and taught. The scapegoat mechanism was the second discovery, which is the age-old unconscious or nonconscious human reaction to the predicament of mimesis. The third moment was when he began to see that the Bible exposed mimetic desire and the scapegoat mechanism, above all in the Passion accounts of the New Testament Gospels. "In the Gospels we have the revelation of the mechanism that dominates human culture unconsciously."[39] The gift of redemption or salvation is received through standing with the Innocent Victim, who was crucified by the powers and principalities of this world and was raised by God the Father from death to life.

All this work of Girard's which we pondered and with which we grappled was not simply a body of research establishing knowledge and data to be transmitted and employed. As Chris Fleming has written, "Girard has proffered not simply *research* . . . but a research *programme*."[40] In *The Bible, Violence, and the Sacred* I called it an "understanding of human culture based on a theory of the Bible's significance that is supported by a social scientific model of explanation."[41] I also quoted Hamerton-Kelly's statement that it was a "heuristic model"[42] and I went on to conclude that the "question is whether the model has great analytic power in interpretation of the data."[43] In retrospect I can see that Hamerton-Kelly and more recently Michael Kirwan are right to emphasize the term "theory." Theory is derived from the Greek *theoria*, meaning sight, speculation, contemplation. It is a way of seeing a certain subject or field of data. Theories should be judged by their power and elegance. Elegance is the achievement of creative insight joined to simplicity and a wide range of explanation. Power is the capacity to pose appropriate questions and generate a wide range of hypotheses that can be tested.[44]

One of the serious challenges to the mimetic theory and Girard's total research program is the status of the Bible. As noted in the previous paragraph, at the very heart of the theory is a concept of the Bible's significance. The basis of the Bible as holy, canonical Scripture is that it is a witness to God's self-revelation. But how can a research theory call itself in any sense "scientific" if its foundation is divine revelation? Girard, as an avowed Catholic Christian, accepts and believes in divine revelation, although not as a literalist or a fundamentalist. That view of the Scriptures is also true of all of those who have been leaders in COV&R since its inception, although a statement of belief is not necessary for membership or meaningful participation. I think that there is a threefold response to this challenge. First, scientific progress, like any kind of detective work, does not take place without the power of intuition, a way of "looking into" a subject and empowering the quest.[45] Reading a biography of great thinkers like Einstein or Freud would confirm this statement. I remember serving on a college committee with a chemistry professor. He used the word "intuition" over and over again as way of talking about those moments that advanced research. There is no doubt that the biblical prophets and other inspired witnesses were persons of powerful intuition. Girard has spoken of his work as based on a "global, massive intuition" (for more on this topic, see "The Annual Conference, 1991" in chapter 2). Even if the researchers do not accept their experiences as having a divine origin, cannot their anthropological insights be examined and tested? This has been precisely Girard's approach in most of his work, to develop an anthropology stemming from biblical anthropology.

As for the second response, experience and experiment are both necessary for confirmation of a theory. The two words both come from the same Greek root that means "to try out, to test." There are life-experiments, which are experiences of faith and community (e.g., different forms of communal living) and there are scientific experiments that employ the methods of modern disciplines of the natural and social sciences. Both of these are sources of knowledge. So the challenge to the mimetic theory is for its advocates to encourage and in some instances engage in (1) empirical forms of anthropological study, in cooperation with other fields of research, and (2) forms of living as communities of love, whether Christian or other forms. Those following a research program inspired by the mimetic theory must look for "proof" or "disproof" from both of these types of validation.

The third response addresses Karl Popper's criterion of falsification: a theory or hypothesis is empirically meaningful, thus "scientific," if it is possible to subject it to a test of falsification by empirical observation. (If I say that my home is located at such-and-such an address in Edmond, Oklahoma, that statement can be falsified if one went to that address and my home were not there.) To pose the question of falsifiability to the mimetic theory is, as Girard has said, a red herring "because we aren't talking about a natural phenomenon that can be tested and debunked in laboratories. In the same way, Darwin's evolutionary theory can't be dismissed by the standard procedure of falsification."[46] He goes on to observe that many true things, for example, the illusory nature of witchcraft, cannot be verified or falsified according to Popper's criterion.[47] There are certainly accepted "truths" that cannot be empirically falsified. I remember from theological seminary that one of my professors, Schubert M. Ogden, while arguing against the position of a certain philosopher (perhaps it was Anthony Flew), asserted the proposition that "the universe exists" cannot be falsified. It should be noted, however, that Popper presented other criteria for scientific status that amount to basically the same thing as his criterion of falsification. These are testability and refutability.[48] Hypothetical aspects of the mimetic theory could be subject to arguments of refutation in the areas of social scientific research. Girard himself has at least provisionally refuted his prior conclusion that sacrifice of humans preceded animal sacrifice, which began as a substitute for humans. As for testability, it depends on what kind of testing or experimenting is conceived. Note my comment on life-experiments, above.

Girard's work in developing the mimetic scapegoat theory convinced and enthused us to focus on his project. Many of us in BINAC felt ourselves pulled into Girard's discoveries as we began to read, write papers, converse with each other. When Girard met with us in the spring meetings of 1988 and in 1989, we became even more convinced that we were on our way toward a new hermeneutics that simultaneously opened the Judeo-Christian Scriptures and foundations of human cultures before our very eyes.

Therefore the birth of COV&R was a hermeneutical revolt, as we tried to find our way out of the impasse of a culture that seemed at every point to be turned against its own foundations and that even produced biblical scholars and theologians who led the way in trying to shatter the rock from which they were hewn.

Spring at Stanford, 1990: The Formation of COV&R

My wife Yvonne and I left our home in Phoenix, New York (a village twenty miles north of Syracuse) to drive to Palo Alto and Stanford on January 3, 1990. We had had our usual cold weather and snow in central New York, and we were worried about the weather we would encounter across the country. About the time of our departure it snowed heavily that week in the mountainous areas of New Mexico and Arizona through which Interstate 40 passed. We were taking that more southern route rather than Interstate 80 to the north because our itinerary included a stop to see relatives in Tulsa, Oklahoma, and a visit with our son and his family in Fresno, California. It turned out to be one of the most pleasant trips we have ever taken. The weather turned sunny and the roads were clear by the time we reached the western states.

We arrived in Palo Alto around January 16 or 17 and soon found an apartment that we could rent by the month. We planned to be there for about three months. Some Danish colleagues had arrived about the same time to work with Girard also, and they rented an apartment in the same apartment complex. They were Hans Jensen, Jørgen Jørgensen, and Claus Thomas Nielsen. Within the first week or so the Danes and I had lunch with Girard and Hamerton-Kelly at the Stanford University Faculty Club. It was a gesture of hospitality on Girard's part and an opportunity to talk about the months ahead. The Danes and I were going to audit Girard's course on Shakespeare, but we all wanted some more personal and intense interaction with him. Over lunch I asked him whether we could meet with him regularly to report on our research and discuss it. He readily agreed, and Hamerton-Kelly offered the facilities of the Center for International Security and Arms Control (CISAC), where he was a research fellow. We decided that we would meet every two weeks and take turns in presenting our ongoing work. As I recall, the initial group was made up of Girard, Hamerton-Kelly, Jensen, Jørgensen, Nielson, and me. Hamerton-Kelly's research assistant at the time, Byron Bland, sometimes met with us, and others joined us from time to time. The seminar is still meeting at this writing. Sometimes only a small core group is present; at other times there are visitors from the Stanford community or visiting scholars from other institutions in North America and Europe who take part.

My routine on weekdays was to go to one of the libraries at Stanford and work in a carrel. The carrel was assigned to Girard, but he did not use it so he turned it over to me while I was there. There were many pleasant breaks for lunch at the student center, Tressider Memorial Union. By the month of March the weather was always sunny and warm by afternoon, so the Danes and I ate at the tables outside. Yvonne often joined us, as did Gil Bailie, who drove down from Sonoma to Stanford for Girard's Shakespeare class. Those were special days in my memory. Not only did we all have the opportunity to pursue research in Stanford's excellent library facilities and enjoy the beautiful campus (while learning how to walk safely on a campus crossed constantly by hundreds of students and many faculty riding their bicycles!), but we also enjoyed collegial fellowship with one another over coffee and lunch. Of course, at the center of this total experience was the accessibility to Girard himself and the good offices of Hamerton-Kelly in facilitating our time there.

My work there established the basis of my book, *The Bible, Violence, and the Sacred*. The writing went slower than I expected because I had to do more background research than I had previously assumed. I also attended the Shakespeare seminar and had to keep up in the reading for that, and in addition our new informal seminar met twice monthly. Moreover, Yvonne and I took advantage of being in California by traveling many weekends to see our son and his family in Fresno, and I had a number of guest lectures at various academic institutions. I ended up only writing a chapter and a half, and later I extensively revised that material. However, the experience was invaluable for the intellectual stimulation and the fellowship and friendship that developed among those who were working together. René and Martha Girard offered us all a warm reception, and the beginning of our friendship with them is a cherished memory.

One of my tasks in the first three or four weeks at Stanford was to plan the meeting that would, we hoped, be the beginning of a new group dedicated to hermeneutics and culture criticism revolving around the mimetic scapegoat theory. Girard's secretary, Margaret Tompkins, gave me able assistance in the clerical part of the work, and I received input from Charles Mabee and Robert Hamerton-Kelly. The conference was sponsored by Girard's Program of Interdisciplinary Research, which was funded by his Mellon grant. We decided to invite scholars who were on their way to the spring meeting of Westar seminars (the Jesus Seminar, BINAC, and a literary criticism group) in Sonoma, plus those already working with Girard at Stanford, and a few others. There were twenty-one in all who attended that first meeting.[49] The date set was March 1. We would meet only that one day. As already indicated, Girard's Mellon funds paid for meals and one night's lodging for the participants who were at Stanford just for the conference. The hospitality included a reception hosted by René and Martha Girard in their home and lunch for the participants at the Faculty Club. Robert Hamerton-Kelly gave a short talk after lunch about CISAC and his work there. It was CISAC that provided the seminar room for our meeting.

The first part of the meeting was primarily devoted to Bruce Chilton's presentation of the chapter on Girard's analysis of sacrifice in Chilton's manuscript in progress *The Temple of Jesus,* which was followed by Girard's response to the paper and group discussion. Girard gave an illuminating and passionate response to Chilton's paper and in the ensuing discussion Hamerton-Kelly, a person who never minces words, sharpened the issues in a dramatic fashion. Particularly at issue were Chilton's argument that human sacrifice began as a communal meal and, concomitantly, that sacrifice of victims had nothing to do with violence. The response of the mimetic scapegoat theory is that it makes much more sense to construe the eating of meat as having stemmed from sacrifice of animal victims substituted for humans and that the whole process from its beginnings to its ultimate ritualization is best understood as a cultic repetition of slaying the victim and celebrating its benefit of peace and order for the community.[50] Chilton stood his ground in a gracious manner during the debate, although part of his hypothesis was not plausible to those of us who already accepted the mimetic scapegoat concept. In fact, one aspect of his position seemed incredible to us, for he held that sacrifice of a victim is a nonviolent act.

After the academic part of the program we turned to the practical matter of starting a new professional organization. I began by proposing that we launch a new society, and offered a brief statement as to its purpose. I no longer have a record of that initial rough statement, but after some discussion the following concept was adopted:

> Our purpose is that of exploring, extending, and criticizing the theoretical model of René Girard concerning religion and culture. The Colloquium will be concerned with research and the social implications of research. Scholars from various fields are encouraged to participate, but the focus of the activities will be the relevance of Girard's thought for the revitalization of religious studies and theology.

This definition was modified at the annual meeting in May 1991 and the resulting statement has since been printed on the masthead of *The Bulletin of COV&R*. An important change was to delete the name of Girard from the statement of purpose. Important as he was and is as the originator of the mimetic scapegoat theory, encouraging and inspiring it to move into new areas of scholarship and application, we did not want the new society too facilely identified as a kind of academic cult organization rendering devotion to one person. Girard did not have, nor has he ever had, any problem with our early attempt to protect the subsequent development of COV&R from becoming a personality cult. At the same time, as the title of this history indicates, the central importance of Girard and the feeling of affection for him is shared by most of those who have taken on an active role in COV&R.

We had a discussion on the name of the new entity just as lengthy as the one on the statement of purpose. My notes indicate that at the meeting we initially hit upon COVARS as the name. According to a note I made on the name, COVARS stood for Colloquium on Violence and Religion and Society. The two "ands" reflected our intention to emphasize the relation of the three subjects, rather than simply to focus on the violence *in* religion and society. However, by early April 1990 when I sent a memo to the colleagues who we thought might be interested in the new professional society, the name had evolved to COV&R, the Colloquium on Violence and Religion. I do not remember how the final form of the name and acronym came about, but I surmise that Bob Kelly, Charles Mabee, Gil Bailie, and I discussed it further after the meeting on March 1 and made the final decision. If my memory serves, Margaret Tompkins had some input in coming up with the final form of the name, but I can no longer recall the specifics of any of the conversations.

At our initial meeting there was a consensus that it would be essential to have a European section of COV&R, for we knew of the interest in Europe.[51] Girard had already had a friendship and collegial relationship with Raymund Schwager for at least fifteen years. Schwager was a Jesuit priest and professor of systematic theology. After the Danes on sabbatical at Stanford, Schwager and his young colleague Wolfgang Palaver, both at the University of Innsbruck, were the first Europeans with whom I had contact about COV&R.

Another decision we took was to hold two meetings within the next year. One would be a shorter meeting in conjunction with the American Academy of Religion (AAR) and the Society of Biblical Literature (SBL), November 17–20 in New Orleans. That has since become an annual event, especially for those already attending the big annual congress of AAR. In the early years it took place for half a day or a full day prior to the beginning of the convention. While I served as executive secretary, from 1990 to 1998, I handled the arrangements with the AAR and the SBL. Eventually that responsibility became a separate position in COV&R. Martha Reineke has served in that role in recent years and she has brought about a sea change for the better in the program planning.

The other conference would be our annual meeting, which would focus on important topics and would include a meeting of the advisory board and a business meeting open to all members. Our first three annual conferences, 1990, 1991, and 1992, took place at Stanford.

At this early stage Charles Mabee, Robert Hamerton-Kelly, Gil Bailie, and I had high hopes and a vision, not just of the growth of the Colloquium, but of the spread of the insights of René Girard's mimetic scapegoat theory for the benefit of the world. We could not anticipate, probably fortunately, what obstacles and bumps in the road lay in the future. On the other hand, at this writing both aspects of the vision have been realized, at least to a great extent.

Brief Biographies of COV&R Leaders

Robert G. Hamerton-Kelly

Robert Hamerton-Kelly was one of the three cofounders of COV&R. After obtaining his B.A. and M.A. from Cambridge University, he completed his Th.D. degree at Union Theological Seminary. He was a Humboldt Fellow at the University of Munster in 1972 and the University of Munich in 1977. He taught at Scripps College and McCormick Theological Seminary, and he served as Dean of the Chapel at Stanford University from 1972 to 1986. He was trained and has taught in New Testament studies and the classics. After he met René Girard in 1981 he became a leading interpreter of the mimetic theory. He was a senior research fellow at the Center for International Security and Arms Control from 1986 to 1997 (now the Center for International Security and Cooperation) and served thereafter as senior minister of the Woodside Village Church until he retired in 2004. He is the author of six books and the editor of four. The two books he has written on the mimetic theory are *Sacred Violence: Paul's Hermeneutic of the Cross* and *The Gospel and the Sacred: Poetics of Violence in Mark.*

He was the first president of Imitatio, Inc., which he started in collaboration with Peter Thiel and René Girard. As one of the founders of COV&R he was invaluable as a resource person. He served on the advisory board for six years and was the organizer of the 1996 conference at Stanford. On the recommendation of the advisory board of COV&R, the members present at the business meeting at St. Mary's University College, July 10, 2009, unanimously voted to make him an honorary lifetime member of the advisory board.

Charles Mabee

Charles Mabee was one of the three cofounders of the Colloquium on Violence and Religion. After undergraduate studies and seminary work, he went on to earn a Ph.D. from Claremont Graduate School in Old Testament studies. His interests and commitments, both theoretical and practical, are quite diverse, so his teaching and writing have not followed the typical path of an Old Testament scholar. He is the author of *Reimagining America* and *Reading Sacred Texts through American Eyes,* both dealing with the possibilities and problems involved in reading the Bible in the American cultural context. He has taught at Radford University, Marshall University, Oakland University (where he has also served as a campus chaplain), and Ecumenical Theological Seminary, where he is the director of the Master of Divinity Program. His fields of interest are the historical-critical study of the Bible, the comparative study of religion, and, in more recent years, the study of war, particularly the religious support and symbolism often associated with it.

Mabee was the chairperson of the Bible, Narrative, and American Culture seminar of the Westar Institute (1986–1990) and was a key person in the formation of the Colloquium in 1990. He served on the advisory board until 1995. On the recommendation of the advisory board of COV&R, the members present at the business meeting at St. Mary's University College, July 10, 2009, unanimously voted to make him an honorary lifetime member of the advisory board.

CHAPTER TWO

Early Development of COV&R, 1990–1993

From New Orleans to Innsbruck

Meeting in New Orleans, November 16, 1990

COV&R was now a fledging organization, although it was not yet fully formed because it had yet to agree on a constitution and gain membership approval of a slate of officers. That would occur in the annual meetings of 1991 and 1992. Meanwhile, its first semiannual meeting in conjunction with the American Academy of Religion in New Orleans occurred with a group of nineteen or twenty gathered to discuss five papers and talk about Colloquium business. I remember that meeting in New Orleans as a time of cordial fellowship and optimism. Some of us were bubbling over with plans and dreams for the future of COV&R. The weather was warm and sunny, the ambiance of the city was pleasant and stimulating, and we were reaching out in confidence to the future. Some of those plans and dreams would eventually come to fruition and some would not. But my memory of those days, undoubtedly tinged with a kind of romantic nostalgia, is that it was one of the high moments in the history of COV&R.

Walter Wink presented a paper on "Breaking the Spiral of Violence: The Victory of the Cross," drawn from his book *Engaging the Powers*. I reported on "Prophets and Kings" from my book in progress (the title of the book at that point was *Brothers in Conflict*). Michael Hardin gave a paper on "René Girard and Biblical Interpretation." Edwin Hallsten presented "The Commandment That Kills: Paul and Prohibition." And Wolfgang Palaver gave a paper on "A Girardian Approach to Hobbes' Use of the Bible." With the participation of Palaver, it was the first personal contact we had with any of our Innsbruck colleagues since the beginning of COV&R.

COV&R Publications

One of the decisions at the founding conference of COV&R had been to start a journal, to be called *Journal on Violence and Religion*. In fact, some of us attending the meeting in New Orleans had a meeting with the editor of Fortress Press about publication of a journal. An arrangement with Fortress did not come about, and as it turned out the project of a journal did not get off the ground for several years. When a new journal was finally launched it would have a quite different name.

Publishing a newsletter was another proposal that we discussed. That was approved at the second annual conference in 1991. It was named *The Bulletin of the Colloquium on Violence and Religion,* and the first issue appeared in September 1991. Wolfgang Palaver was the editor, with the assistance of Józef Niewiadomski. The first issue was quite modest by comparison to the *Bulletin* published now. A major feature of the newsletter was the bibliography of secondary literature concerning the work of René Girard. This bibliography was provided by the Theology Faculty of the University of Innsbruck. Raymund Schwager succeeded in getting a new post added in theology at Innsbruck, which was created to support his research. Dietmar Regensburger was appointed to that post. One of Regensburger's tasks was to oversee and publish a bibliography concerning Girard, which he has done ably since late in 1991.

At Syracuse University

From the beginning of COV&R in 1990 until the summer of 1992 I did not yet have email, but my correspondence was heavy, mainly by fax and "snail mail." I exchanged a number of memoranda with James Wiggins, my department chairperson at Syracuse University and then executive director of the American Academy of Religion. One request I made was for support of mailings and fax messages from the Department of Religion. He approved my request for a subsidy. Unfortunately, I began to surpass the proposed budget by some time in 1991 or early 1992. He summoned me to his office for a discussion, which included a mild reprimand. My mailings, he informed me, made up 20 percent of the departmental budget in that category (I was one of a dozen faculty). I don't remember the details of the agreement we made, but I recall that COV&R was to reimburse the department for all mailing expenses above a certain amount.

Wiggins was also helpful in enabling me to work out an arrangement with the American Academy of Religion whereby the Colloquium could hold meetings prior to the beginning of each year's convention. Those yearly meetings at AAR/SBL involved a lot of paperwork and what seemed to me unduly great expenses for coffee and refreshments.[1]

If Wiggins was helpful in relatively minor administrative matters, I knew that I could not count on him for a large financial outlay, such as supporting an annual meeting of COV&R at Syracuse University, for example. My place in the Department of Religion at Syracuse was one of grudging acceptance on the part of the faculty who dominated the politics of the department. There was a bloc of colleagues who were definitely "postmodern" in orientation.[2] Wiggins was one of those. They were opposed to a Christian theological orientation in teaching and research. It was acceptable to be an advocate, or at least make positive statements, about various religious or intellectual commitments, but to be an avowed Christian or an advocate of a theory associated with roots in the Christian tradition was not kosher. An incident at a special event sponsored by the Department of Religion during the mid-1990s will illustrate this. The lecturer was well known for his work in psychoanalytic theory and religion, especially the Jewish religious tradition. In the discussion that followed I raised a question whose exact content I do not recall; if memory serves, it had to do with a critical appraisal of Sigmund Freud and the "myth" of the Oedipus complex. I remember the first sentence of his response word for word: "You have to understand, Freud saved my life." There was a hush in the hall, a silence of awe. His affirmation was received with a respect that bordered on the reverent. As I reflected on it afterwards, I felt sure that one could make a statement like that about certain theories that were postmodern,[3] or about a religion of Far Eastern origin, such as Buddhism, but one would be subject to intense questioning if one said something of the kind about Moses and the Torah, or would be the object of hostile interrogation if it were an affirmation of Christ.

Therefore the estrangement from these faculty colleagues only deepened when I became an advocate of the mimetic theory. A majority of those graduate students and the faculty in the graduate program who knew anything about Girard were decidedly anti-Girardian. My perception was that this opposition stemmed from the usual reasons known from long-standing arguments against his work: it purportedly claimed and explained too much as a comprehensive theory and above all it was alleged to be too closely connected to the Christian tradition. Girard's clear avowal of Christian faith "tainted" him. It tainted me, also, in the eyes of certain colleagues and students. However, by the time I came upon Girard's work I was almost forty-nine years old, a full professor with tenure, and I had established myself in the field of biblical studies. So I met with grudging acceptance in my department. I believe it would have been very difficult for me if I had been untenured.

Mabee, Bailie, and Schwager and the Innsbruck Connection

My correspondence and telephone conversations with Charles Mabee and Gil Bailie were extensive at this early stage of COV&R. There were also many fax communiqués between Raymund Schwager and me. As mentioned in the first chapter, I first met Mabee in 1984 at the annual convention of AAR/SBL in Chicago. At that time he was a professor at Marshall University. He later was a chaplain and instructor at Oakland University and joined the faculty of Ecumenical Theological Seminary in Detroit. We had become friends by the time the Bible, Narrative, and American Culture seminar was formed at Notre Dame in 1986. He was someone whom I trusted as a confidant and with whom I could trade ideas. I lent him support in his work as chair of BINAC, and he in turn was valuable to me as an advisor in the early stages of COV&R.

Gil Bailie was our first treasurer. He operated an adult education enterprise called Florilegia (currently named Cornerstone Forum). He eventually became well known for his book, *Violence Unveiled,* and as a speaker at Catholic churches and colleges. We were often in contact about both theological and financial matters. His first wife Kaeti helped him develop the COV&R logo that was used on the COV&R letterhead. Gil had a joyous spirit and a deep commitment to the Christian roots of the mimetic theory.

I corresponded with Raymund Schwager many times before we finally met at the annual conference in 1991. Early on I heard from Girard, Hamerton-Kelly, and others that Schwager was the first theologian to make a strong commitment to furthering Girard's work. Schwager was a professor in the faculty of theology at the University of Innsbruck. He wrote the first theological work applying the mimetic scapegoat theory to the Bible, *Must There Be Scapegoats?,* which was published in German in 1978.[4] When Schwager and some of his Innsbruck colleagues learned that we had started a Girardian society in the United States they sent me their ideas in the form of *Überlegungen*, "considerations," which were suggestions and recommendations concerning the founding of a scholarly journal.[5] At the founding meeting we had briefly discussed publishing a COV&R periodical. The most important of the Innsbruck recommendations was that we undertake two kinds of periodicals. One would be an "in-house" newsletter, which would go out two to four times a year and would include important events and symposia, book and periodical abstracts, bibliographies, short articles, and so on. A separate project would be to put out a scholarly journal of high quality, which would publish carefully refereed articles. The essays published would be written first of all by Girardians, but for the sake of a wider appeal it would be open to non-Girardian scholars also. I went over all the suggestions with Bob Kelly, and I remember that we thought they were all sensible and helpful as we launched the Colloquium.

It was very important to have the support of the University of Innsbruck Theology Faculty. I had read Schwager's book, *Must There Be Scapegoats?*, but until I arrived at Stanford for my academic leave in 1990 I had no idea of the length and depth of Schwager's relationship with Girard, nor of the interest in Girard's thought that Schwager had created among some of the professors and students at Innsbruck. Under Schwager's influence many of those in the theological school of the University of Innsbruck formed a Girardian center of work and interest. On the other hand, we Americans who started COV&R were "upstarts" who had acted quickly on the idea of starting a new professional society focusing on explicating, criticizing, and advancing Girard's mimetic scapegoat theory. To digress for a moment, most of us who started COV&R were not fully cognizant of the following Girard already had, both in North America and Europe. I have heard from Cesáreo Bandera about the 1980s when there were conferences addressed to Girard's work in America and Europe, and when some friends and colleagues would often appear at his lectures and conferences. Those who did this jokingly referred to themselves as the "Girardian circus."[6]

But again concerning our Innsbruck colleagues, it was quite clear that they must have a part at the very heart of our organization and ongoing work. As already stated, our first personal contact was with Wolfgang Palaver when he came to the meeting in New Orleans in November 1990. As a core group got deeply involved in planning for the annual meeting in 1991, it occurred to some of us that Schwager would make an excellent president of COV&R. He had a sterling reputation as a person, scholar, and teacher, he had been a friend of Girard for a number of years, and his leadership qualities would enable us to solidify the partnership with Innsbruck.[7] As it turned out, Wolfgang Palaver was also tapped for an important role as the editor of our newsletter.

Raymund Schwager's response to the proposal of his name for president of the Colloquium was initially one of surprise and hesitation. I still have his fax message to me:

> Ihre Anfrage bezüglich des Präsidenten von COV&R hat mich völlig überrascht. Meine erste Reaktion war, dies dürfte kaum möglich sein wegen meiner mangelnden Kenntnisse der englischen Sprache. Auch eine jährliche Reise in die USA würde mir einige Probleme schaffen, aber dies ließe sich vielleicht regeln. So möchte ich vorschlagen, dass wir diese Sache ausführlich in Stanford diskutieren. Ich werde am 15. Mai dort sein.
>
> Bis bald mit besten Grüßen R. Schwager[8]

> Your inquiry concerning [the office of] president of COV&R caught me completely by surprise. My first reaction was that this would hardly be possible due to my deficient knowledge of the English language. Also an annual trip to the United States would create problems for me, but this could perhaps be worked out. So I would like to propose that we discuss this matter in detail at Stanford. I will be there on May 15.
>
> Until soon, with kind regards, R. Schwager

This message is typical of Schwager's humility. Although his ability in English was not at the level of his French, his second language in which he was quite fluent, his English was certainly competent enough to communicate well. I later learned that he started working diligently to improve his English, even hiring a tutor.

In the event, he accepted the role of president without further resistance, and neither of the obstacles he mentioned in the message to me turned out to be a problem. As for annual conferences in the United States, that was not a policy written in stone. In 1994 COV&R had its first meeting in Europe, in Wiesbaden, Germany, and currently the annual conference is held in Europe about every other year.[9]

What I did not and could not have known at the time was how propitious the beginning of COV&R was for Schwager, both with regard to his relationship with Girard and his dream of helping form a certain kind of community. Coming to Innsbruck in 1977, he was designated as Professor of Dogmatic and Ecumenical Theology. There were complications in completing the appointment, and some faculty members werde displeased about it. According to

Józef Niewiadomski, Schwager had hoped to unite his fellow Jesuits in a close-knit community in which the insights of the mimetic theory concerning the Christian message would be prominent. That unity did not come about. However, when the Colloquium on Violence and Religion was founded, he turned to it as at least a partial realization of his dream of a community uniting the intellectual and spiritual dimensions of human existence.[10]

It was Schwager who led the way in bringing into greater unity the work of North American and European colleagues. Due to his tenure and high status in the faculty of the University of Innsbruck, he was able to procure financial support of COV&R, which came primarily in the form of underwriting *The Bulletin of COV&R*. I found him easy to work with and congenial as a coworker in the Colloquium. As I got to know him better I came to admire his spiritual qualities. He radiated an aura of charity and peace. I began to read more of his published work, and eventually I translated three of his books, *Jesus of Nazareth: How He Understood His Life*; *Jesus in the Drama of Salvation* (co-translator with Paul Haddon); and *Banished from Eden: Original Sin and Evolutionary Theory in the Drama of Salvation.*

The Early Relationship of Girard and Schwager

As already stated, Girard and Schwager first met in 1975. Their extant correspondence goes back to April 1974. Schwager's theological work from 1973 or 1974 until the end of his life was inspired and nourished by the friendship and ongoing discussions he developed with Girard, and the inspiration and intellectual nourishment was mutual. There is no doubt that Girard is one of the great thinkers of the twentieth century, whose thought holds great promise for this century and beyond. His mimetic theory has of course many sources, including above all the Bible, but its development into an overarching theory bears his own stamp in both form and content. However, if there is a dialogue partner who not only encouraged him but also enabled him to test and modify his thesis, that person is Raymund Schwager.

Schwager's own contribution to theology and the mimetic theory was a result of his creative appropriation of Girard's work in combination with the theodramatic theology of Hans Urs von Balthasar. With the assistance of Józef Niewiadomski he developed von Balthasar's concept of "Theodrama" (God-drama) into a five-act schema of Jesus' place in the history of salvation: (1) "Calling to the Wonder of God's Rule"; (2) "Judgment and Self-Imprisonment in Evil"; (3) "Crucified as Victim of the Violent"; (4) "Resurrected—Escaped from the Snare of the Hunter'; (5) "The Holy Spirit and the New Vineyard."[11]

He was very prolific during the last quarter of the twentieth century, beginning with *Must There Be Scapegoats?*, which came out in German in 1978, and including not only the books already mentioned but also *Der Wunderbare Tausch* (The Marvelous Exchange) and *Banished from Eden. Must There Be Scapegoats* was the first book drawing upon the mimetic theory to examine the Bible from the standpoint of its contribution to Christian theology, particularly Christology.

I am fortunate to have been granted access to the extant letters exchanged between Schwager and Girard from 1974 to 1991, and I am grateful to Józef Niewiadomski, dean of the Theology Faculty at Innsbruck University, for permission to read these letters and refer to them in this history. Niewiadomski was authorized by the Society of Jesus to oversee access to the correspondence and other materials in Father Schwager's estate. The Innsbruck Theology Faculty now has a research and writing project under way that will result in the translation of the letters from French into German and a critical edition of both the correspondence and Schwager's unfinished manuscript, *Dogma und dramatische Geschichte: Christologie im Kontext von Judentum, Islam und moderner Marktkultur* (Dogma and Dramatic History: Christology in the Context of Judaism, Islam, and Modern Market Culture).

Schwager wrote to Girard in a brief letter dated April 18, 1974, telling him how impressed he was with *La violence et le sacré*. The letter gives the impression that he had recently read the book. We know that he had just recently written a review of the book when he wrote the letter.[12] He arranged to meet Girard when the latter was teaching in France in the summer of 1975. Girard said that their meeting near Avignon in Sauveterre de Rouerge was very important for him. It was extremely encouraging to encounter a theologian so interested in his work. Moreover, Schwager already anticipated much of the trajectory of Girard's thought in regard to the Bible and Christianity, which he would articulate in *Things Hidden since the Foundation of the World*. The latter was published in French in 1978, at almost the same time as Schwager's *Brauchen wir einen Sündenbock?*

Girard himself does not remember details about that first personal meeting in August 1975. It is quite clear, however, that the prior correspondence, and particularly the long discussion with Schwager, buoyed him considerably. He was tremendously encouraged that a theologian understood his theory so well and accepted it—even anticipating future lines of development. Schwager says in a letter just a month after that first meeting, "It's with joy that I think again about our meeting at Avignon."[13] The personal encounter opened both of them up to begin discussing the mimetic theory in earnest. In that letter Schwager poses a question about the role of the law in violence, citing Romans 7:7: "If it had not been for the law, I would not have known sin. I would not have known what it is to covet if the law had not said, 'You shall not covet.'" And this coveting or acquisitive desire is what leads to murder, adultery, robbery, and lying (false witness) about one's neighbor.[14] Girard says a number of interesting things in reply. It is clear for him that the victim mechanism is prior to the law: when one reaches the stage of law as such, it is abstract and has a symbolic function, whereas the victim mechanism is primordial in human life; it is the efficient cause of hominization, enabling the transition from an animal state to humanity.

Girard goes on to say that the law is necessary in human existence up to a certain point because in specific instances the thing prohibited is actually dangerous. However, if it is carried too far—to the point where it must be exceeded by love—it can indeed foment violence. However, those who too readily impeach and reject law tend to fall into its inversion, which is a state of chaos. He holds that there is a certain Christian failure, which is just the contrary of the legalistic failure, and that involves rejecting the law and claiming the liberty of the Gospel without really assuming a life of love. This is where an apocalyptic situation becomes possible. "I would say therefore that the essence of the modern error is the resentment regarding the law that leads to its reversal, as with Nietzsche, Freud, et al, i.e., to a sacrificial super-crisis."[15]

The epistolary discussion of Girard's book *Des choses cachées depuis la fondation du monde,* which was composed in collaboration with Jean-Michel Oughourlian and Guy Lefort, reveals the nature of his debt to Schwager as his conversation partner. Indeed, Schwager's *Brauchen wir einen Sündenbock?* appeared that same year, 1978, a month or two before Girard's book came out. Girard began reading Schwager's German text, but it was a bit of a struggle for him. He told Schwager in one letter that he was not able to make his way in German nearly to the level that Schwager commanded French. He commended Schwager particularly for his explication of the Psalms as persecution texts that foreshadowed the Gospel witness.

When Schwager wrote to Girard in a letter dated March 29, 1978, he had not quite finished reading *Des choses cachées.* By this time Girard and he had a relaxed, collegial relationship. His opening salutation is "Cher ami" (Dear friend).[16] He congratulates Girard on the book and says that he finds it to be excellent on the whole. At the end of the letter he reiterates his gratitude for all that he has received from Girard.

In between, however, he raises some important questions. One of these concerns Girard's contention that the crucifixion of Jesus is a source of knowledge. He anticipates that theologians will object to that, even though many, perhaps most, will be ready to accept a nonsacrificial interpretation of Jesus' death. Yet for them the cross is a source of life, not knowledge. Even though Girard emphasizes the love of God in the Gospel witness to Jesus' ministry, death, and resurrection, there remains still the possibility of misunderstanding.

Schwager gently chides his friend for not mentioning the Spirit, for the Spirit slowly transforms the hearts of those who become engaged with the gospel of Christ. The Spirit, as the Apostle Paul affirms, is the source of freedom, love, and peace. Then, coming back to the cross as revelatory, he points out that it is a source of life in two respects: (1) Jesus remains true to the message of his Father and does not react to his persecutors with violence, and (2) the Father responds to the violence of the persecutors by sending the Holy Spirit.

Finally, Schwager comments that Girard misunderstands the letter to the Hebrews, which Girard criticizes in *Things Hidden* as a sacrificial understanding of the gospel. Schwager points out that the vocabulary of Hebrews is indeed sacrificial, but the *content* is not; it is quite different. He makes three points in brief fashion: (1) The epistle stresses the difference between ordinary sacrifices and the death of Jesus. (2) The continuity between the Scriptures of the old covenant and New Testament according to Hebrews revolves around *faith*, not sacrifice. (3) The believer is one who bears persecution, like Jesus.[17] Jesus' sacrifice is that he learned obedience and was faithful to the message of nonviolence.

Girard responds in a letter of April 17, 1978. He reminds Schwager that he is located in a situation where literary critics dominate, not in a theological milieu like his friend in Innsbruck. It is Schwager who must do the necessary biblical and theological work to help him complete the mimetic theory. This was a responsibility that Schwager had already in fact taken upon himself.

Regarding the Spirit, he understands his friend's concern, but he points out that at the very end of the book (which Schwager had not yet concluded), he would find a biblical quotation about the Spirit (from Ezekiel 37). The prophet Ezekiel's vision of the valley of dry bones, of the dead Israel, renewed and resurrected by the breath or spirit (*ruach*) of the Lord, was certainly important to Girard as he concluded *Things Hidden*. He says, "I always cherished the hope that meaning and life were one. Present-day thought is leading us in the direction of the valley of death, and it is cataloguing the dry bones one by one." But "it is up to us to resuscitate meaning by relating all the texts to one another without exception, rather than stopping at just a few of them."[18] Nonetheless, Schwager's point was well taken, for the work of the Spirit was not a theme in that work.

However, Girard did deal with the Holy Spirit in his next book, *The Scapegoat,* published in French in 1982. The final chapter of the latter work is devoted to "History and the Paraclete." The Paraclete in the Gospel of John is the Spirit whom God the Father will send (or whom Jesus will send from the Father, John 15:26) when Jesus leaves the disciples. He calls this Spirit the *parakleitos,* the advocate, the defender. Satan is the accuser who "deceives men by making them believe that innocent victims are guilty." The Paraclete is "the chief defender of all innocent victims, *the destroyer of every representation of persecution.*"[19] Therein lies Girard's understanding of the work of the Spirit in human history: the Spirit transforms human history by destroying "every representation of persecution." For Girard, the "transformation of human hearts," as Schwager put it, is a matter of overcoming the persecutory impulse stemming from the scapegoat mechanism, and this is something that should and can happen not only at the level of the individual, but in the larger patterns of groups, movements, and nations that play a part in God's salvific plan.[20]

On the whole problem of sacrifice, Girard begins to concede to his friend that he should think more broadly about sacrifice, particularly in its specifically Christian sense. Perhaps he has been too hard or obdurate with regard to that subject, but the essential thing is to "perceive the abyss between the gospel perspective and that of the persecutors," and indeed between the New Testament and all the religions of the earth. Girard formulates this statement in a complex sentence that indicates that though there is a chasm between the Old and New Testaments and between the New Testament and all the world religions, there is also paradoxically a continuity with respect to human life between Old and New Testaments and between the New Testament and other religions. This continuity serves a mediatory function, but it does not imply any complicity of the gospel message with religions of violence. We see here an expression of Girard's fundamentally anthropological perspective.

On the cross as a source of knowledge, he grants that it cannot be limited to that. However, he affirms that it is also a source of knowledge as well as a source of life, a source unlike the *méconnaissance* (misconception, misreading) of the scapegoat mechanism found in all the primitive religions.

He concludes his letter by noting that there is something "overwhelming" (*écrasant*) in undertaking works like *Things Hidden.* He has had twin negative reactions from Christians and atheists alike. "That is why you are right about the misunderstanding on the subject of apocalyptic language and the sacrificial language of Hebrews. It is your turn to demonstrate that, and I eagerly await your next works."

It should be noted that eventually Girard was completely won over by his friend's understanding of sacrifice in a Christian sense and Jesus as scapegoat, and this included conceding that Schwager was right about the letter to the Hebrews. Girard's clearest published statement of Schwager's influence on his thinking about the mimetic theory is given in the anthology celebrating Schwager's sixtieth birthday.[21] In that essay he cites at length the statement Schwager makes in *Must There Be Scapegoats?* about Jesus as a scapegoat: in contrast to all other victims of scapegoating, whether human or animal, the working of the scapegoat mechanism against Jesus was complete, revelatory, and salvific. It revealed the resentment and all the darkest forces of the human heart. "The collective transfer thus took on a completely new meaning. It was more concrete and more universal than the ganging up against random scapegoats."[22] Girard says, "I certainly comprehended [Schwager's] logic at that time, yet it was not possible for me to accept it. It made me uneasy, giving me a feeling that now seems to be dispelled." He goes on to say, "His intuition was correct."[23]

Girard continues in that essay by explicating two interrelated topics: the mimetic theory and religious relativism and the mimetic theory and the sacrifice of Christ. Both are intimated in the correspondence already cited. The Jewish-Christian tradition is like the other religions in stemming from a crisis. The Jewish and Christian traditions of revelation narrate instances of scapegoating and ganging up on victims who are considered guilty from the standpoint of the majority or dominant persons involved in given situations. Christianity even has a savior who dies and rises again, like the dying and rising god in many archaic religions. But the biblical religions testify to a dissident minority who rebel against the majority view and witness to the innocence of the victim. It is the Christian witness that God raised Jesus from the dead, justifying both Jesus and that minority of followers—and yet this occurred without act or desire of violence against his enemies. "I thought it was in the primary interest of the mimetic theory to engage in apologetics against religious relativism with all my might. . . . The appeal [such as Schwager's] to the concept of sacrifice that characterized the ritual of the archaic religions for describing the Passion of Christ stood in the way of me and my program of research."[24] He was afraid that recourse to that concept would hand over all future arguments to those who would assimilate Christianity to archaic religions; therefore he had previously rejected using that language.

There is a paradoxical unity of all religions in that the concept of sacrifice applies to all of them, which Girard illustrates by referring to the story of Solomon and the two prostitutes who lay claim to the same baby (1 Kings 3:16–27). When Solomon renders his judgment to divide the baby in two and give one half to each woman, the lying woman accepts this but the true mother says no, let him live; she may have him. There is one kind of religion that sacrifices the victim for the sins of the community; there is another, unique, religion in which the innocent victim offers himself to the violent community so that they might live. The gods of the religions are divinized scapegoats; Christ is the divine Son who became *the* scapegoat for humanity.[25] In conclusion, Girard acknowledges that some of the ideas in *Things Hidden* are contrary to Schwager's logic concerning sacrifice and Christ as scapegoat, above all his criticism of the letter to the Hebrews. "Looking back I recognize here a certain hesitation and I understand this flaw. This allows me now, to the contrary, to honor the critical advance made by Schwager."[26] This critical advance is recognized also in *De la Violence à la Divinité,* the volume of four-books-in-one that Grasset published. There Girard adds a long footnote in *Things Hidden* to the subsection "The Judgment of Solomon." He confesses that his opposition between "non-sacrificial thought" that is always faithful to the inspiration coming from the Gospel texts and "sacrificial thought" that is always unfaithful to the spirit of the Gospels "reflète une ultime illusion humaniste et 'progressiste' dans mon interpretation du christianisme" (reflects an ultimate humanist and "progressive" illusion in my interpretation of Christianity). But, he says, "Je ne me suis débarrassé de cette illusion qu'après la publication originelle du present livre. A mes yeux, désormais, la vraie opposition entre le chrétien et l'archaique doit se définir comme opposition entre le sacrifice de soi et le sacrifice d'autrui" (I rid myself of that illusion only after the publication of the present book [*Things Hidden since the Foundation of the World*]. In my view, from then on, the true opposition between what is Christian and archaic religiosity must be defined as an opposition between the sacrifice of oneself and the sacrifice of the other).[27]

Further commentary on the correspondence is a fascinating temptation, but it really requires a book, which is precisely what the Innsbruck Theology Faculty has under way. Suffice it to note that by the end of the decade of the 1970s, Raymund Schwager was an indispensable conversation partner for René Girard, and the two men felt a strong spiritual and intellectual unity. Schwager closes a letter of June 27, 1979, with the phrase, "In the union of prayer." And in his reply of August 1, 1979, Girard affirms, "I feel an intellectual and spiritual communion with you." A great deal of the strength, cohesion, and influence of the future professional society, the Colloquium on Violence and Religion, would stem from that friendship and the spiritual patrimony that René Girard and Raymund Schwager have bequeathed to those who come after them.

The Annual Conference, 1991

The preparation for the conference at Stanford, which took place May 16–18, 1991, entailed a great deal of work. It occurred to several of us that we should have a constitution and by-laws for the new organization. In the spring of 1990 I turned particularly to Charles Mabee, Bob Kelly, and Gil Bailie for advice. None of us had any expertise in the development of rules of governance for an organization. As I looked about for some idea or model, I resorted to the constitution and by-laws of the Society of Biblical Literature, an organization to which I had belonged since the mid-1960s. I adopted a number of features of that document, often revising the wording or provisions to fit our new organization. However, that model was not a happy choice. The SBL was a large professional society with thousands of members, which required a much more complex set of rules and procedures for governance. Some of COV&R's by-laws were revised or eliminated in the following years, and a great part of the constitution was ignored in the later history of COV&R.

In any case, the annual conference in 1991 was when we became "duly constituted." I think there was a general feeling that we were truly launched as a viable entity. We had a *pro tem* advisory board—temporary only in the sense that the members were to be confirmed at the next annual meeting in 1992. René Girard was the honorary chair; Raymund Schwager the president; Wolfgang Palaver the editor of the newsletter; I was the executive secretary; and the other members were Mark Anspach, Judith Arias, Gil Bailie, Cesáreo Bandera, Diana Culbertson, Robert G. Hamerton-Kelly, Jørgen Jørgensen, Roel Kaptein, Charles Mabee, Thee Smith, Mark Wallace, and Walter Wink.

This was an outstanding group of scholars and teachers. COV&R would attract many outstanding people in the coming years, but we could not have had better, more congenial leaders for the beginning of COV&R. I have already commented extensively on René Girard and Raymund Schwager. Schwager was chosen as president by acclamation of the advisory board and confirmed as such at the business meeting. As the initial organizer of the Colloquium I was asked to continue the work I had begun by serving as executive secretary. **Wolfgang Palaver** (University of Innsbruck) was a young specialist in the thought of Thomas Hobbes and Carl Schmitt, as well as

Girard, and was especially concerned with Christianity and social order. He and his family spent the academic year 1991–1992 at Stanford, where he was a colleague of Bob Kelly at CISAC and a research associate of the Austrian Science Fund. (The title of the project was "Der Aufbau eines europäischen Systems kollektiver Sicherheit" (The Structure of a European System of Collective Security). One outcome of the project was a little book in German and an article in English: "Collective Security in Europe and Austrian Neutrality: An Ethical Reflection from the Point of View of Catholic Social Teaching," in *European Collective Security: The Policy of Neutrality.* He was chosen to be the editor of the newsletter. **Mark Anspach** was a young bilingual scholar in literature and anthropology. In the early years he wrote me several letters concerning COV&R that impressed me for the balanced perspective and sage advice. **Judith Arias** (University of East Carolina) had been one of Cesáreo Bandera's doctoral students at the University of North Carolina. Her field was late medieval and early modern Spanish literature, and she was also interested in children's literature. She would eventually perform a great service for COV&R as the first editor of its journal, *Contagion: Violence, Mimesis, and Culture,* launched in 1994. **Gil Bailie** (Florilegia—now called the Cornerstone Forum—his own adult education enterprise) has already been mentioned. His book, *Violence Unveiled,* was the most widely read of books in English by Girardian writers from 1995 into the twenty-first century. **Cesáreo Bandera** was a highly respected University Professor of Spanish literature at the University of North Carolina. He and Girard met in late 1968, and for several years while he was a colleague of Girard on the faculty of the State University of New York at Buffalo he was Girard's conversation partner regarding the mimetic scapegoat theory. He recalls how Girard would come to their weekly lunch meeting with fire in his eyes, "boiling over with *Violence and the Sacred.*"[28] Bandera would succeed Schwager as president of COV&R in 1995. **Diana Culbertson** (Kent State University) was a Benedictine nun whose field was religion and literature. She came to be in demand as a frequent speaker, and she was an ambassador for the mimetic theory within Roman Catholic circles. She would eventually serve as executive secretary and president. I have already written about **Robert Hamerton-Kelly** in the first chapter. He was a New Testament scholar who wrote books from a Girardian standpoint about the Apostle Paul and the Gospel of Mark in the 1990s. His interpretation of Paul's conversion and break with the Jewish religion of Torah ("Law") as a rejection of sacred violence was highly controversial and particularly disputed by Jewish scholars. In the period when COV&R began he was, to my mind, the most astute theological interpreter of Girard in the English-speaking world. **Jørgen Jørgensen** (Hjørring Seminarium in Denmark) was one of the Danish scholars on leave to study with Girard while I was at Stanford in 1990. He eventually published in Danish an anthology of writings about Girard, as well as his own volume on Girard's work. **Roel Kaptein** was a psychotherapist and a minister and former official in the Dutch Presbyterian Church. He had worked with a number of groups in Northern Ireland who sought to understand and resolve conflict and violence and he was a member of the Corrymeela Community. **Charles Mabee** (Marshall University) was the chairperson of the group from which COV&R sprang, the Bible, Narrative, and American Culture Seminar of the Westar Institute. He was the author of two books on American biblical interpretation: *Reimagining America* and *Seeing Sacred Texts through American Eyes*. He was quite active in the organizational and administrative work of the society for its first four or five years. **Thee Smith** (Emory University) did research and wrote about African-American traditions of faith and ritual, and he was also a consultant offering workshops in conflict resolution. He would later host an annual conference of COV&R at Emory. He and Mark Wallace coedited *Curing Violence*, which came out in 1994. **Mark Wallace** (Swarthmore College) was a theologian with an interesting and helpful combination of interests in addition to the mimetic theory: the revival of neo-orthodox theology (Karl Barth) and a new theological approach to problems of ecology. **Walter Wink** (Auburn Theological Seminary), a professor of New Testament, became well known for his trilogy of books on *The Powers*. He and his wife were widely sought for workshops on the Bible and transformation of personal and social life. I don't have records or memory indicating that he attended any of the early annual conferences. However, he was often present at COV&R's annual shorter meetings in conjunction with the American Academy of Religion and the Society of Biblical Literature, and he has maintained an interest in COV&R through the years.

Of these board members, Bailie, Culbertson, Hamerton-Kelly, Mabee, Smith, Wallace, Wink, and I had all been participants in BINAC. It was a group whose collegiality, energy, and (relative!) lack of mimetic rivalry made the inception of COV&R possible. In the ensuing years many other colleagues came into our circle who were outstanding as human beings and as contributors to our work.

The focal subject of the 1991 conference was "Mythology," with particular reference to the work of René Girard. An intellectual, and sometimes religious, reversion to myth was quite apparent in the late twentieth century. The cultural situation in North America and elsewhere in the Western world was such that both postmodernism and adherents of a neopaganism found a field of play in ancient myths and symbols. It was therefore important to clarify the role of myth in the emergence of social order.

There were thirty-nine persons registered for the conference, with a few other auditors for the session at which Girard gave his paper. There were fourteen presenters.[29] The small number, which we had also in 1992, allowed for a certain informality and an opportunity to meet everyone and have relaxed discussions. At the time I had a sense that this time of origins was a golden period, a period of enthusiasm and vision of possibilities for the future.

It was an interesting mix of colleagues and papers. Although all of the papers were good and stirred discussion, Girard's presentation was the centerpiece of the conference: "A Venda Myth Analyzed."[30] Girard analyzed the myth of Python and his two wives, a myth transmitted among the Venda people of South Africa. His methodology and anthropological conclusions were not new; he had already published them in *The Scapegoat*. However, it was an excellent mythical source for the application of his argument that however fantastic and incredible a myth like this may seem to modern men and women, there are two actual events that lie behind it. One is a crisis in the community (in this case, a drought), and the other is convergence of the community on a scapegoat (in this instance, the younger wife who is vulnerable as someone young and female). It is an excellent example of a scapegoat text (oral in origin, of course). As is typically the case, the scapegoat is accused of some crime that threatens the welfare of the community. Without a scapegoat the people's rivalries and suspicions of one another could lead to conflict and a paroxysm of violence. This potential violence is the very paradigm of the social chaos that all societies and cultures try to avoid.

However, the arbitrary violence that generates the scapegoating of the victim is camouflaged in the myth. The victim is always presented as culpable, and the social order that owes its very existence to the originary victimization stands unanimously against him or her. It is ironic that so many in sophisticated intellectual circles find myth and mythic symbols so appealing, while at the same time they are the very ones who are ruled by a dogma of political correctness. This dogma affirms the absolute value of the victim, or of those claiming the status of victim. But of course, they are blind to the victimization engendered by political correctness.

Although it is not my intention to report on all the business meetings of all the annual conferences, I will do so in cases where I have a memory or record of something really noteworthy or important for COV&R. The business meetings are held primarily for purposes of providing information to members and voting on matters recommended by the advisory board. What stands out for me from the business meeting at the end of the conference in 1991 is my recollection that I asked Hugo Assmann if he would extend an invitation to South American colleagues who were involved in "liberation theology" to participate in COV&R. Assmann, a Catholic liberation theologian, had organized a meeting, a dialogue, of theologians and social scientists with Girard, which took place June 25–29, 1990, in Piracicaba, Brazil. Girard was very impressed with the level of dialogue and the knowledge of his work among those who attended. Those gathered were mostly liberation theologians who were interested in considering the mimetic scapegoat theory as offering an alternative paradigm to the socialist tendencies of liberation theology to that point. Assmann edited a collection of papers and selected discussion highlights from that gathering.[31] The last fifty-five pages of this anthology are devoted to highlights of the four days of discussions between Girard and the other participants, as transcribed and edited by Assmann. This record contains some very interesting "autobiographical fragments" from Girard as he put his mimetic theory in the context of his own life. He speaks of feeling at ease in this cordial "Latin" atmosphere of camaraderie, and explains that his natal region of Provence in southeastern France was more Latin or Roman than the rest of France. In fact, he experienced a form of discrimination when he went to Paris to study at Ecole des Chartes during and after the war years. Those from the south or *le Midi* in France were widely regarded as having a strange, uncouth accent. He himself accepted this prejudice as true, and he did not fully understand this discrimination until he came to the United States and observed the treatment of African-Americans.[32] He also gives a description of his intellectual conversion to Christianity, which paved the way for his spiritual conversion. He speaks of a "global, massive intuition," which led to conceiving the mimetic theory. In this experience he knew with certainty "that it is about something that overcame me and that I could neither change nor abandon nor modify, because it is something like an inseparable whole."[33]

Back to that Colloquium business meeting: Assmann replied that he had no official capacity to serve as a spokesman of COV&R to South American colleagues, and he challenged us to find ways to reach out to South American scholars and others interested in Girard and listen to what they had to say. It is my regret that we lacked the requisites for doing that. We had no one in the leadership group who was able to serve as a liaison to South American colleagues, and Assmann did not feel that it was his role to do so. In any case we had too many other priorities to deal with in order to survive as a viable professional society. Moreover, in our early days and for years to come

COV&R had very limited financial resources for reimbursing the expenses of those who had to travel long distances to our conferences. I have always regretted this situation. Although a few participants from Africa, Asia, and South America have attended the conferences, COV&R's membership and sphere of activity have been confined largely to North America and Europe.

The business meeting received reports from the advisory board that were significant for organization structure, communications, and outreach. These included the proposal of a constitution, to be ratified at the next annual meeting; the publication of a biannual newsletter, *The Bulletin of COV&R,* to be edited by Wolfgang Palaver aided by Innsbruck colleagues; and the publication of a scholarly journal, provisionally titled *Journal of Violence and Religion,* to be edited by Robert Hamerton-Kelly. The first number of the *Bulletin* duly appeared in September 1991 and the constitution was ratified, with modifications, at the annual conference in May 1992. Starting a new journal was more difficult. The project of an annual journal was eventually launched at Chapel Hill in 1993, the first issue appearing in 1994.

There is one more thing about the conference that I think is worthy of mention, and it has nothing to do with the official work of the organization. There was a reception hosted by the Girards one evening. It was very pleasant, with many little groups of people engaged in conversation. A kindly looking man with white hair, dressed very informally (most of the men attending the reception were wearing suits), was moving around offering guests hors d'oeuvres from a tray. I inquired of several people who that person was. The first person or two I asked didn't know, but I eventually found out that it was Michel Serres. Serres, who had been elected to the French Academy the previous year, was an old friend of the Girards. He taught at Stanford almost every spring for many years, and he and his wife stayed with the Girards when he taught in the spring quarter. As I came to know more about the Girards and Serres I reflected that Serres serving as a waiter was not only characteristic of the unpretentiousness of Serres himself, but also reflected the Girards' friendliness, hospitality, and humility. Their home was a kind of home away from home for friends, former students, and various ones of us engaged with the mimetic theory.

Symposium in Innsbruck, 1991

A significant event in 1991 was a symposium at the University of Innsbruck: "Dramatische Erlösungslehre: Ein Symposion" ("Dramatic Doctrine of Redemption: A Symposium"). Taking place September 25–28, it was a celebration and critical discussion of the work of Raymund Schwager, and that also meant of course a discussion of the work of Girard. The symposium was organized by Józef Niewiadomski and Wolfgang Palaver, who were also the editors of the collection of papers presented.[34] Those who are concerned to gain a deeper understanding of the symposium theme and can read German would find the published papers very interesting. Schwager wrote a "*Rückblick auf das Symposium*" (Perspective on the Symposium) that gives his responses to critics of the mimetic theory and his own dramatic theology of salvation.[35] His answer to critics who raised the question whether Girard's thought depicts humans as naturally violent is particularly important for the theological ramifications of the mimetic theory.[36] To summarize Schwager's response to the questions raised, Girard does not hold that violence is a natural instinct of humans. His thinking does not tend in the direction of an "essence" or "substance" that defines human nature. Aggression and violence are possibilities in the gift of freedom for the infinite that opened up in the decisive break of the hominids from the level of animal societies, and they became practically inevitable with the origin of culture in spontaneous scapegoating and the development of the scapegoat mechanism and the sacrificial rituals, prohibitions, myths, and various other institutions of human society.[37] Theologically considered, mankind exists in a "fallen" state of mimetic rivalry, but redemption is possible through participation in God's self-revelation that breaks into the human predicament and opens up the way of freedom and love.

The works of Schwager that formed the point of departure for the critical discussion were *Brauchen wir einen Sündenbock?* (later translated into English as *Must There Be Scapegoats?*), *Der wunderbare Tausch: Zur Geschichte und Deutung der Erlösungslehre* (*The Marvelous Exchange: On the History and Interpretation of the Doctrine of Redemption*), and *Für Gerechtigkeit und Frieden: Der Glaube als Antwort auf die Anliegen der Gegenwart* (*For Righteousness and Peace: Faith as the Answer to Contemporary Concerns*). There were three broad categories of papers: biblical perspectives, systematic theology, and discussion of Girard's theory. Robert Hamerton-Kelly and James Williams presented papers on New Testament topics and Roel Kaptein gave a report, evaluation, and a practical application of mimetic theory in his work with patients in a Belfast hospital. Other COV&R members participating were Hans Jensen and Jørgen Jørgensen, as well as Schwager, Palaver, and Józef Niewiadomski. It was the first time that I met Niewiadomski, who would eventually follow his mentor Schwager in serving as dean of the Innsbruck faculty of theology. He was to become quite active in COV&R.

It was a delightful time to be in Innsbruck. I had traveled by air to Zürich, then taken a train from there to Innsbruck. The scenery was breathtaking as the train went through the mountains. About the time of the conference the *Föhn* swept in: a sirocco wind from the south that made it warm—one day it was actually hot. One afternoon Schwager and some of his colleagues took us for a picnic in the Alps near the city. Besides the 'Gemütlichkeit' of the company and the beauty of the terrain, I was fascinated with the crucifixes in every field and the cows everywhere wearing bells. Hamerton-Kelly, Kaptein, Jensen, Jørgensen, and I enjoyed restaurants in town and walking around downtown to take in the sights, including the famous Golden Roof, the balcony and roof that are part of the house built for Tirolean sovereigns by Archduke Friedrich IV in the fifteenth century.

At the conference at Stanford the previous May it was apparent that more long-range planning for future conferences was needed. Those of us on the board attending the Innsbruck conference served as an ad hoc planning committee. We met before the sessions began to outline future conferences.[38] The work of the committee was a success in that the basic topics for the next four annual meetings were conceived, and the advisory board later confirmed them. These were

1992 Ethnocentrism and Violence. At Stanford.
1993 Literary Studies, with a focus on Girard's book on Shakespeare, *A Theater of Envy*.
1994 Social Sciences, with a focus on Jean-Pierre Dupuy's Le *Sacrifice et l'envie*.
1995 Psychology and Psychoanalysis, with a focus on the work of Jean-Michel Oughourlian and Roel Kaptein.

We followed through with these themes for the annual conferences from 1992 to 1995, although there were various modifications to the specific programs.

The First Issue of The Bulletin of COV&R

As already mentioned, the first issue of *The Bulletin of COV&R* was published in September 1991. Wolfgang Palaver took on a considerable task in agreeing to serve as the editor. He was already quite busy teaching, engaged in research and writing, and fulfilling his duties as the father of a young family. He served as *Bulletin* editor for seven years. The first issue had only eleven pages. It included a bibliography of the secondary literature on the work of Girard, abstracts of the New Orleans meeting in 1990, abstracts of the annual conference at Stanford in May 1991, two book reviews, a listing of two new books, notice of the meeting of COV&R at AAR/SBL in Kansas City (November 23, 1991), and membership information. These segments were prefaced by a joint message that Palaver and I wrote on the rationale and goals of the *Bulletin*, with a description of the contents we envisaged. We noted the need to facilitate communication among scholars interested in Girard's theory, quoted the object of COV&R (already printed on the masthead), and stated that although this forum was open to all scholars of varying academic disciplines, "it will nevertheless find its focal point within the domain of the disciplines of religious studies and theology."

From Kansas City to Stanford, 1992 and Beyond

Meeting in Kansas City, 1991

There was a morning meeting of COV&R on November 23, 1991, in Kansas City, in conjunction with the annual congress of AAR/SBL. The topic was a discussion of Eugene Webb's chapter on Girard in *Philosophers of Consciousness*. It was an excellent session, highlighted by Webb's own comments on the chapter and keen responses by Andrew McKenna and Mark Wallace. The issues were several: Should Girard be ranked among philosophers or should his mimetic theory be viewed as an antidote to Western philosophy (McKenna)? Does Girard neglect an existential dimension that is distinct from mimetic rivalry, a dimension of desire for being that is rational and not conflictive (Webb)? Does Girard's contention that God's nonviolent agency is the keystone of the Bible, in a sort of canon within the canon, fail the Bible's readers and hearers because it neglects the many instances of text-mediated violence in the Bible (Wallace)?

It was healthy to get these issues out into the open in a meeting of COV&R because they were to emerge again and again in the years to come. To offer my own brief comment on these issues, those who become in any basic sense "Girardian" in their thinking usually understand the generative mimetic scapegoat theory as an antidote to the illusions of self-generated desire and individual autonomy in philosophy. That is certainly the dominant perspective among colleagues whom I know. The argument that Girard deals exclusively with the mimesis leading to conflict and rivalry has a partial justification in his early focus on that aspect of mimetic desire. However, even in major works prior to 1991 there were more than hints of *transformative* mimesis. Girard had already written of Jesus' true intention, which was centered in positive, salvific mimesis: the misunderstanding of his mission "takes place in proportion to the negative attitude of the only individuals who could have helped Jesus in his mission and initiated the good contagion of good reciprocity."[39] This is mimesis that is good because it is the desire that is formed in interaction with the divine mediator of the Kingdom of God, Jesus Christ. See also *Deceit, Desire, and the Novel*, especially his reading of Dostoyevsky. With the publication in 1991 of Girard's book on Shakespeare, *A Theater of Envy*, this transformative mimesis is spelled out at length in his commentary on *The Winter's Tale*, particularly in chapter 37, "Does not the Stone Rebuke Me for Being More Stone Than It?"[40] As for violence in the Bible, Girard interprets the Bible as a "text in travail," which carries a double sense of a "work in progress" but also a work that labors and proceeds painfully but surely toward realizing the revelation of the loving, nonviolent God that is completed in Jesus Christ. However, this issue had yet to be addressed at length. More recently Mark Heim touches on this at a number of points in *Saved from Sacrifice: A Theology of the Cross*. I summarize my own position in the preface to the reprinted edition (2007) of *The Bible, Violence, and the Sacred*. There I ask about the dynamic of history as revealed in the biblical witness. "In its witness to revelation is it working, is it agonizing to bring forth a new being, a new world, a new community, a new human being constituted by God? Of course it comes out of a past of archaic myth and ritual that has its virtues but also its deep flaws, most notably the ignorance of its own foundations in scapegoating and sacrifice." The biblical witness "is a new disclosure that moves through the remains of ancient myth, symbol, and folkways. . . . Over time and in time it illuminates the predicament of human beings caught up in mimetic rivalry and a sacral blaming process that veils the execution of innocent victims. . . . [I]n the biblical witness to God in history there is unveiled not only the origin of violence in mimetic desire, but also the antidote in the cross of Jesus."[41]

Annual Conference at Stanford, 1992

The work of preparation for COV&R 1992 began in 1991. As previously noted, the ad hoc planning committee at the symposium in Innsbruck had already proposed the topic "Ethnocentrism and Violence." (It turned out to be "Ethnocentrism and the Study of Violence.") I have letters and fax messages in my COV&R files discussing possible speakers. A couple of these declined for various reasons. Late in 1991 or early in 1992 I contacted Tobin Siebers, a professor of literature at the University of Michigan, about giving a talk on the subject of the conference and he accepted. I was particularly impressed with his critique of Lévi-Strauss, Derrida, and Nietzsche in his book *The Ethics of Criticism*.

Siebers was a former student of Girard's at Johns Hopkins University. He had a great appreciation for the role of religion in human culture. He accepted Girard's critique of religion, or transmission of the sacred, in the founding and maintenance of culture, but he did not view biblical revelation and anthropology in the same positive way that Girard did.[42] My sense was that within his own postmodern perimeters Siebers would contribute in a stimulating way to the theme of the conference, and as it turned out I was not disappointed.

One of the advisory board's decisions in planning for the 1992 conference was to hold a "praxis" workshop prior to the conference. That is, it was to be a session devoted to application of the mimetic theory and it would involve interaction between the speakers and those attending. Roel Kaptein and Raymund Schwager were the leaders, although effectively Kaptein took charge because Schwager was reticent, feeling that his English was not good enough to handle a discussion format. The announced topic was "Human Desire, Healing, and the Holy Spirit." It was held at the First Methodist Church in Palo Alto (the home church of the Hamerton-Kellys) and was sponsored by the church's Committee on Discipleship and Spiritual Nurture. A number of the church members attended and conversed with COV&R members.

The event was one of several through the years in connection with COV&R conferences that focused on practice rather than theory. Many individual workshops and seminars on spiritual, ethical, and sociological implications and applications of mimetic theory have been quite good. However, we have not been successful in establishing them as a prominent part of the meetings due to the Colloquium's more theoretical orientation. Yet there have always been some members who desired a combination of theory and praxis. This is one of the main reasons that a new group, Theology and Peace, was started in January 2007. Its leadership and Girardian orientation came directly out of COV&R. I will say more about Theology and Peace in a later chapter.

"Ethnocentrism and the Study of Violence," Stanford, May 7–9, 1992

The conference itself was a memorable one. For one thing, there was a remarkable adherence to the theme of the conference. Tobin Siebers and René Girard gave a general frame of reference with their presentations, Siebers on "The

Ethics of Anti-Ethnocentrism" and Girard on "Ethnocentrism and Western Culture." Siebers concluded that the vogue of "multiculturalism" and "ethnicity" was a way of shifting the question of race relations to the university setting. This in effect scapegoats the university, placing on it problems that were to be solved within the academic setting. The debates over these problems thus take place in the university, but this is exclusionary because very few of those most affected participate in the higher academic setting, namely the racially excluded, the underprivileged, and the poor. If we put this in the best light, the shift from civil rights to multiculturalism reflects the politics of the "trickle down" effect, that is, trying to solve the problem of race relations from the top down. In the worst light, the university becomes the scapegoat, bearing the burden of what federal, state, and local governments should be addressing.

Three of the other four papers directly addressed ethnocentrism in different texts and settings. In addition to these there was a brief intervention on ethnocentrism and Girard's work and a panel discussion of Hamerton-Kelly's recently published book, *Sacred Violence: Paul's Hermeneutic of the Cross*. The panel discussion was to take place on Saturday afternoon. That event, plus the presence of Mikhail Gorbachev at Stanford for a lecture, made that a very noteworthy day indeed. As I recall, we learned of the Gorbachev lecture only immediately prior to the conference, so we had to push the panel discussion and our concluding business meeting later in the afternoon. We were told that those who wished to attend the lecture in the Frost Amphitheater on the Stanford campus should arrive two hours early in order to get a seat. There was great interest at Stanford in Gorbachev's lecture although it did not compare to the excitement in 1990 when Gorbachev first spoke at Stanford. Because the Berlin wall had fallen late in 1989, the ramifications of the end of the cold war were still being felt and discussed in the following year.

The welcome and introduction were scheduled to start at 11:00 in the morning, and by that time the sun was really beating down on us in the amphitheater; it was unusually hot for early May. The temperature must have been close to ninety degrees (Fahrenheit) by noon. I have pictures of various COV&R colleagues sitting in the amphitheater, some of them wearing paper hats, made with whatever sheets of paper anyone had, to protect their heads.

Gorbachev's announced topic was "The Rule of Law: Our New Frontier." It was uncomfortably hot and the lecture had to be translated by an interpreter on the podium. The appearance of Gorbachev seemed to fit in with the theme of our conference, and the topic of international law was certainly relevant. The concept of international law, if arrived at by international consensus, would override ethnocentric prejudices. However, the lecture title was probably the wording formulated by his Stanford hosts. The former secretary of the Communist Party in the U.S.S.R. focused on defending his actions in the breaking up of the Soviet dictatorship. One quotation from a news release on his speech is quite relevant to the mimetic theory: "Therefore, I tried to use tactical moves to gain time to give the democratic movement a chance to get stronger. As president of the country I had many powers, including emergency ones, and more than once people tried to make me use them, tried to push me into an extremist position." He went on to say that "I could not betray myself."[43] The situation of "people" exerting pressure on a leader toward an extremist position is a radically mimetic one. The leader then confronts the options of either capitulating and accepting the position of those pressing him, or reacting against it to the degree that he takes extreme measures, perhaps even violent ones, against his opponents. It is a rare leader who desires and acts to find a third way. Whether or not Gorbachev really acted as virtuously as he claimed, the conviction that one cannot betray oneself has to be based on faith in a supreme sacred authority or sacred source of authorization, whether explicitly articulated or not. Trust in and imitation of a peacemaking divine model is the only position that offers a way out of the mimetic predicament.

The most remarkable event of the COV&R conference itself was a confrontation between Robert Hamerton-Kelly and Sandor Goodhart. The format of the discussion of Hamerton-Kelly's book on Paul and the Torah was that two New Testament scholars would first comment on it, with Kelly responding. They were Paul Duff, who spoke on "Sacred Violence and Social Order in 1 Corinthians," and Neill Elliot, whose topic was "Paul and the Lethality of the Law: Issues in Interpretation"—a paper that dealt primarily with Hamerton-Kelly's work on Galatians and Romans. Hamerton-Kelly then responded, sharply criticizing the two presentations. But that was not the end of the matter. As the moderator, Ted Peters, opened the floor for general discussion, Sandor Goodhart stood up and became in effect a third panelist. A few Jewish scholars (not members of COV&R) had already read Hamerton-Kelly's book and were offended by it. So was Goodhart. He objected to Hamerton-Kelly's treatment on the grounds that the Torah should not be understood as rooted in sacred violence, but is a witness to God that teaches anti-idolatry, opposition to idols, opposition to making anything or anyone other than God the ultimate object of worship and devotion. He also said that Hamerton-Kelly's interpretation of Torah as rooted in sacred violence was especially objectionable in light of the Holocaust.[44] The exchange between the two was very sharp and angry, the first time we had had an experience of that kind in the context of a COV&R event. There were a few others in the gathering who made remarks, but we seemed to getting nowhere in dealing with the dividing wall that had risen up between the two protagonists. At the point that Goodhart brought up the Holocaust as a basis for objecting to Hamerton-Kelly's treatment of Paul, Vern Redekop spoke up and attempted to serve as a mediator. Redekop is a Mennonite, an Old Testament scholar and a specialist in conflict resolution. He asked for everyone to pause and he invited the two combatants to listen to one another's real concerns and discern where they were wounded by the antagonism of the other. Goodhart was sincerely concerned about what he viewed as an accusation of foundational violence at the heart of Judaism, especially in light of the murder of millions of Jews in Europe during the Nazi regime. Hamerton-Kelly objected to this connection of the Holocaust to his hermeneutics, which led him to the conclusion that the Torah represented a double exclusiveness that produced violence: it was responsible for the death of Christ and for the wall of separation between Jew and Gentile.[45] I don't remember in any detail how the two protagonists and all those gathered then talked and listened their way to a cessation of hostilities, but a sort of peace did finally prevail. This is not to say that everything was moonlight and roses for those who participated in the debate, which had been acrimonious until some resolution was achieved. However, Hamerton-Kelly and Goodhart both found a way of working together in COV&R through the years and treating each other with respect. This respect has developed into collegial friendship. This, I think, is partially due to their common friendship with Girard and their acceptance of the mimetic theory, but also and simultaneously a commitment to participating in good mimesis. That is, they have sought to obey the peacemaking mandate and work of the nonviolent God. René Girard himself is nothing more—and nothing less!—than a messenger of this divine voice in human history.

Redekop's intervention was an important practical lesson in the potential for resolution of conflict when an intervening voice offers an option of peaceful mimesis in a situation of mimetic rivalry. But it works only if the parties involved recognize or experience the inspiration or authority undergirding the intervening voice. Redekop's authority derived from the power of the mimetic theory but, as stated in the previous paragraph, that in turn is based on an understanding of the voice of the biblical God speaking through history.

One positive change that this debate triggered was an ongoing Jewish-Christian dialogue. Participants in the early years included presentations by Sandor Goodhart, Charles Mabee, Raymund Schwager, and me. Eventually the conference at Purdue University in 2002, organized by Goodhart and Ann Astell, highlighted Jewish-Christian issues.

In the meeting of the advisory board there were two important matters that affected the future of COV&R. One was amending the constitution, the other was incorporation. With prior input from other board members, I proposed five amendments, which the board accepted and recommended to the membership.

1. Addition of "at Stanford" in Article I: "The Colloquium on Violence and Religion at Stanford." We thought the institutional identification would help us in fund-raising. (I don't know of any evidence that it actually did.)
2. In Article III, the addition of the office of treasurer. Gil Bailie had already been helping me with financial records, and he agreed to accept this position.
3. In Article IV, changing the provision from eight to eleven elected members of the Advisory Board in addition to the officers.
4. Article V provided for a nominating committee. We recommended that this should be eliminated, as a nominating committee was too cumbersome for a small society.
5. In Article VIII, deletion of the last clause requiring three months prior notification of the membership for a proposed amendment. Again, we thought this was too cumbersome for our society at its current stage.

Since the last amendment was recommended under the constitution in place when the conference began, we informed the members present at the business meeting and had the changes formally approved at the 1993 meeting at the University of North Carolina. These amendments simply reflect the awareness of governing rules necessary for the stage of COV&R at the time. As the Colloquium has developed and grown, the constitution should probably be revisited more often than it has been.

The second important matter we discussed was incorporation, which would enable us to seek and receive tax-deductible contributions. I was not initially the person charged with looking into that, but as it turned out the responsibility fell on me as executive secretary some time in the late summer or early fall of 1992. I soon found out that it entailed an extensive amount of telephoning and paperwork. It took several years to come to a satisfactory answer to the question of incorporation. For assistance I consulted my friend Fred Marty, a lawyer in Syracuse. He finally advised me in the spring of 1995 that at the present stage of the organization it was still too small for incorporation. Thus it was deferred until a later time. In 2004 Duncan Ragsdale, a COV&R member and lawyer in Memphis, Tennessee, offered to pursue the matter, and we finally achieved incorporation status in 2006. That is a development to which I will turn later in the book.

So, in many respects the meeting at Stanford in 1992 was important and memorable. A count of members in the early spring prior to the conference indicated sixty persons registered as members; fifteen of these were European. It was estimated that five more had joined by the time of the conference. The growth in membership was slow but steady. In retrospect I can see that it enabled us to get our bearings. We were not overwhelmed with a huge number of people and competing desires and proposals that could have been difficult to sort out and allow us to remain in collegial relationships. At some point in those early years when I was conversing with Girard, I expressed my worry about our slow membership growth. He replied with words to the effect that we shouldn't have concerns about being "popular" and attracting people for the wrong reasons. His comment reflected his own journey with his "idea," his concept of mimetic desire and its effects in the generative scapegoat mechanism, which was roundly attacked by many and put him in a minority position in the academic world, particularly when he began to reveal his Christian commitment in published works. If we had grown quickly in appealing to academic fashion we could have soon become entrapped in the mimetic predicaments and sacred violence that characterized the world about us. Not that we were immune to that because of our focus on the mimetic theory and our numbers were small, but by and large we were able to think and feel our way with a sense of integrity.

Meeting in San Francisco, 1992

The other event in 1992 was a meeting of one day at AAR/SBL in San Francisco on November 20. My feeling at the time was that it was an excellent meeting both in terms of intellectual exchange and cordial atmosphere. Charles Mabee gave a paper comparing Girard and Rudolf Bultmann on the problem of myth, and Robert Hamerton-Kelly responded to Mabee's paper. Both presentations were well done. In the ensuing discussion René Girard made the most telling comment: the Gospels should not be primarily the object of demythologization; rather, they are the source of it. Leo Perdue, an Old Testament scholar well known for his work in wisdom literature and Old Testament theology, presented an appreciative critique of my book, *The Bible, Violence, and the Sacred.* He raised a number of important questions concerning justice and the God of victims. For example, how does God defend victims? How do humans defend victims, apart from acts of violence? As is commonly the case, he focused on scapegoating but did not deal with mimetic desire, which is necessary for understanding the mimetic theory.[46]

But was the meeting that cordial? Later I would find out that it was not congenial for everyone. There was a person present whose experience of the event was quite negative. I did not find out about it until about three years later. I mention it here because the dynamic of COV&R, its very engine, operates effectively to the extent that we not only *study* mimetic desire and generative scapegoating, but that we *act and relate to others* with a minimal level of mimetic rivalry. That is what charity and justice are about; not necessarily "love" in an intimate or affectionate sense, but seeing and acknowledging the other as also the object of divine love whom we do not have to defeat or before whom we have to flaunt superiority or feel inferior.

That person who attended and was "turned off" by the gathering was Björn Krondorfer. I found out about his reaction only when he responded to an article I wrote that was published late in 1995.[47] Though his response to my essay included a few favorable remarks in passing, it was primarily an attack on the mimetic theory, which in the form represented by Girard and me he considered a "remythologization" of Scripture. In his view, we were hung up on "vesting the Scriptures . . . with authoritative, revelatory, redemptive power."[48] He commented in his response-article that he attended the COV&R meeting in San Francisco. "Half-jokingly I told friends after the session that it reminded me of a revivalist meeting among academics."[49] This raised a question for me: were there others there who felt the same way? Had this happened at other meetings?

I wrote him a letter responding (none too gently) to many of the points in his response to my article, and toward the close I asked him whether he had tried to converse with any of us during the breaks or afterwards. I would have been glad to meet him and have an informal conversation. He did not answer that question in his letter replying to me. Part of the problem in perception was probably due to the nature of our discussion in the COV&R sessions. We should be sensitive to those present who are, or feel like, outsiders in the discussion. This is an ongoing problem in any kind of organization or society. But in broader cultural and intellectual terms, the issue was one of postmodernism versus a religious and philosophical position that was basically foundational, that appealed to sacred authority in some fashion. The issues have been well described by Philip Rieff, particularly in his posthumous volumes on *Sacred Order / Social Order*.[50] Krondorfer speaks and writes out of the "third culture," which is a culture that is transgressive, attacking and transgressing the boundaries of the kind of culture (the "second culture") that appeals to foundations and a sacred order. His reading of the Bible does not accept it as a witness to the revelation of God or the saving power of Jesus' death and resurrection. Those who participate in COV&R have to have at least "one foot" in what Rieff calls the second culture, at least enough to engage in dialogue with one another. Almost without exception, as far as I know, they are either religious or have a background disposing them to take the study of religion seriously. So it may appear to thoroughgoing secularist academics whose thinking and sensibilities are "postmodern" (or "third culture") that many of COV&R's meetings have a "revivalist" tone. But within the Colloquium the fact that an intellectual can take religion seriously and even be religious is simply taken for granted.

Later the same day at the COV&R meeting Rebecca Adams conducted an important interview of Girard in which he clarified the goodness of mimetic desire. That is, it is good insofar as it manifests an active, positive desire for the other. Adams asked whether "it's possible within your theory to fully account for this desire on behalf of the Other—for nonviolent, saintly desire." Girard replied, "Wherever you have . . . that really active, positive desire for the other, there is some kind of divine grace present. This is what Christianity unquestionably tells us."[51]

The Annual Conference in Chapel Hill, 1993 and Beyond

The early development of COV&R entered into a new phase in 1993: for the first time our major annual gathering would take place away from our home base at Stanford University, where Girard had generously used his Mellon funds to help us get started. The next conference would be at the University of North Carolina in Chapel Hill. The co-organizers were Judith Arias of East Carolina University and Cesáreo Bandera. Bandera was the host and made arrangements at North Carolina, and Arias handled the correspondence and program planning. The theme of the conference was "Literature and the Sacred." They did a superb job, and the setting at the Carolina Inn was lovely.

The event was propitious for Bandera. A year or two before he had planned an event to be held in Spain, with the funding to come from an office of the Spanish government. It turned out that the funding was not approved. When he learned of our intention to hold a conference in 1993 on the mimetic theory and literary studies, he proposed that we hold it at the University of North Carolina. He had already planned to invite a number of those in COV&R to present papers in Spain, so to hold a COV&R meeting at Chapel Hill dovetailed perfectly with his plans.

COV&R's membership had grown considerably from the previous year, so that by March of 1993 we had ninety-four members registered, in addition to two institutional memberships. We anticipated a somewhat greater attendance for the meeting at Chapel Hill, and that turned out to be the case. There were fifty-two registrants, with others in attendance for some of the sessions. There were eleven participants from Europe, the largest number yet. It was also the first time that there were speakers on the program who had no affiliation with COV&R or any association with Girard or the mimetic theory.

"Literature and the Sacred" University of North Carolina, April 22–24, 1993

The meeting of the advisory board in the home of Cesáreo and Esther Bandera had an important issue facing it. Were we going to launch a journal, as we had first discussed at the beginning of COV&R in 1990? It did not take long to reach the consensus that we would indeed go ahead with it, especially since Judith Arias was willing to head the project and serve as its first editor, with Bandera as the associate editor. It would be published by East Carolina University, where Arias was on the faculty. It was an enormous amount of work for Arias to get the journal started as she carried her normal teaching load and engaged in her own research. Our intention was to publish essays from selected papers at the annual conferences of COV&R, in addition to other papers that were worthy of publication. There would be a refereeing process supervised by the editor. Arias succeeded in having the first volume published in 1994. More on that first issue in the next chapter.

We consumed even more time at the board meeting discussing a name for the new periodical. When the subject was first broached in 1990 we quickly came up with the title *Journal of Violence and Religion*. The problem with that was that it did not give an adequate indication of what the mimetic theory was about. A number of possibilities were discussed, one of which was *Contagion*. Many, including myself, had reservations about it. It was intriguing, for it is a great metaphor of the mimetic process. Indeed, although it is known primarily as a medical term, it may well have had its origin as a word expressing the operation, the "contagion," of mimetic desire. Many terms that are associated with different functions and spheres of life in law, medicine, physics, and so on, originated in aspects of social life.[52]

Still, some among us were concerned that seeing the title *Contagion*, most people would mistake it for a medical journal. During the course of the year the advisory board delegated the authority to make a final decision on the name to those board members attending the meeting of the Colloquium in conjunction with AAR/SBL in Washington, DC. There *Contagion* won the day, on which more shortly.

One notable thing about the conference itself was the interdisciplinary range of the presentations. The titular theme of the conference, "The Sacred and Literature," was reflected in the broadest spectrum of papers we had had at a COV&R conference. Reflections on the divine and the sacred were given in the treatment of texts in French, Spanish, Italian, English, Norwegian, Chinese, Japanese, and biblical literature. There was a paper on a film and one on Girardian theory and feminism. All those presented by COV&R members were very good to excellent. Girard's lecture on anti-Semitism in the Gospels was one of the major presentations.[53] His thesis was that rather than being an attack on the Jews, the Gospel witness to the crucifixion of Jesus proclaims instead an exposure of the scapegoat mechanism in a long series of murders that began with "the foundation of the world." As long as Christians do not understand the meaning and significance of these Gospel passages they will be unable to counter the charge that the Gospels are anti-Jewish.

The organizer, Cesáreo Bandera, presented a paper that represented a major concern in his work as a specialist in Spanish literature with a deep and keen knowledge of classical literature. The title was "Separating the Human from the Divine." This paper stemmed from his outstanding and original work, particularly in research and writing on Miguel de Cervantes and Pedro Calderón de la Barca (known generally as Calderón).[54] It is important to take note of his work because he arrived at an actual *literary* theory, which he developed out of Girard's mimetic theory. Girard's work began with literary texts and he has produced brilliant readings. In the broad range of his thought he almost always returns to these texts, but his interest was never literary as such; it is an interdisciplinary approach whose methodological axis is anthropological and whose generative power is religious and theological.

The question Bandera posed was what happened to treatment of sacred themes and figures in the transition from medieval to Renaissance literature in the sixteenth to the seventeenth centuries. He refers to the "allergic" reaction reflected in Cervantes' prologue to *Don Quijote:* the "'mixing of the human and the divine,' which . . . 'is a kind of motley in which no Christian understanding should be dressed.'"[55] There are numerous examples of this refusal to mix the two. The performance of "sacred mysteries" in particular was affected. Christ and Christian figures and symbols could not be presented in theater or poetry. A series of prohibitions occurred, from the 1548 decree of the Paris parliament forbidding the Confrèrie de la Passion to perform the Passion of Christ and other sacred mysteries, to the gradual disappearance of the *autos sacramentales* (sacred plays) in Spain in the eighteenth century. In fact, the sacred mystery performances in Spain lasted as long as they did only because of the brilliant mastery of Calderón. The dressing up of Christian themes in chivalric literary form was particularly offensive to Christian moralists and theologians. A few such attempts were promptly stopped by the Inquisition, and yet the Spanish Inquisition never officially banned secular books of chivalry, in spite of urgent demands from some of the most rigorous quarters to do that.

Yet if we put this separation of the human and the divine in relief against the work of Dante (1265–1321), we can see that a tremendous change occurred in subsequent years. In the *Divine Comedy* Dante gathers his perception of the historical reality of Florence and Italy in 1300 into his vision of the divine order of all things. Yet two centuries later such a mixing of things human and divine—which was "striking in Dante only for the vastness of its scope—would be totally out of place, indeed shocking and unacceptable."[56] Torquato Tasso (1544–1595) and John Milton (1608–1674) "were as Christian as Dante, and yet they could no longer do what he did."[57] It was the same Christian consciousness that was the obstacle to doing what Dante did.

So what accounts for this rapid change? In response Bandera mentions first the factor of a new historical awareness. However, without completely dismissing it, he observes that the rational character of this explanation is flawed. The change was quick and radical; it was, in his way of putting it, an "allergy" to the mixture of the human and the divine. Something primeval was at work in this development.[58] This something primeval is the differentiation of the sacred and the profane of which Emile Durkheim wrote. The sacred and the profane, says Durkheim, "have always and everywhere been conceived by the human mind as two distinct classes, as two worlds between which there is nothing in common."[59] Durkheim spoke of an "irresistible refusal" of the human mind to confound the two categories. This refusal is what Bandera calls "sacred allergy."

The paradox is that this most basic of all distinctions is at the same time the most fragile. The sacred is set within bounds, separated from the profane, both because it is felt to be absolutely necessary while also the most dangerous reality. It is extraordinarily contagious, so whatever it touches becomes sacred itself. Thus it is that "the sacred, that which is worshipped or revered as the ultimate guarantor of stability in the community, is also the very source of instability or undifferentiation."[60] Now what Girard's theory of the sacred adds to and completes in the understanding of this fundamental distinction in human life is the collective scapegoat mechanism that settles on the victim as the event which bridges the gap between the chaos of undifferentiation and the differentiation that enables hominization, the emergence of mankind.

If the victimizing process is the basis of believing almost instinctively in the "absolute" difference between the sacred and the profane, then the "allergy" becomes only worse if any awareness of this victimizing, leading to doubt about the reality of the sacred, begins to enter into existential involvements of human beings. Like the medical allergy, which is a reaction of the body's defense (immune) system, the human heart and mind defends itself against a breakdown of the absolute demarcation that seems to make culture possible. The developing guilt, the process of "culpabilisation,"[61] results in an erosion of the sacrificial mechanism that is "specifically Christian in character" and "leads to individual introspection, to the turning of the blame from the publicly recognized enemy toward the questioning self."[62] This weakness of the sacrificial mechanism was to be advantageous to the development of modern poetic fiction. Poetic fiction becomes "shaken enough at its sacrificial core to bring such a core into view, but without its terrifying sacrificial power, tamed enough to be looked in the face by the best poets and prompted to reveal some of the oldest secrets of mankind."[63]

This essay left me with a basic question, which I posed to Bandera: Since the Christian revelation subverts the archaic sacred with its absolute differentiation between the sacred and the profane, the "allergic reaction" to the mixing of the human and the divine appears to be a defense *that reverts powerfully to that archaic sacred.* From the standpoint of the Christian revelation, the refusal to confound these spheres since Dante could be viewed as a deterioration in a very basic respect. To put this in another way, the primeval distinction between sacred and profane has largely assimilated the Christian revelation of the divine. Otherwise, why couldn't there be another Dante?

His response was as follows:[64]

> The "allergic reaction" is indeed a reversion to the inherent logic of the most archaic sacred, or perhaps I should say a reversion pointing in the direction of the most archaic sacred. It points in that direction, but it doesn't really get there. It is a typical archaic sacrificial reaction, except

> that it no longer has the strength of the original archaic one. It has been weakened under the influence of Christianity. It is a similar phenomenon to what Girard showed in the case of medieval texts of persecution. Had it not been weakened the "allergic reaction" would have led to the banning of all fiction-making poets from Christian society (something similar to Plato's expulsion of the poets from his ideal republic). As it actually happened, the 16th century Christian poet could clearly see the profound sacrificial roots of his fiction, and, therefore, its equally profound incompatibility with Christ. And yet he did not panic, he did not expel poetry and the poets, because in those sacrificial roots he also saw humanity itself, primitive humanity, unredeemed humanity, and, therefore, the very reason for the coming of Christ. He could see that Christ could never be mixed up with traditional fiction making, poetic catharsis, and all the rest, but sacrificial expulsion was no longer an option, because when he looked at primitive humanity he was looking at himself. Apparently Dante, and the Middle Ages in general, never had this kind of experience, the vision of this profound incompatibility between Christ and poetic fiction. He could dress the most profound Christian truths in totally fictitious poetic attire, and do it sincerely, in perfectly good faith. Nobody could do that after him with a straight face, so to speak, without apologies, not even Milton. Of course, it is not a question of deciding who was a better Christian. They were all equally sincere in their Christianity. It was the Christian revelation itself that did it, as it worked its irreversible way through a human history that never loses completely its link to the archaic sacred: *larvatus prodeo.*[65]

In commenting further about the impact of the Christian revelation on literature, Bandera stated that the sacred-profane distinction does not exist in light of the coming of Christ, the "emptying" (*kenosis*) of God into humanity (Philippians 2:6–8). For Christ "there is no such thing as a boundary between the sacred and the secular." Literary fiction would not exist if the archaic boundary between sacred and profane should dissolve. There would probably be narratives of some sort, perhaps in the style of the Old Testament and Gospel accounts, but there would be no genres such as epics, comedies, tragedies, and so on. As Girard indicated in *Deceit, Desire, and the Novel,* "'the only way for fiction to tell the truth is to . . . renounce itself, to point to something which is . . . beyond itself.' The truth has nothing of the titillating excitement that makes an artistic fiction interesting, as I point out repeatedly in my *Quijote* book."[66]

One other notable presentation in terms of the discussion it stimulated was given by Susan Nowak, a doctoral student at Syracuse University. She presented a paper on Girardian theory and feminism: "The Girardian Theory and Feminism: Critique and Appropriation." It was particularly well received, and it came as a pleasant surprise to COV&R participants to hear a feminist scholar negotiate the way between feminist critiques of the mimetic theory and its potential for feminist theory.[67] Her paper had three parts: elements of Girardian theory that feminists find useful; elements of the theory that feminists judge to belong to an androcentric-patriarchal worldview; and a critique of the feminist critique. Her key point in the critique of the critique was based on Girard's concept of difference, "the model of the exception in the process of emerging." This model is not based on the binary oppositionism that informs structuralism and deconstructionism. The Girardian concept of difference is predicated on the conviction that violence and victimage are not necessary to the process of differentiation.[68]

A concern that arose at this conference was whether it was desirable to have "outside" speakers. There was no doubt that it was valid and necessary to invite speakers who were critical of the mimetic theory as long as they had a basic grasp of the subject and were willing to enter into discussion. For this conference I invited, with the approval of Arias and Bandera, two scholars from Duke University to respond to the biblical papers presented by Sandor Goodhart and me. My idea was that it was good to have a couple of outside scholars who were well known in their fields. A practical economic factor in my thinking was that Duke was located in Durham, close to Chapel Hill, so no travel expense would be required. James Crenshaw, teaching in the Duke Divinity School, had already published extensively on Old Testament subjects, especially prophecy and wisdom literature. Wesley Kort, located in the university department of religion, was well acquainted with biblical literature and well known for his work in religion and literature. But that part of the program was disappointing because not only did they know nothing about the mimetic theory, they were also not remotely interested in a dialogue with the group. I mention it here because it was a problem that would occur more and more as the COV&R membership grew and program organizers, either desired to have, or were required by circumstances to have, speakers who were on the program to do their own thing without regard to the purpose and operative concerns of COV&R. There are arguments pro and con about that. It has remained an ambiguity in COV&R policy. In some instances, such outsiders have become friends of COV&R; in other instances it has been simply another item in their vita. Having speakers from outside has certainly benefited us when they have been willing and able to engage in discussion and dialogue.

The Meeting in Washington, DC, November 1993

The COV&R program in Washington during the convention of AAR/SBL was well attended. There were three sessions. One paper was given by Darrell Fasching of the University of South Florida on "The Ethical Challenge of Auschwitz and Hiroshima: Apocalypse or Utopia?" He was not a COV&R member or familiar with the mimetic theory, but the topic was one of great interest to Girardians. In 1993 he published a book of the same title. Ted Peters was the respondent. Most of the discussion revolved around Fasching's thesis that Martin Luther was the major source and influence in the German capitulation to a higher authority that was believed to be the voice of divinity in history. It is a significant subject, but unfortunately there was little engagement with the mimetic theory as such. In another session Martha Reineke offered a commentary on some of the essays in *Curing Violence*, edited by Mark Wallace and Thee Smith. She proposed a *topological analysis* as contrasted with a *utopian hermeneutics* as the best way of approaching the work of Girard, and on that basis gave an appreciative critique of the mimetic theory in the light of feminist concerns. In a third session Charles Mabee and I made presentations concerning the Suffering Servant of the Second Isaiah. Mabee argued that the Apostle Paul should be interpreted in light of the Servant and held that the songs of the Servant were the key to his self-definition of his ministry. I offered three questions concerning the Suffering Servant for further study and reflection. The most important of these had to do with the relation of the exodus of Israel from Egypt to the new "going out" of Babylonian exile proclaimed in Isaiah 40–55, which is an excellent example of "the exception in the process of emerging": How is this new exodus related to the Suffering Servant of the Lord? Is there a connection between them?

During the days of the convention in Washington the members of the advisory board met as an ad hoc committee authorized to make a final decision on the name of the journal. Judith Arias could not be there, but there were six or seven board members present. A consensus quickly emerged to call the new periodical *Contagion*. However, we had to spend a lot of time ruminating on possible subtitles. All of us thought that *Contagion*, which might be misleading in any event, should go with an appropriate subtitle in order to convey a sense of the range of the mimetic theory. We finally reached agreement on *Contagion: Journal of Violence, Mimesis, and Culture*. I remember that I wanted "religion" in the title, but we could not include all the relevant words. It has had three distinguished, hardworking editors at this writing: Arias served from 1993 to 1996 (although the first issue did not appear until 1994). Andrew McKenna followed her, serving from 1996 to 2006. William Johnsen took over in 2006 and has been the editor until the present. I will say more about McKenna and Johnsen at later points in this history.

Perspective: The First Three Years of COV&R

A few things stand out in the early history of COV&R and can be touched on here. One is certainly the excitement and satisfaction most of us felt in discovering the work of Girard and in seeking to extend and implement it. There was the sense of a journey just beginning, an adventure of work and fellowship as we sought to develop a new professional society.

Along with Charles Mabee, Gil Bailie, Thee Smith, and a number of others, I hoped that it would take form not only as a society of scholars but also of practitioners in various fields, such as clergy, psychologists, social workers, and others. This hope was only partially realized. However, one related organization that was started in 2007, Theology and Peace, owes its inspiration and impetus to the mimetic theory, but it is much more oriented to praxis, particularly in working with churches concerned with peacemaking and helping in theologically or ethically based community development (e.g., in the cooperation of churches in the aftermath of Hurricane Katrina in New Orleans).

Of course, COV&R began and has developed as it has in great part due to the person and work of René Girard. He gave us his blessing from the start, offered his university resources, and he and Martha Girard extended the hospitality of their home to COV&R people. Due to the wide range of the fruitfulness of Girard's mimetic theory in literature, theology, sociology, anthropology, psychology, and other fields, the COV&R meetings must be as interdisciplinary as one would find in any professional society.

Concerning practical matters of group management, on the other hand, Girard has not taken an active part in the administration of COV&R, and I don't know of a single instance in which he has tried to bend some policy decision to his will or blacklist anyone. The only occasion I can recall when he made a public statement approving and advocating a perspective or approach to which he presumed everyone should agree was during the annual conference at Ghost Ranch in 2004. In a panel discussion he said, in effect, that the signature theology, the theology identifying COV&R, should be that of Raymund Schwager. This moment will come up later in chapter 4.

One factor in the successful early development of COV&R was the relative cohesiveness of the work of the leaders. Not only did we have a group of outstanding scholars, but also there was a spirit of a community almost without exception; there was a common appreciation of, and commitment to, the purpose of the Colloquium. There were no prima donnas. We all recognized that the *sine qua non* of our organization was the genius of René Girard, but it was not a genius to be worshipped in a pagan fashion; rather it was a great gift that resulted in a body of work to be analyzed, understood, criticized, and implemented in society and culture. We did not have to worry about rivalry with Girard, and any feelings of hostile competition that existed in our midst were relatively scarce.

In those early years our conferences had the advantage of bringing together a small number of people. We were all concerned about growth, outreach, and influence, although as I have noted, Girard calmed our anxiety about this to some extent by pointing out that it was not our task to become a "popular" movement or group, for that would only fall into the mimetic entanglements and scandals of popular assumptions, fads and fashions that always disguised the violence of the scapegoat mechanism. In any event, the conferences were small enough in the first three years that most participants felt free to speak up in discussions, and they had many opportunities to talk informally with others who held common interests. As far as I know, those who went away from COV&R meetings with a bad taste in their mouth were rare.[69]

The only public incident in which there was offense taken and a really angry exchange was the encounter between Hamerton-Kelly and Goodhart, which I have already recounted. Although that incident did not end completely to the satisfaction of either antagonist, with hurt feelings and issues remaining afterward, the two were able to work together to the good of COV&R through the ensuring years and eventually became collegial friends.

On the matter of membership growth, COV&R seemed to be increasing its registered members slowly but surely. There were almost one hundred registered as members by the end of 1993. In research and publication, many COV&R colleagues were quite prolific, as one can see from scanning the bibliographies given in the issues of *The Bulletin of COV&R*. Of course, the "Bibliography of Literature on the Mimetic Theory" was intended to be as comprehensive as possible, so a number of the books, articles, and reviews were the work of nonmembers. Still, the contribution of members to the extension of the mimetic theory through research and writing was significant. To give an idea of the research and writing by noting only book publications, COV&R authors or editors of books listed in the bibliographies of the *Bulletin,* 1991–1993, included René Girard, James Alison, Stefano Cochetti, Paul Dumouchel, Jean-Pierre Dupuy, Robert G. Hamerton-Kelly, Hans J. L. Jensen, Roel Kaptein, Andrew McKenna, Józef Niewiadomski, Jean-Michel Ougourlian, Wolfgang Palaver, Raymund Schwager, Simon Simonse, Eugene Webb, James G. Williams, and Walter Wink. Some of these writers were credited with multiple titles.

One of the expectations from the beginning of COV&R was that it encourage and support extensive collaborative projects. At the Chapel Hill conference in 1993 a proposal was made to begin ongoing collaborative groups in biblical literature and in psychology. The result was a few meetings of groups and workshops in subsequent years, but these attempts did not flourish and no published work resulted. The collaborative work eventually initiated among colleagues in theology at the University of Innsbruck was more successful. Also, the work of Imitatio, which is an organization related to COV&R that was formed in 2008, has very extensive collaborative research and writing under way. It will be discussed in chapter 5.

Brief Biographies of COV&R Leaders

Gil Bailie

Gil Bailie was an early enthusiast for the beginning of COV&R. He had been offering courses for adults through his Florilegia Institute in Sonoma, California, during the 1980s when Robert Funk telephoned him one day in 1988. Funk, the founder and director of the Westar Institute, told him that the Bible, Narrative, and American Culture Seminar of Westar planned to host René Girard for a day of discussions: could Gil provide a meeting place in his facilities? Bailie had discovered Girard's work not long before, so he jumped at the chance to provide a venue and participate in BINAC. He found Girard in person to be even superior in thought and presence to the persona of his writings. Bailie was subsequently a strong supporter when we got the Colloquium started, and he served as our first treasurer. His smiling, encouraging presence meant much to the early group that formed around Girard.

Besides serving as treasurer and member of the advisory board, Bailie has presented numerous papers at meetings through the years. One of his most notable contributions to COV&R and the spread of the mimetic theory was the publication of *Violence Unveiled: Humanity at the Crossroads,* which appeared in 1995. For a nonspecialist audience it was the most accessible book on the mimetic theory in English that had been published and it is still widely read. Bailie continues his work through his organization, now called the Cornerstone Forum. Drawing upon mimetic theory in his theological commentary and critique of culture, he devotes himself completely to the explication and defense of orthodox Catholic theology in the contemporary world.

Wolfgang Palaver

Wolfgang Palaver, an Austrian, obtained both master's and doctor's degrees in Catholic theology at the University of Innsbruck. He had a special relationship with Raymund Schwager, who was not his dissertation advisor, but who helped him and advised him beginning in the late 1980s. Palaver is a specialist in theological ethics, politics and theology, and Catholic social teaching. He has been prolific in producing articles, essays for anthologies, and editing, and he is the author of three books: *René Girards mimetische Theorie*; *Politik und Religion bei Thomas Hobbes*; and *Die mythischen Quellen des Politischen* (The Mythical Sources of the Political—on Carl Schmitt).

In COV&R he has served as editor of *The Bulletin of COV&R,* executive secretary, president, and member of the advisory board. He is at this writing the chair of the Institute of Systematic Theology in the Theology Faculty of the University of Innsbruck. In 1991–1992 he spent a year in CISAC at Stanford as a colleague of Robert Hamerton-Kelly and as a research associate of the Austrian Science Fund. His service to COV&R has been extraordinary. If there is one person who has been with us at every point along the way as encourager, advisor, and leader, from New Orleans in 1990 to the time of this writing, it is Wolfgang Palaver.

Raymund Schwager

Born and raised in Switzerland, Raymund Schwager entered the Society of Jesus in 1956. After studying philosophy in Germany and theology in France, he worked as a prefect of a Jesuit boarding school in Austria prior to his ordination to the priesthood in 1966. He obtained his doctorate in theology at the

University of Fribourg, Switzerland, in 1969. In 1977 he became Professor of Dogmatic and Ecumenical Theology in the Theology Faculty of the University of Innsbruck. From 1985 to 1987 and from 1999 to 2003 he served as the dean of that faculty. His untimely death in February 2004 was a great shock and source of grief for his many colleagues and friends.

Schwager became acquainted with René Girard in 1975 (their correspondence having begun in 1974). Their friendship and his theological contribution to Girard's work were of great importance to Girard and the development of the mimetic theory. He wrote many books and articles. His books in English translation are *Must There Be Scapegoats? Violence and Redemption in the Bible*; *Jesus of Nazareth: How He Understood His Life*; *Jesus in the Drama of Salvation*; and *Banished from Eden: Original Sin and Evolutionary Theory in the Drama of Salvation*. He was the first president of COV&R (1991–1995), and he was named an honorary lifetime member of the advisory board in 1999. His untiring theological work advocating the mimetic theory, his quietly astute leadership, and his humble, charitable spirit live on as a treasured legacy to COV&R.

Those attending the founding conference of COV&R at Stanford University, March 1, 1990. René Girard in the middle row, center.

Front row, L-R: Ed McMahon, Mark Wallace, Barbara Mabee, Diana Culbertson, Theophus Smith, Robert Hamerton-Kelly, Stefano Cocchetti

Middle Row, L-R: Brigitte Cazelles, René Girard, James Williams

Back Row, L-R: Hans Jensen, Jørgen Jørgensen, Byron Bland, Vernon Robbins, Mark Anspach, Richard Keady, Charles Ozeck, Gil Bailie, Charles Mabee, Robert Bater, Bruce Chilton

René Girard responding to Bruce Chilton's paper, March 1, 1990. To his left, Robert Hamerton-Kelly; to his right, Vernon Robbins; far right, Charles Ozeck.

René Girard (standing) and Cesáreo Bandera, at a reception in the Girards' home, May 17, 1991

James Williams, beginning the founding conference, March 1, 1990. L-R: Bruce Chilton, Diana Culbertson, Williams, Barbara Mabee, Charles Mabee

Raymund Schwager in his paper hat protecting himself from the sun at the Gorbachev speech, May 9, 1992

Waiting for Gorbachev to speak, May 9, 1992. L-R: Wolfgang Palaver, James Williams, Raymund Schwager

CHAPTER THREE

International Meetings and Growth of Membership, 1994–1998

Looking toward Wiesbaden and Beyond, 1994

Moving out from Stanford and meeting at the University of North Carolina in 1993 strengthened the feeling that COV&R was indeed a viable academic society. This momentum gathered force in 1994 as we looked toward our annual conference in Wiesbaden, Germany. As executive secretary of COV&R I already had a fairly extensive correspondence with scholars in Europe, primarily with Raymund Schwager and Wolfgang Palaver, but with others also. Until 1994 most of this correspondence was by letter and fax. I started using email late in 1992, and by 1994 most of my contacts were by email. It was easier and much less expensive. (The number of telephone calls also decreased greatly.) However, there is a unfortunate aspect of this. I didn't tend to save email messages through the years, particularly when I changed computers. The result is that I have a large quantity of letters and faxes from the period 1990–1994, but not too many after that.

Now we would hold our first symposium outside of the United States. The hosts and planners of the conference were our colleagues at the University of Innsbruck, specifically Raymund Schwager, Wolfgang Palaver, Józef Niewiadomski, and Dietmar Regensburger, who worked in cooperation with the Katholische Akademie Rabanus Maurus in Germany. As their planning took shape and speakers were invited and papers were volunteered for the program, it became clear that it would not only be international, but in some respects a global symposium. I have mentioned that at Chapel Hill in 1993 there were presenters focusing on literary texts from around the globe. At the Wiesbaden meeting we actually had speakers and participants from eleven nations and five continents. The program included speakers from the United States, France, Holland, Brazil, Zaire, England, Germany, Canada, Austria, India, and Northern Ireland.

As formulated in a general manner almost three years previously, the focus of the conference was to be on the social-scientific work of Jean-Pierre Dupuy, who is a brilliant critic and a philosopher of the social sciences. Dupuy looked above all to Ivan Illich and René Girard as thinkers who inspired his own research. The Innsbruck planners took his work as their point of departure, but broadened the scope somewhat to "Theology and/or Secular Thinking: Discussion on Political Philosophy, Economy, and Sociology." The featured speakers were to be Dupuy, who would give the keynote address, John Milbank, and René Girard. The meeting would also have three parallel workshops on subjects not directly related to the conference theme. This was a step forward, as many of us worked in areas not usually directly connected with the conference themes.

Meanwhile, the Issue of a Book Series

Meanwhile, I was occupied with establishing a connection with the Syracuse University Press. My idea was that the Press might be interested in a series featuring the mimetic theory. As I recall, discussions with the editors, especially the acquisitions editor, began in the fall of 1993. By the time of the meeting in Washington, DC, in November 1993 I announced a book series entitled "Violence and the Sacred," of which I would be the editor. The scope of the specific subject areas was ambitious: biblical literature, anthropological studies of violence and sacrifice, interdividual psychology, feminist criticism applying the mimetic theory, and literary studies of the premodern roots of modern and postmodern culture. By late in 1994 or early in 1995 there were three works in progress that I thought would get the series off to a good start. James Alison had completed a draft of his book, *The Joy of Being Wrong*, which was an outstanding Girardian study on original sin and salvation. I also had developed plans to edit an overview of Girard's work in the form of excerpts from his books and articles, particularly those pertaining to religion and Christianity. This was eventually published as *The Girard Reader*. I was working also on a translation of Girard's little book on Dostoyevsky in which he brought together and extended, in a long essay, what he said about the great Russian writer in *Deceit, Desire, and the Novel*. The title in the English translation is *Resurrection from the Underground: Fyodor Dostoyevsky*.

However, this book series project suffered the same fate as some of our other early goals and ambitions for COV&R. The working relationship that I initially established with the Press did not last. Early on there was a delay in arriving at a formal agreement because the Press hired a new director, then there was a combination of personal conflicts and misunderstandings, some of them my own fault. There was also the factor of the limitations of the vision and management of the Press. Fortunately, another possibility opened up. Gil Bailie published his book, *Violence Unveiled*, with Crossroad Publishing in 1995. He sent a message on my behalf to Michael Leach, the publisher then at Crossroad. Leach and I hit it off well and had a good working relationship. Crossroad published *The Girard Reader*, *Resurrection from the Underground*, and also Alison's book, for which I was one of the outside readers. However, Leach decided not to announce these books as part of a series.

Meanwhile, by 1995 the Innsbruck theologians had succeeded in starting a book series in German, Beiträge zur mimetischen Theorie (Contributions to the Mimetic Theory) with an anthology edited by Niewiadomski and Palaver, *Vom Fluch und Segen der Sündenböcke* (On the Curse and Blessing of Scapegoats), which honored Raymund Schwager on his sixtieth birthday. I had no inkling, of course, that I would eventually write a history of COV&R that would appear in that series. A book series in English on the mimetic theory would also be established in the United States. In the first decade of the twenty-first century when one was launched with the Michigan State University Press, with William Johnsen as general editor.

The Conference in Wiesbaden-Naurod, June 8–11, 1994

The conference on "Theology and/or Secular Thinking: Discussion on Political Philosophy, Economy, and Sociology" took place in a rural setting at the Wilhelm-Kempf-Haus, a diocesan conference center just outside of Wiesbaden-Naurod.[1] It was a pleasant, tranquil setting for the participants, who numbered 110, by far our largest attendance yet. It was quite a restful conference for me. I had arrived almost a week before the conference and had done a lot of driving. I rented a car at the Frankfurt airport and drove south to visit friends in Kehl am Rhein, Germany and Strasbourg, France. After that I returned to Frankfurt to pick up Vern Redekop at the airport, and the two of us traveled to Hengelo, Holland, to spend a couple of days with Roel and Joke Kaptein. Roel, Vern, and I then drove back to Frankfurt for the COV&R board meeting, which could not be held at the retreat center near Naurod due to scheduling conflicts. I was a tired executive secretary by the time the conference itself began! However, the conference and the concluding tour of historic Frankfurt left me relaxed and refreshed.

The advisory board met prior to the conference, and one matter on the agenda should be mentioned. Raymund Schwager had proposed earlier that we plan an annual meeting to be held in Jerusalem. It was his dream that COV&R would meet some day in the Holy Land, the birthplace of Judaism and Christianity, and Jerusalem is of course one of the holiest places for Islam. In light of this, Charles Mabee and I had done some preliminary work. I had made provisional reservations for lodging and meeting rooms at Tantur, an ecumenical institute on the road from Jerusalem to Bethlehem. Mabee had looked into a tour of the West Bank, with some Palestinian speakers. However, the majority of the board members believed that there were at that time still too many difficulties, due to tensions over the ongoing Israeli-Palestinian conflict and possible problems in getting Muslim speakers together with Jewish and Christian participants. The majority sentiment was probably very realistic, and it certainly would have stretched us to do the planning and come up with the finances necessary to carry off such a conference. However, it is unfortunate that Schwager's dream, which was at the center of the ecumenical aspects of his theological work prior to his death, has yet to be realized. Some of the annual congresses, particularly the one at Boston College in 2000 and to some extent those at Amsterdam in 2007 and London in 2009, have reflected and represented aspects of his broader ecumenical vision, but it remains to the future for COV&R to attempt to realize it.

We had some significant, warm discussions in the various sessions in Wiesbaden-Naurod.[2] Jean-Pierre Dupuy gave the keynote lecture, speaking on "Sacrifice et envie: Le liberalisme aux prises avec la justice sociale" (Sacrifice and Desire: Liberalism Grappling with Social Justice). He stated that modern society stems from a market economy, which is regulated by self-organization. Developing his thesis by reference to the great authors of political economics (Adam Smith, Friedrich Hayek, John Maynard Keynes), Dupuy argued that self-organization arises from mimesis in the Girardian sense. Referring also to mass psychology in Freudian theory and stock market speculation, he concluded that the market society *contains* violence in the double sense: it possesses the elements for potential violence and at the same time it holds it back.[3]

Dupuy's comments on Sigmund Freud's mass psychology were particularly acute and important. According to Freud, a crowd has an imagined *endogenous fixed point* embodied by the crowd's libidinal ties with a leader. By contrast, the mimetic theory maintains that the crowd itself produces these bonds, although it believes itself to be the product of the leader's love and power. Freud postulated that when the internal leader or model no longer functions, an imagined *exogenous fixed point* takes over. This is the belief that the crowd is a transcendent movement or reality that has *autonomy* in relation to individual decisions and actions. It generates its own movements. Dupuy points out that there is "misrecognition," Girard's *méconnaisance,* in this total crowd phenomenon.[4]

To compare the crowd phenomenon to the market, the market's participants believe it is a reality that operates independently. It has as its imagined central fixed point the model of the egotistic human being who is constrained by the automatic or mechanically working constraint of the market (the endogenous fixed point), which will supposedly guard against any destructive contagion of the mass of people in the market. Yet it is apparent that the market can fall apart into panic just like a crowd in panic, in which it is everyone for himself (the relapse to self-love and desire) as the transcendent whole (exogenous fixed point) bears down upon each individual. Therefore, to reiterate, the market society is imagined to hold off violence, but at the same time it can become like a crowd collapsing into a mob.[5] Both Freud's "narcissistic" leader and internal and external fixed points and the modern doctrines of the market mechanism beginning with Adam Smith are deficient in that they do not recognize the operation of mimetic desire, which is what creates these phenomena. The mimetic analysis shows that the points of transcendence are false and the leader's putative narcissistic power is a "pseudo-narcissism."

One of the most interesting segments of the conference was the dialogue between John Milbank and René Girard in a panel discussion. Milbank had made an impact in theology with his book *Theology and Social Theory,* in which he sought to demonstrate that modern sociology stems from Christian social theology and so has both theological and antitheological assumptions built into its various forms. In that book Milbank flagrantly misread Girard's mimetic theory in ascribing to him the postulation of a covetous mimetic desire that is ontological, that is inherent in human being itself.[6] He emphasized in his conference paper that reality is not known apart from interpretation and criticized attempts such as Girard's to construct universal social theories. In the discussion Girard found little common ground with Milbank except on one extremely important point: he agreed with Milbank that the practice of nonviolence was decisive for Christian theology and that all social theories should be criticized from that point of view.

The papers of Paul Dumouchel and Wolfgang Palaver were important for understanding the thought of Thomas Hobbes, who was one of the greatest philosophical progenitors of the secularization of politics. Dumouchel spoke on "Christianity and the Political Problem of Religion."[7] Dumouchel points out that Hobbes's argument about the effect of Christianity is that it results in the secularization of politics. God's kingdom is eternal and cannot be instituted by political power. Its reality and meaning totally transcend political power, so it is utterly separate from politics. It cannot be commanded or legislated. The temporal power, "Leviathan," must demand obedience, but not in matters of religion. Those who do not believe this cannot be coerced (unless, presumably, their beliefs lead them to rebel against the state). However, if their beliefs are transformed to support the Leviathan, the state, that is, to support the secularization of the state, then religion and politics can get along together.

Dumouchel concludes that Hobbes "has sketched what, I think, is the only possible solution to the political problem of religion."[8] Dumouchel's position has certainly been the accepted doctrine in Western democracies, including even the Roman Catholic Church since the papacy of Pius XII. However, it has tended to vitiate appropriate social and political action on the part of the church in the face of the violation of human rights by modern nation-states that have effectively taken the place of religion in the lives of their citizens.[9]

Palaver's paper was drawn from his dissertation research on Thomas Hobbes. In this presentation he focused on the *katechon*. This Greek word is usually translated as "restrainer" or "one restraining," that is, the one (or power) restraining the "man of lawlessness" (2 Thessalonians 2:3). Palaver explicates the function of the state as *katechon*, restrainer of violence, in Hobbes's thought. It is a concept that is basically mythical because it presumes the war of all against all and the necessity of the scapegoat mechanism as restraint of chaos and violence. Hobbes holds that this restraint, the political authority, is imposed by God and so the subjects should obey the sovereign in matters of civil and criminal law, although they should be free to hold and practice their own beliefs. This area of freedom within a commonwealth is necessary because God's kingdom is supreme in another, transcendent realm. The belief in human equality and freedom of religion, which was brought about by the Protestant Reformation, is sparked by the gospel of Christ.

Palaver argues that Hobbes's interpretation of the Bible draws on those aspects of Scripture that are amenable to mythical and sacrificial thought, which is at the foundation of Hobbes's political philosophy. Here Palaver parts ways with Dumouchel, because the solution of the *katechon* as the basis of secularization is unacceptable both to a vision of democracy and to Christian faith. But this brings one to the problem that Girard has struggled with and is at the center of his apocalyptic tendencies: can the Christian revelation succeed in history? For as Palaver says in conclusion, "Without a *katechon* . . . we have to change our ways. We have to give up retaliation, violence, and mimetic rivalry in order to prevent our self-destruction."[10]

For the first time at an annual conference there were half-day "workshops" that were not directly related to the theme of the conference. This allowed a much broader spectrum of participants to engage in discussion of subjects that were often closer to their own areas of specialization. The "Workshop on the Mimetic Model in Psychology and Psychotherapy," chaired by Roel Kaptein, had only eight present. The small number was a positive factor in a very intense conversation that began with the question of how to reduce violence, but which turned into the problem of how to fend off violence or defend oneself against an aggressor. Among the important talking points was the observation that if one did not allow one's fear to be mirrored back to an aggressor, this could increase the chances of a peaceful encounter. The "Workshop on Mimetic Theory and Biblical Literature," which I chaired, had thirty-five persons who were engaged with two presentations: Norbert Lohfink's paper on "The Destruction of the Seven Nations in Deuteronomy and the Mimetic Theory, " for which I was the respondent, and Vern Redekop's presentation on "Ethical Projection and the Torah in Light of the Mimetic Theory," Anthony Bartlett responding. Lohfink argued that there is a *resacralization* in Deuteronomy: the people, not the land as such, is holy, and the people is seen as vulnerable to the danger of imitating the foreign peoples (the seven nations) already present in the land. The focal point of a lively discussion was Deuteronomy's exclusiveness, and whether Deuteronomy represented an advance in the desacralization process generated by the historical transmission of revelation. Redekop presented the understanding of Torah as the process of casting forward in time an ethical vision. In his response Bartlett emphasized the interpretive dialogue in biblical history and literature moving from the God of the sacred to the God of the victim. The "Workshop on Mimetic Theory and Literature," cochaired by Sandor Goodhart and Jacques-Jude Lépine, had about forty participants. There were six brief presentations, all quite diverse in subject matter but each concerned with the dialectics between mimetic theory and world literature.[11]

A Mennonite Conference on "René Girard and Biblical Peace Theology"

By the middle of the 1980s there were various Mennonite scholars and leaders who were paying attention to Girard's work and discussing it. I have already referred to Vern Redekop's contributions. One of these Mennonite scholars was Willard Swartley, who was a professor of New Testament at Associated Mennonite Biblical Seminary (AMBS) in Elkhart, Indiana, and who served as the dean of the seminary in 1979–1981, 1990, and 1995–2000. A prolific biblical scholar, he made connection with COV&R by 1993. I remember meeting him at the COV&R event at the convention of AAR/SBL in November 1993 and briefly discussing a conference he was organizing at the seminary in Elkhart.

The conference, "René Girard and Biblical Peace Theology," took place at the AMBS in Elkhart June 14–15, 1994, just a few days after the COV&R conference in Wiesbaden-Naurod. Sandy Goodhart and I went by plane from Frankfurt to Chicago and traveled together by bus and auto to Elkhart. Rebecca Adams and her husband Robin Collins were also there to give papers, as was Michael Hardin. Other COV&R people also contributed to the volume, *Violence Renounced*, which was generated by the meeting.[12] The meeting itself was a true symposium in that presentations and debates occurred in the friendliest of atmospheres, and this solidarity of spiritual bonds and scholarly purpose was strengthened and articulated in the communion service in which everyone participated on the second day. The communicants included Sandor Goodhart and me. Goodhart had maintained, and still maintains, a strong, very self-conscious sense of his Jewish identity, both religiously and culturally, but it is striking and noteworthy that he felt it appropriate to take part in communion. I also participated, although I had converted to Catholicism in September 1993. A transgressor already in my first year of being a Roman Catholic! I knew, of course, the Catholic teaching that Roman Catholics should receive the host only from validly ordained priests in the proper apostolic succession and only within the institutional framework of affirming the transformation of the bread and wine into the actual body and blood of Christ. However, I too felt that it was spiritually right to participate. The communion service symbolized our solidarity with one another, something that transcended our intellectual concerns and exchanges.

The volume stemming from the conference helps to reinforce the insights, both theoretical and practical, that came from the conference. Swartley's personal conclusions in his preface to *Violence Renounced* are a good indicator of what was at stake and of some directions for further reflection on the mimetic theory and peacemaking. (1) Girard's work places the violence recounted in the biblical narratives in a new light, yet his cleaving of extant mythical projections away from the authentic revelation of the nonviolent God leaves a huge question about the canonical authority of the Bible. (2) Girard has enabled us to see the mimetic scapegoat mechanism at work and biblical revelation's exposure of this mechanism, yet he himself has too easily scapegoated sacrifice itself (as Girard himself has conceded and corrected.) (3) The Girardian project has enormous power to expose the myth of redemptive violence that prevails in all areas of human culture, but he has given little attention to the salvific model of mimesis emanating from Christ, the New Adam.[13] Girard has commented frequently on the shift in his thought occasioned by Raymund Schwager's questioning of his sacrificial reading of the letter to the Hebrews. On the first criticism, the whole matter of Girard's reading of the Bible as a "text in travail" has yet to be thoroughly thought through. My own view is that it is the basis of a certain kind of historical approach that stems from a profound view of what the Bible is and does.[14] Robert Daly's work on atonement or salvation speaks to the third criticism, on which more in the following section of the chapter.

The paper that Rebecca Adams presented falls under the third conclusion, "the salvific model of mimesis emanating from Christ." She raised an important question about the mimetic theory.[15] Her argument has gained a lot of attention, especially in the first decade of the twenty-first century. She briefly mentions objections to Girard's theory such as neglect of the primordial goodness of human beings in the biblical account of creation and feminine desire or the feminine as extrapolated by feminist critics. But her concern is to go deeper than textual and historical data to the basic problem as she perceives it: the scapegoating of "constructive desire" or love. This is the true "scapegoat." She avers, however, that "this 'scapegoat' is not central to the structure of the mimetic hypothesis but is, ironically, an effect created by not following the hypothesis through to its logical conclusion."[16] When Girard says, for example, that following Christ means to give up mimetic desire,[17] he must mean to surrender one's (previous) life of the persecutory self—"giving up scapegoating, or violence, or participating in the victimage mechanism."[18]

Now Adams's standpoint is that the true dynamic of the mimetic theory is movement toward a solution to the human predicament brought about by persecution and violence. Girard has affirmed that of course, although primarily in a general sense of renouncing violence and forgiving those who transgress against us. A solution cannot be reached, however, without accounting for how actual victims of violence may be empowered, that is, enabled to become true agents in their particular circumstances. A complete theory of violence will not only show how to assume the perspective of the theory, "but it must also *show us how* those who have been victims can actually cease to be victims *by ceasing to identify with their victim position*."[19] This is lacking in Girardian theory, so it "fails . . . to escape the kind of mythical structure it seeks to expose."[20]

Adams's intention and concerns are unabashedly Christian and theological, so her constructive proposal is a crucial question about God: "What does God desire?"[21] God (or God in Christ) is the ultimate Subject and Mediator that Girard actually (if not formally) presupposes in his anthropology and the end to whom he intends his anthropology to lead. Adams proceeds to present and diagram three kinds of triangular desire that all rest on a dualistic epistemology and system of representation. This is a dualism of subject-object with its putative inevitable fall into divided thinking and exclusion of the other.[22] She labels these "classic triangular desire," "coquette" or "romantic love," and "colonization." The classical form (Girard's) "automatically leads . . . to rivalry, then doubling, then escalation," and so forth. In the coquette, the (proto) subject's subjectivity is a mere object for the projection of the mediator-coquette's self-image. In colonization, the mediator-colonizer transforms the (proto) subject into an appropriated object.[23] To move beyond this dualism, it is necessary to understand the Mediator in terms of loving mimesis: the Mediator (God) desires for the subject the *subject's own subjectivity,* that is, his or her personal free agency. "In this scenario, if the proto-subject was to imitate the desire of the mediator, then the proto-subject would desire his or her own subjectivity."[24] The double bind, "imitate me"/"don't imitate me," becomes a simultaneous, seamless command.

Adams's paper raises important questions concerning our thinking about mimetic theory. Other female colleagues have contributed further insight to the process of thinking on mimesis and love. Martha Reineke refers directly to Adams's paper when she states in her essay on Girard and D. W. Winnicott, "Loving mimesis breaks open the double bind that has threatened to capture the proto-subject within the constraints of acquisitive mimesis."[25] This concept pictures the embrace of proto-subject and model in "the dynamic of loving mimesis, which is generative of transformation in society, not sacrifice."[26] Ann Astell argues, in referring to Girard's discussion of the good harlot (1 Kings 3:16–28) in *Things Hidden,* that "maternal compassion is actually central to Girard's understanding of the unveiling of the victimage mechanism, because it sees goodness in the very life of every potential victim, regardless of what that person has done *or is capable of doing*."[27] The one woman would rather gain victory over her adversary than let the child live, while the true mother would rather renounce her maternal rights than see the child killed. She is willing to give up everything, including perhaps her own life, so that her child might live.[28]

Now a "solution" for the mimetic theory in the strict sense of providing a proven remedy for violence, something comparable, for example, to the polio vaccine to prevent polio or antibiotics to heal infections, cannot be construed as a fair test of Girard's mimetic theory. However, the theory does have an ethical impulse stemming from its conceptual foundation in the Incarnation, the revelation of the nonviolent, loving God entering into human existence and taking the place of the victim in order to unveil the violently retributive, mimetically triggered scapegoat mechanism. Therefore Adams, Reineke, and Astell are right to the extent that proponents of the mimetic theory should be concerned with both the concept and the practice of *doing* what God intends or desires. Consistency between theological and ethical vision is the only path to the truth of desire.

The desire that creates or affirms the other's proper subjectivity, so that loving the other is being oneself (or specifically, loving God is to affirm one's own subjectivity), is a significant contribution in thinking about the mimetic theory. On the other hand, it should be noted that Girard, Schwager, and others of us certainly have stated and affirmed the freedom that stems from imitating the desire of God or Christ. That "freedom of the sons of God" of which the Apostle speaks is practically the same thing as Adams's subjectivity. She has, however, framed and sharpened an issue that should be further explored.

Part of the problem in grasping the concept of mimesis at the roots of the mimetic theory is that Girard has moved back and forth between *de facto* and *de jure*, between the project of explaining the way human existence proceeds and the task of projecting human possibilities and responsibilities as attested in the witness to God in the biblical revelation. Girard has often spoken or written of "(mimetic) desire" as that which lies behind and informs the scapegoat mechanism and its violent outcomes. Less frequently he has referred to the positive outcomes of mimetic desire—outcomes that predominate in human culture; otherwise we would have killed ourselves off long ago. Here I ask the reader's indulgence as I repeat what I stated about this matter in the first chapter: What Girard describes as the work of mimetic desire is not good or bad in and of itself. It simply is a fact of being human. It is true that in a theological sense it is good as part of creation, as the means by which humans can relate to the world and to their divine origins. However, it is a dynamic possibility that can be actualized in various ways. People familiar with his thought will often speak of "good mimesis" or "bad mimesis." This is understandable, but a distinction must be made between the work of mimesis itself, on the one hand, and the model and the object of desire, on the other hand. The working of mimesis has to be evaluated on the basis of the model and the object of desire that the subject learns to seek from her imitation of the model. Mimesis as such may be considered good or beneficial as a possibility of the created order, but in its actuality everything depends on the kind of model and object of desire and, concomitantly, the kind of relation of subject to model and object. So desiring to have what given models desire is necessary for becoming "humanized" or acculturated, for entering into the human world, for living, loving, working, and playing with others. It is clear, however, that it can and does lead to conflict and violence.

There is, finally, an even greater challenge to Adams's proposal of loving mimesis. It is the question whether humans are so constituted, so "wired" in a bioneural sense, that violent behavior is an inevitable outcome of mimetic desire if we view human behavior on the whole. From a theological perspective this could and should be viewed as a result of "original sin." However, exactly what that means and what God's intention in creation means in a modern sense in light of the mimetic theory taken in conjunction with modern research in the social and natural sciences, remain to be seen. By any account, taking these factors seriously suggests that truly desiring the other's own subjectivity occurs only through a transcendent gift of love and grace. It is not something that one simply decides to do or is able to achieve by accepting a certain idea. I will return to this in chapter 5, where I discuss Robert Hamerton-Kelly's call for the Colloquium to account for violence as a generative principle and to take seriously that the affirmation of the God incarnate, crucified, and risen from the dead means that we are invariably sinners (viz. perpetrators of violence) to whom God offers forgiveness.

The Meeting in Chicago, November 18, 1994

The meeting in conjunction with AAR/SBL in 1994 was significant in terms of both the people who attended the sessions and the content of the papers presented. Among those present were three representatives of book publishers, including the acquisitions editor of Syracuse University Press. The morning and afternoon sessions both had thirty-five to forty persons in attendance.

In the morning session Sandor Goodhart and Charles Mabee engaged in a dialogue about Jewish and Christian approaches to the Bible. Goodhart argued that a "prophetic" reading of the Scriptures emerged in postexilic Judaism. Mabee held that Judaism had no category of thought that would allow it to accept Christian claims about Jesus. They are two different kinds of religion, but a common interpretive ground may be found in the prophetic revelation that God is revealed through the victim, not the victimizer. The respondent, Hans Jensen, replied that the true meeting point for Jewish and Christian theology is the priestly cult as articulated in the priestly writings of the Pentateuch. It is there that one finds the grounding of a theology of creation and concern for the life of *homo religiosus*, which has universal aspects in spite of specific religious differences.

The afternoon session featured Robert Daly addressing the question as to whether Christianity is sacrificial or antisacrificial. His answer to that, based on his research on sacrifice in the Bible and early Christianity, was that sacrifice took on an ethical-spiritual sense in New Testament and patristic Christianity. His respondent, Paul Duff, argued in response that early Christianity did not reject temple sacrifice, even as it developed a spiritual understanding of it. However, even more interesting from the standpoint of the gospel message of salvation is the question Daly raised toward the end of his paper: what is actually happening to those who participate in "sacrifice," understood as atonement or redemption? He did not try to answer the question in that presentation, but in later works he comes back to it. In his contribution to *For René Girard* he sketches the intellectual, moral, and spiritual senses of conversion. Drawing upon experiences in a twelve-hour course in theology and philosophy developed at Boston College, he describes the students' growing intellectual awareness of the sacrificial mechanism and its victims, which is the easiest part of the process, then tells about the fieldwork component that puts students in a situation where they can begin to identify with people who are victims of the social, political, and spiritual effects of scapegoating and violence. That is where actual moral change begins to occur. The full "phenomenology of redemption" for Christians is prophetic, eschatological, and apocalyptic, and so is yet to be consummated. Daly does not attempt to describe its content in detail, but points to the evidence of saintly persons and saintly communities whose lives are lived for others in love and nonviolence. Their witness at least hints at a full phenomenology of redemption.[29]

A Look Back from the End of 1994

Looking back from the end of 1994 one can get an increasingly clear idea of where the Colloquium had been and how far it had come. From our small beginnings at Stanford we had grown slowly but steadily to more than one hundred members and friends in North America and Europe. We were basically "international" from the beginning; we already had a Canadian and two Danish colleagues present in the founding conference and then within weeks we joined with our Innsbruck colleagues in beginning to form the future of COV&R. Moreover, religion, literature, and culture from all parts of the world were already our subject matter. This was in great part due to the inspiration of Girard's interdisciplinary model of research and reflection. Yet now that almost four years had passed since our initial gathering, actually meeting in Western Europe seemed to be a concrete confirmation of our identity, our perspective, goals, and aspirations.

The broad range of subject matter began to be apparent from the beginning of COV&R, and I have already mentioned in chapter 2 the astonishing range of literary and sacred texts that presenters took up at the 1993 meeting at the University of North Carolina. The Wiesbaden symposium furthered this process in setting up breakout sessions or workshops that enabled many participants to discuss topics in or related to their own areas of specialization. Until that event members were tied to the main theme of the conference.[30] Of course, for the majority of participants who already had some grounding, and often expertise, in the mimetic theory, most of the plenary subjects were of considerable interest, but it made a positive difference to be able to engage in discussions related to our specific fields.

One of the early expectations of COV&R was that it would become a vehicle for organizing teamwork in research and writing. This did not happen. Our colleagues in theology at Innsbruck had already begun collaborative research and publication apart from COV&R, although the existence of the Colloquium enhanced their work. The meetings of COV&R did give many of its participants a cordial and stimulating context for discussion and evaluation of their ongoing projects as they learned what others were doing. If one glances over the articles and reviews published by COV&R members from 1990 to 1994, the quantity is noteworthy and the quality of scholarship was of the highest.[31] The number of books published by members, including two by Girard, numbered over two dozen in that period.[32]

Finally, a Jewish-Christian dialogue had commenced. Although the number of Jewish members and participants at meetings has always been small, Sandor Goodhart has quietly but firmly insisted on a Jewish-Christian dialogue in which some others have also been interested. Raymund Schwager and Charles Mabee were among the most active in dialogue with Goodhart during the early years of COV&R. Although it has not continued since then with the same intensity at all the conferences, it has been an important part of our history and one conference would be devoted to it: "Judaism, Christianity, and the Ancient World" at Purdue University in 2002. I think that the Jewish-Christian dialogue was the matrix for the emergence of the discussion of other world religions at Colloquium meetings.

Looking toward Loyola University Chicago and Beyond, 1995

Our next annual conference was to be held at Loyola University in Chicago, June 1–3, 1995. Andrew McKenna, who had studied under Girard at Johns Hopkins University, served as the host. McKenna knew by the time of the Chapel Hill conference in 1993 that Loyola was the designated venue for 1995, and he began preparatory work by the summer of 1993. He and I exchanged a number of letters and faxes about the conference in 1993 and 1994. (We were both online with email by 1993, but I don't remember whether we had email correspondence, nor have I any record of it.) McKenna was the chairperson of Modern Languages at Loyola by then. He spent an enormous amount of time on conference planning and administrative details. A large chunk of his work was spent in applying to the National Endowment for the Humanities for financial support of the conference. The application almost succeeded. Of the seven referees, six gave evaluations that were quite favorable. The lone negative report may have doomed the application. However, the work McKenna did result in an outstanding conference. It was also a conference in which conflict was sparked. To that I will return shortly.

The Publication of Contagion

Meanwhile, we received good news concerning our annual journal, *Contagion: Journal of Violence, Mimesis, and Culture,* which was launched in 1994. It was a finalist in the "Best New Journal" category in the competition sponsored by the Council of Editors of Learned Journals. One judge called it "a bold new entry into interdisciplinary cultural studies; attractively produced with an impressive and wide-ranging list of contents." This recognition was a tribute to the hard and imaginative work of Judith Arias, as well as to the contributors to the first issue.

The first issue of *Contagion* was conceived as a tribute to René Girard on his seventieth birthday (which was actually in 1993). Most of the articles had been given as papers at the annual conference of 1993 in Chapel Hill. It was our idea from the beginning that some of the papers delivered at the annual meetings would be published in the journal, although articles submitted by others would be considered also. The leadoff article in the first issue was contributed by Michel Serres, who was not present at the symposium: "One God or a Trinity?"[33] Arias stated in the "Editor's Introduction" that "Girard's hypotheses on culture, mimetic desire, and human violence provide the common frame of reference for [the] wide range of critical orientations and practical concerns" of "scholars in the humanities, religion, and the social sciences," as well as the concerns of those outside the academy engaged in various forms of psychotherapy, conflict resolution, and inner-city development and the "implementation of new approaches to the problem of individual and community violence."[34] Hamerton-Kelly noted in his tribute that Girard had been an inspiring pioneer of thought not only through books and other formal scholarly contributions, but through personal contact: In the informal seminar begun at Stanford in 1990, for example, "many have been nourished." "In the seminar and out, over meals at the club and coffee in the student union, he has been constantly gracious, kind, and self-effacing." He "has given us a method and many coruscating readings that show its power to illuminate; but for those of us who have had the privilege of his friendship, and the friendship of Martha his wife, the pleasure of their company transcends even the power of their work."[35]

The Conference at Loyola, June 1–3, 1995

The symposium at Loyola University of Chicago highlighted the theme of "Violence, Mimesis, and Responsibility." There were 110 participants registered. The keynote speakers were Jean-Michel Oughourlian, with Rusty Palmer responding, and René Girard, with Martha Nussbaum responding. There were also sections on various subjects, as well as two half-day workshops, one on criminal justice and the other on reduction of violence. Oughourlian had authored *The Puppet of Desire* (translated from the book in French, *Un mime nommé désir*) and was one of Girard's two interlocutors in *Things Hidden since the Foundation of the World.* He discussed some cases from his psychotherapy practice that revolved around mimetic rivalry, and he indicated that sometimes it is better for those involved if the therapist encourages the patient to let the rivalry play itself out further so that the subjects may be put on a more even footing. He indicated that mimetic rivalry is inevitable in human existence, and that in many situations both parties in a relationship must understand and feel that the other person is viewed as desirable by someone else. In response Palmer entertained the gathering with his humor, but at the same time he clarified "interdividuality" by stating that persons are not simply constituted as an autonomous entity called the "self, " but are first and foremost determined and formed in their relations with other individuals who are models or mediators.

In his paper Girard took up the increasing occurrence of eating disorders, anorexia and bulimia, among young women in Western culture, particularly in the United States. He argued that prior hypotheses as to their cause—factors arising from interpretation that is psychoanalytic, Marxist, feminist, and so on—have become bankrupt. The commonsense perspective of the person in the street tells us as much if not more than these ideologies: the problem is the compulsive desire to lose weight. But moving beyond a surface level of analysis will show that the underlying generative factor is the mimetic rivalry that is fed both by a culture of competitive consumerism that is not moored in the affirmation of transcendence, and by reaction to this culture in the touting of models of thinness and athleticism.[36] Nussbaum responded by questioning the statistics concerning eating disorders scrutinized by Girard and by indicating the positive benefits of the emphasis on diet and exercise for women throughout the world. Her remarks were not wrong, but did not really address the truth or value of the mimetic approach.

The meeting at Loyola was the occasion for a new theoretical area of conflict that may have been silently present but that had not clearly emerged before in the sessions of COV&R symposia. On the afternoon of the second day there were at least two papers representing radical positions that could be characterized as "postmodern" in various ways. One was a paper given by Susan Nowak seeking to apply the mimetic theory to feminist thought, particularly for the sake of correcting Christian anti-Judaism among some feminist theorists. The perception of some auditors was that she applied the mimetic theory without an adequate development of its concepts for that frame of reference. It also evinced an assumption about the normative status of "multiculturalism" that many of those present did not share. The paper of Anthony Bartlett on a theology of the church came across as a radical attack on the institutional church that did not recognize its role in transmitting the Christian gospel to succeeding generations, whatever the church's defects. There were no lengthy debates on the floor, but the presenters sensed that part of the audience was unreceptive to their offerings. It would have been a good moment for an attempt at reconciliation like that of the event at Stanford in 1992. I think that the particular place and the size of the gathering were factors weighing against such an attempt. These were plenary sessions in an auditorium, and there were many more in attendance than in 1992 at Stanford. In 1992 there were about thirty-five present in a fairly small meeting room. In Chicago, the mimetic effect of the crowd was certainly a factor in the bad feeling that spread among some of us, and this spilled over into conversations after the sessions. I believe that we lost two or more members because of that occasion. Conflict like that is inevitable in human relations and certainly in organizations, but it is worth our while to reflect on what happened and whether such incidents can be remedied.[37]

The advisory board of COV&R had important business to conduct. Raymund Schwager's two terms as president came to an end, so the board members nominated Cesáreo Bandera as the new presider. Schwager had done an excellent job in every respect, and we were certain that Bandera would also be an outstanding leader. As Hamerton-Kelly remarked, he had a certain "gravitas" appropriate to the position. Bandera was elected by acclamation in the plenary business meeting. The situation was unusual in that we did not have enough time during the regular meeting to finish our business, so an additional meeting of the board on Sunday was convened after the conference had officially ended. Some of the board members had departed, but a majority were able to attend. Judy Arias had made great strides with the journal, *Contagion*, but the additional work was affecting her teaching and research and even her health. Therefore she was ready to hand over the role of editor to someone else. We proposed to Andrew McKenna that he become the editor of the journal, and he accepted. As chair of the Department of Modern Languages at Loyola he had access to resources that would facilitate publishing the periodical. As it turned out, he would have to scramble to find funding and get the editorial work done after he stepped down as chairperson of the department in 1998, but he continued to achieve the same standard of high quality that Arias had started. He served as editor from 1996 to 2006.[38]

The Meeting in Philadelphia, November 17, 1995

The shorter annual meeting in conjunction with AAR/SBL had two sessions. In the first session Sandor Goodhart and Charles Mabee continued their Jewish-Christian dialogue by commenting on Genesis 22, the Akedah or "binding" of Isaac, as it is known in the Jewish tradition. Also in the first session David Odell-Scott presented a paper on atonement, exclusion and orthodoxy in 2 Corinthians 5:16–7:4 in which he focused particularly on 2 Corinthians 6:14–7:1. He argued that the latter passage was not composed by Paul, but inserted by critics of his ministry of reconciliation who were not "heretics" but predecessors of orthodox Christianity. Paul was a critic of the structures of violence. These opponents of Paul advocated a prototype of what would become "Christendom" through the exclusionary use of sacred violence.

The afternoon session on "Violence Conversion" was a kind of workshop led by Thee Smith whose format was lecture, practice, and response. To recover from systemic violence in our cultures and institutions Smith proposed a practicum "designed to model what human community can be like under optimal 'interdividual' (Girard) conditions, and therein to empower practitioners to foster those conditions in their ordinary affairs."[39] What the group gathered there actually did was to reflect on their life stories in response to five questions:

1. When was a time [that] you successfully resolved a situation of rivalry, scapegoating, persecution or conflict without resorting to violence or threatened violence?
2. When was a time [that] you failed to do so?
3. When was a time [that] you yourself were the victim of such treatment?
4. How is item #2 related to item #3?
5. How would you like to replay item #2 without the influences of item #3?[40]

A discussion of one participant's retelling of his story ensued, facilitated by Smith as he elicited the cathartic and healing features of the Girardian model. Then Barbara Patterson and Richard Fenn gave prepared responses, followed by further discussion, with special input from Rebecca Adams, Sandor Goodhart, and Walter Wink.

Other Matters in 1995

As already noted, the book series with the Syracuse University Press that I had envisaged had completely fallen through by the end of summer 1995. However, COV&R was alive and well, Crossroad Publishing agreed to publish some of the works I had in mind, and the theologians at Innsbruck had started a series of books on the mimetic theory.

We also moved more and more into exploiting possibilities with the Internet. As announced in the fall issue of *The Bulletin of COV&R*, it would be thenceforth possible to search for literature on the mimetic theory via the Internet. One could find there a bibliography of works on the mimetic theory, which were integrated into the University of Innsbruck's documentation of theological and interdisciplinary literature of the Theology Faculty at Innsbruck. Dietmar Regensburger has supervised that operation now for many years.

Another development in 1995 was contact with the Ernest Becker Foundation, which was founded by Dr. Neil Elgee and some of his friends early in 1993. Becker was known especially for his book *The Denial of Death*, which was awarded a Pulitzer Prize for nonfiction shortly after the author's death. His other major works were *The Birth and Death of Meaning* (1971) and *Escape from Evil*, published posthumously in 1975. The center and point of departure of Becker's thought is the human anxiety about death that leads to a multitude of personal, social, and cultural defenses against death—an all-pervasive denial of death. There is an area of overlap between Girard's mimetic theory and Becker's formulation of death-denial. Girard has commented that the reality of death is a universal source of anxiety for humans, pervading and presupposed in all that they do and think. He holds that in preliterate and archaic cultures death was viewed as a form of violence perpetrated by evil forces. One could hold that if the fear of death is the primary universal assumption in human existence, mimetic desire and mimetic rivalry are the primary modes by which human beings produce the religious and cultural forms and institutions that attempt to shore up their defenses against death.[41]

The initial contact of Neil Elgee with COV&R was through Gil Bailie.[42] The Ernest Becker Foundation's first major conference, in October 1995, was named "Love of Violence (LOV): Girard and Evolution." Girard's mimetic theory was represented by five speakers: Bailie, Cheryl Kirk-Duggan, Susan Nowak, Eugene Webb, and James Williams. Elgee joined COV&R and attended one or two COV&R conferences.[43] It appeared that there could have been a mutually beneficial long-term interaction of the two entities, COV&R and EBF, but that did not happen. If we were to compare the history and social formation of the two organizations, we would probably find a number of differences that were not conducive to a closer relationship. However, I think the primary reason was mimetic rivalry. Both groups were so devoted to their inspirational-conceptual model, Girard and the mimetic theory for COV&R and Becker and the theme of death-denial for EBF, respectively, that it was threatening to both to seriously consider the contributions of the other thinker to human life and thought. The reading and discussion of Becker did not make inroads in COV&R because most of the members, if they knew anything about Becker, considered him a minor thinker in comparison to Girard. On the Becker side, if any read Girard or knew anything about the mimetic theory, they considered it a minor part of the whole picture of human attempts at self-defense against death. But whatever the truth of the assumptions on either side, the question remains: would it have been better to develop an alliance or working relationship of some sort?

The Return to Stanford, 1996

The next annual symposium was to be held at Stanford University, June 27–29. Some of us who were present at the first three meetings of the Colloquium were looking forward to returning to the campus there. Robert Hamerton-Kelly was the host and the sponsor was the Center for International Security and Arms Control (CISAC). This institute was a kind of think-tank based at Stanford whose mission was to conduct research relevant to government policy and to serve as a consulting agency for governments seeking international security and cooperation. It later changed its name (but not its acronym) to Center for International Security and Cooperation. Hamerton-Kelly was a research fellow from 1986 to 1997. CISAC provided the meeting space for the founding conference of COV&R in 1990 and the ongoing seminar that began in January 1990.

The thematic topic of the conference, "Ethnic Conflict in International Perspective," was similar to that of the 1992 conference, which was "Ethnocentrism and the Study of Violence." The 1992 conference was different from the one four years later in that it focused on ethnocentrism and "multiculturalism" as studied and practiced in the American academic setting, The 1996 symposium took up the topic in the context of international politics. René Girard gave the keynote address. Other speakers included four from CISAC (Byron Bland, Jonathan Mercer, Melanie Greenberg, and Dan Froats), as well as others from interdisciplinary programs at Stanford (William Hurlbut and Lee Ross).

"Ethnic Conflict in International Perspective," June 27–29, 1996

It was a rich and varied conference. Girard's presentation, "Mimetic Theory and Ethnic Conflict," served as a frame of reference for the entire program and auxiliary activities. He surveyed the basics of the mimetic theory, relating it to warfare and the question of the modern post-Enlightenment as to whether warfare could be ended. He then took as his case study the Balkan conflicts during the 1990s. Drawing upon the sociological analysis of Roger Brubaker to illustrate the phenomenon of escalating rivalry, he stated that "an escalation of mimetic rivalry occurred that generated the desire for ethnically homogenous statehood among Croats on the one hand, and on the other hand, among Serbs in Croatia as well as the Serbs in Serbia."[44] This illustrates once more how both individuals and groups in conflict become more like each other in disposition or existential stance as their mutual hostility increases.

Byron Bland gave an interesting and relevant paper on the conflict and violence between Protestants and Catholics in Northern Ireland.[45] The title has to do with the ritual that emerged there: the marching of the Orange (Protestants) in provocative parades and the rising of the Green (the Irish Catholics) to taunt them and throw rocks at them. Bland observes, "Had their mimetic violence fastened on a common scapegoat, the common identity favored by the [Society of] United Irishmen might have come about. However, no external target emerged, and the mimetic violence remained focused within [the] confines of their relationship."[46] Bland concluded the paper with two comments on transforming conflicts from intractable to tractable ones. In other words, establishing the preconditions of reconciliation. One of the paths to reconciliation is to acknowledge the situation, especially the pain and suffering of the other. The other comment is that apology is important, certainly as an area to be explored. Although apology is primarily associated with interpersonal relations, "one group of people can apologize to another. . . . In this way, the moral social bonds needed to reunite the parties are put into play."[47]

The conference also offered four parallel sessions on the last day. This was the greatest number of such sessions since COV&R began. The four subject areas were biblical studies, literature, education, and theology. In the Education group Marie-Louise Martinez spoke on a topic that would serve as the theme for the 1998 conference in St. Denis: "Integration and Ethnic Conflict in French Schools: A Girardian Approach to the Reduction of Violence in Education." In the Theology session Raymund Schwager, Herwig Büchele, Józef Niewiadomski, and Wolfgang Palaver reported for the Innsbruck working group on the application of mimetic theory.

Roel Kaptein (1919–1996)

One of the significant events of the conference was a gathering to mourn the death and celebrate the life of Roel Kaptein. He was the first of our leading members to pass away. He served on the advisory board until his demise, which occurred on May 16, 1996, and he participated extensively in discussions. He led two workshops and gave one paper while a member of COV&R. He believed passionately in our work and was ever the friendly critic.

Kaptein was a Dutch Reformed pastor in Holland. He was associated for many years with the Corrymeela Community and worked in Northern Ireland as a peacemaker through the Centre for the Study of Conflict at the University of Ulster. One of the Corrymeela websites speaks of his "profound influence" on staff and community members. The website narrative notes that he started with a person's questions and responded to them by drawing upon Girard's mimetic model and many pictorial examples.[48] René Girard said in his eulogy that Roel "was aware that the life of the intellect is not enough, that it cannot flourish for long when divorced from 'real life,' which is the influence we all have on one another. . . . He made me realize how much of an intellectual in the bad sense I always was, even and especially in my criticism of the academic world, which I felt placed me outside of it. Seeing this mimetic illusion of mine, Roel simply shrugged his shoulders. . . . Roel believed in the Resurrection and the Life and I believe with him that he is still alive. . . . And he is especially alive here, at our yearly meeting, because he embodies our common Spirit."[49]

Advisory Board Issues

The advisory board had two important items on its agenda. One was a self-review, which I asked Thee Smith to conduct. We had intended to include non-board members in the review, but we encountered difficulties and did not succeed in doing that. Smith formulated two sets of two questions each. Each board member responded to the first set in turn, and then we did the same with the second set. It was an informal process, with a number of requests for clarification and minor digressions, and we arrived at a number of collectively expressed responses. On the basis of these responses, the group agreed on some recommendations for the board and the membership of COV&R:

1. In supporting the inclusion of women's voices in our conference sessions we would remind moderators to call upon women who indicate a readiness to speak.
2. To extend and formalize the processing of papers for *Contagion*, we should use a wider range of designated readers.
3. For the sake of balance and even to extend our approaches to the mimetic theory, we would recognize the following subgroups and allow for perhaps three parallel groups to articulate the themes of our conferences in a four-year cycle: Biblical, Literary, Psychoanalytical, Practical/Transformational, Political/Economic, Jewish-Christian Dialogue, and Theology.

4. We would figure out ways to institutionalize the "turbulence" or "disorder" that attends the growth of an organization like ours, so that it works for the intellectual vitality of our Colloquium and not against it.
5. We would commit ourselves to develop a protocol "for negotiating the turbulence of competing agendas in the organization in a way that is consistent with our non-exclusionary theory but that also secures and advances the legacy of mimetic theory and Girardian thought."[50]

As I look over the results of our self-review and reflect on how it was handled in subsequent years, I would give the advisory board a grade of C+. In supporting women's voices I think that we have done fairly well and improved somewhat through the years. The process of recruiting papers for the journal and refereeing them has certainly been satisfactory. As for acknowledging subgroups that would help us frame the theme of each annual conference, we have not done that, although the variety and scope of subjects has been impressive on the whole. I have been disappointed that biblical studies has not been better represented, given that the Bible has a foundational role in the mimetic theory. The fourth recommendation, harnessing the disorder (which means in part "conflicts") of the organization in order to enhance its growth and intellectual vitality is extremely important. But as we stated it our recommendation it is very general and abstract. Probably we have willy-nilly done a pretty good job in that regard. Which is to say paradoxically that in our disorder we have somehow used this disorder to create a kind of order, a viable professional society that will continue into the future. On creating a protocol to negotiate competing agendas, I don't think anything has been done in a formal way, although good leaders and the general goodwill of those who support COV&R have won out. So in looking back in light of the self-review, I would say that our work to that point had been satisfactory, but not good or excellent.

The fault is mine in great part that the grade, or least my own evaluation, is not more favorable. I should have followed up with our president and with Thee Smith to make sure that we returned to that self-review process, even if it meant critiquing the review and revising our priorities. But as we passed through 1996 and 1997 came around, I was beginning to run out of steam. I had accepted a supported resignation offer ("buyout") at Syracuse University and would retire in May 1998. My wife and I were thus beginning to plan to leave central New York and return to our home state of Oklahoma. I had devoted a great deal of time and energy to COV&R matters for six years—and I would serve two more years as executive secretary—but now my grip was beginning to loosen. Writing this history, however, is a very instructive process for me. With the advantage of the attendant hindsight I would recommend that COV&R returns to the kind of self-review that Thee Smith and I initiated in 1996.

The other major topic for the advisory board was a difficult question, the discussion of which began among some of us before the conference itself. The question was where we would hold the annual symposium in 1998. Most of us shared the understanding that we would meet in North America two of every three years and once every third year in Europe. This seemed to be a fair and balanced rule of thumb, reflecting the fact that at that time a preponderant number of members lived in the United States. We were already set for a conference in Graz, Austria, in 1997 and Thee Smith had invited us to meet at Emory University in Atlanta in 1998. However, Marie-Louise Martinez proposed that we hold the annual meeting for 1998 in St. Denis, just outside of Paris. I was personally opposed to it and most of the board members were initially resistant to a meeting in Europe two years in a row. However, Martinez pointed out that in 1998 there would be municipal elections in St. Denis, and she thought that if the Socialists won the election they would probably not support a conference such as ours in 1999. This contingency swung the consensus in favor of St. Denis in 1998, and I reluctantly went along with it. As it turned out, it was just as well. Thee Smith, who had already begun planning for a conference in Atlanta, was not offended, and in any event it was becoming clear that COV&R was more and more an international society. One-half of our subsequent annual meetings through 2010 would be held in Europe.

"Once in a Blue Moon"

There was an event during that meeting of the Colloquium that was the occasion of much gaiety and laughter as well as unease among those present. It was in fact a twofold event. Our host and primary organizer, Robert Hamerton-Kelly, had announced in the March 1996 issue of *The Bulletin of COV&R* that there would be a "Goat of the Year Award." The criterion of selecting the "goat" would be that member whose writings had been most subject to unfavorable reviews in the recent past. The award ceremony would include a ritual stoning—with "innocuous missiles." I myself had already thought about some such mock ceremony at an annual meeting and mentioned it jokingly to a few colleagues in COV&R. My idea, however, was to make it a random selection, perhaps by drawing of lots. It sounded like a lot of fun. Well, it was and it wasn't.

The "Goat of the Year Award" was to take place at the concluding banquet Saturday evening. When we arrived at the place of the banquet, which was held outdoors in very pleasant weather, we found a pile of "innocuous missiles" on each table. They were small folded socks. Here I will pause for a brief flashback. The meeting at Stanford was excellent in terms of the quality of the program and the convivial atmosphere. However, the sites of the various meetings, lodgings, and meals of the meeting were quite spread out. Even more than that—rather minor—complaint, the charge for lodging and meals seemed unusually high, especially for the banquet meal. (Many of us were not used to prices like those in the Palo Alto–Silicon Valley area.) Of course Bob Kelly, the organizer-host, became the object of discontent and murmuring from participants. It is a rare occurrence in social life when a group experiences difficulties but does not find someone to blame.

After the banquet gathering had time to finish the main course, Hamerton-Kelly went to the podium to comment on the program of the previous days and to announce the remainder of the evening festivities. He pointed out that this occasion was "once in a blue moon." In common idiom, of course, that phrase means infrequently or almost never. Yet in fact there would literally be a blue moon that night according to its calendrical sense of two full moons in one month. At this point there was an occurrence in which, in retrospect, we can recognize the continuity of our lives with those of our very remote ancestors who were just emerging from the state of proto-humanity into what could fairly be called a "human" state. All of a sudden there moved among us a contagion that prevailed over the reflexive consciousness that we identify as one of the prime characteristics of being human. For as Hamerton-Kelly continued speaking there was a spontaneous eruption that occurred so quickly that we were not sure who started it off.[51] One or two persons at one of the tables began throwing socks at him, and immediately everyone (so it seemed) joined in the "stoning."

That spontaneous outbreak was quickly over, ending in laughter and general good feeling. Everyone was having a good time. Our "victim," Hamerton-Kelly himself, seemed to enjoy it as much as anyone. As things calmed down and he continued to speak, it happened again! There was another round of throwing socks at Kelly. This seemed even more spontaneous than the first one because by then any prior inhibitions were gone. It was as though the lynched villain had somehow risen from the dead, so to speak, so now let's finish the job. Not having any other way to get the best of anger during the conference, the crowd took out their frustrations on Hamerton-Kelly, the actual scapegoat. This was a revealing event, for it was not planned or calculated. It seemed that a series of irritating contingencies triggered an outburst that betrayed traces of the primitive sacred—a vestige, perhaps, which is no longer fully functional in social and political life, but which is capable of generating momentary intensity of situations of rivalry and potential violence.

After this second outbreak, the crowd's thirst for (mock?) vengeance subsided. Hamerton-Kelly announced that the goat "award" was given to none other than René Girard. The thinking of Hamerton-Kelly in choosing Girard was evidently that it would be difficult to determine who had the most unfavorable reviews of his or her work and anyway, when is an unfavorable review really "bad"? Sometimes it is better from a certain perspective to receive uncomplimentary reviews from certain reviewers. Moreover, Girard himself, who no doubt had been praised and attacked more than anyone else in our academic world, was beyond any rivalry with COV&R members and would be a scapegoat who would not take offense. Girard tolerated the whole evening, including the stoning ritual, pretty well. The evening was actually conceived to honor him, and his wife and children were all present. I am sure they were all scratching their heads over the strange events. The act of throwing socks at him was desultory, just going through the motions, and in fact, some of those present did not even do that. We were back to our modern state of prohibition and constraint, embarrassed that we were asked to engage in even a mock ceremony that simulated a primitive event of stoning, particularly since the human object was one who embodied our reason for being as a group. The total series of events at the banquet is worthy of serious reflection, in spite of the fact that many of those present would like to forget it.[52]

Afterwards we proceeded to the dormitory where most of us were staying for a reception and informal singing, with Sandy Goodhart, an accomplished musician, at the piano. I remember that at some point I was passing through the hallway to the room Yvonne and I shared when I saw Wolfgang Palaver standing in about the middle of the large reception area. I still had a folded sock as a souvenir and the spirit of the evening came over me again: I threw the sock at him, hitting him squarely, as I recall. He picked up the sock and chased me down the hallway to avenge himself on me, which he did, scoring a hit. What would they have thought back in Innsbruck? Or for that matter, in Syracuse?

Concerning the mock stoning, there is a related matter that merits mention: I have found short classroom skits to illustrate aspects of the mimetic theory to be quite helpful.[53] One time after I retired and my wife and I moved back to Oklahoma, as I was teaching a course on the Old Testament prophets for the Pastoral Ministry Program of the Archdiocese of Oklahoma City, I composed a dialogue that leads to scapegoating. In it two groups of students sitting at opposing tables are neighbors on the same street who become more and more angry with one another over what begins as a few petty annoyances. The exchange comes to a head with a spontaneous convergence on a victim, who happens to be passing by. He is ragged and dirty and walks with a limp. I played the victim. Balled up sheets of paper were the "innocuous missiles." When the "stoning" occurred, I fell to the floor. That was the end of the little lynching drama I had composed, so I said, "Okay, that's enough." As I was getting up another paper ball hit me on the head. "That's enough!" I shouted again, as the class was collapsing in laughter. Then yet another paper ball hit me!

The additional missiles were thrown by a woman who was the best student in the class. She took a number of my courses and has stayed in touch with me. That was all very interesting, and probably a double illustration of mimetic rivalry: the scripted rivalry of the skit and the unconscious rivalry of the student with me. There are various views and models of the teacher-student relationship. Whatever the model, however, rivalry is always part of its dynamics.[54] In the human condition of mimetic desire, a model is always implicitly a rival and a rival a model.

The Meeting in New Orleans, 1996

The American Academy of Religion and the Society of Biblical Literature held their annual joint convention once again in New Orleans, so the annual meeting of COV&R in association with AAR/SBL was held in that venue on November 22 and 23, 1996. There was a rich array of papers. Paul Duff gave an interesting paper on the book of Revelation. He reported that recent studies of the historical context late in the first century a.d. did not support the inference that there was widespread persecution of Christians at that time. His thesis was that there was crisis in the church of Asia Minor revolving around witchcraft accusations against the "Jezebel" of Revelation 2:22. The strategy of John the seer "throughout the Apocalypse is not primarily aimed at condemning pagan culture or Rome specifically. Rather, he uses the apocalyptic tradition of the 'evil empire' to convince the uncommitted majority in the churches that his rival is in league with the forces of evil which control the dominant, external culture."[55] Diana Culbertson and I were respondents to Duff's paper. Culbertson held that John was not caught up in rivalry with Jezebel. "He sees *her* mimetic desire, labels it, and warns of the human catastrophes consequent upon the claim to a sovereignty that belongs only to

God."[56] The most important part of my response was not a direct comment on Duff's thesis, but was stated in a set of questions that troubled me, and still trouble me, about the Apocalypse: "Does the seer understand that the God of the Lamb does not impose violence? Is the real secret of the Apocalypse that the human desire leading to violence is subverted? Does the seer not only discern the apocalypse, but that it is what humans do to themselves? Is the final repayment according to everyone's work (Rev 22:12) a mythological pronouncement stemming from an intuition of our true situation which is already demythologized in the visions? Or does John misunderstand judgment, and see it as Christ's violent division of the good from the evil?"[57]

In the other session there were two presentations. Cheryl Kirk-Duggan held our attention forcefully with her subject: the "Lizzie Bordens" of ancient Israel, that is, women who slay men or who cause wrongful deaths. She focused on Deborah-Jael, Jezebel-Athaliah, Judith and her maid, and Herodias-Salome in the Bible, and two twentieth-century murderers, Lizzie Borden and Susan Smith. "Society tends to be surprised that women do violence, given the way we have merged certain personal qualities disproportionately into gender role identity. Women do kill in the name of God, desire, passion, revenge, [and] in self-defense. Violence is not [a] respecter of gender, class, race, time, or beauty."[58] Julie Shinnick responded to Kirk-Duggan's paper with three interpretive questions: (1) Since two of the murderers mentioned by Kirk-Duggan were victims of incest, were they exacting mimetic vengeance? (2) Could the Old Testament texts cited be a witness to the spirit of truth, or were they simply immersed in mimetism and vengeance like those of other peoples? (3) Related to the last question, do we catch a glimpse of the truth about the scapegoat mechanism in at least two of them: Jezebel's last words to her murderer, Jehu, "Is all well, Zimri, murderer of your master?" (2 Kings 9:31), and the anguish of Sisera's mother in the song of Deborah as she waits for her son to return? In both instances the protagonists are doubles, Jezebel and Jehu as murderers and Deborah, "a mother in Israel," vis-à-vis the mother of Sisera, the Canaanite army commander slain at the hand of the woman Jael (Judges 5:7, 24–30).[59]

William Mishler presented an absorbing paper on Ibsen's use of the Akedah (the binding of Isaac) in his verse drama *Brand*. "Whereas René Girard sees the Akedah and the Crucifixion as texts which progressively reveal the mechanism of mimetic desire in human culture, Ibsen, reading not as a theologian but as an analyst of his contemporary culture, suggests that to the popular mind, at least, the death of Jesus stands as a kind of reversal of the Abraham/Isaac example . . . 'Was God humane to Jesus Christ?' Brand cries as he prepares to sacrifice his own son."[60]

To Graz and Beyond, 1997

As 1997 began one could see that there was still a slow growth in the membership of COV&R. As reported in the March issue of *The Bulletin of COV&R*, the number of registered members was 125. That record of growth was very gradual. However, the effect of the meetings of COV&R and the outreach of its members through writings, lectures, and courses appeared to be considerable. The next two annual conferences, which were held in Europe, would bring even more academics and others into encounter with the mimetic theory.

The next annual meeting took place in the city of Graz, which is located in southeastern Austria close to Hungary and the former state of Yugoslavia. Gerhard Larcher was the host with the Institute of Fundamental Theology of Graz, the Institute of Dogmatic Theology of Innsbruck, and other groups. The theme of the conference was "Film and Modernity: Violence, Sacrifice, and Religion." As it would turn out, part of the program would elicit deep emotional reactions and more heated debates than any of our events since the encounter over Paul's interpretation of the Torah in 1992.

The Conference in Graz, June 23–27, 1997

The symposium in Graz was quite memorable for me. It was the closest I had been to Eastern Europe, as it probably was also for a number of the American participants. For a good many of us the program itself, particularly the films, cut into our basic assumptions about the world and our sense of what "postmodernity" really amounted to, more than anything we had encountered in a professional meeting previously.

A particularly pleasant memory for me was a two-day stop in Innsbruck before the meeting in Graz. It was a chance for me to visit with our Innsbruck colleagues. Cesáreo and Esther Bandera joined us there, and one of my students, Tyler Graham, came down from southern Germany, where he had taken an intensive course in German. The Palavers held an informal dinner party for us in the village where they resided, and from their yard we watched the fires on the mountains that celebrated midsummer. It is also the date that the Christian tradition has assigned to the birth of John the Baptist.

With the Innsbruck colleagues attending COV&R in Graz we traveled by train from Innsbruck to Graz. During that trip Raymund Schwager and I conversed at length. It was the longest conversation I had with him. As we were driven to our lodging after the train arrived in Graz we saw a sight that initially seemed incongruous with the setting at the border of Eastern

Europe and the theme of the symposium—but perhaps it was a reflection of the cultural situation being addressed. There was a billboard proclaiming the entrance to Graz, the home of Arnold Schwarzenegger! This was six years before he become governor of California. What a commentary on modern Western culture permeated by the media!

The Austrian hero had emigrated to the United States and made good in Hollywood, America's Tinseltown, and he was later to become governor of the Golden State, which is California's official nickname. In the nineteenth century it was called the El Dorado State because of the discovery of gold in 1848. It has also been known as the Land of Milk and Honey. The irony of all this was amazing to me, and even more so at this writing when the state has fallen into a great morass of troubles. But perhaps the greatest irony of all is from the standpoint of this book is that COV&R had its birth as a professional society in the Golden State, the El Dorado of America, where the fictional apocalypse of Hollywood joins the real possibility of apocalypse in the twenty-first century.

Gerhard Larcher, with his assistant Christian Wessely and his secretary Elisabeth Kuehrner, did a good job of organizing and hosting the event. There were 115 registered participants, who moved between Mariatrost, a Catholic educational center, and the Schubertkino, a movie theater in downtown Graz. A bonus for the week was the simultaneous meeting in Graz of the Second European Ecumenical Assembly, some of whose participants attended also some of the COV&R sessions. It was interesting for us to have the opportunity to meet people attending the other conference.

The fact of violence in our cultural substructures as represented in film came home to those present as we watched a number of films that were shown. These included *Natural Born Killers*, *Pulp Fiction*, *Bad Lieutenant*, and two films that dealt with questions of historical identity in the midst of ethnic conflict and violence in the Balkans, to which Graz is so close: *Le regard d'Ulysse* (*Ulysses' Gaze*), a film of Theodor Angelopoulos, and *Underground*, written and directed by Emir Kusturica.

Robert Hamerton-Kelly gave the only paper that provided historical background for the comprehension of the conflict and violence in the Balkans: "Ethnic Conflict and Historical Identity in South East Europe." He surveyed the general historical stage in which the Ottoman, Habsburg, and czarist empires confronted one another, focusing on the Ottomans, who played a significant role for about 400 years. In the remainder of the paper he devoted primary attention to Muslim identity in Bosnia and Serbian identity.

Hamerton-Kelly states in his interpretive conclusion that current social science is not helpful in understanding this historical situation because it doesn't take religion seriously, nor does it have any appreciation of the contribution of the mimetic theory. The Balkan crisis is sacrificial, and its problems are dealt with by scapegoating. The causes include the collapse of Communism and totalitarian ideology, the deceitful "construction" of a crisis by political opportunists, and the escalating violence that is a mimetic process that criminal gangs have set in motion. The Christian churches have been rendered sacrificial. "Serbian Orthodoxy and Croatian Catholicism have joined the nationalist cause and thus forfeited much of their theological truth, which should have been to stand against the sacrificial solution to the crisis. The Muslims have been given a religious identity that is more high-profile than their practice warrants and, mimetically enthralled to their Orthodox and Catholic rivals, have accepted that identity and exaggerated it."[61]

So there is a double triangle of identities, Orthodox, Catholic, and Muslim, "corresponding to the old imperial identities of Russia, Habsburg, and Ottoman, and overlaying the nationalist identities of Serb, Croat, and Muslim." The upshot is that "each group has looked outside itself for the scapegoat."[62] Balkan identities are determined in mimetic rivalry as those involved go around in Godless circles in which they become alternately victimizer and victim. These sacrificial identities "are the ghosts of the culture of death."[63]

One of the films shown was *Dead Man Walking*. Its redemptive moment in the last part of the film, where the audience sees the main character's murder of a young couple and hears his confession of guilt and acceptance of personal responsibility, is placed in juxtaposition to the state-sanctioned violence of his execution. This film seemed quite tame in comparison to most of the others shown, particular *Funny Games*, then the most recent film of the Austrian director Michael Haneke. In it we were drawn in but then repelled by the murder of a bourgeois family, who are killed off one by one by a couple of young men. The killers look and act "normal" at first and have no motivation to commit murder that is disclosed to the audience. As Larcher says in his report on the conference, "It is the form of showing violence that is decisive."[64] I think all the viewers would agree that it was difficult to watch, and as a matter of fact a few in the audience left in disgust during the showing.

Filmmaker Haneke made a short presentation on violence and the media in which he gave, without directly saying so, an artistic and ethical justification for that kind of movie. He pointed out three dramaturgic premises that normally have to be fulfilled to show violence to the public: (1) dissociation of the violence from the viewers' immediate life situation (westerns, horror films, science fiction); (2) showing a crisis in the viewers' actual life situation in which violent acts liberate the victims of violence by evil perpetrators (war and police films, individuals seeking righteous revenge); (3) embedding the violent action within wit and satire (e.g., *Catch-22* and *Pulp Fiction*). His justification for a film like *Funny Games*, which met none of these criteria, was implied in his question at the end of his presentation: "How do I give the viewer the possibility of indeed perceiving this loss of reality [i.e., 'being an indifferent consumer of interchangeable empty forms'] and his own involvement therein, so that he may thereby free himself from being a victim of the medium and become its potential partner? . . . [T]he problem is not: how do I show violence, but: how do I show the viewer his own position in relation to violence and its portrayal?"[65]

The film certainly disturbed me, to the point that in a conversation with Raymund Schwager I said that showing a movie like that to the general public could have destructive consequences. How many emotionally unbalanced persons tottering on the edge of violence might want to imitate the young killers who acted almost bored as they murdered the family one by one? In response, Schwager offered another perspective: rather than being offended—or in spite of being offended, which is not a bad thing in itself—we need to come to grips with what the film communicates about ourselves and our contemporary cultural situation. As I reflected back on it, that was precisely the point of Haneke's comments on violence and the media.

Now it was a striking coincidence that the theme of the ecumenical assembly meeting in Graz was reconciliation, the reconciliation of God and humans and human beings with one another. Girard himself spoke on "Christian Reconciliation in the Modern World" and Gerhard Larcher's paper dealt with the question of the function of film in the modern search for identity and reconciliation. The violence that issues from the generative mimetic scapegoat mechanism is what in traditional Christian language is called "original sin." The nonsacrificial understanding of the message of the Christian gospel is that "the Son alone is united with the Father in the fullness of humanity and divinity. But it does not imply that this union is an exclusive one, or prevent us from envisaging the possibility of mankind becoming like God through the Son's mediation."[66] Reconciliation as salvation from our violence is what Christian soteriology and eschatology are all about.

After the experience of the films shown at the conference Robert Hamerton-Kelly, Hans Jensen, and I escaped to attend an opera rather than attending a reception hosted by the mayor in the city hall. It was a performance of Mozart's *Don Giovanni*. Many operas narrate violent acts or presuppose violence. The plot of this one revolves less around the sexual conquests of the protagonist than around his acts of violence, not only in the abuse of women but above all the slaying of the Commandant, Donna Anna's father, in a sword duel. The final scene in which the dead Commandant comes as a dinner guest to Don Giovanni's residence and pulls him down to hell is dark and chilling. This dark and violent side of the opera is muted to a great extent, of course, by the distant time of its setting, the mythical form of the final encounter, and the beautiful music of the whole opera, in turn lyrical, comic, and haunting. It is an example of Haneke's first dramaturgic premise for dealing with violence, dissociation from the audience's immediate life situation.

In any case, it was a lovely "escape" for us. The opera was performed in a school gymnasium with seats on either side of the performers. We were sitting close to the orchestra. It was quite an experience to be so close to the performers, almost like being part of the cast. It was a nice complement to our experience of the conference.

Meeting in San Francisco, November 22, 1997

The meeting of COV&R at the time of the AAR/SBL convention in San Francisco was different from the previous such meetings in two respects: there was only one event on the program and we had a record attendance of about seventy-five. The two respects really amounted to one: René Girard was the speaker. His topic was the meaning of the Gospel Passion vis-à-vis the myths and rituals of primitive and archaic religions. He intended to write a book on this theme. This did not happen, although all his books deal with the subject to some extent, particularly *I See Satan Fall Like Lightning*.

In this paper Girard emphasized that the early religious life of humankind was not meaningless. It was based on a deluded premise, but the behavior and the beliefs flowing from that archaic premise were functional and rational within the cultural systems presupposing it. The deluded premise was mistaking a successful scapegoating event as the epiphany of a new divinity who taught the community how to sacrifice victims and thus prevent the crises that disrupted its life. The originary crisis was the one that this god had terminated through the sacrifice of his or her own life. In mythology scapegoating is effective, it "works," because it is misinterpreted as the disclosure of the sacred that heals the community, "whereas in the Gospels scapegoating succeeds with the crowd but ultimately fails with the disciples because of the Resurrection which rescues them from the mimetic contagion and turns them into true witnesses of Jesus' death, martyrs able to write a faithful account of what happened, and, if necessary, to die the same death as Jesus' death."[67]

To Saint-Denis and Beyond, 1998

As we looked forward to the annual conference of COV&R in St. Denis we could confirm a growth in membership, actually a leap upward for such a small society. Our number increased from 125 in early 1997 to 165 in early 1998. As already indicated, I myself was disappointed that we had not kept to the rhythm of meeting every third year in Europe, but circumstance and opportunity prevailed and everything turned out well.

Saint-Denis is part of metropolitan Paris. It has its own government, but it is located in the northern suburbs of Paris. It had been a Roman settlement, but it got its present name from the first bishop of Paris, Saint Denis, who was martyred about 250 C.E. In recent times it came to the world's attention, in June 1998, when the world soccer tournament took place in the new stadium, le Stade de France, built specifically for that occasion (and just a few blocks from our conference venue). It was the focal point of jubilation in France when the French team won the soccer cup. A well-known and interesting landmark in the town is the Basilique Saint Denis, which dates back to the seventh century and is the home of an abbey. It became a cathedral church in 1966 for the bishop of Saint-Denis.

Apart from concerns for the organization, I was looking forward to spending a week in France. I could refresh my spoken French a bit, and it would be my longest visit to France since that fateful spring of 1985 when I discovered René Girard and the mimetic theory. I even gave a brief opening welcome in French at the opening session.

The tide of specific human events is impossible to predict, even if prophets and poets are able to intuit patterns, trends, and destinies. How could I have guessed or imagined on that April day thirteen years before that my discovery of *Violence and the Sacred* would converge with the passion and vision of Charles Mabee and Robert Hamerton-Kelly and result in the launching of an organization that would meet in France in 1998? As for René Girard, it would have been impossible for him to imagine what would spin out of his subsequent work and experiences as he came as a young man to America in 1947.

The host and organizer, Marie-Louise Martinez, did an enormous amount of work planning and organizing the conference. She first proposed a symposium in 1995. The theme that she articulated was an ecumenical approach from the resources of different fields (theology, anthropology, art, and philosophy) for moving beyond violence. However, in light of the theme and content of the 1997 meeting in Graz she decided to modify the theme to "Education, Mimesis, and Reduction of Violence." She and her conference team sought out contributors from many fields, some of whom were not involved with the mimetic theory, and they also applied to and received funding from a number of government sources. These included her own professional home, the Centre d'Etudes de Formation pour l'Enfance Inadoptée (Center for the Education of Unadopted Children—CNEFEI); the Centre de Recherches en Epistémologie Appliquée (Center for Research in Applied Epistemology—CREA), headed by Jean-Pierre Dupuy at l'Ecole polytechnique; the Conseil d'Europe; the Fondation de France, and others. French and English were the languages of the conference, and simultaneous translations were provided for the proceedings.

The Conference in Saint-Denis, May 27–30, 1998

A large number of participants gathered for the symposium, coming from fourteen countries and representing a broad spectrum of interests and specialties in the humanities and social sciences. The number in attendance was 350, which still stands as a record for a COV&R meeting.

Once more, I could not help but marvel at the distance we had come since our beginnings in 1990. This conference was extremely important because it gave COV&R and the mimetic theory an exposure and an opportunity for interaction with non-COV&R people that we had not had before. At the same time I felt a tinge of regret and nostalgia as I remembered the close camaraderie of our small and humble beginnings. But we did not form a new scholarly society simply in order to fraternize among ourselves; what propelled and lured us belonged to the world.

The organization of the conference and many of its papers reflected Marie-Louise Martinez's concern for nonviolent education of persons and the formation of children. She places her vision of the educational process within the field of the mimetic theory to propose ways out of a mimetic triangle of violence. These include seeing the teacher as a kind of nonobstructive mediator of knowledge and methods of learning who does not consciously or unconsciously try to focus the student's desire on herself as teacher. The teacher should make use of prohibitions in a structure that facilitates concern for the other, and maintain an attitude of confidence based on reason within this structure.[68] There were dozens of papers dealing with violence and education, as well as many other topics. Among the notables in attendance were Girard himself, of course, who spoke on the mimetic theory in its entirety; Paul Ricoeur, whose subject was religion and symbolic violence; Henri Grivois, chief medical officer of the Hotel-Dieu in Paris, who presented on adolescence, indifferentiation, and the onset of psychosis; Antoine Garapon, director of the Institute-Supérieur de la Justice in Paris; and Michel Serres of the French Academy, who spoke on education and the handicapped. Of great importance for Girard and COV&R was Paul Ricoeur's affirmation of the mimetic theory.

Ricoeur, a leading philosopher of the twentieth century and important hermeneutical thinker and interpreter of Freud, stated that the mimetic theory provided a missing link in his own philosophy of religion. This missing link is the expelling of a third person as the basis of reconciliation in the antagonism engendered by mimetic rivalry. The groundless ground of being, "God," becomes a "blurred object . . . of desire and fear" for the "instructed community" as its members project their own appropriative desire onto the divine source that summons them into being and gives them life. In their perverted desire they do not understand that this superabundant source is actually the bestower of gifts. The Christ symbol as the revealer of the scapegoat mechanism "is not necessarily the only one possible." What "this means is . . . that the reception of the source or groundless ground as pure gift is henceforth, for us, inseparable from criticism of the victimary process that radically corrupts the reception of the fundamental source and transforms it into entrapment in the rivalry with all the other communities that themselves were receptive communities that became entrapped."[69]

A question remained as to whether Ricoeur completely understood the mimetic theory. In speaking of the "Christ symbol," he held that Jesus as the Christ is a symbol of what is present or latent in other historical traditions. That could be partially correct, but one could not assert that without taking into account the prophetic history exposing desire and the scapegoat mechanism, a history of which Christ is the embodiment. Ricoeur sounded very much like Paul Tillich in speaking of the "groundless ground of Being"; it is a puzzle as to how an abstraction like the "groundless ground" would reveal anything. His language comes across as referring to philosophical discovery that negates revelation in a religious context. Nevertheless, Ricoeur's approval and acceptance of the fundamental elements of Girard's work was certainly a welcome moment, and has probably contributed at least to some degree to greater acceptance of it.

One of the highlights of the conference for a number of COV&R people and their guests was a reception at the Girards' apartment in Paris. I have a vivid recollection of getting some of people up to their floor by shifts on the extremely slow elevator. In the convivial conversations I recall trying to carry on a conversation in French with a young Italian man. Between my American and his Italian accent our communication was not smooth but it was a friendly meeting, nonetheless. Another vivid memory from that evening is seeing the informal shrine of flowers and notes for Princess Diana near our train stop in Paris. Her death in a horrible auto accident had occurred nine months before. It was a striking contemporary instance of a public model of desire whose death was mourned by millions of people in the world.

At the business meeting of the conference I announced my resignation as executive secretary. We had no one ready to hand who had been willing to take over the role in 1997, so I served one year beyond the two terms permitted by the constitution. My participation in COV&R for the next several years was limited due to my retirement, the process of selling our home in Phoenix, New York, a village north of Syracuse, and our move back to our home state of Oklahoma. The move and settling in a new area required considerable time and energy.

Diana Culbertson agreed to assume the role of executive secretary for a year, after which Sandy Goodhart became executive secretary and Culbertson became president. Another addition to the officers of the Colloquium, a very important one, was Julie Shinnick. She was a musicologist specializing in the late medieval period who had joined COV&R in 1994. She was elected to serve as treasurer when Gil Bailie's terms expired. She would serve faithfully for ten years in that office, often performing tasks beyond the job description of treasurer.

The Semiannual Meeting in Orlando, Florida, November 21, 1998

Our semiannual meeting in association with the American Academy of Religion met for half a day in Orlando, not far from Disney World. Of course, many of the participants took advantage of the opportunity to visit Disney theme parks. The topic of the gathering was "Fieldwork in Sacred Violence." The first speaker was Fred Boehrer, one of my doctoral students at Syracuse University and co-leader with his wife of the Catholic Worker Community in Albany, New York. He spoke on the work they and their colleagues were doing on behalf of the poor, homeless, and marginalized people in the urban setting. Much of his effort was devoted to publicizing problems and mediating conflicts, and inviting those otherwise unaware of the issues to join with the Catholic Workers as they stood with the scapegoats in the American economic and political systems. He left the convention early to travel to Fort Benning, Georgia, to protest with thousands of others at the School of the Americas, the site of the U.S.-sponsored paramilitary training for Latin American soldiers.

The second speaker was Paul Bellan-Boyer of All Nations Lutheran Church in Jersey City. His subject was a scapegoating experience within a church and parish setting. The community crisis illustrated in detail all the elements of mimetic rivalry and expulsion. The respondents were Rusty Palmer, Thee Smith, and Walter Wink. Their comments were the occasion of a lively discussion.

For me an interesting event that weekend was a daylong meeting in which I led discussion of the mimetic theory as a mode of biblical interpretation with a small group of Mormons, who were brought together by Dr. Mack Stirling of Traverse City, Michigan. Stirling had participated in COV&R for several years, and he in particular had become well informed about the mimetic theory and envisioned its usefulness in reforming and revitalizing Mormon biblical theology.

Perspective on the Years 1994–1998

By the end of 1998 it was quite clear that COV&R had become a thoroughly international society. This was reflected in the fact that seven of the seventeen advisory board members were European, located in Belgium, Italy, Denmark, France, and Austria. In addition our honorary chair, René Girard, was French and our president, Cesáreo Bandera, was Spanish, although their primary residence was in the United States.

Perhaps the use of the word "international" should be qualified. As Michael Kirwan has observed, "René Girard and mimetic theory have been, for the most part, a transatlantic phenomenon."[70] Although Girard met with Brazilian theologians in 1990, the mimetic theory has evidently sparked interest very slowly there. So the spread of the mimetic theory was so far primarily transatlantic.

In communication with our membership and sharing of research we were certainly doing fairly well. Our newsletter, *The Bulletin of COV&R*, had been published twice yearly since the autumn of 1991. By 1998 it was typically fourteen to sixteen pages long, containing reports on meetings, notes from the officers, book reviews, and bibliography on the mimetic theory. The COV&R

journal, *Contagion: Journal of Violence, Mimesis, and Culture*, was an annual that published articles of high quality. The *Bulletin* announced the publication of over fifty new books on the mimetic theory during this period, 1994–1998, most of them written by COV&R members.

A Jewish-Christian dialogue was one of the recurring events at many of the COV&R meetings. This was largely due to the concern and energy of Sandor Goodhart, but others were ready and willing to take a leading part in the discussions, especially Raymund Schwager and Charles Mabee. The Jewish-Christian discussions were a foreshadowing of the conference at Boston College, which revolved around the relation of Christianity and the mimetic theory to the great world religions.

The range of themes of the annual conferences through these five years was certainly impressive. We had explored ways in which the mimetic theory casts light on social theory (1994), psychology and cultural criticism (1995), ethnic conflict in an international context (1996), film and sacrificial violence in modern culture (1997), and reduction of violence in education (1998). I have found it quite a re-educational experience just to review these themes for this writing. Yet what difference did our understanding make in our lives and in the world plagued by violence? The relation of theory and practice would continue to concern many of us as we moved into a new century.

Brief Biographies of Leaders

Cesáreo Bandera

Cesáreo Bandera was the president of COV&R from 1995 to 1999, and otherwise served on the advisory board for many years. He came to the United States in 1960, shortly after graduating from the Law School at the University of Seville. He changed careers a couple of times, eventually receiving an M.A. (1963) and a Ph.D. (1965) from Cornell in Spanish literature (Latin American and Peninsular). Back in Spain from 1966 to 1968, he earned another degree in Romance philology from the University of Salamanca (1968). In 1969 he moved from Cornell to the State University of New York at Buffalo where he and Girard became friends—a friendship that would last a lifetime. In 1985 he joined the faculty at the University of North Carolina, Chapel Hill, from which he retired in 2002. His academic field has been medieval and Golden Age Spanish literature, as well as comparative literature and literary theory. His personal interest, especially through association with Girard, has been in the historical relationship between literary fiction and

Christianity. His first book was a reworking of his doctoral dissertation, *El Poema de Mio Cid: poesía, historia, mito*. His first "Girardian" book was *Mímesis conflictiva: ficción literaria y violencia en Cervantes y Calderón* (Conflictual Mimesis: Literary Fiction and Violence in Cervantes and Calderón). Two more books followed years later: *The Sacred Game: The Role of the Sacred in the Genesis of Modern Literary Fiction*, published also in Spanish by the University of Sevilla Publications; and *The Humble Story of Don Quixote: Reflections on the Birth of the Modern Novel*. A slightly longer version of the latter was published with the title *"Monda y desnuda." La humilde historia de Don Quijote* ("Naked and Unadorned": The Humble Story of Don Quixote) in Madrid and Frankfurt the year before.

In addition to his outstanding scholarship and his insights concerning the mimetic theory, his personal "gravitas," as Hamerton-Kelly described him when he became president of COV&R, and his practical good sense when he served as a board member and president, have contributed much to the welfare of COV&R.

He was named an honorary lifetime member of the advisory board in 2006.

Sandor Goodhart

Sandor Goodhart received his Ph.D. in 1977 from the State University of New York at Buffalo, where René Girard was his mentor and dissertation advisor. He is a specialist in dramatic literature, literary theory, and Jewish studies. He has been on the English faculty of Purdue University since 1997, and he is currently the director of the Interdisciplinary Classics Program. He is the author of *Sacrificing Commentary: Reading the End of Literature* and the editor of *Reading Stephen Sondheim: A Collection of Critical Essays*, and he has written many articles interpreting texts from the standpoint of the mimetic theory and the thought of Emmanuel Levinas. In his work with the Hebrew Bible he emphasizes the connection of its prophetic dimension to mimetic theory.

Goodhart has been active in COV&R since 1991 and is a founding member of Imitatio. He has served COV&R as an advisory board member, executive secretary, and president. In addition, he has contributed to COV&R not only by presenting many papers and his active involvement in discussions, but also as a kind of goodwill ambassador with his openness to dialogue with other positions and his friendly wit.

Andrew McKenna

McKenna was one of Girard's early graduate students who went on to teach and publish in the area of mimetic theory. Girard directed his dissertation,

"Baudelaire and Sartre: A Study in Comparative Analysis," which he completed at Johns Hopkins to earn his Ph.D. in 1970. He has taught French language and literature since 1971 at Loyola University Chicago, and served as chair of the Department of Modern Languages and Literatures in 1992–1998 and 2004–2005.

He was elected to the COV&R advisory board in 1994, and followed Judith Arias as editor-in-chief of *Contagion*, working in that capacity from 1996 to 2006. In addition to many articles and book reviews, he is the author of *Violence and Difference* (1992), the only book as yet written that compares and contrasts the work of Girard and Jacques Derrida. He is a founding member of Imitatio and a board member of the Raven Foundation. His contribution to COV&R is much appreciated, particularly his intelligent and indefatigable editorial and other work to keep *Contagion* afloat until we began to see better days financially in the twenty-first century.

CHAPTER FOUR

Stability and Transition, 1999–2006

I call the next eight years a period of stability and transition because COV&R had definitely established itself and functioned fairly well during the early years of this period, and growth in membership and changes in policy direction and outlook were not considerable until toward the end of this time. In fact, there was a sort of lull during the middle of this period in which certain things did not get done. One symptom of this situation is that reports are lacking on some of the annual meetings of COV&R in conjunction with AAR/SBL. This is because there are no written sources on those events in *The Bulletin of COV&R* for 2000, 2001, 2002, and 2003. This lacuna came about because of certain editorial transitions and the impact of September 11, 2001, on one of the editors. There were, in fact, some problems with getting the *Bulletin* published. These problems were worked out toward the end of this period.

The challenge of coming to grips with Islam began even before the calamitous events of 9/11 with a session on Islam at the Boston College conference in 2000. Moreover, the latter conference and the 2002 symposium at Purdue brought Judaism to the fore as it had not been before. New leadership in the last few years of this period and the process of gaining further support in funding and outreach through becoming incorporated, and thus legally able to receive tax-deductible contributions, were major factors in starting the transition to another phase of the Colloquium's history. This part of the story will be related later in the chapter.

The Conference in Atlanta and Beyond, 1999

Theophus ("Thee") Smith had begun initial planning for the conference at Emory University in Atlanta, Georgia, over three years before. It had been provisionally projected for 1998, but given certain circumstances, as related in the previous chapter, the advisory board decided to defer the meeting until 1999. Smith, a historian of African-American religion and liturgy and a conflict resolution specialist, was particularly well situated for this conference on "Violence Reduction in Theory and Practice: From Primates to Nations." The resources of Emory University are ample. Two of Smith's colleagues from other areas of research and teaching participated in the conference and made important contributions. These were Frans de Waal, director of the Living Links Center at Emory and associated with the Yerkes National Primate Center in Atlanta, and Bruce Knauft of the Department of Anthropology, an expert on the rain forest people in Papua, New Guinea.

Atlanta itself is an American city of great interest. Located in the Deep South, it was all but completely destroyed by the attack of the Union forces in 1864 during the Civil War, but after the war it became an even more important commercial hub than before. It is not among the largest of American cities but the metropolitan area is huge, the eighth largest region in the United States according to 2008 census figures. The city metropolitan area has thirty colleges and universities, including a consortium of Black colleges and universities. The latter includes Clark Atlanta University and Morehead College, one of whose graduates was Martin Luther King, Jr. The (Jimmy) Carter Presidential Center and the Martin Luther King, Jr. National Memorial Foundation are both located in Atlanta. Thee Smith had expected that these two institutes would send representatives to the conference. However, the Carter Center people informed Smith that they were interested only in practice and ethical application and the King Foundation had long before fallen on hard times in leadership and funding. Neither sent an official representative to address the conference.

"Violence Reduction in Theory and Practice: From Primates to Nations," June 3–5, 1999

The conference was well organized, congenial, and participants were well treated. Thee Smith enjoyed the support of Fred Smith (no relation), a COV&R member and a staff member of the Carter Center Interfaith Health Program, as well as the able assistance of Maggie Kulyk, his graduate assistant and the conference manager.

In his introductory remarks as host, Smith raised a number of questions. Do theorists of violence, such as most of the members of COV&R, have the imagination, vision, or fortitude for attempting to reduce violence, an effort that engages most practitioners? Should we not become "more publicly accountable concerning the consequences for practice of the theories of violence that we explore"?[1]

There was an interesting combination of papers in the plenary sessions. Eric Gans spoke on his thesis that the emergence of our species—the process of "hominization"—occurred by means of the deferral of violence through language. Frans de Waal demonstrated with slides and research data that reconciliation in situations of conflict and violence occurs already among primates. René Girard commented from the audience that these two presentations illustrate important differences between the humanities and the social sciences in the selection of data, methods of study, and modes of persuasion. To the enjoyment of the audience, Gans walked from the other side of the stage and gave de Waal a lighthearted embrace, thus symbolically "reconciling" the two approaches to research.

Of particular relevance to the theme of the conference was the presentation of Charles Villa-Vicencio, a South African theologian and researcher for South Africa's Truth and Reconciliation Commission. He called the assembly's attention not only to the obvious perpetrators of violence, but especially to the passive, hidden perpetrators who quietly acquiesce to this violence and permit it.

An especially instructive lecture was given by Richard Koenigsberg on the increasing development of similarity between German soldiers and their Jewish victims during World War II. The soldiers were, in the own way, the sacrificial pawns of the Nazi regime, just as the Jews and other ethnic groups so obviously and horribly were. There was a kind of "perverse unity" between them as their lives were put at the disposal of the state. Many in the audience seemed outraged by this thesis, which blurred or even obliterated distinctions and moral differences, but at the same time they could see and appreciate the mimetic structure of violence that lumped victims and the agents of oppression together.

In his presentation René Girard emphasized that theories of violence, and lifestyles that seek to implement these theories, do not necessarily reduce violence. Jesus brings "not peace but a sword" and tells his followers they must "be wise as serpents and innocent as doves" (Matthew 10:34 and 10:16). The scandal of the cross causes sacrificial crises that aggravate violence as well as ameliorate it. As he later said in *Evolution and Conversion*, "Any great Christian experience is apocalyptic because what one realizes is that after the decomposition of the sacrificial order there is nothing standing between ourselves and our possible destruction."[2] Even though the deeper meaning of Christianity is compassion for the victim, we are unable to live without scapegoats in the world as we know it. Therefore, "Christianity is a source of disruption."[3] Still, we are not completely and necessarily determined by mimeticism. "We do not have to engage automatically in mimetic rivalries. We do not have to accuse our neighbor; we can forgive him instead."[4]

After the conference Eric Gans composed an interesting commentary about the significance of the conference and Girard's mimetic theory. Here I will quote the final paragraph of his reflections, which are set within his own alternative to the mimetic theory, which includes the postulate that our understanding of origins does not have to include reference to supernatural revelation, even though religion is indeed important in the development of human culture.

> Thus the ultimate contribution of the Girardian thinking that inspires the Colloquium on Violence and Religion is the opportunity to understand the origin of the sign in terms exclusively of the paradox of mimesis, that is, without the intervention of "supernatural" forces. But the originary hypothesis explains at the same time why such forces are necessarily evoked. To understand the origin of the sign, we must understand the sacred quality of its referent. The sign is the name-of-God; the sacred, what is designated by the sign. Paradox is the minimal explanation, but there is no higher criterion by which to decide if paradox by itself is explanation enough, if our connection to the community through language can be understood otherwise than in terms of a subsisting mediating being. Whichever may be the case, an invisible barrier will always separate the purely empirical study of human behavior, including that of the brain, from the human essence revealed in the birth of language. If there is to exist a true science of the human or "science humaine," it will be through the acceptance rather than the denial of the revelation that COV&R has chosen as its mission to preserve.[5]

A true human science, an integration of knowledge and methods of gaining knowledge, is one way of describing what COV&R is all about. Even though there is an "invisible barrier" between "purely empirical study of human behavior" and "the human essence revealed in the birth of language" (or the birth of culture through the scapegoat mechanism, as more orthodox Girardians would put it), those engaged in the more empirical branches of research and those working in branches dealing with the transcendent essence of the human should be able to erect a bridge across this divide to converse with each other and take seriously one another's approach and findings.

The meeting in Atlanta was a time of transition in the leadership of COV&R. Cesáreo Bandera completed two terms as president. He was succeeded by Diana Culbertson, who was one of those colleagues present at the founding meeting in 1990. She accepted the position of executive secretary for a year until Sandor Goodhart could become established at Purdue University, whereupon he would move into that role. As it turned out, Goodhart became executive secretary the following year and Culbertson the president. Both Goodhart and Culbertson had already made significant contributions to COV&R. As for Bandera, he was an important colleague in the governance of COV&R during the 1990s. See the discussion of his contribution to mimetic theory and literary theory in chapter 2 and the brief biography at the end of chapter 3.

Finally, the advisory board honored Raymund Schwager and me by nominating us to become lifetime honorary members of the board and of COV&R. This was approved in the business meeting of COV&R members.

The Semiannual Meeting, in Boston, November 20, 1999

There were three papers in the meeting in conjunction with AAR in Boston. The only one to which I have access is the one given by Anthony Bartlett. Bartlett's topic was mimetic anthropology and the Holy Spirit, which led him to a radical understanding of the Crucified Christ. His radicalization of mimesis allows him "to propose the figure of the Crucified as the possibility of myself-as-other, the self as the Christ who has entered by compassion into the depth of my situation. Through the alterity of Christ the self experiences 'alteration,' dies to its old self (with Christ) and repeats the self-giving other, that is Christ, in a new, liberated self. Following from this we can then say it is Christ's act of abyssal compassion that gifts the Spirit to humanity: a new principle of human relationality experienced as the reality of the self enters human affairs."[6]

The Conference at Boston College and Beyond, 2000

As we came to the turn of the millennium, it was apparent to Robert Daly, S.J., and his colleagues at Boston College that an authentic dialogue, that is, a real attempt to speak to and understand the major religious traditions, was necessary to achieve any semblance of peace in the world. But not only that, an authentic dialogue dares to presuppose that greater insight into the destiny of human beings in their transcendent essence is at stake. Of course, the grief and horror of September 11, 2001, lay still over a year into the future, yet there were already many signs of impending apocalyptic catastrophe as human history was moving into a stage where the former positive benefits of the scapegoat mechanism were crumbling by virtue of the Christian revelation and secularization, while the dynamic of sacred violence was breaking out of its religious and cultural bounds. Is there any prospect of peace on earth within history itself, or must this hope remain a purely eschatological, otherworldly longing?

In addition to the specific planning for the conference, there was an important professional environmental factor in theology. This was the Boston Theological Institute, which was founded around 1969 and has been in full operation since then. As Daly told me, it did not have a direct influence on the COV&R conference, but it certainly had an indirect and strong "contextual" influence. "As one faculty administrator of the BTI put it . . . , 'We don't do ecumenical theology—but we do theology ecumenically.'"[7] In other words, the project was not to engage in comparative studies in the history-of-religions sense; it was rather to do comparative theology, in which what is at stake in different traditions in terms of core beliefs, symbols, and rituals is the object of open discussion, analysis, and meditation. Its mission is not to evangelize or proselytize but to understand other traditions and gain deeper knowledge of one's own tradition. For the Christian participant, the objective would be faith that seeks understanding. Whatever the direct connection of the BTI to the symposium, part of its vision was realized in the format and content of the conference whose theme was "Violence and Institution in Christianity, Judaism, Islam, Hinduism, and Buddhism."

A subsidiary theme of the conference was a "Girard-Lonergan Conversation." Bernard Lonergan (1904–1984) was a great philosophical theologian in the Thomistic tradition. A Canadian and priest in the Society of Jesus, he spent the last part of his career at Boston College. His most well known works are *Insight: A Study of Human Understanding* (1957) and *Method in Theology* (1972). He was particularly interested in human consciousness and relationships and the experience of conversion or fundamental change in thought and behavior. Therefore it was thought to be fruitful to give participants an opportunity to become better acquainted with his work vis-à-vis that of Girard.

Boston College itself was founded by members of the Society of Jesus in 1863. It was originally located in Boston, but in 1909 it was moved to Chestnut Hill. About six miles from downtown Boston, it was a very rural area at the time. Initially a liberal arts college with an emphasis on languages, philosophy, and theology, it has become a major private university with about 15,000 students. The Jesuit presence is still felt there in many ways, and there are about fifty Jesuits who serve as members of the faculty, staff, and administration.

"Violence and Institution in Christianity, Judaism Hinduism, Buddhism, and Islam," May 31–June 3, 2000

The format of the conference was a plenary session devoted to each of the five major religious traditions, with the time divided in each for the presenter's summary of his paper, the comments of a respondent, and open discussion. In addition, there were breakout sessions, many of which were very significant according to comments made by conference participants.[8] The major papers were given by Robert Daly, S.J., "Violence and Institution in Christianity," Paul Nuechterlein responding; Reuven Dimmelman, "Working Warfare and Its Restrictions in the Jewish Tradition," Sandor Goodhart responding; Qamar-ul Huda, "The Problem of Violence and Conflict in Islam," Robert Hamerton-Kelly responding; Francis X. Clooney, S.J., "Violence and Non-Violence in Hindu Religious Traditions," Julia W. Shinnick responding; and Christopher Ives, "Dharma and Deconstruction: Buddhist Institutions and Violence," Leo D. Lefebure responding. The presenters were expected to summarize their papers in twenty-five minutes because their papers had been circulated prior to the conference.

One factor that cleared the way for more instructive discussion and learning was the contribution of the plenary presenters, especially Daly, Clooney, and Ives, in addressing the actual violence committed by adherents of the respective traditions, in spite of their ideal spiritual visions of peace and nonviolence. Daly in particular paved the way for discussion by making the methodological distinction between *normative* and *descriptive* approaches to the institutions of the religious traditions.[9]

The conversations grew in congeniality and insights offered over the period of three days. The discussions were abetted by the program structure, which allotted fifty minutes for open discussion in each plenary session, and also a generous amount of time was scheduled for meals and coffee breaks. As the discussions grew, two themes seemed to emerge with particular emphasis.

One was *conversion*, a fundamental change or transformation of humans from a perspective and lifestyle of self-society-world rooted in retribution and the working of the scapegoat mechanism to a nonviolent perspective and lifestyle. This was not, however, a prominent subject in the major presentations. Daly raised the question of conversion in his leadoff paper, particularly by referring to Lonergan's analysis of conversion as intellectual, moral, and religious.[10] It was perhaps implied in Clooney's discussion of the Hindu emphasis on the person as agent who is to avoid violence and killing.[11] He quoted a translation of the Tamil *Tirukkural*, which includes these verses: "The sum of virtue is not to kill. / All sin comes from killing. . . . Even at the cost of one's own life / One should avoid killing."[12] It is all but explicitly articulated in Christopher Ives's comment that "Buddha subverted violence . . . , not by revealing once and for all the innocence of the scapegoat, but through a non-theistic psychological analysis, moral discipline, and meditative praxis."[13] In his response to Ives Lefebure linked Buddhism to the sociological, interdividual theme of self-other relations in the mimetic theory by observing, "From the beginning, Buddhism saw the reordering of human consciousness as inextricably linked to the reordering of society."[14]

Although conversion was not highlighted in the plenary papers, it was certainly on the minds of participants in the discussion of Buddhism and in the wrap-up discussion. It came to the fore especially in the comment Wolfgang Palaver made comparing the ways in which Christianity and Buddhism try to deal with desire, as well as in Billy Hewett's juxtaposition of Zen Buddhist techniques in a Christian situation and the conversion process in Ignatius of Loyola's *Spiritual Exercises*.[15] Sandor Goodhart thanked Paul Nuechterlein for mentioning the Jewish idea of conversion, which is "the abandonment of sin and the return to the way of God," which is to say the movement from idolatry to anti-idolatry.[16] In his epilogue Robert Daly concluded that "We gained, I think, a deeper awareness of the role of conversion in the move from violence to nonviolence."[17]

Another theme that preoccupied many participants was that of *language*, specifically our Western language of philosophical and theological terms. Daly acknowledged this in his concluding reflections: "Mimetic theory is a Western theory." He goes on to say, "That granted, our conference did suggest that mimetic theory might be helpful to non-Western cultures, as long as it is not applied in a procrustean manner."[18] To illustrate the problem I will return to what two of the participants said, both cited above. If, according to Ives, the Buddha subverted violence through nontheistic psychology, discipline, and meditation, does this entail more or less the same process of conversion as we speak of in the Western language of repentance and conversion (Greek *metanoia*)? Wolfgang Palaver, in the context of his remark, points out that "Buddhism seems to try to overcome desire completely. Christianity, however, tries to aim one's desire at God, and to invite one's friends to do the same."[19] However, according to the Girardian interpretation of desire (which is basically the Augustinian concept), one form of desire *is* to be overcome completely by conversion through identification with the Innocent Victim—namely, the perverted, metaphysical or idolatrous desire that ends inevitably in scapegoating and violence. The desire directed to and informed by the Divine Other is not to be rejected, but is salvific, as Palaver intimates.[20]

It is clear that we need to take care with our language and not to presume that we are necessarily talking about the same thing. Girard addressed this, I think, toward the end of the discussion of Buddhism. Schwager asked Lefebure to explain his assertion that the Girardian interpretation of the Christian revelation threatened to block dialogue. Lefebure answered that he was thinking about an exclusive claim to the truth and a concomitant blindness to violent patterns of behavior. Girard's comment in response was that "There is an exclusivist claim, but it's not an individual claim. It's not a question of who does or doesn't have the truth; that leads to mimetic rivalry. Rather, it's a question of language we all have to use. . . . So it is not a question of whether any theory is absolute truth, but, who can present an alternative, present another language."[21] This was a very interesting and quite ambiguous statement. Does it mean that the Christian revelation is *the* truth, but so far no one has succeeded in translating the Christian language, which affects us at a level beyond philosophy, into a language that speaks to the hearts and minds of Jews, Muslims, Hindus, and Buddhists (not to speak of Christians!)? Or does it mean that Christian language is rooted in a revelation whose truth is actually shared or present in all the great traditions, if we just had a language that could articulate this?

This conference demonstrated a number of important things. Given the right kind of structure and supportive setting, real dialogue and learning can take place. In this regard, it is a model of what conferences should be and accomplish. Although members of COV&R are not exempt from the impulse to scapegoat, we can see that we have the resources to become aware of the scapegoating impulse and the possibility of the spiritual discipline necessary to hold it in check to a great extent. It seemed clear that even if the mimetic theory is a Western theory, it could be helpful to non-Western cultures if it is not presented and applied in a rigid, dogmatic manner. Also, most of the participants became more deeply aware of the role conversion plays in the movement from violence to nonviolence. Complete conversion is intellectual, moral, and religious (so Lonergan), and a symposium like this contributes at least to intellectual conversion. As the discussions continued and grew in intensity and insight, they pointed to the need for a more sophisticated analytic methodology in the application of the mimetic theory.[22]

The Semiannual Meeting, in Nashville, Tennessee November 18, 2000

This meeting was listed in the convention book as "Mennonite Scholars and Friends and COV&R." The program was a panel discussion of *Violence Renounced: René Girard, Biblical Studies, and Peacemaking.* The panelists included Ted Grimsrud, Sandor Goodhart, Willard Swartley, Vern Redekop, and Rebecca Adams. This volume was discussed in chapter 3.

The only panelist response available to me was that of Goodhart, who responded to Girard's response published in the volume. Goodhart argues that the discovery of the sacrificial mechanism and the divine revelation through the innocent victim is already found in Isaiah 52:13–53:12, and that the Gospels texts reflect and represent this concept. The uniqueness of the Christian revelation, avers Goodhart, is the witness to the resurrection of Jesus. Now the intention of God is completed in the resurrection of the innocent victim, for it is a justification and affirmation of the Servant and so sets God's intention for the world in the proper light. Goodhart quotes Girard's statement about the resurrection in *I See Satan Fall Like Lightning* to show that this is really Girard's own position: "Only the Resurrection, because it enlightens the disciples, reveals completely the things hidden since the foundation of the world, which are the same as the secret of Satan, never disclosed since the origin of human culture: the founding murder and the origin of human culture."[23] Goodhart maintains, in other words, that in fact the whole revelation is there already, "prophetically" in the text of Isaiah, but it is extended and brought to full light through the resurrection of Christ.[24] The last three verses of the Servant passage, Isaiah 53:10–12, point to the restoration and vindication of the Servant. Whatever the intention of the original writer concerning the identity of the servant figure, one could say that prophetically it already includes the resurrection of the Suffering Servant of the Lord, so the gospel is already there *in nuce*.

To Antwerp and Beyond (2001)

The annual conference in 2001 was held at the University of Antwerp in Belgium. The city of Antwerp is very important in the Belgian economy and culture. Located in Flanders, it is a city of just under 500,000 inhabitants with about 1,200,000 people in the metropolitan zone. It is known throughout the world for its busy port, its diamond trade, and fashion industry.

Johan Elsen was the host and organizer of the symposium. He served as editor of the *Bulletin* for two years, 1998–2000, then resigned from that position in order to devote himself to organizing the annual conference, which promised to be quite significant in the history of the Colloquium. The theme was "The Mimetic Theory and the History of Philosophy." We had heard and interacted with one of the great contemporary philosophers, Paul Ricoeur, at St. Denis in 1998, and of course Michel Serres, a "Renaissance" thinker whose work encompasses philosophy, literature, history, and mathematics, was a friend who participated in some of the conferences. But for the first time Girard's work was set within a wider philosophical context. His primary conversation partners for the meeting were Charles Taylor and Gianni Vattimo. Taylor, a practicing Roman Catholic, is an outstanding Canadian philosopher known as an expert on Hegel and Wittgenstein. His most well known book is *Sources of the Self*. Vattimo is an Italian Heideggerian philosopher who studied with Karl Löwith and Hans-Georg Gadamer; he is known for his socialist politics and affirmation of secularization as a product of Christianity. He described his return to Christian belief in 1996 in a short book, *Credere di credere,* translated into English as *Belief*. There were numerous other papers on the program dealing with a diverse range of topics related to philosophy and the mimetic theory.

"The Mimetic Theory and the History of Philosophy," May 31–June 2, 2001

Guido Vanheeswijck's presentation on Girard's place in the history of philosophy is helpful as background for understanding the discussion among Girard, Vattimo, and Taylor.[25] Vanheeswijck presents salient points of contact between Girard and modern philosophers, particularly Kojève, Hegel, Nietzsche, Heidegger, and Derrida. He notes the great difference, however, that Girard is more influenced by the Bible, Greek tragedy, and modern literature than by the philosophers.

Vanheeswijck observes the importance of Alexandre Kojève as an interpreter of Hegel and the appreciation of dialectic and desire that his contemporary generation held for Hegel's thought as mediated by Kojève. I think that Vanheeswijck is wrong, however, in stating that Girard simply borrowed the Hegelian-Kojèvian concept of desire as desiring the desire of the other. For one thing, Hegel and Kojève construed desire as a metaphysical reality of consciousness, which Girard does not. For another, Girard emphasizes the importance of the desired *object* in desire. If desire becomes attached to the being of the other, so that there is a longing to have or be the other, then that is deviated or perverted desire in Girard's view. In theological terms it would be idolatry.

Girard values Heidegger's work for articulating the difference between the logos of Heraclitus and the logos of the Gospel of John, but he cannot accept Heidegger's attempt to validate the identification of violence (*polemos*) as the ultimate logos of the world because he understands the world as the creation of the God who is love, not violence. "Girard intends to show that Heidegger's 'sacred being' is nothing but the product of interhuman violence."[26]

As for Nietzsche, Girard views him as the greatest thinker of the nineteenth century. He was able to isolate all the issues concerning God, religion, and the human condition, but from the standpoint of the mimetic theory he took the wrong turn on all of them. In spite of being antiromantic and antisentimental, he fell into a romanticizing of Dionysus and the will to power—sacrificial thinking, in other words. Heidegger simply ignores Nietzsche's declaration of the collective murder of God in his interpretation of Nietzsche's work. The covering up of the violence of the sacred is what stands out for Girard, and in this regard he thinks of Nietzsche and especially of Heidegger when he refers to the death of philosophy or philosophy as a dead end.[27]

Derrida's work was important for Girard as he formulated the mimetic theory from the late 1950s into the decade of the 1960s. The point where he made the greatest contact with Derrida's thinking was in the latter's treatment of the *pharmakon*, the remedy-poison that he highlighted as writing in his interpretation of Plato's *Phaedrus*. But we can glimpse the difference between them in Derrida's treatment of the human instance of the *pharmakon*, namely the *pharmakos*, the scapegoat, the one who is expelled from the city-state and lynched. In "The Pharmacy of Plato" he deals with the scapegoat only in footnotes. Derrida, at least in his earlier work, was concerned primarily with texts, not with human social reality. Or to put it another way, Derrida *is* concerned with social reality as it is affected by theory. As Andrew McKenna says, "Whereas Girard advances a theory of violence, Derrida is concerned with the violence of theory."[28]

Vattimo draws upon Girard to develop his view that the Christian affirmation of the Incarnation, God entering into human life and human history, leads to the emergence of secularization and the spirit of charity. Thus ontology, a doctrine of being, has to be "weak" in that God, Ultimate Being, has fully entered into the world. Any Absolute, any claim to ultimate truth, must be rejected.

Vattimo credits Nietzsche and Hegel with the process of uncovering *ressentiment* (the spirit of vengeance) and metaphysics as predications of absolutes (God as omniscient, omnipotent, etc.) that cut the human spirit off from Being itself. Thus Vattimo construes Girard's critique of the pagan sacred as applying also to the absolutes of medieval metaphysics. God's entrance into human existence means traditional "God-talk" and ritual are unnecessary.

In fact, Vattimo's "weak ontology" comes across as very much like the perspective of the death-of-God theologians who became notorious in the 1960s. Frederiek Depoortere observes a number of noteworthy similarities in the interpretation of the Incarnation between Vattimo and Thomas Altizer. These include Karl Barth's idea that there is a clear distinction between Christianity and natural religiosity; focus on the Incarnation as the key to Christianity and secularization; the contemporary disclosure of the true meaning of the Incarnation; any notion of transcendence as necessarily violent and oppressive; and the death of God not as a metaphor but an ontic reality.[29] Although Vattimo rejects association with the death of God and secular theologians,[30] the affinities are certainly there and they put him at odds with Girard, who continues to affirm the reality of the transcendent God and the necessity of affirming the reality of truth and living in the truth. This truth is fundamentally the truth of the victim. Christ, the Innocent Victim, has always to be the point of reference for understanding what is true.

Interestingly, in *Belief* Vattimo credits Girard for helping him return to Christianity. Girard's criticism of Heidegger's understanding of the logos in *Things Hidden since the Foundation of the World*, in which the logos of the Incarnation is the deity who comes into the world and allows himself to be expelled from it, was the crucial insight that led Vattimo to his form of Christian belief, which is to advocate the spirit of charity that Christianity (not Christendom) has introduced into the world.

Charles Taylor, like Girard, is a Roman Catholic. Taylor chose the Catholic Church as a young man. One of his parents was Catholic, the other Anglican. He turned to the Catholic Church through his reading of Catholic sources prior to Vatican II. Girard, however, whose mother was a very devout Catholic, and also liberal and intellectual, was a cradle Catholic. However, he effectively left the church at the age of twelve or thirteen and returned only after intellectual and religious conversions that occurred in 1958–1959.[31] Vanheeswijck notes some basic affinities between Girard and Taylor. Both uncover and criticize the modern belief in the autonomous human subject and both are post-Hegelian in their intellectual orientation. Although Taylor is first and foremost a philosopher, in *Sources of the Self* he refers to a literary canon (Flaubert, Proust, Dostoyevsky) that is very similar to Girard's, and they both insist on the major role of Christianity in modern Western culture.[32]

In his presentation Taylor offered an appreciation of Girard's seminal work, particularly "for giving a non-reductive explanation of human violence and for exemplifying how Christian faith might be integrated into a rigorous theoretical hermeneutic."[33] In a book published six years later he would describe Girard's work as "pathbreaking."[34] Taylor spent most of his time, however, in posing questions about the mimetic theory. I will skip over those that had already been asked over and over again and mention only those that seemed original in his reflections. One was whether modern violence was actually similar to violence in the ancient world; has this modern violence become ritualized and does it offer a kind of moral inspiration to modern people? Do modern states offer their citizens the opportunity to experience themselves as good by violently expelling or punishing evil? Is there an ennui, a kind of boredom with the rationality of modern life that leads moderns to hunger for violence, for breaking out and breaking down?

In his report on the conference William Mishler ended with a note that is an important comment on Girard's mimetic theory and something very important for COV&R members to keep in mind. Mishler referred to Sandor Goodhart's paper, "Response to Willard Swartley's Book" (*Violence Renounced*). In a very respectful yet firm manner Goodhart clarified his difference with Girard regarding the respective roles of Judaism and Christianity in revealing and undermining sacred violence. An important aspect of Goodhart's position has already been indicated above. He demonstrated the possibility of remaining true to Girard's central insights while coming to different conclusions. Mishler comments, "In my view (and judging from onsite response to Goodhart's paper, I was in abundant company), Goodhart gave an inspiring example, from deep within the Girardian circle, so to speak, of the continuing openness and vitality of René Girard's thought—for as Charles Taylor remarked a propos of our understanding of modernity: 'We need to complexify our views.'"[35]

Mimetic Theory and Pastoral Ministry at Ghost Ranch

One of the interesting experiments of bringing together the theoretical and the practical was the seminar on pastoral ministry and the mimetic theory, which met for five or six days in the summers of 2001, 2002, and 2003 under the auspices of Ghost Ranch. Ghost Ranch is a continuing education retreat center operated by the Presbyterian Church. The ranch itself, comprising 21,000 acres, was given to the Presbyterians by the owners in 1955. Its address is Abiquiu, New Mexico. In 1990 the church acquired Plaza Resolana in Santa Fe, which had been a retirement center. In recent years it has been renamed Ghost Ranch Santa Fe. The groups that gathered over the three summers met twice in Santa Fe and once at the original ranch near Abiquiu.

Hiking could be arduous at Ghost Ranch, Abiquiu. The year we met there the class went for a hike to Chimney Rock, a climb of about 600 feet (from 6,500 to 7,100 feet) and a round trip of three miles. Not that strenuous for the athletic and for experienced hikers, but quite arduous for most of us over sixty, especially as we had only been at Ghost Ranch two days and so had not completely adapted to the altitude. I remember that I felt tired and achy all the next day.

The seminar was the brainchild of Britt Johnston, a Presbyterian pastor then located in Santa Fe. He had become a passionate proponent of the mimetic theory several years before. He organized the meetings and was one of the leaders in the conversations that took place.

Johnston conceived of the events basically as conversations. There were to be no "papers," no formal presentations, but a series of conversations whose topics the participants proposed at the beginning, with various persons in the group volunteering to lead off on the topics by making brief remarks, asking questions, staging an interactive game or dialogue, or whatever they chose. I participated as a facilitator who helped keep the conversations and thinking oriented to the mimetic theory. We have audiotapes from the first two summers. In principle, one might think that it would be very boring to listen to hours and hours of recordings of conversations, which sometimes rambled a bit. However, in listening I was surprised: they held my attention throughout.

The COV&R connection was represented by three members who participated in all three seminars: Johnston, Tom Michael, and I. Jean Turgeon attended twice, and Kent Johnson and James Alison (who was cofacilitator with me in 2003) were present for one of the retreats. We had small groups: ten persons participated in 2001, nine in 2002, and fifteen in 2003.

"Seminar," like the related word "seminary," derives from the Latin *seminarium*, "seed plot." I like to think of a seminar as a process of planting seeds—ideas, thoughts, and concerns—which one hopes will grow, thrive, and flourish in their "soil," the participants in the conversations. The topics discussed were very wide-ranging. They included interpretation of the Bible, liturgy, disease and spiritual healing, church family systems, evangelism, social dreaming,[36] scapegoating of pastors, the significance of truth as contrasted with opinion or subjective interpretation, child and adult development, Christianity and Islam, and the Eucharist and creativity.

So many topics seem quite scattered—which of course is a function of "how the wind blows" and plants the seeds, or how the Spirit moves in a group. However, as I reviewed the tapes I found that at least four themes were sustained: interruptive praxis, the Bible as a text in travail, mimesis and healing, and the meaning and practice of the Eucharist.

"Interruptive praxis" is a phrase I borrowed from a paper given by Tony Bartlett in a graduate seminar at Syracuse University. The intent of the phrase is to specify a form of moral and spiritual practice that seeks to avoid complete rupture and disruption insofar as possible, but whose purpose is to bring about a pause in a situation or sequence of thought and action that produces new reflection and reorientation. The precondition of interruptive praxis is dying to the old self in the sense of ending self-justifications for grudges and scapegoating, acknowledging that only God can save us, and finding ways of taking our own spiritual inventories. The practice of it is essentially that of intervening to raise the voice of the victim and to tell the truth in a nonrivalrous way. Sometimes it involves steering conversations in other, better directions (e.g., interrupting a given narrative in a nonrivalrous way with humor or silence).

The Bible, particularly the Hebrew Bible, is a "text in travail," a phrase used by Girard to describe "a process under way . . . a struggle that advances and retreats."[37] In other words, the Bible is a text for which the metaphor of the birthing process is appropriate. The actual revelatory struggles that gave birth to it were often times of anguish and pain.[38] In the terms of the mimetic theory, the biblical text gives birth to a new anthropology in which the God's eye view is to look from the standpoint of the victim. In fact, there is a twofold metaphor here, for in talking about the Scriptures in French Girard often refers to *le travail du texte*, "the work of the text." He originally meant it as a metaphor simply suggesting a work in progress and history still moving forward toward completion. Our word "travail" comes from the French word. In French it usually means work or labor, and it is also used of women in childbirth. In English it can denote very hard labor, but also pain, and is particularly associated with the pains of childbirth. When *le travail du texte* was rendered in English as "text in travail," Girard accepted the English connotation as also appropriate. The important thing in this view is that the biblical text is not a static reality, but a reality that works, that functions, that brings forth a new reality out of a frequently painful history, which is its inner form. In that sense the reader who has faith seeking understanding is part of that history and integrates the text into his or her life.

The theme of mimesis and healing began with reflection on passages in chapters 8 and 9 of the Gospel of Matthew. There we see healing as a process of good mimesis in which those healed trust in Jesus' authority and compassion. The Gospel of Matthew is the gospel record that gets to the deep meaning of healing: Jesus takes the disease of the ill person upon himself. He touches the unclean, the leper, for example, thus making himself unclean before the Law. "He took away our infirmities and bore our diseases" (Matthew 9:17, quoting Isaiah 53:4). We agreed that whatever the organic cause of bodily disease, one may well suspect that a mimetic spiral into frustration, envy, and resentment is often a huge factor in illness. One of the implications of the Matthean witness to Jesus is that those who follow Christ in pastoral ministry are summoned, within the bounds of their human limitations, to take the infirmities of others upon themselves, not for the sake of self-flagellation but as the burden of love and service.

As for relating Jesus' healing ministry to the Eucharist, it is important to understand that participating in the Eucharist is to take part in the life of Christ, who enters into a kind of communion with those he heals.[39] In the Eucharist, as Britt Johnston put it, there is a model of exchange utterly different from the secular economy of exchange, debt, and retribution. The secular market is the center of idolatry, whereas the Eucharist is based on generosity, God's generosity in Christ. It offers the model of sharing, the sharing of God with human beings and of human beings with one another. Jean Turgeon extended this line of thought by emphasizing that the model of God in Christ is that of forgiveness, which is even more important religiously than affirming God as creator. The forgiveness of human sin through God's generosity is the core of the new covenant, which in turn is the center of the Eucharist. The Gospel of Luke brings this out explicitly in the narration of the Last Supper: "This cup is the new covenant in my blood, which will be shed for you" (Luke 22:20).

The Catastrophe of September 11, 2001

It is striking that the annual conferences in the years immediately following the catastrophe of 9/11 did not offer a focus or even a great deal of attention to this devastating event. Actually, the conference in 2000 was more relevant to that topic, in that some attention was given to understanding Islam as one of the great religious traditions. There were also attempts to come to grips with Islam and related areas of concern in the modern world in the annual conferences of 2007 and 2009. Is this relative lack of emphasis a symptom of academic or intellectual paralysis in COV&R, or more positively viewed, is it an indication that it took time for the organization and its leaders to begin to grasp the enormity of Islam's implications?

However that may be, our Innsbruck colleagues invited postings on the COV&R website managed by Dietmar Regensburger. These are available on the home page under "Discussion Board: 'War on Terrorism?'" One of the postings was an interview René Girard gave to Henri Tincq of *Le Monde*, which was reproduced both in French and in English translation. Girard's comments were typical of his humility and insight. He admitted his inability completely to fathom the Muslim attitude toward death in the phenomenon of the suicide martyrs and in acknowledging that American free enterprise is not a solution to the dynamics of competition fueled by mimetic rivalries. On a cultural level, "what is occurring today is rivalry on a planetary scale" in which those who seek to destroy Western institutions and influence are at the same time imitators of what they desire to destroy. On the level of interreligious relations, Girard affirmed the prophetic insights of the prophet Muhammad concerning violence and sacrifice (e.g., the Quran's narrative of Abel sacrificing the ram that was the same ram that Abraham would see caught in the bush when he was about to offer Isaac), but for Christians these insights are not comparable to the nonviolent divine love revealed in the crucifixion of Christ.

One of Raymund Schwager's contributions to the discussion, "September 11, 2001 and a Theology of the Signs of the Times," points out the problems of violence and inner conflict both within and between Western and Muslim cultures. The Western societies have their origin in Christianity but have become secularized as they trust in democratic forms of government and the generally positive outcome of anonymous market mechanisms. This means that Western societies inevitably engage in confrontation with the traditional Muslim tendency to assert the necessity of Islam's religious dominance in any ideal form of political governance. Nonetheless, there are many points at which Christians and Muslims can carry on a dialogue, even though it is valid to recognize the significance of the fact that Christianity arose as belief in God's presence and action in Jesus, the innocent and peacemaking victim, whereas Islam follows the Prophet who at times was a leader in war.

There were many contributions from the faculty at Innsbruck: besides a half dozen postings from Schwager, there were three from Wolfgang Palaver and one each from Józef Niewiadomski and Willibald Sandler. Andrew McKenna also contributed a piece. Plus, there were a number of comments by non-COV&R people.

My own contribution was a brief set of reflections that included the recommendation that we calm the rhetoric of war, back away from cries for revenge, and practice prayer for our enemies as Jesus taught us to do. Gil Bailie, on his website, affirmed that Christ was present with the victims in the fiery stairways and collapsing buildings, immolated once more by those who know not what they do. But, I would add, we Americans acted in the same destructive ignorance as we lost over 4,000 troops in Iraq, in a war and civil strife that killed tens of thousands Iraqis. (Could we ever estimate the children that would never be born because of these deaths?)

A New Research Initiative at the University of Innsbruck

At the University of Innsbruck Raymund Schwager initiated in 2002 a long-range response to 9/11 and what it represented. Confronting his colleagues there with the question of an appropriate response to the crisis precipitated by religion fundamentalism and violence, he proposed that the faculties engage in cooperative research focused on the subject. Faculty members from theology, history, literature, philosophy, and the social and political sciences responded to this initiative. The cooperative discussions and research that ensued resulted, in 2007, in the formation of a research platform, "World Order—Religion—Violence." Recently "Communication" has been added to this platform. Publications in the book series published by LIT as "Beiträge zur mimetischen Theorie" (Contributions to the Mimetic Theory) carry as a subtitle "Religion—Gewalt—Kommunikation—Weltordnung" (Religion—Violence—Communication—World Order).

According to the statement posted on the university's website, "The research-platform coordinates various research efforts in the field of religion and politics by groups and individuals at the University of Innsbruck. Methodologically, our work includes the study of relevant cases of the interplay of religion and politics in the past and the present, comparative history of ideas, and normative political theory. Interdisciplinarity and a culture of discussion and exchange between various theoretical approaches are central to our work. The platform is organized in thematic research-clusters that meet regularly. Activities include workshops, conferences, and discussion-groups. The successful lecture series in honour of the late Raymund Schwager furthermore contributes to the profile of the research-platform."[40] Wolfgang Palaver served as the first chairperson of the faculty representatives who form the platform committee.

The Annual Conference at Purdue University, 2002

The annual meeting for 2002 was held at Purdue University in West Lafayette, Indiana. The organizers and hosts were Sandor Goodhart and Ann Astell, with support particularly from Thomas Ryba. Goodhart and Astell were both on the English faculty. Goodhart was also involved in Jewish studies and became the director of the classics program. Ryba taught courses in religious studies. As already noted in this history, Goodhart was the prime motivator of Colloquium discussions of the place of the Hebrew Bible and Judaism in the mimetic theory. Now at Purdue much of this energy and work came to fruition in the symposium on "Judaism, Christianity, and the Ancient World."

Purdue University is located about sixty miles northwest of Indianapolis and only about thirty-five miles from the Illinois border. Under the Morrill Land Grant Act signed by President Lincoln in 1865 the Indiana General Assembly established a land grant university in 1869. It was to be situated in the area of West Lafayette, Indiana. The legislature did not have to appropriate any state money. The primary benefactor was John Purdue, who is buried on the campus, and the town of West Lafayette gave a gift of land. The first classes were offered in 1874. It has since become the flagship university of the Purdue University System, with six campuses in Indiana that have a student enrollment of almost 40,000. It is well known and highly rated for its College of Engineering, but its business school is also ranked high among American universities. I think most of us attending the conference had heard of the engineering school, but we found the total university to be quite impressive, not only in engineering, business administration, and the sciences, but also in the liberal arts.

Goodhart and company brought together an impressive program, including René Girard, Eric Gans, Michael Fishbane, Alan Segal, and Gerard Rosse. Goodhart also used the occasion to honor three of us with discussions of our work: Eric Gans, Raymund Schwager, and James Williams.[41] For Goodhart it was a very special occasion. He is the most devoted of Girard's former students. As he told me, he felt it was a great honor to bring his longtime mentor to Purdue and gain university support for this conference.

The 2002 Meeting at Purdue: "Judaism, Christianity, and the Ancient World: Mimesis, Sacrifice, and Culture," June 5–8, 2002

Given the history of conflict and misunderstanding between Judaism and Christianity, the planners of the conference had as their objective to reduce the potential for violence by using the mimetic theory to explore what these two traditions have in common. In Girard's work he affirms the basic continuity of the Hebrew Scriptures and the New Testament. That continuity revolves around prophetic insight that illumines the witness to revelation in the Jewish Scriptures and comes to a full disclosure in the Gospel testimony concerning the Passion, death, and resurrection of Jesus.[42] The prophetic insight is based on revelation "from below," from the standpoint of the victim: it pulls apart the veils obscuring the scapegoat mechanism and penetrates to the origin of this victimary mechanism in mimetic desire. Analyzing and conceptualizing this prophetic insight is the anthropological basis of Girard's interpretation of the Bible.

The mimetic theory as conceived by Girard is opposed to all anti-Semitism. He states that Christian anti-Semitism is "based on an inability to understand the true nature and eminently typical character of the Passion."[43] In fact, his primary modern example of the *méconnaissance*, the "misrecognition" at the heart of the mythical thinking that revolves around persecution victims, is the case of Alfred Dreyfus. Dreyfus was a Jew, a captain in the French army, who in 1894 was falsely accused of passing military secrets to the Germans. "In fact, anti-Dreyfusism was a true myth, a false accusation that the accusers confused with truth."[44] It was a myth fueled by anti-Semitism. His primary medieval example was the persecution and murder of Jews in France in the fourteenth century, who were accused of causing the bubonic plague by poisoning the drinking water in wells and rivers.[45] These examples of his point out that myth is a narrative form that typically stems from persecution and scapegoating and they reflect at the same time his feeling and thinking about anti-Semitism.

Two biblical scholars presented lectures that were particularly pertinent to the objectives of the conference because their scholarship is an attempt to get to the very heart of Judaism as it emerged from the Bible. One was Jewish, Michael Fishbane, who did not comment directly on Christianity but whose paper is indirectly very important for understanding the rabbinic religious vision that was so important in Jesus' cultural and religious milieu. The other was Christian, Bruce Chilton, a professor and Episcopal priest, whose work consistently seeks to show how Jesus and the early church both reflect and differ from their Jewish milieu.

Fishbane spoke on "Transformation of Sacrifice," specifically the changes in rabbinic Judaism's approach to sacrifice after the destruction of the Jerusalem Temple in 70 A.D. The rabbis were concerned with the time "in-between," the time between the present age and the reconstitution of the Temple in the messianic age.[46] For the rabbis sacrifice continued to be important, but the "place" of sacrifice was now the individual Jew, who was expected to practice fasting and self-abnegation. The rabbis developed a doctrine of *ke'ilu*, "as if": when one offers and humbles oneself through fasting, one's desire leads to a higher plane of existence and actually diminishes oneself through the loss of blood and fat. It is "as if" one is offering sacrifice in the Temple through giving up one's physical substance for God.

Being occupied with the Torah (*'osek ba-torah*) is another transformation of sacrifice into a different religious mode. It is as if studying the Torah is to give offerings to God. To be occupied with the text about the sin offering, for example, is to make a sin offering. Also the blowing of the shofar (ram's horn) on New Year's Day, according to the Talmud tractate Rosh Hashanah (New Year), awakens both human beings and the divine mercy and attentiveness. Therefore it binds one to the altar of the Temple.

These transformations of sacrifice as highlighted by Fishbane help us understand how the early followers of Jesus were both similar to and different from other Jews. In the Gospel of Matthew, for example, Jesus emphasizes the primary demand of purity or wholeheartedness of individual intention toward God and neighbor (especially in Matthew 5). The disciple's intention is lived out by self-giving to the just and loving God who is met through the other, the neighbor.[47] When working on the Gospel of Matthew during the 1980s I called this a kind of "ethical mysticism." This spiritual orientation is very close to the rabbinic vision that Fishbane describes. But in this Christian transformation of sacrifice, one binds oneself not to the Temple, but to Christ, who is Immanuel, "God with us" (Matthew 1:23; see Isaiah 7:14), who tells his followers that "where two or three are gathered together in my name, there I am in the midst of them" (Matthew 18:20), and promises the apostles, "I am with you always, until the end of the age" (Matthew 28:20).

Chilton gave an interesting survey of sacrifice and the function of communal meals in the early church, as well as his own historical reconstruction of why Jesus was crucified. Jesus could have got away with his visionary perspective in Galilee, which involved inclusion of nonobservant Jews in Galilee and Judea in his circle, and also women and tax collectors. However, he put himself in mortal danger in Judea, where he was dangerously close to the Temple and the Roman governor. Chilton holds that the cleansing of the Temple was a kind of occupation of it. It stemmed from Jesus' sense of his mission and was based on his interpretation of a text in the book of Zechariah. When the Temple occupation failed, Jesus interpreted the meaning of his last meal with the disciples in that light: in the absence of a pure holy place to offer sacrifice, Jesus made meals with him into a rival altar, so to speak. This interpretation of the origin of the Eucharist is related to Chilton's thesis that the phenomenon of sacrifice itself has its origin in the communal meal, rather than vice versa as in Girard's mimetic theory.

Many of us found Chilton's paper interesting and provocative. However, the problem with his thesis about the Temple and the Eucharist is that it is a cultic interpretation as he described it, that is to say, it had its origin simply in the narrow convictions of a rival religious group in Judaism. The upshot of his view is that it tends to reduce the origin of the Eucharist to a petty political-historical rivalry stemming from Jesus' disappointed expectation that he would take over the Temple in Jerusalem. In light of the mimetic theory, however, faith in Christ holds that a certain intelligence, an illuminative understanding, is passed on from Jesus to the disciples and from the disciples to the tradition resulting in the composition of the Gospels. Christ's offering of himself at table and on the cross extends beyond a conflict over the Temple in Jerusalem; it is universally inclusive and transcends local religion and politics.

The session devoted to a lengthy conversation between René Girard and Michael Fishbane was especially informative. Their dialogue ranged from the Bible and ancient Near Eastern mythology to Freud and Lévi-Strauss and the violence of World War II. Before listening to this discussion I knew that Girard was beholden to Charles Darwin to some extent, but I had not realized just how deeply Girard's approach to the Bible, religion, and mythology was rooted in Darwin and evolutionary theory. I knew that he had read in these sources, as one sees at the beginning of *Things Hidden*, but I did not know the extent of it.[48] This would come into fuller view two years later when *Les origines de la culture* appeared. (It was published in English in 2007 with the title *Evolution and Conversion.*) Girard remarked that victimization and sacrifice probably have a biological substratum, and this is eventually retold in myth. This does not mean, however, that he believes a biological determinism is the final word about human existence. Otherwise, the prophetic thread of the Bible and the Gospel witness to Christ would be meaningless. From the Christian standpoint, God becomes the scapegoat to show that the sacrificial mechanism is not the divine intention for human existence.

The conversation between Girard and Fishbane exemplified what dialogue should be. As Vern Redekop said from the floor in the ensuing discussion, Michael Fishbane's openness to learn more about Girard's thought was a model for all of us in our approach to other theories and points of view.

Finally, one note on an action at the business meeting. On the recommendation of the advisory board, the members present approved Eric Gans as an honorary lifetime member of the board. Gans, a former student of Girard's, has employed the mimetic theory in conceiving his own theory, which he and his followers call "generative anthropology." In fact, a professional group devoted to generative anthropology (GA) has held annual meetings in recent years. The relationship with COV&R is amicable, and any rivalry between them is friendly. Some of the GA people attend COV&R meetings and vice versa.

Death of William Mishler

Late in 2002 members of COV&R learned of the death of William "Bill" Mishler. He died tragically at his home in Amherst, Massachusetts, on December 9, 2002. Bill Mishler was an active participant in COV&R from 1993 until his death. Prior to his retirement he was professor of Scandinavian studies at the University of Minnesota. A productive scholar, he served on the advisory board prior to his death. He also served the Colloquium as a translator and he wrote the report of the 2001 conference at Antwerp for the *Bulletin*. Those of us who knew Bill Mishler were shocked and saddened when we received news of his death. We have missed his presence at meetings and his many contributions to our work.

The Annual Conference at Innsbruck, 2003

Innsbruck is one of the most beautiful cities, small or large, in the world. I have already said something about it in chapter 2. In his impressions recorded in the *Bulletin* Per Bjørnar Grande stated, "I knew [Innsbruck] was picturesque, but that it had such old world charm and dramatic beauty . . . was a pleasant surprise."[49] Wolfgang Palaver was the organizer, aided by Raymund Schwager, Józef Niewiadomski, and others on the theological faculty at the University of Innsbruck. Palaver had just been promoted to full professor, and this was the first big event for which he was responsible. That made it even more disappointing to him that one of his keynote speakers, Jean Bethke Elshtain, could not be present, canceling almost at the last minute. However, she did send her paper on Augustine's understanding of passion and politics, which was published in the conference papers. In the event, Jean-Pierre Dupuy took the leadoff slot in the conference program and everything turned out well.

"Passions in Economy, Politics and the Media—in Discussion with Christian Theology," University of Innsbruck, June 18–21, 2003

There were many superb papers at this conference. Strange as it may appear at first, René Girard's paper, "The Passionate Oxymoron in *Romeo and Juliet*," established a basic frame of reference for the theme of the conference. Girard showed that Shakespeare uses the political passions in the ongoing feud between the Capulet and Montague clans as a fiction to communicate through Romeo and Juliet his brilliant insights into mimetic rivalry. An oxymoron is a rhetorical figure that combines opposing or contradictory images or ideas. For example, when Juliet learns that Romeo has killed her cousin Tybalt she calls him a "Beautiful tyrant," a "Fiend angelical," even a "Wolfish ravening lamb." The ostensible meaning of her outburst, which is a cover for the ambivalence of mimetic desire, is her love for both Romeo and her cousin and her loyalty to her family. Girard argues, however, that in the courtly tradition of "true love" on which Shakespeare drew and with which his audience was familiar, the ideal authentic love between man and woman did not permit expressing any ambivalence about the other, the object of desire. The ambivalence in Juliet's words suggests a mimetic entanglement of emotions that breaks through the rhetoric of courtly love. Shakespeare had a tremendous dramatic intuition for mimetic desire, which in intense forms moves so easily into jealousy, rivalry, and even physical violence.

All human passions are informed by mimetic desire, which can be changed and directed more and more to "things that are above" (Colossians 3:2), but which are inevitably subject to rivalry, envy, and jealousy. Juliet's use of oxymora betrays more than a hint of distrust of Romeo, which conflicts with her deep attraction to him. After all, had he not shortly before, previous to wooing her, courted Rosaline and turned away from her when she rejected his advances?

So Girard's presentation was very thought provoking. There were at least three insights in his presentations that were particularly relevant to the specific theme of the conference:

1. "In a world full of hypermimetic individuals, such as the Elizabethan court, or our own consumer society, the principle of frustration is inexorable."[50] This is due to the phenomenon of mimetic desire that cannot or will not recognize its own mimetic character.
2. Following from the previous point, "All mimetic addicts, both males and females, are really addicted to indifference and rejection."[51] This is not

modern masochism, but the work of the mimetic mechanism that engenders inaccessibility to the desired object because that in turn increases its value. (As Groucho Marx said, "I wouldn't join a club that would accept me as a member.")

3. Inasmuch as the oxymoron conveys the ambivalences of mimetic desire, it "may be regarded . . . as the literary forerunner of the deluge of violence and pornography that is submerging nowadays much of what is left of our culture."[52] Its classical form can denote, or connote, the rivalry and potential for conflict and violence that are present in all erotic or acquisitive desire.

Jean-Pierre Dupuy's lecture was basically a slightly extended version of his presentation at Wiesbaden-Naurod in 1994. One additional point that is quite interesting was his comment on the fundamental role of imitation in market speculation as set forth by J. M. Keynes. Keynes's thesis was that in playing the market "the only rational form of conduct is to imitate others."[53] What Keynes hit upon was the fundamental ambivalence of information in the market economy. An example is the knowledgeable investor who knows that a given security is seriously undervalued in the market. Can he ignore the value placed on it by the uninformed? No, he cannot, for the investor's own portfolio could well be at risk some day. It is not sensible from the standpoint of self-interest to pay a given amount for a security that you know is worth more than the going price if there is a possibility that it will drop below the current price. Two guidelines emerge from Keynes's analysis. One is that it "is too risky to depart from the majority evaluation."[54] The second is that the smart speculator is able to "guess better than the crowd how the crowd will behave."[55]

Dupuy also made some instructive remarks in a discussion at the end of the conference. Human agents in the modern world usually exist at a greater distance than persons in the past from the central action of exchange leading to the fulfillment of their perceived needs. The process of victimization is now more indirect. "In the case of sacrificial victims we are concerned with *mimetic victimage* and the *focus of attention* lies on the victim. In contrast, economic victimage means *third person victimage* . . . [T]he prevalent relationship towards them is *indifference*." They are not lynched and sacralized like victims in archaic societies, and they remain within the social system, though at its margins. They often experience intense resentment toward those who are winners in the system, and this fact often leads to "violent acts of terrorism, . . . confronting people with their own violence and causing *secondary, derivative victims*."[56]

Wolfgang Palaver's paper, "Envy or Emulation," argues that envy and emulation cannot be divided into bad and good, respectively, a distinction that goes back to Aristotle. Both are rooted in mimetic desire. Emulation itself would have no meaning apart from the sense of desiring to equal or surpass someone or something else. In his concluding section he comments on the relation of Catholic social teaching to an economy and social order driven by envy. Positing that economic activity is a matter of exchange or transaction in a social context that is based on our religious nature, Palaver points out that the tradition of Catholic social teaching, beginning particularly with Leo XIII's encyclical *Rerum novarum* in 1891, "has emphasized the necessity to give religious values precedence over temporal interests."[57] It and other Catholic documents emphasize that only if the "infinite desire of human beings is directed toward God" can the danger of the Hobbesian war of "all against all" be avoided.[58] Although we should not support the idea of a theocratic government in which the Catholic Church or any other religion rules society, still the church, and perhaps similar institutions of the other world religions, should play an important role in civil society. The church stands particularly as an opponent of the dissolution of the moral distinction between means and ends in which the economy becomes an end in itself.[59]

Have the media of communication become the new "church," outside of which there is no salvation? Józef Niewiadomski spoke to this question in an inspiring and provocative manner in "Extra Media Nulla Salus? Attempt at a Theological Synthesis." The Catholic Church's claim that outside the church there is no salvation has been variously interpreted, especially in the modern era. Niewiadomski points out that the church came into being due to God's passion for humanity; at its foundation is the Incarnation, reflecting God's intention of universal communication with and among human beings. However, the "dream of Constantine" whereby the church pretended to be "God's only religious form" led to the paradox that the "the church gradually debased the traces of God acting in the world. . . . The mystery of God's universal salvific will thus mutated into a social mechanism of exclusion."[60]

Niewiadomski holds that we now live in a "global society . . . structured by the mass media and that poses the same problem [as the tradition of Constantianism]: unifying structures that aspire to bring about the dream of universal human communication"; this society threatens to exclude "all those who are victimized by the media and the dimension of bodily existence," while at the same time "it perpetuates the unredeemed structure of human existence."[61] It is a new "dream" that has brought global society about, the dream that informs information technology and the free market of Adam Smith's putative "invisible hand."[62]

But the invention of global cyberspace has brought its own demons and its own entangling paradoxes. Its enticement is that all institutions, including the market and the interconnection of all kinds of communication, "appear as mere preconditions for the individual's experience of freedom."[63] It is the old satanic seduction: to be autonomous, to be one's own god. One of the great rewards of being like gods is that cheap cyberspace brings with it the possibility of the dearest gift of all: *attention*, perhaps even adoration. The cybernetic gift of attention means that a universal theme of the Christian legacy, concern for the victim, affords more and more people the opportunity to exploit it by presenting themselves as victims and releasing their resentments over the Internet. "The ritual of accusation and the hunt for scapegoats" has taken on a new form.[64] A kind of global society has indeed been created, but "at the same time it has atomized its members and made them lonely."[65]

In the face of this cultural situation, the Christian theologian's task is to confess, "I know my redeemer lives" (Job 19:25) and to demythologize the media on the basis of his or her faith in the Triune God who "descends into the world of human *profundior et univeralior appetitio* [more profound and universal human desire], submits himself to [human] passions, becomes a victim of rivalry and envy in order to reveal . . . what is true fulfillment of desire, and to redeem humanity from the trap of mimetic desire."[66] This is the true divine passion, which is not mimetic desire, but the participatory way of relating that characterizes the three Persons of the Trinity. Thus it is that true body, true matter, the true enjoyment of God's creation is revealed, as seen through the prophet's eyes:

> On this mountain the Lord of hosts will provide for all peoples a feast of rich food and choice wines, juicy rich food and pure choice wines. On this mountain he will destroy the veil that veils all peoples, the web that is woven over all nations; he will destroy death forever. (Isaiah 25:6–7)[67]

The Conference at Ghost Ranch in 2004

The 2004 meeting of COV&R was scheduled for Ghost Ranch in Abiquiu. As we looked toward that gathering, there was an air of anticipation for many of us about meeting at such a magnificent setting in the mountainous desert of New Mexico. This anticipation was at the same time intermingled with an air of sadness over the sudden death of our beloved friend and colleague Raymund Schwager in February of that year.

Ghost Ranch Abiquiu is located in a beautiful desert setting about thirty-five miles west-northwest of Santa Fe. The setting is ideal for nature lovers, and the ranch facilities are quite rustic, as aptly described by Petra Steinmair-Pösel in the *Bulletin*: "The red-glowing stone formations invited to go for a hike, e.g., to the close-by Chimney Rock. The Ranch itself contributed to [the impressions of natural beauty]: rooms and bathroom facilities were really basic, which perhaps was inconvenient for some participants, but probably added to and intensified the experience of natural beauty and wilderness."[68]

Britt Johnston, who initiated the pastoral ministry seminars at Ghost Ranch, was the organizer, aided by a program committee made up of Robert Daly, James Williams, and Andrew McKenna. The theme of the symposium was nature and human nature in light of the mimetic theory. Although there is a tendency easily to romanticize venues like Ghost Ranch as bringing people "closer to nature," no doubt the environment there confronts one with a starker sense of the difference between the total environing world and the routine social worlds with which we are familiar.

It was a year of events that had great impact on COV&R. One event that many of us found hard to believe at first was the sudden death of Fr. Raymund Schwager on February 27. It was hard to believe, first of all, because he was such an important presence for us. Never imposing himself, always humble, working incessantly whether front and center or behind the scenes, his scholarly work and collegial contribution were of significance second only to René Girard's.

Moreover, at sixty-eight years of age Schwager was apparently healthy and full of plans to complete a new manuscript, as mentioned in chapter 2. He also had new interfaith projects in mind. However, because an image taken as part of a physical exam seemed to reveal a dark spot on his lungs, the physicians recommended that he undergo a new procedure for finding out whether a tumor was developing. It involved arresting the action of the subject's lungs while attached to an apparatus providing oxygen. He died during the procedure of a heart attack. It turned out that nothing was wrong with his lungs.

Schwager's Innsbruck friends and colleagues were particularly grief stricken at the news. But all of us who had worked closely with him, not least of course René Girard, were in a state of mourning. I had been in frequent email contact with him as I finished translating the final draft of his book on original sin and evolutionary theory. With the support of the Innsbruck theological faculty, particularly Nikolaus Wandinger and Dietmar Regensburger, the final manuscript was completed and published in English in 2006 as *Banished from Eden: Original Sin and Evolutionary Theory in the Drama of Salvation.*

At the Ghost Ranch conference the program began with a memorial tribute to Schwager. There was a reading of Psalm 124, one of his favorite Psalms. He particularly loved verse 7: "We have escaped like a bird from the snare of the fowlers; the snare is broken, and we have escaped." He had drawn on this verse for his literary recounting of the life of Jesus: *Dem Netz des Jägers entronnen: Wie Jesus sein Leben verstand* (Escaped from the Net of the Hunter: How Jesus Understood His Life). Petra Steinmair-Pösel read some of Schwager's own comments on this verse of the psalm. Using the model of five "acts" that Schwager had articulated, with the assistance of Józef Niewiadomski, both in his narrative life of Jesus and in his later magnum opus, *Jesus in the Drama of Salvation,* the tribute was divided into five parts: act 1, biography and the theme of dramatic theology in his writing, presented by Niewiadomski and Wandinger; act 2, his new experience of leadership in America as the first president of COV&R and the translation of some of his books into English, presented by James Williams; act 3, his service as churchman and Jesuit, presented by Andrew Marr; act 4, an overview of his contribution to mimetic theory and to COV&R and his qualities as a teacher, presented by Julie Shinnick, Wolfgang Palaver, and Sandor Goodhart; and in act 5 René Girard spoke about his relationship with Schwager. *Zeker tsaddiq livrakah*, "the memory of the righteous is for a blessing."

"Nature, Human Nature, and Mimetic Theory," Ghost Ranch, June 2–5, 2004

Among the notable papers, Michel Serres presented his own intriguing variation on the thesis that the New Testament, and specifically, the Apostle Paul, is at the origin of the Christian concept of the self that informs Western culture. He confesses in this paper, "Before reading Saint Paul, I did not cognitively understand how a philosopher-son thought, nor did I understand the meaning of the religion of the Son. The entire West descends from this son and finds itself in him."[69] The constituting of the human self by faith, *ego credo,* faith in God, as the basis of adoptive sonship in and through the Son is the new thing that emerges from Paul's witness to Christ.

On "nature," which was one of the main subjects of the symposium, Paul Dumouchel and Jean-Pierre Dupuy made a provocative presentation on "Nature as the Excluded Third." Defining nature from the perspective of mimetic theory as "what is neither subject nor object of mimetic rivalry,"[70] they argued that nature has no place in mimetic theory; indeed, "nature" no longer exists as nanotechnology increasingly takes over what used to be called nature. There was quite a lively discussion over their argument. For one thing, if there is no nature, then it becomes impossible to conceive of a "human nature," at least in any traditional sense. Jean-Paul Sartre, for example, rejected the idea of a universal human nature. He attacked the theological notion of philosophers like Descartes and Leibniz that the work of God is analogous to that of a craftsman. He uses the example of a paper cutter: first the manufacturer has a form that is drawn up, and the production proceeds exactly according to this form.[71] The Bible is a fundamental source for thinking and speaking of human nature as that of an evolving, multifarious self that has definite characteristics through all its changes and adaptations.

On nanotechnology, a search of the literature appears to indicate that Dumouchel and Dupuy's argument was rhetorical hyperbole, perhaps for the purpose of provoking our thinking about nature and the human world. It seems doubtful that a majority of those involved in nanotechnology are ready to cast aside the concept of nature; they tend to separate it completely from their concept of nanotechnology. Nature for those involved in this kind of scientific investigation is that realm of the empirical world that cannot be produced or replicated by human action. However, there are borderline areas where nanotechnology modifies nature. To take Gregor Schiemann's work as an example, he addresses this question in an essay on nanotechnology and nature. Defining nature in two ways, narrowly as what does not originate in human action and more broadly as the empirical content of the laws of nature, he builds upon the narrow sense of nature to reach the following conclusion:

> I proposed an epistemic criterion according to which an object is natural if it is impossible—using all available scientific methods at a given time—to ascertain that it was produced by human action. This criterion makes it possible to distinguish—analogously to the Turing-test of artificial intelligence—between natural and artificial components of most nanotechnological processes and products. Given the multifariousness of the relationship between nanotechnology and nature, there are cases where it becomes problematic to distinguish between the two. *I assume, however, that these cases are exceptions.* Nanotechnological objects are mostly hybrids of nature and art; only in a few cases would they be said to be wholly natural because their artificial origin could no longer be confirmed.[72]

Simon Simonse presented an interesting paper comparing the ecological function of the kings and gods of people on the east and west banks of the upper Nile in Africa to the understanding of God, people, and environment in Old Testament religion. In his research he found that among the Lulubo and the Lokoya, where the "king" is the rainmaker, this leader is responsible for the control of natural resources. If a crisis like drought is too severe, the king or queen may be slain as a sacrificial event, and this is supposed to release the rain. There is a certain continuity between monarchs and divinities. Where gods are the ecological agents, they are beyond human control, although they may be supplicated in prayer and the sacrifice of animals. Simonse summarizes that in "the kingship scenario, victimhood alternated between the community (suffering disaster) and the king (suffering regicide). In the divinity scenario, humans are always at the receiving end of victimhood."[73]

Simonse notes similarities between these Nilotic features of myth and ritual pertaining to environmental crises and ancient Israel's responses to crises. The big difference is that there is a historicization of crisis in the Old Testament. "In the Old Testament, the natural environment as a key concern in transactions between God and humans retreats further into the background to give way to concern about moral purity and justice. . . . The text [of Genesis 1] emphatically repeats that what God created was very good. There was no more need for humankind to play a side role in managing cosmic order."[74] Apropos of the mimetic theory, there is a historical development toward prohibition of the scapegoating of humans, and the sacrificial slaughter of animals is restricted to calendrical rituals.

Simonse's argument concerning the Old Testament would have been strengthened if he had placed greater emphasis on the theme of covenant. The covenant concept in Israelite history was the theological and religious basis of law, with prohibitions (most of the Ten Commandments) protecting the people in their religious and social transactions. However, at the center of this covenant is a relationship with the deity that is presupposed in the freedom that various great voices assumed in arguing with the God of Israel (Moses, Jeremiah, Job, many of the Psalms; Jacob wrestling with the "man" at the ford of the Jabbok). The covenant was an essential part of Israel's revelatory breakthrough in history, and eventually this understanding of divine presence and guidance would break across the boundaries of law and prohibition in the mission and message of Jesus and his followers who formed the beginning of Christianity.

A discussion and evaluation of the conference took place on June 5, with René Girard, Anthony Bartlett, Sandor Goodhart, and Sheelah Hidden as speakers on the panel. The panelists and many of those present expressed their sense of the vitality of the conference and the general rapport of those attending. The success of the conference was due in large part to the work of the local host and organizer, Britt Johnston, who, it should be mentioned, practiced an inspiring resistance to responding in kind when one speaker (an exception to the rapport) used very derogatory and disrespectful language in attacking a piece on abortion he had written.

Concerning theology and the mimetic theory, Tony Bartlett expressed the need for a new theological initiative that reached out in a new evangelical mode beyond the framework of the institutional church. René Girard replied that Raymund Schwager's work should continue to be our theological lodestar. Here is Bartlett's own comment on that moment, written some years later:

> At the final evaluation session I suggested . . . Girardian thought was grounds for a new spring of evangelism. Girard verbally hushed me and said, "No, No." Again I understand why he did this. Jim Williams told me afterward that Girard had said, in reference to the interchange, that mimetic thought needs to be a "Trojan horse" in culture. In other words it is a matter again of preserving the formal academic or intellectual contours of his thinking, and once accepted at this level the deeper implications might impose themselves. However, this is not the way theology works. Theology speaks directly and coherently out of revelation. I understood then that I was doing something quite different from Girard and many intellectuals around him. Roman Catholic theologians . . . have—it's true—flourished around him but that is because they are working within an overarching tradition of discourse that does not depend on Girard. They creatively appropriate him to it. I, in contrast, am not working within this framework, but more immediately with the phenomenology and ontology to which Girardian thought gives rise.[75]

There is an enormous issue here for those doing theology while engaged simultaneously with the mimetic theory. This is, as already mentioned in chapter 2, the one instance of which I know that Girard imposed himself on the direction of COV&R'S work. It is quite clear from the Schwager-Girard correspondence that Girard sees an almost perfect meshing, a theoretical-theological symbiosis, between his articulation of the mimetic theory and Schwager's appropriation of it for Christian theology. That has been and is a powerful impetus in the movement of the mimetic theory out into the world. Nonetheless, the question remains, can COV&R sustain multiple theological frameworks and perspectives? Must it be restricted to one theological canon of its own making?[76]

In the event, this friction within COV&R between the academic and the more practical or experiential kind of theologizing is one of the important factors leading to the creation of a separate organization, Theology and Peace, founded by Bartlett, Tom Nicoll (an Episcopal priest), and Michael Hardin, and now led by an expanded board. This is not an unfortunate development, especially since the relationship between COV&R and Theology and Peace has been a good one as far as I know. This relationship has been abetted by a third entity that has formed in part due to the existence and influence of COV&R, Imitatio. Imitatio was led by Robert Hamerton-Kelly from 2007 to 2010 and is funded by the philanthropic work of Peter Thiel.

But the emergence of Theology and Peace and Imitatio lay in the future as we met at Ghost Ranch in 2004. It was an exciting time, with a dawning sense for many of us that we were, indeed, living in an apocalyptic age. There was a sense of great vitality in what we were about, but at the same time a foreboding of disaster with respect to the future of the human and the natural world. This conference, in my view, was the beginning of the transition into a new phase of COV&R's history.

An important decision taken at the business meeting expressed the practical organizational aspect of the growth of COV&R's influence in the world. Robert Daly gave a detailed report on incorporation as a nonprofit organization and recommended on behalf of the advisory board that the members approve incorporation and that the board constitute itself as the board of directors for incorporation purposes. The members present unanimously approved the change. This matter had come up in the previous decade, as already noted, but it had been shelved as too early in COV&R's development. Now the time was ripe. Duncan Ragsdale, a COV&R member and lawyer from Memphis, Tennessee, volunteered to see the process through, with the assistance of our treasurer, Julie Shinnick. We were now large enough as a professional society to make incorporation feasible, and it would clearly be to our advantage to be able to receive tax-exempt donations.

Another important piece of business was the selection of Nikolaus Wandinger as the new editor of the *Bulletin*, succeeding Paul Bellan-Boyer. With his institutional setting at Innsbruck and commitment to the task, Wandinger would bring the semiannual newsletter to a new level of quality in its coverage and the information it contains.

The transition to another phase had begun.

Politics and Apocalypse: A Meeting at Stanford

Another happening in 2004 was a significant workshop involving six days of discussion that took place June 12–17, 2004, at Stanford University. In his report on the meeting Robert Hamerton-Kelly named the group the "Stanford Girard Circle." It was apparently the forerunner of Imitatio. Peter Thiel, the managing partner of Clarium Capital Management and a member of the circle, sponsored the event. Thiel majored in philosophy at Stanford University and earned a law degree there. He made his mark in hedge funds and derivatives and started PayPal, which he eventually sold.

Participation was by invitation only in order to achieve a more leisurely and focused discussion. There were thirteen participants, nine of whom presented papers. Seven of these essays are published in *Politics & Apocalypse*, edited by Hamerton-Kelly. This was the first publication in the series Violence, Mimesis, and Culture from Michigan State University Press. The discussion centered on the thought of Girard as related to Carl Schmitt, Leo Strauss, and Eric Voegelin with papers also on biblical apocalypse and apocalyptic and modern theology. The editor wrote a helpful introductory essay for the volume. Apocalypse, in its biblical root meaning of the "unveiling," the unveiling of God's will, is not construed in Girard's mimetic theory as the final revealing of the destroying judgment of the wrathful, vengeful God, but as the vision of what humans are bringing about given that they now have invented instruments of global self-destruction.

To Koblenz and Beyond, 2005

The Election of René Girard to the French Academy

An auspicious event early in 2005 was the election of René Girard to the French Academy. In France, l'Académie Française represents the apex of official recognition of an individual's contributions to French language and culture. The work of its members is usually acknowledged as having great significance beyond the boundaries of the culture and institutions of France.

The French Academy was founded by Cardinal de Richelieu in 1635, during the reign of Louis XIII. It is composed of forty "immortals," as Richelieu called them. Its primary function is to monitor the French language and to engage in the ongoing work of updating its French dictionary.

Girard was elected on March 17, 2005, and officially received in a ceremony on December 15 of that year. In that ceremony Girard gave a discourse eulogizing the life and work of his predecessor, Father Robert Carré, who had occupied Chair 37. Then Michel Serres, a member of the Academy since 1990, pronounced the discourse of welcome to the venerable institution. Serres, whose formal speech and written work is replete with poetic imagery and aphoristic insight, gave a speech of the sort that must be rare from *sous la Coupole* (under the Cupola) at the French Academy. It was simultaneously a review of the scope and insights of Girard's work, an encomium to his genius, and a personal outpouring of feelings of friendship. He proclaimed that "what you say in your books is true; what you say gives life."[77] He acknowledges the conversion, in effect, that Girard's friendship and influence has brought about in his life.

> Du coup, vous m'avez appris ceci, qui a changé ma vie, de distinguer le saint du sacré, ni plus ni moins que le faux du vrai. Theólogie, éthique, épistémologie parlent, en trois disciplines, d'une seule voix.[78]

> As a result, you taught me this, which changed my life: to distinguish the holy from the sacred, neither more nor less than the false from the true. Theology, ethics, and epistemology speak, in three disciplines but with one voice.[79]

Neither does Serres neglect the contribution of Martha Girard, who has been so important in her husband's life and work. Serres says, "Few people know that without you, without your inimitable presence, the great theories that I have the heavy charge to praise this evening assuredly would not have seen the light of day."[80]

As Sandor Goodhart, writing as the president of COV&R at the time, so aptly stated about the election of Girard to the French Academy, "René Girard's work, now recognized at the center of cultural life in France, can finally accede to the end for which in my own it was destined: namely, its recognition in posterity as the primary articulation in our time of the sacrificial logic of all human groups and the relation of that cultural, religious, and perhaps even biological logic to a sacrificial violence that, if not efficaciously managed, will destroy us utterly."[81]

The Annual Conference Near Koblenz, Germany, 2005

The annual conference near Koblenz, Germany, held in store a new kind of setting for the Colloquium: the monastic complex of Marienland, where Sisters of Mary reside. Marienland is the largest complex of the buildings and grounds on Berg Schönstatt. Schönstatt (literally "Beautiful Abode") is the center of the international Schönstatt Movement founded in 1914 by Fr. Joseph Kentenich (1885–1968). According to the information compiled by Nikolaus Wandinger (with the aid of Ann Astell and Wikipedia), Pope John Paul II called Father Kentenich "one of the great spiritual leaders of this century." He "courageously opposed Hitler and suffered as a political prisoner in the concentration camp in Dachau from 1942–1945. Fr. Kentenich conducted pedagogical conferences in Schönstatt in the 1930s and envisioned Schönstatt as a site for academic meetings, such as COV&R 2005."[82]

Ann Astell, herself a Schönstatt Sister of Mary, was the COV&R organizer in collaboration with the resident Sisters of Mary. The theme of this symposium was "Mimetic Theory and the Imitation of the Divine." Situated at the confluence of the Rhine and Mosel rivers, both the city of Koblenz and Berg Schönstatt are rich in beauty and tradition. Koblenz has a number of buildings and places of historical and aesthetic interest, including two churches in the Romanesque style. Schönstatt has gained renown as a place of religious pilgrimage as well as for the Schönstatt Movement.

The work of planning and organizing of the conference was carried out in the face of two difficulties. One was the pressure of time. Usually the annual conferences are scheduled two or three years ahead. However, just a year before, the COV&R board learned that the scheduled venue in Italy was no longer possible. Ann Astell and her order quickly offered to host the meeting at Schönstatt-Koblenz, but this was obviously short notice for the kind of planning and organizing that had to be done. The second problem was that Astell, who was then on the English faculty at Purdue University, had to communicate with the Schönstatt Sisters by long distance. However, things came together marvelously well. Astell traveled to Schönstatt a week prior to the meeting and found a warmly receptive and diligent team ready to make the final preparations. Astell and her conference team—Sr. Angela Macari, Sr. Mattia Amrhein, Sr. Doria Schlickmann, Sr. Vernita Weiss, Sr. Maria Julia Agüero, and Sr. Marisa Spickers—quickly swung into action to take care of all the final details.[83]

There were 160 participants from twenty-six nations.[84] Besides the nationalities represented, there was the greatest ecumenical mix—priests, nuns, the religiously committed and secular scholars, Catholics, Protestants, Muslims, and Jews—that we have been favored with at a COV&R symposium.

The conference events included an optional dinner excursion by boat on the Rhine, musical concerts, and a film about Father Kentenich. One of highlights was the singing of two songs in which known melodies carried new lyrics composed specifically for the conference. One of these was a salute to

Schönstatt and Koblenz, which those gathered there for the COV&R meeting sang to the tune of "The Happy Wanderer." The other was a song of congratulations to René Girard on his election to the French Academy. It was sung to the tune of "I Have to Leave Ol' Texas Now" (!). It has many stanzas; here are the final four:

René Girard,
Eighty years plus one!
A life so rich
Makes a mighty sum.

René Girard,
Honoree of France,
Our joy for you
Makes us want to dance.

René Girard,
"*Im*-mortal" now!
Your countrymen
Honor you—and how!

René Girard,
On Mt. Schoenstatt's height,
We celebrate
On this special night.

"The Imitation of the Divine," July 6–10, 2005

The conference brought together a number of distinguished scholars from outside of COV&R, including Margaret Miles and Jean-Luc Marion. It will help to clarify what lies behind the theme of the conference in the Marienland setting by referring first to Ann Astell's paper. Her presentation in one of the plenary sessions, "Symbols of the (Other) Self: Joseph Kentenich and Edith Stein," articulates in brief form the iconic center and depth of the Schönstatt movement and at the same time it comments on the thought of Father Kentenich and Edith Stein (Sr. Benedicta of the Cross). Father Kentenich's Marian theology and the worship and work of the Schönstatt Sisters are informed by a kind of "visual piety." In her paper Astell compares "Father Kentenich's linkage of a proper use of images in identity-formation, on the one hand, to

Edith Stein's analysis of the role of images in the life of St. John of the Cross, on the other." She notes that "Father Kentenich and Edith Stein (1891–1942) had reached similar insights into the role, positive and negative, of images in personality formation—insights that have yet to be sufficiently implemented in the life of the church, despite René Girard's acute delineation of mimetic social structures and the prophetic call of scholars like Margaret R. Miles for an educational theory and practice that recognizes and utilizes the personal 'insight' that is granted through the attractive force of a religious image."[85] Although the Nazis tried to obliterate both the image of Mary at Schönstatt and the message of Father Kentenich that the Sisters internalized, they were not successful. Even while Father Kentenich was imprisoned at Dachau, he and the Sisters remained true to the Marian ideal that he taught. His key Gospel text was the scene in John 19:26–27, where Jesus, on the cross, sees his mother and the beloved disciple standing nearby and tells his mother, "Woman, behold your son!" and to his disciple he says, "Behold, your mother!" Astell says, "Identifying himself with that disciple, Father Kentenich looked upon Mary as his mother and model of discipleship, in obedience to Christ, whose features he saw veiled in hers."[86] The idea is not that Mary replaces Christ, but that each points to the other, and in devotion to her the disciple sees Christ. This image of Mary, the "original" who is veiled in her icons, was the central object of faith for the Novitiates in 1939, who vowed their fidelity to the Appearance of the Thrice Admirable Mary. In their affirmation of faith and opposition to the Nazi regime this "ideal spread with new intensity through the ranks of the Sisters."[87]

When Father Kentenich was imprisoned Edith Stein, Sister Benedicta of the Cross, was in the process of writing *Studie über Johannes a Cruce: Kreuzeswissenschaft* (A Study of John of the Cross: The Science of the Cross). Stein was a Jew who converted to Christianity and entered the Discalced Carmelite Order in Cologne in 1933. Even as she wrote her final book while residing in a Carmelite convent in Echt, Holland she anticipated her own arrest. She and her sister were taken by the Gestapo early in August of 1942 and deported to Auschwitz on August 7. According to the tradition of that Carmelite convent, the last words she uttered there were spoken to her sister Rosa: "Come, we are going to join our people."

In her thought and meditation St. Benedicta, who was canonized in 1998, became fascinated by the role of images—cross, night, bridal chamber—in the identity formation of the great Spanish mystic, St. John of the Cross. "In the innermost chamber of her soul, there was, she knew, an 'other self' at the hither side of her conscious knowing." As it was for Father Kentenich, who called this hidden self the "personal ideal," finding her way to it "depended . . . on the attractive force, the gravitational pull, the anagogy of symbols that were simultaneously images of God and the true self, the other self, which is found only in God."[88]

So in the setting of Marienland at Schönstatt, the life and teaching of these two great mystics form the background to understand the theme of the conference. Father Kentenich taught that each one of us is endowed deep within us with a picture of what God wishes us to become. This is the original "image of God," which cannot be replaced and which is the key to our authentic identity.[89] In a similar vein, St. Theresa Benedicta, following St. Theresa of Avila, spoke of the "seventh chamber of the soul," the innermost chamber where God is found. It is here that freedom is experienced in radical surrender to God. The new "I," the new self that is formed, is radically intersubjective.[90]

Father Kentenich and Sister Benedicta were both taken on journeys of death from the standpoint of the Gestapo captors, who believed that the death of all Jews and Christian rebels who remained stalwart for the Jew Jesus, among others unworthy of life in the Third Reich, would bring about a new order of things. Astell comments in the conclusion of her paper that Father Kentenich and Sister Benedicta saw in these journeys an utterly different narrative pattern and a different set of symbols and ideals: "the cross, the night, the pilgrimage, the chamber, the shrine. Who dares to say that the images we use don't matter, don't make us 'other,' even to ourselves?"[91]

Józef Niewiadomski gave the opening keynote address, comparing Raymund Schwager's pre-Girardian thinking on Christian discipleship to the understanding held by Dietrich Bonhoeffer and René Girard.[92] He concludes that Schwager's interpretation delineates discipleship as sharing the fate of Jesus, walking in his life or footsteps by participating in his surrender to God, which opens the way to freedom and love. This imitation is not simply made up of external acts but is a transformation made possible by the Holy Spirit. Girard's understanding of following Jesus is similar in that he asks how the mimetic rivalry of the world can be broken and transcended. It cannot in human terms. A transcendent power is required. The transcendent power is the work of the Spirit that puts the disciples in the way of a new contagion, the contagion of love, which is the power of reconciliation and healing. Bonhoeffer's perspective could be understood as very similar. In his *Ethics* he writes of the "great change [that] takes place at the moment when the unity of existence ceases to consist in its autonomy and is found, through the miracle of faith, beyond man's ego and its law, in Jesus Christ. This means that I can now find unity with myself only in the surrender of my ego to God and to men."[93] On the question raised at the beginning of the paper as to whether imitation of Christ is an activity of human beings or a matter of God's grace, the alternative of either-or turns out to be false in the Christology that emerges from the reflections of these three thinkers. "We have tremendous parallels between Bonhoeffer, Schwager and Girard. And that is almost a miracle!"[94]

Seminnual Meeting, in Philadelphia

The meeting in Philadelphia with the American Academy of Religion, November 19, 2005, featured four strong papers. William Morrow gave a paper in which he held that the Torah's narration of the conquest of the land of Canaan, especially the Deuteronomic Reform, is more mythological than historical.[95] Ann Astell spoke on Nathan's parable to King David in 2 Samuel 12:1–6. Drawing upon the work of David Daube, she described a complex network of mimetic rivalry that forms the background of the parable. The tale of the rich man with many sheep and the poor man with one pet sheep, which the rich man takes by force in order to feed a guest, is a parable that obviously refers to David stealing Bathsheba, wife of Uriah. But there is probably at a deeper narrative level an allusion to David's rivalry with Saul. David's wife, Michal, daughter of Saul, had been taken by Saul and given to another man. Now David was becoming like Saul![96]

The papers of Nikolaus Wandinger and Robert Daly overlapped to the extent that they both stressed the imitation of Jesus as the way to know God, at least from a Christian point of view. In "No One Has Ever Seen God: Problems in Imitating the Invisible God," Wandinger drew upon Girard and Schwager in stressing that finally it is only through the Son that we find the way to the Father; in other words, we come closest to "seeing" God if we imitate the desire of Jesus, who did not exalt himself but was completely open to receive the overflowing gift of God, the Father's gracious love. Daly's presentation was taken from his ongoing research on atonement theory, which has occupied him since the early 1990s and which was published in 2009 in his book, *Sacrifice Unveiled: The True Meaning of Christian Sacrifice.*[97] In that book Daly states, "If . . . we, precisely as human beings, are ineluctably by nature imitating someone else's desire, then the mimetic activity by which, through which, in which we will be saved is the activity of imitating the desire of Jesus."[98]

The Celebration of Raymund Schwager's Seventieth Birthday

Raymund Schwager, who died in February 2004, would have been seventy years old on November 11, 2005. To celebrate this occasion the Innsbruck Theology Faculty held a two-day academic event on November 24 and 25. The two guest speakers were Aleida Assmann and Jean-Pierre Dupuy. Professor Assmann lectured on "Violence and the Collective Unconscious in the Eucharist." She argued that the Eucharist validates an unconscious anti-Judaism, legitimating violence against the Jews. The response of the theologians was that both priestly hierarchy and laypeople throughout the history of Christianity have typically held a sacrificial misconception of the Lord's Supper, a misconception that Assmann herself shares. Jesus endured violence rather than exercising it himself, and neither in suffering nor in the victory over death of the Resurrection did he or his disciples call for vengeance on the Jews.

Unfortunately, Dupuy could not make it to the conference. Due to fog at his connection in Munich he was left stranded at the airport in Paris. However, he had sent his paper in advance, so Nikolaus Wandinger read it in his stead and Wolfgang Palaver responded to questions out of his general knowledge of Dupuy's thought. The paper was centered in two theses and an open-ended thought. The first thesis is that human beings no longer master technology; they are rather subject to it. In the second thesis he recurred to what he and Dumouchel argued at Ghost Ranch in 2004: nature is drawn into science and technology so that it more and more becomes—or is viewed as—something that we humans make, an artifact. His open-ended thought is that technology cannot or should not replace persons as objects of love for one another. A listing of traits gathered together in a perfect simulation of a human being could still not replace the other as person. But he confessed that he was unable to formulate this as an ethical rule.[99]

Dupuy asserted that the biblical roots of Judaism and Christianity offer no ethical guidance in the face of the danger of putting ourselves in the place of God, for it is precisely the biblical religions that have desacralized nature and so removed "every taboo, prohibition, or limit" that stands in the way of modern technology. But it should be noted that he is wrong about that. There is indeed a demythifying and desacralizing that takes place in the biblical witness, but there is at the same time an affirmation of God as creator and savior—which entails a respect for the created world and the beings that inhabit it. Adam created in the image of God means that Adam (man and woman) is to rule as representative of God, the implied imperative being that mankind is to maintain it in good condition on behalf of God. The Ten Commandments (eight of which are prohibitions) and the summary of the commandments in Jesus' two great commandments (to love God and to love your neighbor as yourself) set the limits required for ethical guidelines. You cannot put yourself in the place of God if you sincerely obey the law of anti-idolatry.

Now of course, those who do not believe in a divine Giver of boundaries and limits are confronted finally with a great quandary, for then there is no authority by which one can settle the meta-question: Why be ethical at all? Why, with regard to the subject under discussion, should one be concerned with the environment? If there is no ultimate Authority, we are left with no limits, no prohibitions that can be universally accepted due to competing desires and interests. Any laws, rules, and limits that are socially accepted without this ultimate Authority then become either the expression of social custom or the imposition of some dictatorial power.

French Girard Association

The first official French organization focusing on Girard's work was launched late in 2005, l'Association pour les Recherches Mimétiques. Here I will simply reproduce the report of Simon de Keukelaere that appeared in *The Bulletin of COV&R*.

> It looks as if René Girard's home country is finally giving him the (belated) recognition he deserves. The seventeenth of December, only two days after his official entrée into the French Academy, the first important French Girard-association was set up. The constitution of the "Association pour les Recherches Mimétiques" was voted in Paris in the sumptuous "Palais de l'Institut." The new group will act in close collaboration with COV&R, but it has its own accents. As we can read in article three of its constitution, the primary goal of A.R.M. will be to "structure the research" linked to the mimetic theory of "René Girard, member of the French Academy, and organise its diffusion in the French Language." Contrary to COV&R the primary focus of activity will not be the relevance of the mimetic model for the study of religion, although that will be a significant area of research.
>
> The project looks very promising. Among its honorary members it has Sandor Goodhart, the [current] president of COV&R, five "immortals" from the French Academy, the chancellor of the French Institute (Pierre Messmer) and even prominent people from the political and financial world, as for instance Jacques Delors (former president of the European Commission), Claude Bébéar (president of the AXA-group) etc. Thanks to the financial backing a specialised center for mimetic studies will soon be

> opened in Poissy, a town on the banks of the Seine, a little outside Paris. Benoît Chantre has been elected as the first president of the association. René Girard is the honorary president.

After the voting the honorary and foundational members were treated to a talk by Mark Anspach on the [current relevance] of mimetic theory and to Benoît Chantre's attention-grabbing discussion with René Girard. Anspach commenced his short presentation on Girard's actuality with a remarkable observation: "Who could imagine a less topical subject in the seventies than 'Violence and the Sacred'? Who could conceive of a more relevant subject today?" Mimetic theory is never the topic of the day, but the topic of the day is often surprisingly mimetic. [Current events] persistently demonstrate the underestimated power and pertinence of the mimetic hypothesis. Girard agreed and pointed to recent findings in neurosciences and experimental psychology that corroborate mimetic theory in a sometimes spectacular fashion. He even encouraged the new association to do some experimental research. One of the focuses of the investigations should be the problem of reciprocity. According to Girard nearly all our human interactions are reciprocal. Even our refusal of reciprocity tends to become reciprocal. This primacy of reciprocity is typical for humans. When animals fight, for instance, they never look at each other. To look at one another, eye-contact, is a beautiful example of reciprocity, of mimetic behaviour. The new "immortal" invited his audience to do a little test with their pets: "try to look into the eyes of your dog or cat: they will get bored after a while." Not only eye-contact, but also violence has everything to do with reciprocity. Here Girard referred to the Prussian war-theorist Clausewitz whose writings on war contain many interesting "mimetic" intuitions. The assembly ended with a reception and a toast on the new association. It is not unrealistic to think it will usher [in] a new era of Girardian studies in France and the francophone world. And with so many "immortals" among its members the (French and international) Girard-associations are predestined to live a long life.[100]

Since the beginning of this new Girardian society it has developed an impressive series of conferences and lectures.

To Ottawa and Beyond, 2006

The 2006 conference was held in at St. Paul University in the city of Ottawa, Ontario. At the time of the conference Ottawa was a city of over 800,000 people, having experienced tremendous growth in the previous thirty years. It is the capital of Canada, and therefore the Canadian Parliament and various offices of federal government are located there. It is situated on the southern banks of the Ottawa River, and the Rideau River and the Rideau Canal run through it. St. Paul is a bilingual (French and English) Catholic University whose grounds back into the Rideau River. Its facilities are excellent and the organizer obviously had extensive cooperation from faculty and staff in planning and holding the conference.

The organizer, Vern Redekop, was recognized in chapter 2 for his intervention in a conflict situation. He is an Old Testament scholar and a specialist in conflict studies. He has been especially interested in the problems of and relations with native North Americans who were inhabitants of the Ottawa region and other parts of Canada long before Europeans arrived on the continent. The major theme of the symposium was "Mimesis, Creativity, and Reconciliation." Sessions were planned on "creative mimesis" and the imagination, peace building, the self, and traditions of the indigenous peoples of North America. Redekop's intention was to emphasize the creative, positive side of mimesis rather than violence. He also sought gender parity in planning the program and made it a point to invite colleagues who had not attended conferences in some time. Gender parity was not quite achieved, although there was a much greater number of women presenting papers, and we did see quite a few friends and colleagues who had not been with us in recent years.

So the overall planning was good, with many interesting topics and sessions. However, there was one drawback. As noted by Nikolaus Wandinger in his report, "there was no room or time assigned for socializing."[101] Otherwise, Redekop and his St. Paul team did an outstanding job.

"Mimesis, Creativity, and Reconciliation," May 31–June 4, 2006

This annual meeting not only brought together a variety of topics and people, including Native Americans, but it also featured dramatic modes of presentation, one of which I will comment on below. One of the most striking and potentially significant subjects related to the conference theme was that of "positive mimesis." Questions are raised over and over again about mimetic desire as conceived in Girard's mimetic theory. Is mimesis only a source of conflict, releasing destructive energy and leading to violent rivalry? Does Girard, in fact, view violence as ontological, a kind of essence in the makeup of human being? The answer to both questions is an emphatic "No!" There have been understandable misconceptions, as dealt with along the way in this history, but there should no longer be reason to raise these particular objections.

As early as 1994 Rebecca Adams criticized Girard for his putative inattention to positive mimesis, and she has refined her articulation of this in variants of basically the same essay over the ensuing years. Martha Reineke's paper cites Adams extensively, as already noted in chapter 3.[102] Reineke examines the mimetic theory in juxtaposition to D. W. Winnicott's notion of object relations and a "transitional space" of necessary aggression and ruthlessness in childhood development and creative living, and shows how it can be viewed as complementary in thinking about a creative and loving mimesis. This complementarity belies Girard's statement that in object relations "there is nothing but conflict."[103]

For her analysis and positive thesis Reineke draws on Ann Bedford Ulanov's interpretation of Winnicott in her book *Finding Space*. Winnicott indicates that there is a "transitional space" between the infant's reaching out to fulfill basic needs and its developing into an adult. Even with "good enough" parents the child will sometimes experience a sense of loss, even a kind of temporary disintegration, as it is subject to changes and transitions such as significant persons coming and going, needs not met as soon as they are felt, and so on. However, in a good enough holding environment, that is, "holding the child when it cannot hold itself,"[104] and with the early aid of a transitional object that is a "first symbol" of protection in the transition,[105] the child has a good chance of developing into a mature adult who enters into positive relations with others. But if the holding environment fails, "a subject splits, longing for protection against further loss."[106] If the person has experience of what Winnicott terms "relational distortions of transitional space,"[107] she could become masochistic, or sadistic, or in some ways very successful in adult life, but the success may be based on a false (empty) self. This is where conflict and objects of blame kick in, a situation that approaches Girard's victimary mechanism.

One of most important aspects of this transitional period is that there is a certain ruthless aggressiveness in which the infant or child engages until it finds its equilibrium in its environment and feels that it is protected in its world. This recurs also for adults who are creative. The energy of struggling for being—or new being, as the case may be—will ideally be channeled in ways that are not injurious to others, but obviously others are often violated in the rivalries that come about in a relentless commitment to achieving certain ends. The point is that from this standpoint the ruthless aggressiveness is an inevitable aspect of childhood development and human relations. The question is, what are the best ways to channel this striving for being?[108] Is there a certain kind of rivalry that is beneficial? We see a mythical example of this in the ancient Mesopotamian epic of Gilgamesh. After a battle between Gilgamesh and Enkidu that ends in a stalemate, the two recognize one another as equals and become fast friends, sharing many adventures together. It is Enkidu's death brought about by the goddess Ishtar that moves Gilgamesh to grief. This in turn is the impulse for his search for the secret of immortality as he travels on a fantastic journey to Utnapishtim, the primordial ancestor who survived the great flood that destroyed all humans except him and his family. But in quotidian terms, is there a form of rivalry that is expressed through working within the bounds of friendship, collegiality, kinship, or simply agreement on common goals, that is a positive, creative factor in human existence? Yet even if that is the case, the mimetic dynamics of human relationships can quickly break out of the boundaries of fruitful cooperation.

So Winnicott's work does contribute to mimetic theory as it seeks to fill in a gap that comprehends early childhood development, and in doing so it poses the question as to whether a certain kind of conflict and aggressiveness is necessary in good, normal human development. In turn, Girard's illuminating concept of the importance of the model/mediator and the sacrificial mechanism in human social existence articulates what is not fully expressed in the thinking of Winnicott, who sees the outcome of conflict, both creative and destructive, as inevitable in human life.

Moving from this analysis of the two great thinkers, Reineke refers to Ulanov, Jim Fodor, and Rebecca Adams in proposing that we turn our attention to a creative, loving mimesis, especially in the framework of religious symbols and experiences. The predicament of aggressiveness, mimetic rivalry, conflict, and violence can be illuminated and remedied in the context of thought and practice informed by the Christian concepts of Christ's *kenosis* (self-emptying) and the *agape* (spiritual love) that is a divine gift which can be shared with others. "Holding fast in the face of destructiveness, the one who expresses *agape* facilitates the transformation of aggression into imaginative work and creative living."[109]

Petra Steinmair-Pösel enhanced the topic of positive mimesis from the theological side with her paper on "Original Sin, Grace, and Positive Mimesis." Drawing particularly on Girard, Schwager, and Adams, she develops a case for the conclusion that mimetic desire enables humans to be open to other humans and to God. As Girard has said, "If desire were not mimetic, we would not be open to what is human or what is divine."[110] From a theological standpoint the corollary is that human beings are endowed with the capacity for transcendence as creational grace. A second conclusion is that negative mimesis may be understood theologically as "original sin" as it affects humankind. As Peter Sloterdijk has said, conceptual mimesis is the "scientific version of original sin."[111] Taking the place of the model is originally and primordially to take the place of God. A third conclusion is that violent imitation can only be answered in terms of soteriology and grace. "Positive mimesis is based upon God's prevenient grace."[112] As Girard affirms toward the end of *I See Satan Fall Like Lightning*, only a power superior to violent contagion will break the power of violent unanimity against the victim.[113]

An essay that is noteworthy and relevant to this discussion of positive mimesis, although it was not presented as a paper at the Ottawa conference, is Pablo Bandera's critique of Eric Gans's generative anthropology (GA).[114] Bandera holds that generative anthropology is really a theory of language and thus in at least one basic respect it is fundamentally different from the mimetic theory. According to Gans, language defines transcendent thought as a theory of language; this is by contrast to Girard's mimetic theory in which the primordial mimetic crisis resulting in the slaying of a victim inspires awe, which is the initial aspect of the experience of transcendent thought. Gans postulates an abortive gesture that turns the group away from the victim that is designated in an ostensive act, establishing the difference between "us" and "it," the designated object. This gesture defers violence by essentially transferring the mimetic crisis to the transcendent realm of the sign. This is the beginning of language. However, how could this abortive gesture have effect if there were no prior mimetic conflict resulting in violence that would be registered in their brains and thus serve as a warning as the group of hominids gathers around the desired object, whether it be animal, human, or whatever? Moreover, Gans states in *Signs of Paradox* that "as imitation [of the model's behavior] becomes more intense, [it focuses] less on the model's behavior and more on the object to which it is directed."[115] Bandera points out that the effect of this would logically lead to Girard's mimetic crisis, not Gans's scenario, for how could this imitation between subject and model increase in intensity if both are increasingly focused on the object, not on their relation? And if somehow the relation of the subject and model increases in intensity, how could it lead to anything but violence [between them] unless their aggression is redirected against a third party? One could see, of course, that a series of such incidents in a given grouping of hominids or proto-humans could lead them to the point of an abortive gesture such as Gans posits. But that is to return to the point previously made, that there must be conflict, violence, and victimization concealed behind the putative originary gesture.

One of the most important insights that Bandera's article offers is that Gans's understanding of love cannot be distinguished from resentment. He quotes statements in *Signs of Paradox* and *Chronicles of Love and Resentment* to demonstrate that for Gans love has the same basic structure as resentment. He does not conceive loving someone in such a way that the object of love would be happy without his care, and he blurs love and eroticism in a tangle of mutual seduction and ironic self-consciousness.[116] Girard, by contrast, views mimetic desire as basically good to the extent it is dependent on a good model and particularly when directed toward God. To take this further beyond what Bandera says in his paper, and as Steinmair-Pösel emphasizes theologically, Girard affirms that only the power and grace of God at work in human desire can overcome resentment, break the power of victimization, and bring about self-giving love among human beings. This divine power is at work in the love or positive mimesis that is a potential even within our human societies, which are generated by violence in the events leading to their formation. For as Bandera says, "Strictly speaking, humanity is not born out of violence but out of the transition from violence to peace. It is precisely because humanity exists at this crossroad that our desires can be directed toward the good or toward the bad."[117]

Finally, among the events of the conference a special experience for many was the series of skits on Matthew 5:38–42, Jesus' injunctions about nonresistance to evildoers. They were conceived and led by Walter Wink, with the aid of colleague helpers. They were very funny and very serious, and they were much appreciated by the plenary gathering. (One of the skits involved responding to someone who demanded the person's outer garment by stripping off *all* layers of one's clothing and offering them while the demanding person was shouting, "No, no! That's enough! Stop!") They illustrated a kind of proactive nonresistance to oppressors. They could also be viewed as a form of rivalry, a way of getting "one up" on opponents. Is this also a kind of good rivalry, a way of utilizing the "evil imagination" for the sake of something good in the world?

Important Organizational Matters

In 2006 two more leaders of high quality emerged. William Johnsen succeeded Andrew McKenna as editor of *Contagion*. McKenna served as editor from 1996 to 2006. I have already noted his sterling work in that role. With Johnsen as editor, the publication of *Contagion* was taken over by his university, Michigan State. Also, under his direction as general editor a new book series was eventually started, Violence, Mimesis, and Culture. Johnsen is also an advisory board member of Imitatio and its publications chair. He is professor of English at Michigan State, and is the author of *Violence and Modernism: Ibsen, Joyce, and Woolf* and numerous essays on modern and contemporary European writing and history. His energy, reflective approach to his work, and dependability have been a great boon to the Colloquium. We can see one sign of it in the cover design, careful editing, and quality of content under his direction in the issues of the journal.

At the Ottawa conference of COV&R in 2006 Martha Reineke was named as coordinator of COV&R meetings at the annual convention of the American Academy of Religion. I had handled this work of coordination when I was executive secretary from 1990 to 1998, and the executive secretary or president was responsible for it thereafter. It was a significant improvement to appoint a responsible person whose specific task would be to do that work. With Reineke's clear thinking, administrative ability, and connections in the AAR, the meetings have reached a new stage of quality.

Finally, it was a big boost to COV&R as a professional society when we received word during the summer of 2006 that our application for incorporation had been approved by the Internal Revenue Service. We now had the status of a not-for-profit organization, so that contributions would henceforth be tax deductible. We are grateful to Duncan Ragsdale and staff, and to our treasurer Julie Shinnick, for their work in seeing this through. We are indebted also to Robert Daly for his well-researched report on incorporation that led to the decision in 2004 to seek the tax-exempt status.

Semiannual Meeting, in Washington, DC

This meeting on November 18, 2006, was the first conference organized by Martha Reineke, the newly appointed COV&R coordinator with the American Academy of Religion. It featured conversations with the authors of two significant books: David Frankfurter and Willard Swartley.

Frankfurter, who is not a member of COV&R, spoke about his recent book, *Evil Incarnate: Rumors of Demonic Conspiracy and Ritual Abuse in History.* He did not refer to Girard or the mimetic theory in this work, which made it all the more intriguing for COV&R participants. Mark Juergensmeyer was the respondent. Willard Swartley commented on his recent work, *Covenant of Peace: The Missing Peace in New Testament Theology and Ethics*, with Michael Hardin responding. This is an important, wide-ranging book, which includes three chapters devoted to the work of Girard and Girardians.[118]

Perspective on the Years 1999–2006

As we look back over the eight-year period covered in this chapter we can see some recurring themes and highlights.

Tension between Theory and Practice

One theme that we find from the beginning of COV&R is a *tension between theory and practice*. For the most part, the Colloquium has been driven by passion for theoretical clarity. Girard himself has certainly been clear that this is his primary concern, and a survey of the conference programs will bear this out. However, questions and concerns about practice, application, and ethical implications have recurred through the years. The mimetic theory clearly has an ethical impulse; indeed, that is one of the main aspects of its attracting power. To repeat what I reported about Thee Smith's introductory remarks at the 1999 conference in Atlanta, do theorists of violence, such as most of the members of COV&R, have the imagination, vision, or fortitude for attempting to reduce violence, an effort that engages most practitioners? Should we not become "more publicly accountable concerning the consequences for practice of the theories of violence that we explore"? The Pastoral Ministry Seminars at Ghost Ranch in the summers of 2001, 2002, and 2003 were directed toward the implications of the mimetic theory for pastoral ministry. The statement that Tony Bartlett made at the Ghost Ranch symposium in 2004 about the need for a fresh theological impetus toward evangelism was informed by both theoretical and ethical concerns, and the emergence of Theology and Peace is an expression of those concerns. Walter Wink's comedic sketches at the 2006 meeting in Ottawa are also an expression of this impetus moving a significant number of COV&R participants. As I noted in *The Bulletin of COV&R*,

> Girard did not comment directly on the dramatic enactment. Instead, he emphasized that his work was a quest for truth, and that quest could not be drawn into specific stratagems and modes of behavior. Girard has pursued that quest now for more than fifty years, and he has done so with persistence and courage.
>
> Yet the quest for finding and knowing the truth cannot be simply separated from doing the truth. In the biblical sense of truth, it is something that is both known and done. "If we say we have communion (*koinonia*) with him while we walk in darkness, we are lying (*pseudometha*) and are not doing the truth (*ou poioumen ten aletheian*)" (1 John 1:6). Unveiling the truth

> is an awesome thing, but then so is doing it. And can we unveil it without doing it?"[119]

It should be noted, of course, that Girard's personal character and practice of holiness make his theoretical work even more appealing to those who know him, but the theory-practice tension remains as a consequence of his thought. His emphasis in his latest book, *Battling to the End*, on renunciation of mimetic desire, both the desire of the other's object of desire and the desire to be imitated, meshes well with his apocalyptic outlook and bespeaks a remote stance toward any kind of activism. Yet his personal spirituality and theoretical direction, significant as they are for those influenced by his thought, are not the only models for Girardians. Girardians are not compelled by their teacher to emulate him in all respects.

Dialogue among the Great Religious Traditions

A promising theme at the beginning of the decade was the perception that COV&R should facilitate *authentic dialogue among the great religious traditions.* "Dialogue" is a term that has been devalued by overuse. The perspective of leaders of COV&R on dialogue is well represented by Diana Culbertson. Speaking of the dialogue between Judaism and Christianity that was central to the 2002 conference at Purdue, Culbertson, who was then president, said, "The memory of this shared patrimony must draw these two children of Abraham into courageous and honest dialogue. This is not the dialogue of tolerance, which so often disguised condescension, but is the dialogue that seeks deeper understanding and the fundamental acceptance of another which transforms human relationships."[120]

The conference at Boston College in 2000 was at least indirectly influenced by the vision of comparative theology held by the Boston Theological Institute. To reiterate what was stated earlier in the chapter, "what is at stake in different traditions in terms of core beliefs, symbols, and rituals is the object of open discussion, analysis, and meditation. Its mission is not to evangelize or proselytize but to understand other traditions and gain deeper knowledge of one's own tradition." In the exchanges that took place at that meeting it became more evident to many of the participants that some of the basic convictions and concerns of Christianity and the mimetic theory were shared by the other religious traditions. The human need for transformation or conversion from the mimetic trap of scapegoating and violence to relations of spiritual connection and peace was one of these convictions, although there was a consensus that finding a way to communicate this in language that is not Western or ethnocentric is a tremendous challenge.[121]

A number interesting exchanges occurred between Girard, Alan Segal, Bruce Chilton, Gerard Rosse, and Michael Fishbane at the 2002 conference on "Judaism, Christianity, and the Ancient World: Mimesis, Sacrifice, and Culture." In this context I would like to mention my own work in the Hebrew Bible and the New Testament. In the appreciation of my work that Tony Bartlett presented, he described my concept of the relation of the Hebrew Scriptures to the New Testament as follows: "The Gospels represent a non-ambiguous disclosure of non-violent love while the Hebrew Scriptures are still engaged in a critical struggle between the old transcendence of violence and an emerging transcendence of love. Here at once is the core interpretative horizon . . . and its significance is not to be located in a pseudo-hierarchy between the Hebrew and Christian scriptures, but in the critical perspective of an organic, historical, self-radicalizing tradition, finding its radical anthropological term in the figure of Jesus."[122] Bartlett's characterization is well stated and exactly correct: my use of mimetic hermeneutics in interpreting the Bible is at the same time an affirmation of the validity of the mimetic theory and of the revelatory insights borne in that history of ancient Israel and early Christianity. It is thus an ecumenical act affirming the biblical origins of both Judaism and Christianity and denying that one is superior to the other. It is rather the interpretive description of a "self-radicalizing tradition," as Bartlett puts it, which reaches its deepest roots in the revelatory configuration (the church and the New Testament) whose center and influence emanate from Jesus of Nazareth.

In terms of understanding the changes in Jewish notions of sacrifice, I thought Michael Fishbane's presentation, "Transformations of Sacrifice," offered a basis for better understanding of both rabbinic Judaism and the emerging Christian concept of sacrifice. He noted that fasting (giving up one's body fat to God), study of Torah (the study of the sin offering for example, which itself becomes a sin offering), and the announcement of the New Year with the blast of the shofar (binding oneself to the altar) are instances of a new mode of sacrifice stemming from individual intentionality. The centrality of individual intentionality is found quite strikingly also in the Sermon on the Mount (Matthew 5–7), in which the subject's intention is directed to God through the neighbor (see also Matthew 25:31–46). But in the primordial Christian sense the "site" of sacrifice is not first of all the individual, but Christ, whose life, Passion, and Resurrection become the mediating reality of the individual's self-sacrifice. This site of sacrifice is further extended in the Church understood as the Body of Christ reaching out into the world. It seems to me that such comparative study enhances the kind of dialogue that informed the earlier symposium at Boston College in 2000.

Passions (or Desire) in the Economy and Communications

The theme of *passions (or desire) in the economy and communications* was the topic of the Innsbruck conference in 2005. It was not prominent or explicit in other meetings during this period, but it does overlap the themes of the 1997 meeting in Graz ("Film and Modernity") and the 1994 conference in Wiesbaden-Naurod ("Theology and/or Secular Thinking"). The latter conference highlighted economic theory and sociology in relation to theology.

In the Innsbruck symposium the most basic and all-encompassing question was raised by Józef Niewiadomski: have the communications media become a kind of substitute for the church, a new institution outside of which there is no salvation?[123] Desire now takes the form of a mimetic rivalry that knows no bounds as people become frenzied users of the Internet, proclaiming their autonomy as they act like gods (or satans) vis-à-vis one another. In the face of this cultural situation, the theologian must affirm that the Redeemer lives, he who entered into the world of the scapegoat mechanism, exposing it and calling all humanity to participate in the passion of the Trinity, which is beyond mimetic desire.

In that Innsbruck meeting Dupuy revisited his critique of the myth of the autonomously working market that he presented in 1994, and he noted Keynes's observation that to be a wise investor in stocks and all speculative aspects of the market it is necessary to anticipate crowd contagion and invest accordingly. In other words, the point is not to value stock at what one thinks it's worth but according to one's best prediction of mass behavior, which of course is mimetic to the core. Dupuy also remarked in discussion that victimization has changed in the modern world of the economy and mass communications. "In the case of sacrificial victims we are concerned with *mimetic victimage* and the *focus of attention* lies on the victim. In contrast, economic victimage means *third person victimage* . . . [T]he prevalent relationship towards them is *indifference*."

This condition of indifference to victims in world of human beings, who believe they are autonomous and yet contradictorily participate in a network of economic and communications mechanisms that they assume will work automatically for their benefit, is consonant with what Michael Haneke said about his filmmaking vocation at Graz: How can he enable viewers to perceive both the reality of their world, which is formed by indifferent consumption of interchangeable empty forms, and their own involvement in it, so that they may be able to free themselves from being victims of the media, which in Haneke's work is the cinema? The "problem is not: how do I show violence, but: how do I show the viewer his own position in relation to violence and its portrayal?"

How to Understand Mimetic Desire

One of the basic questions recurring through the years is that of *how to understand mimetic desire.* That is, is it fundamentally or essentially a destructive force? There is no doubt that it is a force in human existence. As Jean-Michel Oughourlian has indicated, it is a "force of attraction, interest, and attention."[124]

Can one make a case, starting from the basic insights of Girard's mimetic theory, that there is a "positive" mimesis, not just in the utilitarian sense of providing practical benefits connected with bringing about cohesiveness in social order, but also at a higher level as the key to true self-surrendering love and spiritual communion? I will not rehearse the ongoing discussion because the question has come up so many times in the course of this history. Allow me simply to refer the reader to the various relevant passages: in chapter 1, the definition of mimetic desire in "René Girard and the Mimetic Scapegoat Theory"; in chapter 3, the section on Rebecca Adams's paper, "Loving Mimesis and René Girard's 'Scapegoat of the Text,'" in "Mennonite Participation . . . René Girard and Biblical Peace Theology," and with references also to papers by Martha Reineke and Ann Astell; in this chapter, Józef Niewiadomski's concept of the divine passion of the Trinity, which is beyond desire, in the discussion of the Innsbruck conference, "Passions in Economy, Politics and the Media—in Discussion with Christian Theology" (there Roel Kaptein's position as stated during the 1992 conference is also mentioned); and finally, also in this chapter, the various approaches to positive mimesis articulated by Martha Reineke, Petra Steinmair-Pösel, and Pablo Bandera.

Robert Hamerton-Kelly challenges assumptions lying behind the affirmation of a good or positive mimesis, and Girard in his most recent book, *Battling to the End*, seems radically pessimistic about the function of positive mimesis in history. Both positions will be discussed at length in the next chapter.

COV&R as a Professional Society and a Community

A few important topics should be mentioned that have to do *with COV&R as a professional society and a community.* It could be that I have gone too far in calling the Colloquium a "community." Membership and participation in meetings does not offer the shared common life and daily or frequent interaction that would be characteristic of communities in the most basic sense. However, I think it is accurate to say that a majority of participants in the organization share common beliefs, intellectual concerns, and values and think of meetings as time of getting together with friends. That is a big part of the patrimony bequeathed by René Girard and Raymund Schwager, which I noted in chapter 2. Most of those who initially made commitments to COV&R as an ongoing academic-professional society looked to Girard and Schwager not only as mentors but also as friends. And in turn, most of those who came into COV&R after the earliest years became friends of the friends, who were significant models in mediating the personal reality of our two great intellectual and spiritual models.[125]

So the dimension of community, or friendship if one will, owes much not only to Schwager and Girard, but also to those who have held steady at the helm of leadership in COV&R. The seriousness and faithfulness of Cesáreo Bandera, president from 1995 to 1999; the friendly outreach of Sandor Goodhart as president; the firm good judgment of Wolfgang Palaver during the years he has worn many hats for COV&R; the persistence of Andrew McKenna in keeping *Contagion* afloat through some difficult years when he carried a heavy load at his own university; the dependability and friendliness of Julie Shinnick who served as treasurer for so many years; the commitment of Józef Niewiadomski to carrying on the legacy of Raymund Schwager as he succeeded his mentor as dean of the theological faculty at Innsbruck—these and many others embody the mind or spirit of the organization that we call the Colloquium on Violence and Religion.

In this period we also saw the emergence of new leaders, such as Ann Astell, William Johnsen, and Martha Reineke. But their influence was to become apparent in the ensuing years after 2006, so an appreciation of their contribution will be given in the next chapter.

Three other events from this period of time should be mentioned as highly significant for the existence of COV&R as a kind of community. One was the death of Raymund Schwager. Not only did it come as a shock because he was not extremely old and appeared to be in good health; his passing and the age of Girard, who at that time was eighty years old, confronted us with the need to begin thinking about a time when our primary intellectual and spiritual models would no longer be with us. What responsibility does this reality lay upon us if COV&R and the various aspects of work stemming from the mimetic theory are to extend their influence into the future?

The second event was the election of Girard to the French Academy in 2005. That is the highest honor for a French intellectual. It also reflects the awareness of the academy that his work has had a tremendous impact in other parts of the world, particularly in certain European countries. In the United States and Canada his reputation has not reached that status, although it is definitely growing. Now with the research enterprises inspired by his thought, especially those under the umbrella of Imitatio, his work is at the point of blossoming in this country. This is all to the benefit of the mission of COV&R.

Finally, the incorporation of COV&R has opened up new opportunities for funding. This was a special accomplishment, brought about through the work behind the scenes and before the advisory board (now "board of directors") by Duncan Ragsdale, Julie Shinnick, and Robert Daly. It is also a reminder to me, the writer and sometime historian, that in all of life there is always so much going on "behind the scenes" and "below the surface" that is necessary for the existence of any entity and that seldom comes to our awareness. I am aware that I have probably left out any number of events and the contributions of committed people working out of the spotlight and behind the scene. *Mea culpa* for those things and persons I should have made known but did not, or did know but have forgotten.

Two Other Topics of Importance

One more comment pertaining to this chapter. In looking back over this eight-year period, I think of two topics that have been treated in COV&R meetings, but they don't form consistent themes. Nonetheless, they are extremely important. One is the role of the mimetic theory in understanding the apocalyptic tendencies of the Western world. This may be a task above all for our philosophers, although it must almost certainly depart from traditional philosophy. (Greater input from the side of biblical theology is also a desideratum.) Perhaps it must take the form of a kind of sociological philosophy. We have already certain precedents set by the work of Jean-Pierre Dupuy and Paul Dumouchel, and a number of others appear to be inclined in this direction, for example, Jeremiah Alberg, Charles Bellinger, Joachim Duyndam, Stephen Gardner, Per Bjørnar Grande, Giuseppe Fornari, John Ranieri, Martha Reineke, Maria Stella Barberi, and perhaps many others. After all, the father of modern sociology, Emile Durkheim, was a kind of philosopher who sought to understand and explicate not only the origins of social order and institutions, but also the beginnings of human knowledge, as one can clearly see in his introduction to *The Elementary Forms of Religious Life*—knowledge that is rooted in social life and consciousness. Now we are facing the *end* of traditional social forms and knowledge as the West is turning in on itself in frenzies of mimetic rivalry reaching the extremes of self-destruction. Philosophers must now join together with theologians and scientists across the spectrum of human knowledge to help us understand the events playing out the consequences of apocalyptic and perhaps to help us, *Deo volente*, to find new paths of meaning into the future.[126]

I would like to resort to Durkheim again in bringing up the subject of nature and technology, to which COV&R should devote more attention. Dupuy and Dumouchel have provoked us with their thesis that "nature" is more and more being absorbed into nanotechnology. There is undoubtedly a partial truth in what they contend. Yet the fact is that we—and most scientists and philosophers involved in the subject—continue to find the concept of nature meaningful. Is it really the case that we will lose the concept of a reality which environs us and in which we humans participate but do not invent? That seems doubtful in my view. Durkheim is again relevant to this question. He states toward the end of the introduction to *Elementary Forms* that "the ideas of time, space, class, cause or personality are constructed out of social elements," and "their social origin . . . leads to the belief that they are not without foundation in the nature of things."[127] This belief will take on new forms as social life undergoes mutations. But can we do without a concept of the "nature of things," which must mean in a fundamental sense a concept of "nature"?[128] In any case, whatever the theoretical controversies may be, can philosophy and social science aid us in understanding this apocalyptic process, and perhaps contribute to the new world that is being born?

Brief Biographies of COV&R Leaders

Diana Culbertson

Diana Culbertson, O.P. (Ordo Praedicatorum—Order of Preachers), is professor emeritus at Kent State University. She received her Ph.D., in comparative literature from the University of North Carolina at Chapel Hill, and a M.A. in theology from Aquinas Institute in St. Louis, Missouri. She is the author of *The Poetics of Revelation: Recognition and the Narrative Tradition* (1989) and the editor of *Invisible Light: Poems about God* (2000) and *Rose Hawthorne Lathrop:*

Selected Writings (1993). Her articles have appeared in numerous journals. She has lectured and published extensively and is currently an editor and writer at the Center for Learning in Villa Maria, Pennsylvania. Her published works at the Center include a booklet, *God in a World of Violence*, which is widely used in small adult study groups. She recently served as the vicaress (vice president) of the Sisters of St. Dominic of Akron, Ohio. She is at present a member of the Dominican Sisters of Peace, founded in 2009 as a union of seven religious congregations.

She was one of our most faithful and hardworking members from the beginning of COV&R, until early in this century, when she began to devote much of her time to the religious office she held. From 1990 to 2002 she served on the advisory board of the Colloquium, then as executive secretary and president. She continues to speak on the mimetic theory to various Catholic organizations and groups. She has always impressed her COV&R colleagues with her scholarly work in literature and religion, willingness to serve, and good humor.

Robert Daly

Robert J. Daly, S.J. (Society of Jesus), is professor emeritus in theology, Boston College. He earned masters degrees in philosophy and English literature at Boston College and the Catholic University of America. Thereafter he earned his licentiate in theology at Boston College before moving to Italy for spiritual and pastoral work, and then on to Germany where he was granted a doctor of theology degree from the Julius Maximilians Universität Würzburg in 1972.

The onetime chairperson of the Department of Theology of Boston College, he has served on many university and organizational committees. In the Colloquium on Violence and Religion he has been an advisory board member and was the organizer of the 2000 conference at Boston College. He is the author, editor, or translator of some fifteen scholarly books, several dozen scholarly articles, and a number of smaller pieces of a more pastoral nature. His writings initially focused on the area of the early development of doctrine, on patristics, and on biblical theology and biblical ethics. He wrote a classical work on Jewish and Christian sacrifice: *Christian Sacrifice: The Judeo-Christian Background before Origen* (1978). In recent years his research and writing have turned more to liturgical worship and related subjects, as can be seen in his editing of the posthumous work of Edward J. Kilmartin, S.J., *The Eucharist in the West: History and Theology* (1999), as well as various other articles. Even more recently he published *Sacrifice Unveiled: The True Meaning of Christian Sacrifice* (2009).

Daly has been a loyal colleague in COV&R who has provided important theological verification of mimetic theory, especially with regard to liturgy and sacrifice. He has been always willing to serve in a number of ways, both great and small.

Józef Niewiadomski

Józef Niewiadomski is a native of Poland, where he studied theology and philosophy at the Catholic University of Lublin. He continued his studies in the Theology Faculty of the University of Innsbruck and was ordained a priest. From 1977 he worked as an assistant to Raymund Schwager, who joined the faculty in that year. He was initially very critical of the mimetic theory and Schwager's appropriation of it. However, Schwager won him over not through discussion and debate, but by his spiritual integrity, which included openness to questions and criticism. From 1991 to 1996 Niewiadomski taught at the university in Linz, Austria. Returning to Innsbruck in 1996, he has since worked there as professor of dogmatic theology and succeeded his mentor Schwager as dean of the theological faculty in 2004. He has written many articles and reviews and is the author of *Faszinierendes Geheimnis* (Fascinating Mystery) (with M. Scharer) and *Herbergsuche: Auf dem Weg zu einer christlichen Identität in der modernen Kultur* (Seeking Shelter: Toward a Christian Identity in Modern Culture).

Niewiadomski's contribution to COV&R has been substantial. With Wolfgang Palaver he was coeditor of *The Bulletin of COV&R* from 1993 to 1998 and sat on the advisory board from 1999 to 2004. Above all, in his office as dean he has reaffirmed and continued Schwager's commitment to the central role of COV&R and the mimetic theory in the theology faculty of Innsbruck. This support, along with his theological acumen, spirituality, and friendly wit, is much appreciated by his COV&R colleagues.

Theophus Smith

Theophus "Thee" Smith obtained his Ph.D. from Graduate Theological Union in 1987. His dissertation was titled "The Biblical Shape of Black Experience." He is the author of *Conjuring Culture: Biblical Formations of Black America,* for which he received a Book Award for Excellence from the American Academy of Religion in 1994. He is also the coeditor, with Mark Wallace, of *Curing Violence*, an anthology of essays on religion and the mimetic theory. This book had its genesis in the Bible, Narrative, and American Culture seminar

(BINAC) of the Westar Institute. He is an associate professor of religion at Emory University, where he has taught since 1987. An Episcopal priest, he works also as a consultant in conflict resolution and workshop facilitation.

Thee Smith was a member of BINAC and he strongly supported the formation of COV&R. Greatly involved in the work of the Colloquium during the 1990s, he served on its advisory board for six years and was the organizer of COV&R's annual conference at Emory University in 1999. He was an important colleague not only for his official contributions, but also especially for his expertise in group dynamics and his authentic spirituality.

CHAPTER FIVE

New Outreach and Possibilities, 2007–2010

To Amsterdam and Beyond, 2007

The events and activities of COV&R and COV&R people in 2007 vividly reflect the title of this chapter. The annual conference in Amsterdam, certainly one of the most important and remarkable cities of the world, must be placed at the center of this year's history, but there were other consequential occurrences as well.

Lonergan-Dramatic Theology Workshop in Innsbruck

Organized by Roman Siebenrock and Nikolaus Wandinger, a workshop bringing together the Dramatic Theology group in the Research Focus Religion—Violence—Communication—World Order platform with other theologians was held January 8–10, 2007, in the facilities of the Theology Faculty. The participants "discussed methodological questions in theology and philosophy, theology in a political mode, and questions of Trinitarian theology."[1] The discussants kept in mind pressing problems of the relationship of religion and violence. In some respects this event was a follow-up to the Lonergan-Girard part of the program at Boston College in 2000 and the Girard-Lonergan panel at the 2006 conference in Ottawa.

Theology and Peace

A new organization, a kind of offspring of COV&R, saw the light of day in January 2007. I have already referred to the discontent of Anthony Bartlett with COV&R's theoretical and theological orientation (see chapter 4). He and some others have felt the impact of Girard's thought but wanted a commitment more experientially and praxis-oriented to the New Testament roots of Christianity. In the summer of 2006 Bartlett and Tom Nicoll conceived the idea for a new group made up of participants who were convinced of the pressing need and committed to thinking and working out the consequences of the Christian faith in North America. Michael Hardin, director of Preaching Peace, became involved in this project as organizer and person in charge of publicity.[2]

A selected group was invited for a theological conversation under the name of Theologia Pacis. The name was subsequently changed to Theology and Peace. It first met in Akron, Pennsylvania, on January 9 and 10, 2007. There were over twenty present, with the notable participation of the peace churches, especially the Mennonites. A board was appointed, and annual conferences began in 2008. Its primary purpose is expressed in its self-description on its website: "An energizing movement seeking the transformation of theological practice through the application of mimetic theory."[3]

Elizabeth Bailie in Memoriam

Along with the death of other prominent members through the years (Roel Kaptein, William Mishler, and Raymund Schwager), the passing of Elizabeth Bailie was an occasion of great sadness for those who knew her. Elizabeth, wife of Gil Bailie, died on February 18, 2007. Gil, a friend of many of us from the beginnings of COV&R, found through her love and spirituality a companion who graced and inspired his life and work. As Martha and René Girard expressed it in their remembrance, "We were inspired by her spirituality, warmed by her friendship and awed by her courage. Her voice, stilled too soon, lives on in her poems and in our hearts, and for that we are grateful."[4]

Templeton Advanced Research Program at Stanford

An exciting new research project was launched at Stanford University on April 28–29, 2007. Sponsored by the John Templeton Foundation, the Metanexus Institute, and the Travis Research Institute of the Fuller Graduate School of

Psychology, this was a two-year research project bringing together scholars in social science, religion, and philosophy. The principal investigator was Scott Garrels, a member of COV&R who is on the faculty of the Fuller Graduate School of Psychology. The object was to deepen dialogue and achieve greater integration between mimetic theory and empirical research on imitation. The three groundbreaking areas that were introduced and discussed were mimetic theory, led by René Girard; imitation theory, led by Andrew Meltzoff; and mirror neuron investigations, led by Vittorio Gallese. COV&R colleagues attending the meeting, in addition to Girard and Garrels, were Jean-Pierre Dupuy, Paul Dumouchel, Mark Anspach, Robert Hamerton-Kelly, Jean-Michel Oughourlian, and Trevor Merrill.[5]

This research project was one of the important developments that led to the formation of Imitatio, which was formally established at Stanford in April 2008.

The Annual Conference in Amsterdam and Soesterberg

The annual conference in the Netherlands was a noteworthy event because of its setting in one of the world's most interesting cities and metropolitan areas, the social and political turmoil that formed part of the backdrop of the symposium, and the group that brought it about, the Dutch Girard Society.

The Dutch Girard Society

An exceptional circle of people in Holland planned and organized the 2007 conference. The Girard Circle, as it was then called, dates back to 1981. Roel Kaptein suggested to Father André Lascaris and others that they start a study group to discuss the work of Girard. Sandor Varga, who was on the faculty of the Free University of Amsterdam, also played a key role in the beginning of the group. Kaptein and Lascaris were both involved in peacemaking work in Northern Ireland. Participants began meeting in Utrecht and Amsterdam, and later the group was hosted by Seth Boonstra, then the university chaplain at the Free University of Amsterdam. Among the early members of the group were also Matthew Schoffeleers, Aat van Rhijn, Martin Hiebrink, Martijn Leopold, Ernst Stern, Nico Keijzer, Simon Simonse, Hubert Darthenay, Hans Weigand, and Michael Elias. Elias was the convener for a number of years (1994–2004), managed their website (2004–2009), and is the chairperson at this writing. Thérèse Onderdenwijngaard is the current convener and secretary. Berry Vorstenbosch has taken over as overseer of the website, and serves in that capacity as a second secretary. Sonja Pos has also been a participant, although her health in recent years has prevented frequent attendance. Thanks to a grant from Imitatio, the group was officially registered in October 2009 as the "Stichtung Girard Studiekring" (Foundation Girard Study Circle), according to Dutch law on charitable and nongovernmental organizations. However, since in English the usage of the word "foundation" for organizations implies an entity that finances projects and awards grants for education or charitable purposes, "Dutch Girard Society" is probably the best name in English. Other officers, in addition to those mentioned above, are Simon Simonse as vice chairman and Hans Weigand as treasurer.

There are usually fifteen to eighteen persons who attend. They meet about five times a year at the Free University of Amsterdam. The university provides a room and the service of mailings to members. The gatherings are always on Friday from 10:00 A.M. to 12:30 P.M. Either the chairperson or someone who has prepared a presentation starts off the session with introductory comments, and then the rest of the group speaks freely in a wide-ranging discussion. Sometimes they have an assignment to read certain chapters in Girard's books; sometimes they read and discuss other Girardian materials. Occasionally they have a guest speaker who starts off the session. Now and then they focus on crucial current events, for example, the 2002 murder of a gay politician and sociology professor, Pim Fortuyn, by an animal rights activist, and the slaying in 2004 of Theo van Gogh, a publicist and filmmaker, by a Muslim fundamentalist. Both murder victims pushed the boundaries of traditional Dutch tolerance—Fortuyn, by expressing uneasiness about immigrant minorities, and van Gogh, by what he said about Muslims and Jews. Each person in the group wrote his or her reflections on the killings and the social and political dismay that ensued, and these reflections became the basis for discussion when they met.

It is remarkable that the group, which currently has only about forty people on its mailing list, has held together all these years. Those who attend come from all over Holland, so the dedication to meeting for learning and fellowship is strong. When I asked a number of them what held the Circle together for so many years, their unanimous response was that the discussions were very interdisciplinary, in keeping of course with being followers of Girard and the mimetic theory. The meetings are casual and relaxed, and persons of widely varying backgrounds feel free to enter into the conversations.

One of the Society's proud moments occurred when Girard was given an honorary doctorate, his first, by the Free University in 1985. It is unclear whether the Society directly brought that about, as a university professor not in the group made the actual nomination. However, it is likely that the group had some influence, directly or indirectly. Girard met with the Society and talked to them at length while he was in the city for the academic ceremony.

Many members of the Dutch Girard Society have been active in research and writing about the mimetic theory, as well as actively participating in COV&R. Of these members, Simon Simonse, André Lascaris, and the late Roel Kaptein published books that have been reviewed in the Colloquium's *Bulletin*.[6]

The idea for a COV&R conference in the Netherlands began with Simon Simonse and André Lascaris as they were conversing at the 2005 conference in Koblenz. Their colleagues in the Dutch Girard Society took up the idea and were the ones primarily responsible for organizing it. Following up on an essay by the Dutch novelist Margriet de Moor, who discussed the idea of the Netherlands as a potential laboratory of tolerance, the steering committee for the conference came up with "Vulnerability and Tolerance" as the conference theme. The initial concept was more about vulnerability in social and political life, but during the actual symposium the emphasis in papers and discussion shifted to tolerance.

The Society worked in cooperation with the Dominican Study Centre for Theology and Society and l'Association pour les Recherches Mimétiques. The institutional hosts were the Blaise Pascal Institute of the Free University of Amsterdam, IKV (Interkerkelijk Vredesberaad [Inter-Church Peace Consultation]), and Pax Christi. The members of the steering committee were Mark Anspach, Gied ten Berge, Wiel Eggen, Michael Elias, André Lascaris, Thérèse Onderdenwijngaard, Edwin Ruigrok, Simon Simonse, Laura Stoorvogel, Jan Weenink, and Hans Weigand.

"Vulnerability and Tolerance," July 4–8, 2007

The keynote address was given by Ian Buruma, himself a native of the Netherlands. A member of the faculty of Bard College in the state of New York, Buruma is well known as an author and essayist. Two of his recent books were directly relevant regarding the conference: *Murder in Amsterdam* and *Occidentalism,* the latter coauthored with Avishai Margalit. His paper was very engaging because he not only addressed the current social and political crisis but also recognized patterns of imitation and resentment, although these were not processed through the mimetic theory. If he had been familiar with mimetic theory, he might have raised a question about tolerance as a virtue. But those present could certainly agree with his conclusion: "The only thing that all citizens should be bound by is the renunciation of violence, in political, religious, or social conflicts."[7] The only question is whether the renunciation of violence goes far enough.

Wolfgang Palaver responded to Buruma's presentation and did his usual good job of clarifying major points for COV&R colleagues within the framework of the mimetic theory. Palaver, who expressed general agreement with Buruma, explicated three theses. (1) It is mimetic rivalry, not religion as such, that leads toward violence. He acknowledged with appreciation that Buruma, as well as Margalit, his coauthor of *Occidentalism,* shows great insight in indicating the role that mimicry and resentment play in Islamist fundamentalism. And he does not overlook that dogmatic secularist reactions to this fundamentalism can easily fall into the same extremist trap (Marxism, Maoism, Third World liberationism, multiculturalism, etc.). (2) Human beings are religious beings; they are both homo mimeticus and homo religiosus. As Girard has pointed out, and as Buruma acknowledges in his own language, we imitate what we adore, and secularists are certainly not immune to this, even if they are not "religious" in a traditional sense. (3) Concerning religion and the Enlightenment, it has been the "Abrahamic overcoming of the scapegoat mechanism [that] embodies the true spirit of the Enlightenment." However we evaluate Voltaire, for example, he was an authentic representative of that phenomenon when he sided with the Protestant Calas against his Catholic executioners, who falsely accused him of murdering his own son. "Enlightenment means to side with the victim of collective persecution." Palaver concludes that Buruma himself represents the true spirit of the Enlightenment, as instantiated in his comment about Ayaan Hirsi Ali. He strongly disagrees with her rather rigidly doctrinaire embrace of the Enlightenment heritage, but despite this "he protests against the fact that she was forced to leave the Netherlands. The last sentences of his postscript to his book *Murder in Amsterdam* show his siding with the victim: 'Theo van Gogh is dead. Mohammad Bouyeri is locked up in prison alone with the words of his holy books. And Ayan Hirsi Ali has had to leave the scene. My country seems smaller without her.'"[8]

One of the presenters, Joel Hodge, addressed the conference theme within a framework of a political theology rooted in an understanding of the Eucharist, and in so doing he touched on the ideas and concerns of several other speakers. Drawing upon Girard, Charles Taylor, and William Cavanaugh, Hodge questioned common notions about the modern democratic state, which is based on the convictions and scapegoating tendencies of secularism. The secular state is based essentially on a negation of religion, particularly Christianity and the Catholic Church. Its primary scapegoat is the Church, which it sees as virulently intolerant (against women, homosexuals, Jews, heretics, indigenous people, other religions). The state seeks to inculcate tolerance—the basis of politic correctness—by isolating the individual. The dependency of the individual "on the state legitimates the conflicting mimetic desires of citizens, which the state uses to construct a system of exchange held together by transcendent nationalistic fervour that supports its own power."[9] One of the most important characteristics of the modern nation-state's secular character is the taboo against intolerance. "Tolerance is a distortion of the virtue of justice" and it "is the minimal requirement to control one's own desires and lifestyle."[10] Tolerance does not seek the good and the just but the avoidance of violence. It is an attempt to mediate between envy and rivalry.

This understanding of tolerance and intolerance is a partial response to a position like Buruma's, who accepted the idea of tolerance as based on renunciation of religious, social, and political persecution. One can agree with Buruma on renunciation of persecution. However, he doesn't seem to discern the invidious condition of envy and resentment that the state promises to mediate with the imposition of tolerance. The state, whose ultimate sanctions are exclusion and death, thus imposes violence as the arbiter of human life; its implicit claim is to be the savior, saving and protecting its citizens from conflict and violence. It may be liberal, a democratic republic, but its sanctions are violent, for it may declare war when its serves its interests, legalize the killing of unborn children, allow capital punishment, practice secret surveillance if it is seen to be in national security interests, and in general encourage scapegoating in some form or the other for politically incorrect speech. It is implicitly, and sometimes openly, the enemy of most forms of Christianity, which hold that God is the final arbiter of human relations and human destiny.

Henri Beunders agreed with Buruma that since the 1960s a spoiled, materialistic, individualistic "Bohemian" elite had dominated Dutch culture and politics, and these same people harshly criticized the public when symptoms of dissatisfaction and grumbling about cultural changes that affected so many aspects of national life began to erupt. However, he states, "Many people were just longing for new boundaries and were demanding clear answers from the government to the questions and problem that they had to deal with every day."[11] Tolerance does not suffice. One could say, as Hodge implies, that the people of the Netherlands needed to sense a true commitment to justice from their leaders, and however justice is defined it would have to include respect and responsibility for one's fellow citizens as neighbors.[12]

Justice is not tolerance; it is responsibility for and before the Other. As Joachim Duyndam pointed out in his challenging paper on Girard and Levinas, both thinkers articulate the biblical demand to recognize that humans are chosen for responsibility for the other within a network of interrelations. In the account of the women taken in adultery (John 7:53–8:11), Girard's brilliant interpretation of the passage elucidates that "Each accuser holding a stone in his or her hand is holding the first stone. This makes each 'the only one,' unique. . . . All of a sudden you are called to account for your responsibility," and thus "you are singled out."[13] Jesus himself withdraws from the crowd, the hordes (Heidegger's *Mitsein*), and refuses to participate in the mimetic trap his opponents were laying for him. He stands in for the adulterous woman, who is indeed guilty of adultery—but he offers her forgiveness and new life rather than acquiescing in her condemnation and death. Here there is no conflict between mercy and justice, for Jesus' gracious act of defending her and not joining the persecutors is simultaneously an act of justice. For as the psalmist puts it in proclaiming God's will to save God's people: "Love and truth will meet; justice and peace will kiss" (Psalms 85:11).

To return to Hodge's presentation, he proposes a Eucharistic political theology as an alternative to the modern democratic republics that conceal their violence and scapegoating under a doctrine of tolerance in the national governing entity that provides security and offers prosperity. With Girard's thought always in the background and drawing explicitly on William Cavanaugh's political theology and ecclesiology, he illustrates a way of life rooted in imitating Christ and living out the reality of the Body of Christ by telling the stories of Timorese martyrs who have acted nonviolently in witnessing to the Christian revelation.[14] The final paragraph of his paper is worthy of quoting in full:

> In this paper, I have attempted to show that secularism is intimately tied to the rise of the nation-state. The State bases its power and influence on dividing and isolating its citizens, especially in limiting their faith, and allowing them to individually determine their desires within certain limits. The State guarantees its own order based on an exclusive nationalism. The illusion that the secular nation-state gives a free space for people to determine their own selves is exposed when the State becomes increasingly violent and dictatorial. In these circumstances, the Church's unique nature as a Body founded on the victim Christ becomes a stark contrast and challenge to the State. The Church's Eucharistic witness awakens and fulfils the mimetic nature of the human being who seeks relationship with God and stands alongside those victimised and oppressed by the State.[15]

In apparent opposition to any truth claims about the Eucharist or to the belief that Christian witness is a remedial response to cultural conflict and decline, Erik Borgman issued a plea for the affirmation of truth and value in other religions and criticized Girard for his putative claim for the absolute truth of Christianity. The title of his paper, "The Weak Presence of Grace: A Theological Plea for the Return to the Ambivalences of Modernity," reflects his borrowing of Vattimo's "weak ontology" and his own view that a Christian theology should humbly relativize all truth claims. He argued that "Christianity is not a theory claiming to be absolutely true nor a culture propagating unflawed values."[16] Borgman's voice is one that should be taken seriously. However, questions about the accuracy of his position may be raised. In a set of comments published on the postconference website, Simon de Keukelaere refuted Borgman brilliantly: "Modesty has settled upon the organ of conviction."[17] The title of his reflections comes from a sentence in G. K. Chesterton's book, *Orthodoxy,* published in 1909. He quotes two sentences that give Chesterton's thought in full: "Modesty has settled upon the organ of conviction, where it was never meant to be. A man was meant to be doubtful about himself, but undoubting about the truth; this has been exactly reversed." Girard does not make a claim that Christianity as a historical tradition is unflawed and that all other religious traditions are devoid of truth. What is essential is its origin in the biblical revelation that was given anthropologically, through human desire and human relations in various circumstances. The central, founding event for the Christian tradition is the self-surrender of Christ, his "rendering up" (from middle French *surrendre*) of himself to the violent scapegoat mechanism so that the love and power of God the Father would be revealed. Christ is the model/mediator of the Christian's life and relations. That means we should doubt ourselves, our doctrines and narrow perspectives, but not the conviction that God has come among us. The truth is there, but the love of God is the reality that is primary, not any claim to absolute truth that any human being completely understands and controls. This is the authentic Christian conviction, that Christ the convict (Gil Bailie), the "convicted one," is worthy of our trust and belief.[18]

Gil Bailie summed up the whole point about the Christian tradition in a question at the heart of a postconference letter that was sent to a Dutch newspaper: *How to honor the historic commitment to cultural openness and generosity without eviscerating the religious and moral sources of that very generosity?* It is ironic and instructive that this key sentence was omitted by the newspaper that published the letter.[19]

Finally, a few words should be said about the work of the steering committee and all who helped in the organization of the conference. By all accounts, the organization was excellent. Quentin Delval reported that the method of organizing parallel sessions was particularly good. "Small sessions were often more intense than plenary sessions to me, and dialogue way easier with the speaker."[20] Moreover, this writer will attest to the quality of the Dutch Society's record-keeping. Thanks to the work of Michael Elias, all of the abstracts and most of the papers have been made and kept available online, both on the COV&R website and the Dutch Society website.[21] This is a great boon not only to anyone interested in specific papers but obviously also to future historians.

Semiannual Meeting, with AAR/SBL in San Diego

The 2007 meeting of COV&R in conjunction with the American Academy of Religion and the Society of Biblical Literature took place November 17, 2007. Not many attended. This was a chronic problem due to our lack of status with the organizations. Since we were not a "Related Scholarly Organization," our programs were not listed in the regular program schedule. However, Martha Reineke was at work to change this, and our status changed by 2009, as reported in the previous chapter. Reineke urged those few who came to drink lots of coffee, for which we paid $70 a gallon.

Nikolaus Wandinger read a paper on "'Sacrifice' in Harry Potter from a Girardian Perspective." Some of those present wondered whether the Harry Potter series was worthy of such treatment or whether it was appropriate to bring into play a grand theory like Girard's to interpret such works. Wandinger himself evidently thought it merited consideration for the sake of understanding popular culture. A number of questions were raised according to Britton Johnston's report, including whether "J.K. Rowling manage[s] to transcend primitive sacrifice and achieve something genuinely transcendent, or does Harry's fate in the final volume fall short of such redemption?"[22]

Michael Hardin and Brad Jersak led the second part of the program on the recently published anthology they edited, *Stricken by God? Nonviolent Identification and the Victory of Christ*. Seven of the contributors attended the meeting. The title of the volume gives a good sense of the content. Representing a wide range of denominations in the Christian tradition, the contributors are united in their opposition to the atonement doctrine of penal substitution.[23]

To Riverside and Beyond (2008)

2008 was a year when new developments in the work of COV&R and its members began to multiply. In fact, it seems that all of a sudden so much was happening that I wonder whether I can give even a sketch of it all. But in a deeper sense it was not "all of a sudden"; the events in which COV&R and the mimetic theory were caught up grew out of seeds of thought and work planted long before. Yet like the poppies in their riot of color appearing on the Southern California hillsides in spring, the manifestations of engagement with the mimetic theory seemed to be popping up all over.

Mimetic Theory and Neuroscience at UCLA

This conference took place at the University of California at Los Angeles on January 15–16, 2008. It was sponsored by the Center for the Study of Religion at UCLA. Britt Johnston's report in the Bulletin describes the content discussed as "stimulating—even thrilling."[24] Scott Garrels made a presentation that included an outline of points of convergence between mimetic theory and mirror neurology. "Mirror neurons" are nerve cells in the brains of humans and some higher primates that become activated not only when the individual performs certain goal-directed actions, but also when they see another individual perform that action. They are the neurological basis of imitation. The structure of the ensuing conversation emerged from his paper: an opposition "between the neuroscientists' ignorance of the social implications of imitation, and the mimetic theorists' ignorance of neuropsychology," and an opposition "between the neuroscientists' desire to embrace mimetic theory as empirical science and Girard's impulse to use the discoveries in neuroscience as rhetorical support for his theory."[25] Other contributions included Antonio Damasio on the work of mirror neurons, Marco Jacoboni on the social implications of mimesis, and Jean-Pierre Dupuy on the scientific validity of the mimetic theory, independently of whether it is empirically supported by neuroscience.

Imitatio

Imitatio is an incorporated organization started by Robert Hamerton-Kelly, René Girard, and Peter Thiel for the purpose of extending the mimetic theory in the various fields of the humanities, the social sciences, and the natural sciences. Its work is supported by the philanthropic arm of Thiel's enterprises.[26] The initial meeting took place Friday, October 26, 2007. This was the founding meeting of Imitatio, which was held in the Salle de Regence in the Four Seasons George V hotel in Paris. At that time the group gathered chose the name, Imitatio, Inc., appointed five fellows who would be granted stipends for their work, and outlined the organizational structure. Hamerton-Kelly convened a gathering at Stanford University April 28–29, 2008, that brought together forty people, who formed a core group that he called the "founding forty." The Stanford meeting involved restating and discussing the purpose of the organization and assigning the work to be done.

The honorary chair of Imitatio is René Girard. Robert Hamerton-Kelly served initially as the chairman. The editor is Andrew McKenna and the platform representative is Wolfgang Palaver.[27] Peter Thiel is the benefactor as well as a participant. Committees were appointed for the three areas of work that Imitatio would undertake: research, publications, and education. Jean-Pierre Dupuy was named head of the Research Committee. Its immediate agenda included continuing the collaboration on mimetic theory and the neuro- and developmental sciences, and sponsoring additional conferences on war and terrorism and evolution and the mimetic theory's interpretation of religion. Publications, headed by William Johnsen, the series editor of Violence, Mimesis, and Culture (Michigan State University Press), would see to publication of the English translation of Girard's most recent book, *Achever Clausewitz* (Finishing [Off] Clausewitz), and would consider translation of books from Italian and Spanish, including a volume authored by Giuseppe Fornari, one of the Imitatio fellows. Education, led by James Alison, another Imitatio fellow, would put its emphasis on collaboration with other organizations already doing work within the range of Imitatio's goals and concerns: supporting the conferences of COV&R, cooperating with Suzanne and Keith Ross of the Raven Foundation in their educational projects, collaborating with the Dutch Girard Society in planning summer schools and providing teaching materials for faculty, and working with the Association de Recherches Mimetiques in Paris. Also, Alison would plan a pilot project in Brazil as a model of "embassies" for mimetic study. Longtime COV&R members who participated in the Stanford meeting, in addition to René Girard and Robert Hamerton-Kelly, were James Alison, Ann Astell, Jean-Pierre Dupuy, Giuseppe Fornari, Sandor Goodhart, William Johnsen, Andrew McKenna, Martha Reineke, and James Williams.[28]

For those of us who have been part of COV&R from its early years the founding of Imitatio has affected us in two regards. On the one hand, it is the realization of a dream to have the financial resources that Imitatio has in its budget due to the philanthropic generosity of Peter Thiel. Of course, the money and the research programs of Imitatio are not under the aegis of COV&R, but Imitatio has provided aid to COV&R and COV&R members, and there is obviously mutual recognition of the relationship of the two organizations. On the other hand, many COV&R colleagues were concerned that COV&R and some of its individual members would become too caught up in seeking financial support and recognition through Imitatio, to the detriment of its own statement of mission, which is a free, unencumbered investigation of the relationship between violence and religion in the genesis and maintenance of culture in light of the mimetic theory. Anything that distracts us from focusing on "the relevance of the mimetic model for the study of religion," as stated in the COV&R object on the masthead of the *Bulletin*, would cause us to deviate from this mission. But to this point no problem has materialized, and the leadership of COV&R had stood firm in its integrity.

Workshop in Florence

A workshop at an old estate of Lorenzo de Medici, "the Magnificent," was held April 10–13, 2008. The subject was "Analyzing Cases of Mimetic Violence." It was a sacrificial setting amid the hunting trophies and reminders of the Medici family, which ironically had become a Pax Christi Peace House. The Dutch Girard Society sponsored the event, which was conceived as a follow-up to the 2007 COV&R conference in Amsterdam.

With a smaller gathering of ten participants and plenty of time to discuss the presentations, the participants departed at the end with a renewed sense of the power of the mimetic theory to understand ethnic conflict and warfare. Here is a list of presenters and topics:

Simon Simonse: Described the role of Pax Christi in the attempts to negotiate between the Ugandan government and the Lord's Resistance Army and pointed out the mimetic rivalry in this African political setting.

Peter Zvagulis: Summarized his study of ethnic rivalry in Latvia between local groups and the large Russian community.

Thérèse Onderdenwijngaard: Commented on the Sri Lanka impasse with the Tamil Tigers, focusing on a human rights activist who was murdered, probably because she broke with the Tigers.

Wiel Eggen: Highlighted the tripolar rivalry of Islam, secularism, and Christianity in Holland and mentioned the case of Ayaan Hirsi Ali, who left the Socialist Party because it did not condemn Muslim treatment of women and who was subsequently scapegoated to the point that she fled the country.

Hans Weigand: Presented his investigation of the appropriateness of a complex systems methodology to mimetic studies and applied it to the Rawandan genocide.

Mark Anspach: Presented an inquiry into how certain patterns of ritual violence and victimization detectable in suicide bombings, school shootings, and epidemics of anorexia might be influenced by media reports.

Philippe de Keukelaere: Commented on a deviation of the archaic sacred in suicide killings of an enemy that is demonized.

Michael Elias: Discussed how English analytical philosophy on speech acts could work in tandem with the mimetic theory to discern the element of mimetic rivalry or agreement in cultural activities.

Roberto Farneti: Stressed that "the mimetic theory is to be framed as the approach to the entire field of human sciences."[29]

The Raven Foundation

The work of COV&R, Imitatio, and in general the dissemination of the mimetic theory has been enhanced by the Raven Foundation, which was founded in January 2007 by Suzanne and Keith Ross. Suzanne first attended a COV&R conference in 1999, and she and Keith both have attended since 2005. Raven has provided financial support to COV&R and practical advice to both organizations. The slogan of Raven is "Making religion reasonable, violence unthinkable and peace a possibility."[30] A statement of purpose on the Raven website reads: "To think in a constructive and life affirming way about conflict, violence, human nature, the role of religion, and the origin of human culture." Suzanne Ross chose the raven as the symbol and logo of the foundation because in myth and legend it has been maligned and scapegoated as an evil bird that does harm to humans, whereas in fact it is a harmless creature.

Keith Ross succeeded Julie Shinnick as the treasurer of COV&R in 2008, and Suzanne Ross has worked with Martha Reineke in curriculum development for teaching the mimetic theory. Andrew McKenna is a member of the advisory board of Raven, and René Girard and Robert Hamerton-Kelly are honorary members. Sandor Goodhart has been active in Raven's educational outreach on the mimetic theory.

Indeed, Raven's perspective, its way of seeing and filtering the problem of violence and possibilities for peacemaking, is indebted to the mimetic theory.

Suzanne Ross has written a book, *The Wicked Truth,* which draws upon the mimetic theory to clarify and enhance insights from the popular musical *Wicked,* which originated in a novel by Gregory McGuire and later a play by Stephen Schwartz. The story is conceived as a prequel to the *Wizard of Oz.* Andrew McKenna has described Ross's book as "a fertile addition" to those books that address a nonacademic audience for the mimetic theory.[31] Raven is involved in exploring a variety of possibilities for communicating the mimetic theory for all age levels, but particularly for children, teenagers, and college students.

The Annual Conference in Riverside, California

The 2008 conference of COV&R was held in the Riverside, a fast-growing city of about 320,000 in Southern California, approximately sixty miles east of Los Angeles. The climate is semiarid, with an average annual rainfall of about ten to eleven inches. The average high temperature in June is 94 degrees Fahrenheit, but the days were much hotter than that during the conference.

The host institution of the symposium was the University of California at Riverside. The organizers were Sabine Doran, a member of the faculty of Comparative Literature and Germanic Studies, and her husband Robert Doran, who was then on the faculty of Modern Languages and Cultures at the University of Rochester (New York). They became the parents of twins during the period of preparation for the conference. This was a happy and much noted event during the conference. As Simon de Keukelaere remarked in his report, "Girardians know that in quite a few archaic cultures the birth of twins forebodes catastrophe. The physical resemblance is associated with the imminent danger of mimetic catastrophe, the terrifying resemblance of mimetic antagonists." However, in COV&R, this was seen as "the augur of a so-called 'eu-catastrophe,' a neologism coined by J.R.R. Tolkien that reappeared quite a few times during the colloquium. The word refers to the good ('eu') conclusion of a drama's plot."[32] The Dorans and their team did a very good job of planning and organizing. The general feeling of participants seemed to be that they left the imprint of their openness and friendliness on the conference as a whole.

The venue itself was extremely interesting: the Mission Inn, where most of the meetings and all the meals were held. The original owner, Frank Miller, opened the first wing of the hotel, the Mission wing, in 1903. It was built in Mission-Revival architectural style. Miller went on to add three more wings, the Cloister, Spanish, and Rotunda. The Presidential Lounge boasts of ten U.S. presidents who came to the inn, going back to Theodore Roosevelt in 1903. The inn also includes a museum, an art gallery, and an aviator's shrine.

There was an impressive list of plenary speakers, including René Girard, Jean-Pierre Dupuy, and guest speakers Jack Miles, W. J. T. Mitchell, and Richard Cohen. Gianni Vattimo also gave a plenary talk, although he was not new to COV&R meetings, having attended before and being familiar with some of Girard's writings.

"Catastrophe and Conversion: Political Thinking in the New Millennium" June 18–22, 2008

This was a conference in which important issues were joined and some new avenues were opened up. There was also one plenary speech that was a debacle. In support of those statements I have chosen to report and reflect on precisely those papers that Simon de Keukelaere cited in his notes for the *Bulletin*.[33] After hearing these presentations and the discussions they generated and reviewing the materials pertaining to the conference, I have concluded that it is imperative to recognize, summarize, and comment on a convergence of mimetic thinking on the religious and cultural crisis that we now face, a situation that may truly be described as apocalyptic. In that sense, the Riverside conference represented a new stage both in the direction of the work of COV&R and in René Girard's thinking about the human condition for the last decade.

Jean-Pierre Dupuy presented and defended the thesis that he argued in *Pour un catastrophisme éclairé* (On Behalf of an Enlightened Catastrophism). He argued that we need a "Jonah," a doomsayer, because rational analysis in and of itself will not enable us to avoid world catastrophe. This doomsayer must believe what he proclaims and he must be plausible to those who hear the message. Therefore, as in the case of the biblical Jonah, the audience is converted and thus paradoxically the proclaimed apocalypse does not happen. (Dupuy didn't mention that Jonah was bitter that God graciously preserved those damned Ninevites, hated enemies of Israel in the eighth century b.c.e.) The prophet's prophecy is falsified, but it would result in saving human life.

Dupuy talked on this subject in two different sessions, but unfortunately he left no time for discussion. In agreement with de Keukelaere, I think it is worthy of a thorough examination and discussion with theologians, philosophers, and social scientists. De Keukelaere says that Dupuy's presentation of technico-scientific calculations, particularly his paradoxes, "is not an elegant way to elude the very Christian consequences of Girard's apocalyptic thinking (be it to clearly refute them)."[34] I am not sure that Dupuy was trying to do that. Certainly in other contexts he seems to see the Christian consequences of Girard's apocalyptic thinking very clearly, whether or not he can accept them. And he does not exactly refute them—he simply has his doubts. In the homage volume for Girard, *For René Girard,* he clarifies his position by discussing the conceptual fruitfulness of Ivan Illich's "logic of the detour of production" and juxtaposes it to Girard's mimetic theory, with particular emphasis on Girard's apocalyptic thought.[35] The paradox of the detour as a sacrificial concept is that it is necessary to make a move away from one's goal in order to achieve it. Put as a metaphor in spatial terms, it is necessary first to get farther away from the destination in order to arrive there. One example is that of an athlete in track who must back up a certain distance in order to make a good run and jump farther. Or you might be standing on one mountain peak and desire to climb to another peak you can see. But to get there you have to descend to a valley and take a winding path, thus hiking a greater distance, in order to climb to the other peak. This detour is the logic of sacrifice in various spheres of life. Everyone can see that there are some things that must be given up to attain certain ends, but often they become hot issues: the detour of production is work (giving one's time, energy, skill), but it can become the travail of difficult or unhealthy labor. Having long-lasting products like autos, washing machines, and so on, is usually thought of as beneficial, but for the sake of jobs and profits companies plan for products to become obsolete in short order, which often places a hardship on people who lose their jobs because of this and on those who use the older, outmoded product and cannot afford to replace it. There are many examples of the detour as a decision or strategy that manifests the logic of sacrifice in ordinary life.

The detours in economic life are now too many, having long been justified as necessary for the greater economic and social good. The modern market economy, according to Dupuy and his friend and frequent collaborator, Paul Dumouchel, is exclusionary to the poor and disadvantaged in a way and to an extent never known in premodern societies.[36] "The point of departure of [Dumouchel's] analysis is the idea that the economy is fundamentally powerless to illuminate the enigma and the scandal of exclusion because it constitutes the problem and not the solution."[37] Girard's mimetic theory enables the interpreter to understand this. The biblical deconstruction of the sacred, and in particular the Gospel witness to the crucifixion of Christ, which exposes the sacred as mimetically driven violence, brings with it a knowledge that has undermined the sacred in any traditional sense. There is no longer a sacrificial mechanism that reacts to impose order on the very violence it has unleashed. So people who lose out in the modern market economy are not objects of attention because the "economic order is the social construction of indifference to the unhappiness of other people." People are related to one another as "external third parties." Those who are "'excluded' are not sacrificial victims, because, far from being the focus of general fascination, they succumb to the indifference of everyone else."[38]

So what does all this have to do with "the Christian consequences of apocalyptic thinking?" Dupuy points out that Illich saw only the negative consequences of the economy of modernity, a panicked flight beyond the boundaries that hold society together. Girard, on the other hand, sees ambiguity. The knowledge the gospel has bequeathed to the world remains partially realized at present. If the undoing of the sacred brought about by Christianity continues apace without the responsible acceptance and fulfillment of the gospel message of God's love that binds us all together, then the apocalypse as total violence will occur, a doom that we will bring upon ourselves. But with the acceptance and fulfillment of the message of love, the rule and reign of God will be realized. However, what comes across in Dupuy's thinking is a fear, which could be called either "pessimistic" or "realistic," that events will be such that Girard's logic falls back into theodicy, which means in this case a justification of exclusion and violence as necessary means to an end that is ultimately good. This would put us back into the predicament of the modern economy as the problem of exclusion, undifferentiation, and indifference. "If evil is ultimately in the service of good, we might as well let it have its way and wash our hands of it."[39]

So as I appraise Dupuy's position on catastrophe and conversion, he stares the Christian consequences of Girard's apocalyptic thinking squarely in the face but cannot believe in their realization. This could be an instance reminiscent of the man in the Gospel account who cried out to Jesus, "I believe, help my unbelief!" (Mark 9:24). Many of us, if we be honest, would at least sometimes and perhaps all the time stand with Dupuy in this condition.

It is appropriate at this point to turn to Robert Hamerton-Kelly's presentation on Heraclitus and the recent crystallization of his thinking about violence and mimesis. Hamerton-Kelly shares this pessimism regarding the course of history in which the economy is the primary motor of social relationships and politics. Indeed, it appears that he has been influenced not only by Girard, but also by Dupuy and Dumouchel. He has also turned more and more to the theology of John Calvin, the great Protestant reformer who is well known for his doctrine of the predestination of the elect. In Hamerton-Kelly's Methodist heritage there are two primary theological strains in its beginnings. One was that of John Wesley, the founder, who was an Anglican priest. He, his brother Charles Wesley (the great hymn writer), and most of their followers were inclined to the thought of Jacobus Arminius (1560–1609). Arminius was a Dutch pastor and at one time a student of Theodore Beza (1519–1605), who was Calvin's successor in Geneva. However, Arminius rejected Beza's teaching that God predestined some for salvation and some for damnation.

Although the Arminianism of the Wesleys predominated in the future development of Methodism, the theological perspective of George Whitefield (1714–1770) was a significant influence in Methodist origins. He held to a kind of "moderate Calvinism" of the Thirty-Nine Articles of the Anglican Church. He believed that God was the sole agent in conversion and salvation. In actual practice, however, this was not an obstacle to him in preaching, for he always exhorted and invited his audiences to accept the good news that Christ graciously reaches out to lost souls. He was probably the most popular preacher in the eighteenth century, drawing thousands of people wherever he traveled in America. He was the single most influential preacher responsible for the revival movement called the Great Awakening in 1740.

Hamerton-Kelly's model within the Methodist tradition is Whitefield. In terms of the actual course history has taken, he agrees with Dupuy that the economy is the bearer of the sacrificial mechanism that is the main manifestation of the human predicament. From a theological standpoint, human being is "fallen," and it has no recourse of its own volition. Therefore, as the participants in the Riverside conference became well aware—and this was also quite clear at the 2009 conference in London—he announced that violence, that is, the link of mimesis and violence, should be the primary object and focus of our work, and that many of us had become unwisely attached to emphasizing a positive, loving mimesis. He did not name names, but as I have highlighted in this history, quite a few colleagues, in their respective ways, have focused on the positive possibilities of mimetic desire in social and religious life, including Rebecca Adams, Martha Reineke, Pablo Bandera, Ann Astell, and of course the Innsbruck school (Raymund Schwager, Wolfgang Palaver, Józef Niewiadomski, Nikolaus Wandinger, Petra Steinmair-Pösel, among the Innsbruck theologians most well known to us).

So Hamerton-Kelly has thrown down the gauntlet, as it were. Whether or not we agree with him, his exhortation on violence is something we must think through carefully and understand before we accept or reject it. The point of departure would be his paper at Riverside, "Heraclitus Hierophant: A

Mimetic Reading of Two Fragments," but he has spoken on this also in various contexts.[40]

Concerning mimesis, Hamerton-Kelly begins with the fundamental Girardian concept that mimetic desire itself is the human mode of being in the world. Desire, which is mimetically structured and directed, is our "nature," that is, it is what is not created by human effort or achievement and it is essential to the basic characteristics and faculties of human being. This mode of being tends toward violence in the sense that violence is inevitable in human life because desire is a force that works through unconscious imitation of other humans who become models and rivals. A model is always potentially a rival, a rival is always potentially a model. They easily slide back and forth into each other, almost like the 0–1 polarity that is fundamental to cybernetic technology. The very biology of the human brain—the neural network in particular—is a combination of feedback loops and mirror neurons, which place our existence always in polarities of tension and inevitable conflict between self and other.[41]

Pre-Socratic philosophers, particularly Heraclitus in the fifth century b.c., recognized the dynamic, polar combat of opposites. War (*polemos*), declares Heraclitus, is the father or source of all things and all human relations. Heraclitus's maxim, which is repeated in various forms and applications in the extant fragments, was evidently influenced by the wars between the Greeks and the Persians as well as Persian dualistic thought, along with the reflections of earlier philosophers. He held, in other words, that violence is the generative principle of both nature and the world of man.

Now how does this discovery of violence as generative principle square with Christian theology? Does it deny the Christian doctrine of original sin or is it a modern form of Gnosticism? That is, does it posit an evil creator or creation and a special spiritual knowledge that is gained only through a particular interpretation of the revelation centered in the crucifixion and resurrection of Jesus? Hamerton-Kelly's answer to both questions is no. The cross of Christ is the historical event of the divine disclosure of the scapegoat mechanism, which is the operation in human life of the elimination of a victim through whom the contending beings gain relief from the mimetic rivalry that threatens to destroy them. The event of Jesus Christ is the entrance of God into this world of violence: God the Son suffers the violence, the misery, the hell ("he descended into hell") that God's creatures suffer. In a process that may have taken place over thousands, even millions of years, the human species attained to human being, in the form that we know humankind, in which victims slain by hominid groups became the focal point of all sorts of differentiation and the threshold of hominization. That means certainly that language and culture have their origin in the victim.

But what about the Jewish and Christian affirmation of a creation that is good? God, according to Genesis 1, created the world, including Adam, First Man, and everything in it was very good. Hamerton-Kelly holds that the way to understand this affirmation of God's creation, which in some form is necessary to Christian faith, is to view it as mythic or symbolic; it does not describe a "history" or process of events succeeding one another in time. Creation of the world as very good should be understood as an eschatological reality in the mind of God, as it were. That is, creation is good in the "end," as it is meant to be. Understood in that way as the apocalypse, *the apokalupsis* or unveiling of the transcendent reality of the world, creation is unveiled in the crucifixion and resurrection of Jesus, the Second Adam, the Alpha and Omega, in his victory over Satan, the Accuser who is the god of this world. This revelation of creation is indeed proleptic, yet to be fully revealed, but it is vouchsafed to us through a great chain of witnesses in and through whom the Holy Spirit moves. This Spirit is the present dynamic reality of that Mind of God. The Divine Mind is the gracious Spirit that gives us our minds and the possibility of love and peace, beginning with the defense of victims, as a prolepsis of the true apocalypse, the restoration of all things.

The primary task of the mission of witness to the gospel is to proclaim and teach the freedom of the children of God, who though sinners may be freed paradoxically as servants. For when they bind themselves to the service of the Savior-Creator God, they are most free. They come to know, then, the truth of Paul's testimony, that the whole creation is groaning in travail until now, awaiting the glorious revelation of the sons of God (Romans 8:18–23).

Therefore, in short, Hamerton-Kelly stresses that the generative principle of the world is violence, but the *telos,* the *eschaton,* the end toward which it moves is the Logos, the gathering together of all things in salvific unity and in a community of the acknowledgment of guilt and of repentance, of joy and hope in divine forgiveness. A community, in short, of those formerly lost to the dead ends of division and violence. So then, is violence in the primordial sense good? Only insofar as it is directed toward its end, the (re)creation of the world that is its eschatological reality in the Mind of God. Two biblical texts come to mind as characterizations of Hamerton-Kelly's perspective. One is where Joseph reassures his brothers, who feared he would have them executed because they had sold him into slavery: "Even though you meant evil against me, God meant it for good, so that now many people might live" (Genesis 50:20). The other is the Apostle Paul's exhortation to the Philippians: "Have this mind among you that was in Christ Jesus" (Philippians 2:5).

The issues involved in Hamerton-Kelly's anthropology and theology bear serious import. The question of good and bad mimesis is one of the "founding" topics for the mimetic theory.[42] It is essential, in other words, for members of COV&R to discern what they think can be held and what must remain very questionable, within a context of free thought and discussion, as they take the Colloquium into the future. Here are a few of my thoughts as a contribution to that. They are given under the rubrics of the following questions. (1) Is Hamerton-Kelly's theological perspective a kind of Gnosticism? (2) Does his position come perilously close to the satanic theodicy about which Jean-Pierre Dupuy warns us? (3) Can human beings act as agents to affect and change the course of conflict and violence? (4) Has Christianity actually influenced the direction of Western culture, not only toward apocalyptic disaster but also toward transformation for the betterment of personal and social life? It would be inappropriate to take up all these questions for a lengthy discussion at this point. I will treat them briefly, however, in reporting on my critique of Hamerton-Kelly at the Notre Dame conference in 2010.

Two other events merit mention here for the contribution that they made to the total conference. One was Stephen Gardner's paper on Philip Rieff. He did not give it in a plenary session, but the paper and ensuing discussion left a significant impression that seldom happens in the parallel sessions.[43] Rieff is one of those modern thinkers with whom it is worth the time and effort for Girardians to become acquainted. A sociologist and critic of culture with a brilliant mind of great interdisciplinary range and depth, he leveled devastating criticisms of modern Western culture; indeed in ways that brought him to a tragic impasse in his life, he was deeply imbedded in it without fully seeing a way out. He apparently became so discouraged in his perception of contemporary culture that he practically stopped publishing his work and speaking out as a sort of public intellectual for about the last twenty-five years of his life (b. 1922-d. 2006). He left so many unpublished manuscripts when he died that four books under his name have come out posthumously.

Rieff was occupied with thinkers whom he considered nihilistic, ones that he described as "feeling intellects" who reflected and influenced the antinomian tendencies of modern culture. These included particularly Weber, Freud, Nietzsche, Kierkegaard, and Kafka. Rieff held that the foundation of culture is a system of prohibitions. These are interdictions that are "eternally commanded . . . constituting a system of constraint." They "must be not only clear and well-defined but unalterable."[44] "Interdicts are directly commanded truths in sacred history."[45] The whole inclination of modern culture is transgressive, going beyond the boundaries of prohibitions that are necessary for culture to be sustained. In this sense, he viewed certain thinkers as anticultural. Sigmund Freud is the chief of those responsible for modern "psychological man," who rebels against all limits and who cannot achieve virtue but is able to affirm only "values" that constantly change. Freud inducted modern Western humanity into "the triumph of the therapeutic."

The present culture, which Rieff calls the "third culture," an "anti-culture," revolves around self-realization, making oneself or making oneself over. Rieff characterizes it as a culture of fiction, of making up meaning. The first culture was one of myth, taboo, and the gods, characterized as a culture of fate, whereas the second culture is that of a sacred history, characterized by faith and obedience. Fate, faith, and fiction are the shorthand terms for the three cultures.

Even though Freud cannot be blamed for everything that psychoanalysis and its offshoots became, he started the process of a form of treatment that simply helps humans to conform to individualism and loneliness and to endure it. But if Freud is intellectual ancestor of the therapeutic, Rieff attacks Max Weber just as harshly as responsible for giving intellectual approval to transgressive culture by his hostility to the second culture's theme of charisma, which is a gift of grace that is manifest in authority and obedience to the divine will, as in the Old Testament prophets. Weber's sociology highlights "exceptional" individuals. In place of the power and authority of divine revelation evoking faith and obedience, as in the prophets and Jesus, Weber set forth the dominating power of personality, the magnetism of a "superior" will. This is in effect a thinly disguised legitimation of a superficial democratic culture.

For those engaged with the mimetic theory, what Rieff has to say about culture, particularly the function of prohibition and transgression, should be of great interest. He was well aware of the function of myth and symbol, and there is no gainsaying that in some regards he was very aware of rivalry and competition. However, he was so much a person "in-between," caught up in the conflict between the "second" and "third" cultures, as he described them, and so engrossed with those great thinkers of the past who were his model-obstacles, that he was never able to pinpoint the generative role of mimetic rivalry and violence. As Gardner says about him, "Rieff exemplifies a structure aptly described by René Girard as 'mimetic rivalry': his 'rivals' are his 'models.' But he does so in a way that reveals it too as constitutive, if also destructive, of democratic culture. For Girard, the basis of rivalry is, paradoxically, identification; it is the rival's perception of himself in the mirror of his adversary that expresses itself in antagonism and animosity. The model is a competitor, if not an enemy, just because he is a model. Likewise, Rieff's cultural adversaries were his inspirations, and his inspirations exuded an adversarial element." Gardner goes on to say, "The radicalism of Rieff's anti-modernism is a reflex of his own modernism; it is a Jekyll to modernism's Hyde. His critical 'animosity' to his cultural rivals is governed in part by his felt identification with them, as purveyors of modernity."[46] He is simultaneously the cool analyst and the fiercely hostile enemy of the culture that he studies and that is so much a part of him.

The last person whose work is to be highlighted in this account of COV&R 2008 is René Girard himself. Here I will treat Girard's contribution to the symposium in two respects. First, Girard surprised us by making a presentation on Catalhöyük, a Neolithic site in Anatolia, the part of Turkey that is often considered "Asian" geographically. The settlements at Catalhöyük go back to about 7500 B.C.E., if not earlier. This settlement did not look like the sort of town or village with which we are familiar. Without streets or a central plaza, it had more the appearance of a beehive.

Using slide pictures to enable the audience to get a better grasp of his lecture, Girard discussed the pictures drawn on the inside walls of houses at the site. The depiction of the animals is quite realistic, except they are often many times larger than the humans in the pictures. Ian Hodder, the present director of work at the site, describes the men as "baiting and teasing" the animals (deer, boars). Girard, who was basically proposing hypotheses because of many uncertainties about this Neolithic art, pointed out that there is visual evidence of sexual teasing, but the people were probably hunting to kill the animals in a process that appears to have become ritualized. The hunters are scattered around the animal victim like a mob, and some of them show signs of injury. The comparison of certain pictures of a hunted deer show the animal alive and then probably slain: the moment of killing is not directly shown, but in the succeeding picture the animal's forelegs and part of his horns are cut off. The animal was eaten in what was evidently an early kind of festival. Human waste from the site indicates that the wild animals were eaten only at these occasions, whereas the normal consumption of meat depended on the domesticated sheep and goats.

The pictures of the hunts were on the north walls of the houses, before which there was a bench on which inhabitants sat. Ancestors were buried under the bench. The houses, in other words, were sacred precincts. Only later did altars and temples develop in human civilization. So we find here at Catalhöyük what may be the earliest form of scapegoating, the scapegoating of animals that are eaten at a kind of sacrificial occasion. The manner in which the animals are drawn on the walls and their proximity to the residents and the buried ancestors reflects the emergence of the primitive sacred.[47]

Through the years Girard has occasionally changed his mind about some aspect of the mimetic theory if he is convinced that the evidence warrants it. His eventual agreement with Raymund Schwager concerning the continued relevance of the figure of the scapegoat and the function of sacrifice in Christianity is well known: they still have a central function in the Christian gospel, but in a transformed mode. As I shall note shortly, his thought in *Battling to the End* represents a revised view of mimesis and history, particularly the history of Christianity. And here, in reflecting on the Neolithic site, he conceded that the ritual killing of animals may be older than human sacrifice. Therefore, Walter Burkert may be right about this.[48] However, this revision is not of great significance for the mimetic theory. If animals were sacrificed first in some or all of the circumstances of human beginnings, it is certain in any case that after the scapegoating and sacrifice of humans emerged, animals were eventually substituted for humans. Either way, the sacrificial mechanism was generative of religion and culture.

The second event pertaining to Girard's work was a panel discussion immediately after the lecture and discussion on Catalhöyük. The subject of this event was Girard's most recent book, *Achever Clausewitz*.[49] This work may surprise many COV&R members and other Girardians. In it we encounter Girard the historian especially concerned with European history of the last two centuries. He also confesses to revising his perspective on the possibility of standing as an objective observer outside of the sacrificial flaws of historical Christianity and criticizing it from that vantage.

In earlier years, certainly in the earlier years of COV&R's existence, most of us wanted Rene Girard to address current social and political problems and crises in a more direct way. He refused to get drawn into that, holding that his life objective was the search for truth, not immediate applications of the mimetic theory. To him, these desires and pressures must have seemed like a contemporary Western, especially American, addiction to "quick fixes" for social, politic, and religious ailments of the modern world. Yet now in *Battling to the End* he has made a 180-degree turn to speak directly on the crisis of Western culture and world civilization, although not in a hopeful, activist fashion at all. In his career he moved from the identification and analysis of mimetic desire in literary texts to violence and the sacred in archaic religion, and then to finding the key to knowledge in the crucifixion of Christ and his resurrection, thus exposing the scapegoat mechanism and God's withdrawal from the world of violence. Now finally he offers a total interpretation of world history. Drawing upon the biblical witness to revelation as the basis of the mimetic theory, he envisions the world moving toward apocalypse in *Battling to the End*. This apocalypse ("unveiling") will be human self-destruction or the kingdom of God.

Girard's point of departure is, as always, a text, an extremely important text, yet one that was not finished: Carl von Clausewitz's treatise *On War*. Clausewitz never finished it, revising it repeatedly; he was obsessed with it, but never able to complete it before his death in 1831. The French original of *Battling to the End* was titled *Achever Clausewitz*. *Achever* in the French title means both "finishing" and "finishing off, getting rid of." Focusing primarily on book 1 of the work, "On the Nature of War," Girard argues that Clausewitz represents the beginning of the modern predicament of carrying violence to extremes.[50]

It would take too long to summarize Clausewitz's theory of war in this overview. To give a capsulized introduction, it involves understanding the duel as the primary metaphor of war and a tension, if not actually a contradiction, between war as a political end controlled by the state and as violence escalating to extremes. The actions of the parties in war are reciprocal, which Clausewitz analyzes acutely as subject to enhancement as the antagonists react to one another. The side initially defending itself can be more violent, in that the initial aggressor wants to conquer and achieve peace, but the defender does not want peace with the aggressor. Rational thought is caught in a paradox, in that it purports to control strategy and the ends of war and yet can easily conceive of absolute war and destruction of the other. Neither reason nor passion can avoid the entanglements of mimetic rivalry and escalation.

First of all, we should observe that the overarching and ever-present theme of this book is apocalypse. Girard says so in the first paragraph of the introduction.[51] Apocalypse is the reality of a world escalating to extremes "because there can no longer be unanimity about the guilt of victims."[52] There is now literally nothing between mimetic adversaries; they have only their respective identities, which cannot be mediated by the scapegoat mechanism. It is not that God's rule is absent. "The Kingdom is already here, but human violence will increasingly mask it. . . . Apocalyptic thought is thus contrary to the wisdom that believes that peaceful identity and fraternity is accessible on the purely human level."[53] The great secret of violent identity is that peaceful identity exists at its heart; it is "its most secret possibility. This is the secret strength of eschatology."[54] What will be absolutely new is the Second Coming of Christ, and the triumph of Christ "will take place in a beyond of which we know neither the time nor place."[55] This apocalypse, however, "has to be taken out of fundamentalist hands," for fundamentalists do not understand that "Human violence produces the sacred, but holiness leads to the 'other shore.'"[56]

Girard and Chantre, a French philosopher and dramaturgiste who is the president of l'Association Recherches Mimétiques, set up the chapter on Hölderlin with a long section on apocalyptic thought. Girard avers there that the relevance of apocalyptic texts is striking and paradoxical: "They say that Christ will return when there is no hope that evangelical revelation will be able to eliminate violence, once humanity realizes that it has failed."[57] He stipulates that those who pass through this into the new reality of God's Kingdom can do so only from a distance, a distance that is mediated by Jesus Christ. "The imitation of Christ provides the proximity that places us at a distance. It is not the Father whom we should imitate, but his Son, who has withdrawn with his Father."[58] This positive imitation of Christ as withdrawal prepares the way for the conversation about the poet.

Now to turn to a synopsis of *Battling to the End* that follows the course of the book. In the initial stage of their conversation Girard and Chantre discuss Clausewitz's notion of war as a duel; it is a mimetic manifestation of escalation to extremes which can be precipitated (if the parties act immediately) or suspended (if one or both parties stop to speculate on the strategy of the other side). Clausewitz tries at times to postulate reason as controlling war and putting the military objectives under the control of the state, but he will then turn in another direction and speak of the possibility of escalation to extremes.

Clausewitz perceived war as a blend of a "remarkable trinity": "passion, calculation, and intelligence," which he associated with the people, the army commander, and the government, respectively.[59] He noted the relation of this combination of elements to the dynamics of commerce. He seems, in fact, as Chantre observes, to have intuited "the duel as the hidden structure of all social phenomena."[60] Monetary exchanges are also war, a kind of war that avoids, at least temporarily, the violence of actual war. Girard comments on Montesquieu's pacifying vision of trade, although modern economists who refer to him "often have no idea that money's purpose is to neutralize risk of war."[61]

Clausewitz's understanding of war was much more true to historical reality than that of Hegel, whose concept of *Aufhebung* or nullification in the movement of the Spirit in history enshrined sacrificial violence as necessary, but in a kind of euphemistic way that covers over violence. One of Girard's watchwords is the conflict of truth and violence. Violence is contained—in the twofold sense of contain—within the archaic sacred and its modern remnants. In the heritage of Hegelian thought there is an increasingly positive attitude toward violence for the achievement of historical purpose in the movement from Hegel to Marx to Lenin.

However, Clausewitz was caught up in a predicament of mimetic rivalry, which is probably why he was unable to complete his book. He was obsessed with Napoleon, who was his actual model and rival. Girard points out that "Clausewitz thinks over against Napoleon."[62] Whereas Hegel, working in Jena in 1806 when Napoleon won an important battle there, wrote in a letter that he had seen "the World-Soul [Napoleon] pass on horseback under his window,"[63] Clausewitz vacillated between hostility for the legendary French emperor and identification with him. In book 2 of *On War* he even imagines himself as advisor to Napoleon during the emperor's valiant but finally losing campaign in 1814 against the allies who attacked France. He could have counseled him on how to defeat the allies. Girard comments that Clausewitz "is so close to his model that he no longer tries to acquire the model's property, but his being itself, his 'luck' in Clausewitzian terms."[64]

I have already alluded to the conflict between violence and truth. One way to view the underlying theme of Girard's thinking is that of a struggle between two kinds of undifferentiation: the undifferentiation of mimetic rivalry escalating to the extreme of ultimate violence, which is chaos, and the undifferentiation of mimetic desire imitating God the Son, who imitates God the Father, which results in the undifferentiation of love in the divine community. So if Clausewitz is seen as representing the modern escalation to extremes, Girard looks to the poet Friedrich Hölderlin (1770–1843), a contemporary of Clausewitz, as a sign of the awareness of the divine response to the new stage in human history. The poet withdrew from public life in 1807, the year after the battle of Jena. He had been declared mentally unfit, and was taken in by Ernst Zimmer, whose family cared for him for the remainder of his life. Girard holds that his withdrawal was not due to mental unfitness, but to his religious and poetic intuitions. He cites a number of Hölderlin's poems, in particular the opening of "Patmos":

> Near is,
> And difficult to grasp, the God.
> But where danger threatens
> That which saves from it also grows.[65]

The power of God is shown in nonviolence, in weakness; that is his power, which is a function of his love. The divine withdrawal paradoxically increases the reality of the divine presence. Hölderlin's silent sorrow was in imitation of Christ, who withdrew from the world nonviolently in imitation of God the Father. "[Christ] withdraws at the very point when he could dominate. . . . To imitate Christ is to refuse to impose oneself as a model and to always efface oneself before others."[66]

In the last two chapters the interlocutors turn to the mimetic rivalry between France and Germany and the historical relation of pope and emperor. The former chapter begins with an interesting discussion of Germaine de Staël (1766–1817), another contemporary of Clausewitz, as well as of Napoleon, Hegel, and Hölderlin. In her essay *D'Allemagne* (On Germany) de Staël tried "to open the way to a Catholic modernity: that of a dialogue between France and Germany."[67] Although she glorified individuality in the Romantic spirit, she nonetheless had a good intuition about the social role of religion.[68] Her work is significant because French-German interactions are "one of the most virulent seats of undifferentiation in the history of Europe." Indeed, this "rivalry ended up producing the monstrous sacrificial blunder (dérapage) of the Holocaust."[69]

Girard's main point in the chapter on "The Pope and the Emperor" is that the papacy has won out over any emperor or imperial pretensions. Indeed, it embodies the "meaning" of Europe itself. This victory is highlighted by John Paul at the Wailing Wall in Jerusalem, engaged in an act of repentance for the church's treatment of the Jews during its long history. Here "the papacy triumphed over itself and acquired worldwide significance. Before our eyes it succeeded in expelling all imperial ideas."[70] This victory has paved the way for the idea of the identification of all people. "When the pope took up this idea, he unceasingly and stubbornly reminded us of the divine nature of that identity."[71] Girard also defends Pope Benedict XVI in the Regensburg controversy. He argues that Benedict's mission is the laudable one of bringing together faith and reason while eschewing fideism and fundamentalism in the dialogue with other religions and cultures.

We should note, too, that Girard's perspective has changed somewhat in the last decade or so. As mentioned previously in the discussion of Hamerton-Kelly's thinking on mimesis and violence, he has become disabused of the belief that one could stand outside of the mimetism of history and isolate an "essential Christianity" from "historical Christianity." "We are immersed in the pitfalls of our desire, which is always desire for what the other possesses. I repeat, absolute knowledge is not possible."[72]

A major component of this shift in perspective is Girard's stronger and stronger sense of the element of archaic religiosity that forms a polarity with the currents of modern culture. Although he does not come to the point of explicitly stating this, he implies that together they constitute modernity as a state of *polemos*, of combat between opposing, contradictory forces. This continually reappears as the underlying theme that moves through the entirety of *Battling to the End*. Both archaic sacrifice and Christian sacrifice should be considered "sacrifice."[73] "I think that the two great institutions of archaic religion, namely prohibitions and sacrifice, have played an essential role in the passage from pre-human to human societies."[74] "Christianity has archaic religion as its only horizon."[75] Nonetheless, he modifies the meaning of the archaic in the introduction by stating, "The sacred, which has been 'returning' for 2000 years, is thus not an archaic form of the sacred, but a sacred that has been 'satanized' by the awareness we have of it."[76] He characterizes Islam as in some basic sense archaic when he says, "I have the impression that [Islam] has used the Bible as a support to rebuild an archaic religion that is more powerful than all the others."[77]

The panel discussing *Achever Clausewitz*[78] was made up of Girard, Robert Hamerton-Kelly, Wolfgang Palaver, and Jean-Pierre Dupuy, with James Alison as moderator. After Girard's opening comments, Hamerton-Kelly stated that like Clausewitz, he feared that war might disappear; that is, with the emphasis on positive mimesis violence might disappear from mimetic theory, and with the disappearance of violence original sin might also be eliminated. The truth of Heraclitus, of Clausewitz, and of the mimetic theory, he averred, is that "War is the father of all things and the king of all" (Heraclitus).

Hamerton-Kelly went on to say we are a species capable not only of torturing animals, but also human beings. There is a good mimesis, but this is the realm of God's kingdom, the new creation. In the meantime, those anticipating the reign of good mimesis await the Second Coming of Christ by living in imitation of Christ.

Wolfgang Palaver commented on the polarity of Clausewitz's concept of war. On the one hand, it is relatively benign and instrumental as a continuation of the politics of the state, but on the other hand he has great insight into mimetic rivalry and the escalation to extremes. Palaver noted that we are living in apocalyptic times, as seen in the escalation of terrorism, but there are possibilities for de-escalation in the great religious traditions, and certainly in Christianity. We should look for these possibilities in other religions of moving away from the mimetic mounting to extremes. He pointed out that the Quran is being read in a new light by some Muslim interpreters, who are willing to emphasize passages that have not been in the forefront of Muslim thought. For example, it is striking that in the Quran Abel tells Cain that even if Cain stretches out his hand to slay him, he will not retaliate, "for I do fear God, the Cherisher of the worlds."[79]

In fact, without minimizing important differences between Christianity and Islam, Palaver points out in "Abrahamic Revolution," just cited, that the two great traditions share many insights and teachings that are very similar, if not the same. One of these similarities is the human condition of mimetic desire, to which the Quran and Muslim sages frequently refer. Above all, both traditions share a concern for the victims of persecution and injustice. Therefore we should be in competition for the good, engaged with one another in emulation, that is, positive rivalry.[80] As Pope John Paul II said in 1985, speaking to young Muslims in Morocco, "I believe that God summons us today to lay aside our old customs. We should have mutual respect and spur one another to good works on the way of God."[81] A further comment on the desirability and feasibility of dialogue with Islam will be given below in the discussion of the 2009 conference in London.

Jean-Pierre Dupuy, after lauding Girard's presentation on Catalhöyük earlier in the conference, began his comments on the book by explaining the meaning of *achever* in the French title. It is a false cognate, not meaning "achieve" but "finish" or "finish off," that is, to kill. He pronounced this a magnificent book but confessed that it gave him a chill down his spine to read Girard's statement that Christianity will have failed.[82] Dupuy then used most of the rest of his time to complete his earlier presentation by commenting on the paradoxes of nuclear deterrence. One amusing moment was when Dupuy, evidently glimpsing someone pointing to his watch or tapping it, exclaimed, "Don't terrorize me" by doing that. As always, he was completely caught up in his subject.

In Girard's response he agreed with Dupuy that it was in general a pessimistic book, but he wanted people to worry more about the subject and less about partisan politics. Hamerton-Kelly thanked Dupuy for stressing the central fact of violence and our need to respond to it. Palaver was the only panelist who viewed the possibility of positive mimesis in other religions and cultures as a source of hope.

One unfortunate event at the conference was the diatribe delivered in the presence of Girard by Richard Cohen in a plenary session. Cohen was clearly ignorant of Girard's thought. Not only was it rude, it was egregiously erroneous in charging Girard with being a Gnostic of a modern type and, closely related to that, with Christian heresy of a dualistic sort. As Ann Astell commented, "[Sandor] Goodhart's indirect, deliberately anti-mimetic response succeeded in defending Girard's mimetic theory in a masterful way both practically (by refusing to answer Cohen in kind) and theoretically (by showing the theory's relevance to the thought of one of the twentieth century's greatest ethicists [Emmanuel Levinas])."[83]

Having a speaker like Cohen reflects the problem of inviting outside speakers that are not adequately vetted. It is not that speakers must be in agreement with Girard or any adherent of the mimetic theory. However, except in rare cases it would be wise to follow a policy that includes at least these two criteria: (1) The outside speakers should have some acquaintance with Girard's work. (2) The number of such outside speakers will be very few, perhaps only one or two.

In the business meeting COV&R 2008 two very important suggestions were made for future conferences. One was that more of our younger scholars be scheduled for plenary sessions. The other was that we make sure to post papers online.

Also, in addition to thanks tendered to those who rotated off the advisory board, a special word of thanks and a gift were given to Julie Shinnick, who served the Colloquium so faithfully for many years.

The Meeting with AAR in Chicago, November 1, 2008

The COV&R session at the American Academy of Religion, which met October 31–November 3, 2008, was memorable in several respects. The new status of COV&R as a Related Scholarly Organization had been confirmed, although it was too late to include our program in the main section of the program book. Nonetheless, the small meeting room was packed, so that many people had to stand or sit on the floor.

The program was one session in which two books were discussed, and it was a good dialogue on sacrifice, violence, and atonement. Kathryn McClymond introduced those present to her book *Beyond Sacred Violence: A Comparative Study of Sacrifice*. The general topic of her talk was the way in which sacrificial traditions viewed and interpreted sacrificial practices, with examples drawn from Vedic and Jewish traditions. She stressed two points: (1) Nurturing the gods or giving them a gift, rather than destroying the victim, is central to the theology of sacrifice of these traditions. (2) Sacrifice involves a cluster of activities, not a single, unified act. The respondent, Thomas Wilson, highlighted the divergence of perspective and intention between McClymond's work, which sought to explicate the original participants' understanding of their practices, and Girard's mimetic theory, which finds violence at the core of sacrifice. The ensuring discussion revolved around the difference between a modern approach from the outside, which sees the practitioners as enveloped in mythology, and the view from inside the original religious practices. Nikolaus Wandinger, the writer of the report for *The Bulletin of COV&R*, comments, "I personally felt the search for criteria for when to accept the self-understanding of a tradition and when to override that self-understanding with exterior insights has not come to a successful end."[84] A question relevant to that discussion is whether it is true that in the Bible the criticism of ritual sacrifice as rooted in violence originates in the sacrificial tradition's own historical development, as I argue in chapter 5 of *The Bible, Violence, and the Sacred*.[85]

The second main presenter, Mark Heim, commented on his hermeneutics of the cross in his book *Saved from Sacrifice: A Theology of the Cross*, in which he draws upon the mimetic theory in rejecting the theology that construes the cross as penal substitution or divine satisfaction due to human sin. These classical views retain the mythological-sacrificial element from pagan religiosity. Heim proposes rather that the suffering of Christ on the cross is the medium of God's saving purpose working subversively in the world, and that this results in the empty cross, that is, in internalizing and practicing a positive mimesis that saves people from the sacrificial mechanism stemming from mimesis and violence. Józef Niewiadomski compared Heim's interpretation to that of Raymund Schwager and said their atonement theologies were very compatible. However, Schwager realized and emphasized that "even positive mimesis was not safe from deteriorating into rivalry."[86] Moreover, Niewiadomski argued that one aspect of Schwager's theology of the cross stood outside the framework of what Heim presented: "the idea that there still is need for a self-sacrifice of love," which is occasioned not by divine vindictiveness or violence "but by the human inability to live positive mimesis as it should be lived.[87]" Heim agreed with Niewiadomski, and he said that this was not included in his book because he wanted to focus on and address the theological and existential problems that believers experience in encountering the usual sacrificial accounts of Jesus' death on the cross.

Finally, on November 4, 2008, a day after the AAR congress, Wandinger and Niewiadomski were still in Chicago and rejoiced in the opportunity as Europeans to participate in "the positive state of emergency" in Chicago, as Wandinger put it.

They joined the immense throng at Grant Park to see and hear the newly elected American President Barack Obama deliver his acceptance speech.[88]

MLA Award for René Girard

On the evening of December 28, 2008, just three days after his eighty-fifth birthday, René Girard received a Lifetime Achievement Award from the Modern Language Association (MLA). It was only the fifth time that this award has been given in the MLA's long history, stretching back to 1883. It has over 30,000 members, one of the oldest and largest scholarly organizations in the world. Its object is "to promote the study of language and literature in the United States and to provide a forum for intellectual exchange for scholars from around the world."[89] The award came as a surprise because Girard has had a strained relationship with American literary critics, particularly in their poststructuralist phase. However, the realistic mimetic approach of Girard appears to be gaining greater favor now on the literary scene. Those present for the event included Girard's daughter, Mary Girard Brown, and COV&R members Robert and Sabine Doran, William and Rosemary Johnsen, Sandor Goodhart, Robert Hamerton-Kelly, Chris Carter, and Tom Cousineau. A panel discussion of Girard's work was held the following day, chaired by William Johnsen. Presentations were given by Yves Champinot (in absentia, read by Johnsen), Robert Doran, and William Johnsen, with Girard responding.

Such recognitions of Girard's work are not only a tribute to him, but also a source of satisfaction to all of us who have committed ourselves to his intellectual and spiritual vision as formulated in the mimetic theory. We are part of something historic that is working slowly but surely like leaven in the history of humankind.

To London and Beyond (2009)

In 2009 we met in London, one of the great capital cities of Europe. My wife and I had been there briefly in 1995 and we were looking forward to traveling there again, after brief visits with friends and colleagues in Spain and Austria. The annual conference took place at St. Mary's University College in Twickenham, just southwest of central London in the London metropolitan area. It was sponsored by St. Mary's and Heythrop College of the University of London. Michael Kirwan, known to COV&R members particularly for his books on Girard (*Discovering Girard* and *Girard and Theology*) was the organizer. He was ably assisted by Sheelah Hidden and Birute Briliute. It was a pleasant and stimulating four days, including a lovely banquet Saturday night and an excursion on Sunday to Hampton Court, where we could see "Henry VIII" strolling around in the various courtyards and gardens.

St. Mary's University College has had an interesting history. It was founded in 1850 by the Catholic Poor Schools Committee for the education of teachers who would instruct an increasing number of poor Catholic children. It was initially located in Brook Green in Hammersmith under the charge of the Brothers of Christian Instruction. In 1899 the Congregation of the Mission (Vincentians) was asked to take over the administration of the college. In 1925 St. Mary's purchased Strawberry Hill in Twickenham. The college went through various stages, and it is now classified as a "university college." It can apply for full university status when it fulfills further criteria.

Strawberry Hill had been a cottage on a few acres of land by the River Thames. Horace Walpole (1717–1797) purchased the property in 1747. Walpole was the son of Robert Walpole, who was the de facto first British prime minister from 1721 to 1742. He enlarged the house and added to the land, which now totals thirty-five acres. It is a beautiful setting. Our opening reception and concluding banquet were held in the Waldegrave Drawing Room, named after Frances, Lady Waldegrave. In 1846 she came into possession of the house, which she restored and extended.

The dormitories at the college we found to be adequate. We were surprised by the quality of the food at the college cafeteria; it was certainly superior to the fare at most American colleges and universities. The Italian summer students were a bit noisy and not very well mannered, but they didn't seem to bother our COV&R group too much.

"Fearful Symmetries': Religion, Co-Existence, and the Secular," July 8–12 2009

Michael Kirwan chose as the poetic point of departure for the theme of the conference the image of the tiger from William Blake's poem in *Songs of Experience* (1789):

> Tyger! Tyger! burning bright
> In the forests of the night,
> What immortal hand or eye
> Could frame thy fearful symmetry?

In what distant deeps or skies
Burnt the fire of thine eyes?
On what wings dare he aspire?
What the hand dare seize the fire?

And what shoulder, & what art
Could twist the sinews of thy heart?
And when thy heart began to beat,
What dread hand? & what dread feet?

What the hammer? what the chain?
In what furnace was thy brain?
What the anvil? what dread grasp
Dare its deadly terrors clasp?

When the stars threw down their spears,
And watered heaven with their tears,
Did he smile his work to see?
Did he who made the Lamb make thee?

Tyger! Tyger! burning bright
In the forests of the night,
What immortal hand or eye
Dare frame thy fearful symmetry?

There are innumerable reactions and interpretive responses to the poem, ranging from a focus on Blake's apocalyptic mysticism to construing it as a comment on the Industrial Revolution in England. For the conference the main configuration of the meaning seemed to be the contrast between the predatory violence of the tiger and the lamb, associated with peace and innocence (and for Blake, with Christ). Christopher Rowland, professor of exegesis of Holy Scripture at Oxford, gave a slide presentation on Blake's work that was interesting and very enjoyable, as noted by Nikolaus Wandinger in his report for *The Bulletin of COV&R*. Blake (1757–1827) "struggled with the question of a God of victims versus a God of victimizers, and he did so with biblical stories that are important to scholars of mimetic theory as well: Cain and Abel, Joseph and Mary, and not least of all Job. Blake wrestled with different images of God, one benign, the other almost Satanic. He saw Job as a man who started out as a creature of habit, in the same old way of traditional religion, but who then is transformed, leaves this old religion behind and breaks through to an anti-sacrificial message."[90] It is clear that for Blake the fundamental mystery of God is that God created both the tiger and the lamb, the lamb in the poem calling to mind Christ as the Lamb of God who takes away the sins of the world. The "fearful symmetry" of the "Tyger" in the poem is the combination of beauty in its form and shape with its lethal violence as a predator. "It is that symmetry and the need to take account of both aspects that is crucial for understanding both 'the two contrary states of the human soul,'" to quote the title page of *Songs of Innocence and Experience*, "and the nature of the divine."[91] It seems evident from this that Blake's thought, his "theosophy," poses some huge questions for Jewish and Christian theology, in particular for an understanding of how God acts in human history.

Given the conflict between Muslim cultures and the Western world, especially with the emergence of Islamist terrorism in reaction to the economic and political incursions of Western nations in the Middle and Far East, as well as the threat of their cultural influence, it was an accomplishment to have Islamic scholars addressing plenary sessions of the Colloquium. This was an important follow-up to the Boston conference in 2000 on mimetic theory and the great religions, and it was related to the 2007 conference in Holland on tolerance and vulnerability. There were four Muslim scholars who were present and made a significant contribution: Tariq Ramadan, Shaika Halima Krausen, Ahmad Achtar, and Reza Shah-Kazemi. This section of the chapter would become much too long if I reported on all four speakers, so I will limit these remarks to Ramadan's lecture and Wolfgang Palaver's response.

Tariq Ramadan, professor of contemporary Islamic studies at the University of Oxford and prolific Islamic scholar and leader, gave the Raymund Schwager Lecture. Ramadan exhorted the participants to reject stereotypes and acknowledge that Islam is multifaceted and complicated, just as Christianity and Western culture are. He called for intellectual empathy and criticized views of justice and the penal code that are formalistic. He proposed that the way to achieve this approach was by distinguishing between means, ends, and conditions. For Islam, the end or goal is peace, which is the meaning of the word "Islam."[92] Justice is a means to peace and one of its conditions, along with love and mercy. Justice, as represented in the penal code, should not be construed formalistically, but understood as a means to the ultimate end. Comprehending the inner meaning of the penal code means to understand that cutting off the hands of people who have committed theft is not truly to fulfill justice if they were forced into a desperate situation by poverty. Of course, prohibitions and their prescribed punishments exist to prevent offenses and keep peace and order. He noted that the rule for stoning someone to death, as prescribed in the Sharia (literally "path"; sacred law in Islam), is quite strict, requiring at least four witnesses of the transgression. This requirement is seldom met, so executions can hardly ever be done legally. Ramadan, in fact, has called for a moratorium on corporeal punishments, which he says has met with widespread misunderstanding and distortion of his position, both among the sages and leaders in Islam and Western intellectuals. As for Islam, he explains in *Radical Reform,* "The proposal was not directed against Islam's teachings or against [its] texts—quite the contrary. In the name of the higher objectives of the message that call for respect for the life and dignity of women and men, equality, and justice, it was urgent to put an end to an instrumentalization of religion through literalist, formalist implementations that continued to affect poor people, women, and political opponents who have never had the means to defend themselves."[93]

Wolfgang Palaver emphasized in his response that Ramadan associates himself de facto with the Abrahamic revolution. The Abrahamic legacy is centered in the understanding of divine revelation that pulls its adherents away from the sacrificial culture that is generated by the scapegoat mechanism. Palaver noted Surah 12 in the Quran, which is named Yusuf or Joseph. Very much like the Joseph story in the book of Genesis, it represents the monotheistic rejection of scapegoating and divinization of the victim. He observed that Ramadan frequently refers to Surah 4:112, which condemns blaming the innocent for a delinquency or crime. Ramadan is also aware of the cycle of blame and revenge, which involves what Girard has called "a hunt for scapegoats to the second degree, a hunt for hunters of scapegoats."[94] This battle against persecution can become a persecutory extension of the scapegoat mechanism that may be even worse than the wrongs it seeks to redress because of its blind self-righteousness.

Religious and cultural pluralism is one of the "hot" issues in discussions between Western Christian thinkers and Islamic intellectuals. Palaver observed that Ramadan, and one of the other speakers, Shah-Kazemi, referred in their writings and their lectures at the conference to Surah 5:48 of the Quran, which speaks of a law and a path that God has prescribed for different peoples. It was not God's will to make just one people. God's plan is "to test you in what He hath given you: so strive as to race in all virtues."[95] Palaver said, "This means that we are asked to engage in positive mimesis, a form of emulation that follows if we direct our deep desires, our hearts, towards the one God whose infinity overcomes all scarcity and no longer entraps the various religions in their destructive mimetic rivalry."[96] Our rivalry, in other words, should be solely to compete in positive mimesis.

However, a word of caution is in order about Ramadan. There are some, perhaps many, scholars and commentators in Europe and North America, representing various religious and political positions, who view him as hypocritical or as having a "forked tongue," taking different positions in speaking to different audiences.[97] Most of what he said in his lecture sounded good to Christian and Jewish ears. However, if we consider, for example, his proposal to Muslims that a moratorium be declared on corporeal capital punishment: wouldn't a radical reform call for its elimination? In an exchange with President Nicolas Sarkozy of France over Ramadan's alleged anti-Semitism, the latter recommended, for example, that there should be a moratorium on the stoning of adulterous women, Sarkozy reportedly exclaimed, "A moratorium? What does that mean? We're in 2003!"[98] Ramadan's comment could mean that moratorium would be a step toward abolition of such practices. However, the picture that emerges from depictions by his critics is that of an Islamist, or at the least a quite conservative Muslim. He would be characterized as a Scriptural fundamentalist in the West because he does not believe that any kind of critical scholarship should be brought to bear on the Quran.

It is in the context of concern, indeed of anger, about such questions concerning Muslims and Islamic thinkers like Ramadan that Gil Bailie's paper should be placed. In an unusual kind of event for a COV&R conference, Bailie presented an argument in a parallel session that called the whole conference—or certainly the thematic part of the conference—into question. His paper, "Christian Virtues Gone Mad," was taken from G. K. Chesterton's statement, "The modern world is full of old Christian virtues gone mad."[99] His concern in the talk was to issue a warning against inauthentic cultural diffidence and deference to other cultures, and he scolded COV&R leaders for not following Girard's example, but instead for being caught up in the old liberal-leftist tendency to "blame the West." The so-called "dialogues," particularly with Muslim scholars, are exercises in congeniality, not a search for truth. He conceded that Christianity has made a "few" transgressions of conscience in its history, for which, he claimed, it has universally repented. However, he averred that "cherry-picking" the most congenial, compatible verses in the Quran in trying to establish dialogue is a vain pursuit. Celebrating a few passages as religiously and culturally reassuring in an otherwise chilling and bloodthirsty, homicidal sacred text only leads to cultural surrender.

The "fearful symmetries" in the conference title called to his mind the attempt to establish moral equivalences between the two scriptures and their religious traditions. Meanwhile, those who are named Christians are not protecting their heritage and passing on the tradition to their children. The failure to choose one kind of social morality over another is not tolerance but indifference. The United States has been aptly described as a "melting pot" in which people of various ethnic backgrounds and races have come together and become more or less integrated. By contrast, the ideological multiculturalism that is so prevalent among the elite classes in universities and liberal political circles functions to destroy the sociocultural structure that makes this integration possible. It is the melting of the pot itself.

Bailie stated that in general there are three basic topics at issue in the encounter between Islam and Western democracies: religious freedom for non-Muslims in Islamic countries, the fate of the Jews, and the freedom and dignity of women. Of these, he placed particular emphasis on the Jews as Islam's scapegoats of choice. Hostility toward Israel and the Jews is the Muslim "political narcotic."

Bailie certainly had many perceptive things to say both about the dangers Christians and Western democratic governments are bringing on themselves and the questions that must be posed to Muslim thinkers and leaders. In turn there are certain questions that should be posed to him. One concerns the raison d'être of COV&R itself. Is it wrong to invite Islamic scholars to speak to Colloquium members?[100] Given the object of COV&R, which includes to "explore, criticize, and develop the mimetic model of the relationship of violence and religion," are we to avoid talking to those of a rival religion and culture?

Another question is related to Bailie's intention of telling the truth, of "calling a spade a spade," as we say in American idiom. While telling the truth is it not better to refrain from derogatory, inflammatory language, which only creates more enemies? For example, his description of the Quran is so fundamentally insulting to devout Muslims that it prevents any kind of civil intercourse. The role of the Quran in Islam as divine revelation is comparable only to Jesus Christ in Christianity. Bailie's language tends to invite and incite a mimetic reaction: "What about your text? Is there nothing horrible and blood curdling in the Old Testament? How about the book of Revelation in the New Testament?" This is not to say that there is no truth in his charges, but a certain kind of rhetoric provokes mimetic reactions in the form of explanations and defenses of one's text from the other side, and so the mimetic cycle goes. If indeed the relation of the religions and cultures is that of rivalry, a kind of duel (to allude to Clausewitz and Girard's *Battling to the End*), is it possible to compete in positive mimesis?

Finally, is it wise to cast aspersions on the motives of our colleagues who quote certain Quranic passages with the goal of finding common points of insight that could be shared and developed? Should we reject the concept of an "Abrahamic Revolution" in which Islam has a part along with Judaism and Christianity? It is a subject that requires careful, deliberate study and reflection.

On the positive side, it is to Gil Bailie's credit that he has raised another one of the topics that should be pursued and debated in COV&R. He referred in the early part of his presentation to the example of René Girard, which is certainly important. Similarly, we should not overlook the example of Raymund Schwager, whose legacy includes the desideratum of interreligious dialogue. All in all, there is too much at stake to sweep these issues under the table.

Bailie's paper, along with the lectures of the Muslim speakers and Palaver's response to Ramadan, raise two fundamental questions from the standpoint of COV&R. One is a question of immediate sociopolitical consequence. Do Ramadan and other Islamic intellectuals believe that Islam should be the dominant mediating link that connects politics, religion, and culture in the process of globalization that is occurring? This is a conviction which Ramadan is certainly suspected of holding. That would mean, in effect, the world rule of Islam. Therefore, it would only be right and fair to have the time and format to ask him about this and to see whether he would give a straightforward answer.

The other question is more theoretical, but it is enormously important in the long run: is Islam, as Girard has put it in *Battling to the End,* essentially a rebuilt version of archaic religion, or a religion whose fundamental identity and dynamics are rooted in sacred taboo and prohibition, which conceal and protect a scapegoating mechanism, even as they are intended to protect against violence? The way I have stated this is certainly arguable, but it should be researched and discussed at length. If the answer should be yes, it would be difficult to hold a real dialogue with its representatives.

One of the important issues for Christianity and Islam is that of the status of gay and lesbian people. In this regard, James Alison gave a plenary talk that was both thoughtful and poignant on "Brokeheart Mountain: Reflections on Monotheism, Idolatry, and the Kingdom." He addressed the minority, outsider status of gays and lesbians, not only in the Roman Catholic Church, but in the Muslim world also. He pointed out that Christian, Jewish, and Muslim leaders seem to come together in the greatest unity in hatred and exclusion (not at all unlike the human race generally). This has certainly been the case when it comes to attitudes and teachings concerning homosexuals. He invited his audience to join him in thinking through a hypothetical test case. What if it were true that "being lesbian or gay is a regular and non-pathological variant in humanity?" And Muslims might imagine an analogous test case.

Setting this test case within the context of monotheism, creation, and idolatry, the basis of any answer to the question has to be affirmation of the one God. God is not one being among others, whether human or divine. God does not belong to a genus. God is God, "not an object within our ken." In the monotheistic frame of reference we do not worship any thing. So how can we learn the difference between idolatry and worship? The answer for the Catholic faith—and Christianity generally—is that God must reveal the answer, or the basis of any answer, and God has done that. God has given us God's own criterion, and that criterion is God: God as lived out in human form, Jesus. In him God discloses the death-dealing of the scapegoat mechanism, and we learn through him that "Idolatry . . . is an involvement in the human cultural reality of death from which God longs for us to be free." Moreover, God's own interpretation of the divine criterion for true worship and a nonidolatrous life is, according to the Church, the Holy Spirit. It is true that God is utterly Other and beyond our ken, but we are capable of recognizing "symptoms" (signs or indications) of God's criterion (Jesus) and God's interpretation since we ourselves are signs of the Creator and so also of Jesus and the Spirit, who are of the same personal reality as the Creator.[101]

The criterion for God gives us to understand that if we gang up on some vulnerable person or group of people, we are engaging in idolatry. We are not able really to ask the question about idolatry until we remove ourselves from such false and easy forms of unity. Catholic authorities, including the Magisterium (teaching office represented above all by the pope), are implicated in this idolatrous orientation because they refuse to become engaged with the question whether the doctrinal statement that gays and lesbians live in a "disordered condition"[102] is true, and they have refused in principle to engage in association with them.

Alison went on to pose the same question to our Muslim brothers and sisters, mutatis mutandis. That is, supposing it is possible to discuss this subject at all, is there a criterion that enables them to address such a hypothetical case in the Muslim context? Could they ask, "how might this be applied to the possibility of our learning that gay and lesbian people are simply a regularly occurring non-pathological variant of human being rather than a defective form of an intrinsically heterosexual humanity?"

The second and shorter part of Alison's presentation revolved around the meaning of the "end game," the Kingdom of God. "That the One God wants us to be one as God is One is not in doubt. But the shape of that oneness, and the criterion for it, are hugely in question. There is all the difference in the world between the sort of oneness that is the product of shared hatred over against an 'other' who is being annihilated and the sort of oneness that is made available by someone humiliating themselves, offering themselves as a peace offering whose gesture is then gently received by all present."

One of the happy moments in the business meeting was William Johnsen's announcement during his report that the celebration volume honoring René Girard, *For René Girard: Essays in Friendship and in Truth,* had been printed and would be sent to all COV&R members.[103] A notable event in the business meeting was the nomination of Robert Hamerton-Kelly and Charles Mabee as honorary lifetime members of the advisory board. These two colleagues, along with me, were the founders of COV&R in the sense of sharing the desire, conception, and work involved in getting COV&R started. The other colleagues who have been honored as honorary lifetime members are Raymund Schwager (d. 2004), Eric Gans, and Cesáreo Bandera.

COV&R at the American Academy of Religion in Montreal, November 7–10, 2009

Since COV&R began, this was the first meeting during the annual congress of the American Academy of Religion in which COV&R enjoyed the status of Related Scholarly Organization (RSO).[104] This status enables us to list our program in the main body of the AAR program book and to hold joint events with other groups in the Academy. The result of this new status is apparent already this year: there were three sessions, one of which was a joint event with another group, as well as COV&R speakers in another session who made presentations related to the work of COV&R.

The speakers in the first session were Bruce Chilton and Cleo Kearnes, who made presentations about their recent books. Chilton illustrated the thesis of his book, *Abraham's Curse,* by making a slide presentation of archaeological excavations. Kearnes spoke on her work, *The Virgin Mary, Monotheism, and*

Scripture, with Martha Reineke responding. The general discussion focused on the view of Islam held by Girard and as construed by mimetic theorists.

In the joint session with the Christian Spirituality Group there were three presentations. John Roedel, aided by the mimetic theory, explicated the difference between principled and strategic nonviolence. Gregory W. Love criticized the views of Girard and some of his followers, holding that they overemphasized the Passion of Christ and neglected his resurrection. This stirred a warm discussion with acute responses by Mark Heim and Nikolaus Wandinger. Denise Starkey spoke on "The Spirituality of Natality," applying it to the care of severe trauma victims who are survivors of violence.

A third session was devoted to a panel discussion of *Achever Clausewitz* by René Girard. (This was just before the appearance of the English translation, *Battling to the End.*) It offered a spectrum of information and views that placed it within its frame of reference and indicated its ramifications. Sandor Goodhart gave an overview of the book, noting that Girard concludes by sounding an alarm about the dominance of violence in the world and articulates a bleak view of the escalation to extremes in modern history. William Johnsen, editor of the series in which the English translation appears, commented on the difficulty of translating the work and observed that he had not *achevé* (finished—presumably he didn't mean "finished off"!) Girard when he lamented in his 2003 book, *Violence and Modernism,* that Girard had not analyzed modern violence. Paul Dumouchel concentrated on Clausewitz's dual concept of war as "a limited duel that tends to the extreme of the ultimate destruction of the other or as an institution that never leads to the destruction of the enemy but to a stable peace because its violence can be limited."[105] Charles Mabee began by pointing out that Girard demythologized religion in its archaic form as a cover-up for scapegoating, and he concluded by asserting that the nuclear bombing of Japan ended "history" in the sense of events having a meaning and a purpose. It shattered the pretention that God was concerned with human political structures and attempts to manage violence. Stephen Gardner expressed his unease about Girard's apocalypticism and the ambiguities of his view of political responsibility. Gardner also defended Raymond Aron's principle of rationality in political life.

Subsequently he went on to extend his defense of Aron's political thought and offer a penetrating analysis of Girard's apocalyptic perspective and renunciation of politics in two essays.[106] Gardner observes that Girard's rejection of Aron, who argues for a rational political philosophy as an alternative to total war, will seem perverse to many conservative readers, especially to Christians. Girard leaves his readers confused. He is an apocalyptic thinker, and as such he runs the risk of contributing to the chaos that he divines. He seems simultaneously to gesture toward a prudent avoidance of war that is unnecessary and unjust, which is not the same as a pacifist position. The question remains: are we exempt from obligations and responsibilities to inherited institutions, even if they appear to be collapsing?

The alterity of the sacred and profane in the modern world, as conceptualized by Durkheim and further explicated so brilliantly by Girard himself, is reflected in a somewhat altered and diminished fashion in the conflict between the Right and the Left in politics.[107] "It is the breakdown of this oscillating balance of opposites—when [it is] a healthy rather than an absolute opposition—within European nations between the Wars that made the last World War inevitable. This is what Raymond Aron argued, though on a political rather than anthropological level." Gardner recognizes that it is an oversimplification to identify the sacred and the profane completely with given political parties. The Bolsheviks and the Nazis "were both 'archaic' and 'modern' at once. When the cultural divide becomes a direct political battle, the difference itself is corrupted." Politics as such cannot resolve this difference. "The aim of politics in Aron's philosophical sense is to forestall this from happening, if it can, in part by recognizing the difference between politics and culture and the limits of politics."[108]

Other important aspects of Gardner's engagement with *Battling to the End,* especially in the article for *Contagion,* include the following: (1) As intimated in the discussion of Aron's political thought, he highlights the rivalry and clash between the archaic and the modern in Girard's thinking.[109] (2) He notes Girard's perspective on Islam as a reassertion of archaic religiosity. This raises the question whether Islam can properly be placed in the "Abrahamic revolution," as argued by Wolfgang Palaver. (3) Gardner also observes that although Girard speaks of a "good mimesis," there seems to be no evidence that he acknowledges a good "mimetic desire." This would put Girard in at least partial opposition to a significant number of COV&R colleagues.[110]

Finally, in an event related to COV&R, Martha Reineke and Suzanne Ross were joint presenters in the Teaching Religion Section of AAR. Their presentation was titled "Thinking Globally, Teaching Locally." Reineke talked about a course she offered in 2008 in which she showed a YouTube introduction to Girard. She explained that the mimetic theory is a powerful analytic tool for the study of violence at a global level, but it also offers insight into relationships, conflicts, and violence at the local level. Ross presented information about the medium of YouTube and the educational philosophy of the Raven Foundation. She pointed out that the Mimetic Theory 101 videos produced by

Raven work to overcome resistance to learning due to their informal, familiar character. The Foundation also offers a series of introductions to the Bible called "Bible Matters."

Reineke reported that the attendance was good, about forty-five people present. Their presentations generated many questions and comments for discussion. Their overall impression was that those in attendance were very interested in teaching Girard in religion courses and were intrigued with the possibilities of YouTube instruction.[111] Ross said she felt a "genuine enthusiasm for the mimetic theory and a hunger for teaching strategies to use with young undergrads who have as much to unlearn as to learn [about] violence in the Bible and the world."[112]

Ending the Story at Notre Dame, 2010

This history of the first twenty years of COV&R ends with the annual conference at the University of Notre Dame. For some of us it was an occasion to reminisce about the beginnings of COV&R, for the setting at Notre Dame was where the first seeds were sown for its beginnings, although those involved had scarcely any intimation of what the plant they tended would eventually become. As recounted in chapter 1, the Bible, Narrative, and American Culture seminar was formed at Notre Dame in the fall of 1986 during a semiannual meeting of the Westar Institute, whose most prominent group was the Jesus Seminar. Chaired by Charles Mabee, BINAC continued until March 1990. Knowing that Robert Funk, the Westar founder and director, intended to terminate it at the March meeting in Sonoma, California, Mabee and I began to plan for the beginning of an independent seminar in November 1989. As our plans developed, Robert Hamerton-Kelly joined us in founding a new group revolving around the work of René Girard. Gil Bailie, Diana Culbertson, and Thee Smith were other BINAC colleagues who had a significant role in the early days of COV&R.

The campus of Notre Dame is situated at the northern edge of South Bend, Indiana, whose name comes from its location on the south bend of the St. Joseph River. It is about ninety miles east of Chicago. It is not a large city, with a population just over 100,000 and a metropolitan area of more than 300,000. It is unusual not only due to the presence of Notre Dame, one of the outstanding American universities, but also St. Mary's College and an extension center of Indiana University are located there. The South Bend area was visited by French explorers and traders from the seventeenth into the nineteenth centuries. It had its beginnings as an organized political entity in the 1830s.

The University of Notre Dame had its beginnings in the 1840s. In 1842 Rev. Edward Sorin and seven companions, all members of the Congregation of the Holy Cross, took possession of land that the Bishop of Vincennes had given them in the mission fields.[113] They named the new school in their French language Notre Dame du Lac, Our Lady of the Lake. It was so named because there are two lakes on the land. By the end of the decade the school was awarding degrees, although it did not become a true university for a considerable period of time.

In time this institution founded by French priests of the Congregation of Holy Cross would be identified with the Irish in the United States. There were many people, not only Irish Catholics, who supported the university. Nonetheless, the great influx of Irish people, particularly in the nineteenth century, and the eventual success and prosperity of many of them in the United States, would contribute hugely to the academic success and overall prosperity of the university. It is an extremely large, magnificent campus with stone buildings and memorable architecture. The facilities are comfortable and generally in excellent condition. Those attending the conference found that even beyond the facilities, all the personnel, young and old (many of them student employees), were unfailingly courteous and helpful. We had the impression that an ethos of kindness and service prevailed. Just as important as the physical and social environment was the generous support of a number of sources: academic units of Notre Dame, Imitatio, and the Raven Foundation.

The organizers of the conference were not the least of those who served and made our time at Notre dame so enjoyable. Ann Astell and Margaret Pfeil, both professors in theology at Notre Dame, not only had worked out the program beautifully, but were always ready with a smile and a helping hand when assistance was needed. Astell was originally host and organizer. When she became ill for a period of time, Pfeil stepped in and assumed responsibility as co-organizer, which lifted a great burden from her colleague as she recovered from her illness. The task was demanding. There were close to 200 persons registered, the largest number yet for a COV&R conference in North America. There were eight plenary sessions, with ninety presenters in plenary and parallel sessions. In addition there were films, a theater performance of a one-act play written by Anthony Bartlett, an excursion to a Mennonite site, a walking tour of campus, and Sunday Mass at the Log Chapel on campus. Plus the concluding banquet—a subject in its own right to which I will return below.

One of the most obvious and promising aspects of the conference was the number of younger scholars participating in the conference, ranging from graduate and postgraduate students to those in their middle years. (To me, anyone below fifty now seems young!) An especially nice event was the Raymund Schwager Memorial Student Essay Contest, which featured the three winners presenting their papers: Anne McTaggart (first place), Vanessa Avery-Wall (second place), and Pasquale Maria Morabito (third place). All three papers were excellent.

"Transforming Violence: Cult, Culture, and Acculturation," June 30–July 4, 2010

Meeting from 9:00 A.M. to 3:00 P.M. on June 30, just before the conference began, the advisory board had a full docket of items on its agenda. Of the matters discussed, four are of general interest to report in this history. (1) European treasurer Dietmar Regensburger reported 110 active (dues paying) members in Europe, with 30 inactive members. North American treasurer Keith Ross reported 170 active members—but 300 on the inactive list! In the discussion it was suggested and accepted that in North America in particular we would send a letter to all inactives that would emphasize the advantages of paying dues each year. Besides the current benefit of a slight reduction in the conference registration fee, the semiannual newsletter, and the annual journal *Contagion,* active members will receive a free copy of every book published in the book series Violence, Mimesis, and Culture (the latter funded by Imitatio). (2) William Johnsen announced that *Contagion* is now listed in Project MUSE, which is an online database that provides full text and subscription access to scholarly journals in the humanities and social sciences. (3) Thérèse Onderdenwijngaard shared the information that fourteen students (coming from the United States, Columbia, Portugal, Poland, Ireland, the Netherlands, and England) would participate for the first time in a school in mimetic theory in Amsterdam this summer. It is supported by funds from Imitatio. (4) The next annual conference would be held June 15–18 in Sicily. Pasquale Morabito was present to discuss the organizational work and take questions. Jay Alberg proposed that the 2012 meeting be held at the International Christian University in Tokyo, Japan, where he is on the theology faculty. The board voted to approve the proposal.

The conference began with a plenary session that offered an appreciative critique of the thought of Robert Hamerton-Kelly. It was a session that came at an appropriate time and, as it turned out, formed a significant part of a total event, although I was unaware of this in January 2010 when I proposed the session. Hamerton-Kelly announced in the spring his retirement as chair of Imitatio. Imitatio held a dinner honoring him the evening of June 29, with an ambiance of gratitude for his work and a spirit of conviviality. Among the memorable moments of the dinner were the presentation of unusual gifts to the honoree (including a football signed by the coach of the football team!) and Bob Kelly's a capella rendition of "O Danny Boy."

The critical discussion the next day at the beginning of the conference centered on my paper, "Hamerton-Kelly on Violence and Mimesis: An Appreciative Critique." Martha Reineke was the respondent and Diana Culbertson served as moderator. The session spoke, at least in a general sense, to the theme of the entire conference. In the human process of participating in *cult* (worship based on sacrifice, prohibition, and myth), *culture* (the transmission of social order stemming from cult), and *acculturation* (the learning, adaptation, and revision of the transmitted order), is it possible to transform the mimesis inevitably resulting in conflict and violence?

My paper, posted beforehand on the conference website, was too long to read, so I condensed the oral presentation to some key points. After a brief introduction I emphasized three points in Hamerton-Kelly's thinking about violence and mimesis. First, we are wired for mimesis, which the form and dynamic of human desire. In human culture this entails that violence is inevitable, if not necessary. Second, the creation of the world is good *as an eschatological reality* in the mind of God. The revelation of this—the apocalypse or "unveiling"—is definitively given in the advent of Christ and the formation of the church. Third, the preliminary or proleptic embodiment of the new creation is the *ekklesia,* the gathering of those who are called, the Body of Christ. Only within this community can positive mimesis take place.

I raised four questions, as indicated previously in this chapter. First, is Hamerton-Kelly's thought a form of Gnosticism? The answer to that is definitely not, although the question itself leads to important issues concerning the relation of morality to human origins and the possibility of divine disclosure and presence not only in the specific biblical revelation but also in the environing natural and social world. Second, does his position on mimesis and violence come perilously close to the satanic theodicy described by Jean-Pierre Dupuy? (See above in this chapter.) That is, given his view of violence and his acceptance of a kind of Calvinistic determinism, is it Hamerton-Kelly's position that the end (fulfillment of God's will, the kingdom of God) is justified by means that are violent? The biblical witness to revelation, especially the revelation of Christ, attests that God does not cause violence but does *transform* it into ends that produce condition and love. This is one of the main points where the theme of the conference was engaged. The third question is one of human initiative or freedom. I agreed with Kelly that freedom of the will as it is commonly understood is nonexistent from a Christian standpoint. True freedom is a gift of divine grace. Here is where I diverged from his position, for I understand divine grace and imitation of God also at work in some ways and forms *outside* the empirical church and biblical revelation. Fourth and finally, has Christianity actually influenced the direction of Western culture and spirituality in ways of good mimesis (as well as bad of course, but the point is a "deposit," as it were, of lasting institutions and traditions propagating a good contagion)?[114] Whatever the sins and flaws of historical Christianity, the Christian revelation has brought the mandate and possibility of mutual love and forgiveness to the attention of the world in innumerable ways. If we cannot affirm this, then the general theme of the conference, "transforming violence," has to be viewed as impossible in the sacrificial history of the human world in which we live; it would be partially realized, if at all, by only a few people within the framework of the church. In effect, it would be only an otherworldly possibility for those who believe in life after death.

In her response Martha Reineke focused initially on two of the questions raised in my paper, those concerning Gnosticism and human agency. Without disagreeing with me that Hamerton-Kelly's theology is not Gnostic, she suggests that the issue of creation and eschatology he sparks stems from a type of Protestantism; this is a Protestant perspective that Girard also shares, in spite of his Catholicism. It is a perspective "that sees a world wholly pervaded by sin rather than a Catholic perspective which sees that creation is geared toward the good though distorted by the fall."[115] For Girard, this is a type of Catholicism one finds in Blaise Pascal, who was a Jansenist, or who was certainly at least influenced by Jansenism. Concerning human agency, Reineke observes that Stephen Gardner's fourfold model of mimetic desire is helpful in comparing Hamerton-Kelly's position to what Girard has expressed. That is, there is good and bad mimesis and good and bad desire. For instance, one might imitate the positive mimesis of another, but one's desire is realized in bad faith. Perhaps, for example, I see my model praying to God, apparently with great humility, and I imitate her by praying, but I only *appear* to be praying humbly. Really I want to be seen as praying by an audience, above all by my model. Gardner holds that Girard does speak of a good or positive mimesis but not of a good mimetic *desire*.[116] In any case, Girard seems much more generous than Kelly in affirming positive mimesis and good desire, and not necessarily only in the context of Christian faith and the church.

In the second part of her response Reineke turned to suggestions for carrying on dialogue drawn from Heraclitus and Julia Kristeva: Heraclitus's style of teaching and Julia Kristeva's "ethic of strangeness." She points out that Heraclitus recommends an approach to the logos or understanding that we seek by his use of a style featuring analogy, paradox, and ambiguity. Thus the greatest value of his thought for us is not the content of his thought (the founding *arche*—the "father"—of generative violence), but his example as a teacher challenging those who take up his words. As for Kristeva, the main point is a question as to how we see ourselves before a sacrificial economy. To move beyond that, Kristeva recommends that in psychoanalysis both psychoanalyst and analysand focus "on that in me that wants the truth," and at the same time "to entertain a strangeness before the truth," which involves seeing oneself first of all as the stranger who wants the truth.[117] The model for this has its roots in the biblical paradigm of the ethic of the stranger, as we see, for example, in the account of Ruth and Boaz in the book of Ruth. Reineke points out that in a community of scholars recognizing this "ethic of strangeness" there will be openness to truth shared with the other. If we are capable of the self-reflexivity to accept our own lack of being, "a strangeness to ourselves," which could lead us to distort the truth, then it becomes possible "to create a space for conversation that includes our own acknowledgement that the desire we have to be the ones who are supposed to know cannot be met with certitude," and the "we can be more generous with one another."[118]

This plenary session provided an important part of the basic background for discussing and reflecting on the theme of the conference. It provoked a lively discussion, with a number of auditors, including Hamerton-Kelly, coming to one of the microphones to offer comments or pose questions. Among the interesting remarks in Hamerton-Kelly's response were these two: he does not limit the extent and effect of the grace of God to the church,[119] and for him, as for René Girard, his conversion experience is the center of his work from which all else radiates.

Cyril O'Regan, a distinguished theologian and specialist in apocalyptic thought at Notre Dame, gave a plenary address on "Girard in the Spaces of Apocalyptic." (His most recent book is *Theology and the Spaces of Apocalyptic.*) He delineated the modes of apocalyptic thought that Girard rejects and those against which he speaks and writes. Girard rejects a degenerate form of literalist interpretation of biblical apocalypse and he opposes Hegelianism and Marxism (the left wing of philosophy of history stemming from Hegel) as well as Nietzscheanism and Heideggerianism (the modern pagan or Dionysian mode). O'Regan's discourse on modern thinkers with whom Girard has some affinity, namely Johann Metz and Emmanuel Levinas, was particularly interesting.[120] However, it was not clear whether O'Regan really grasped the force of the inner logic of Girard's position, which is the movement of mimetic desire escalating to extremes since Clausewitz. Tony Bartlett's comment was related to the force of this inner logic when he commented in the open discussion that he missed a sense of the *undertow* and the *underside* of history in O'Regan's paper, that is, the condition of those oppressed by violence and poverty for whom and among whom God has entered into history.

Overall, the paper was valuable in providing a perspective on Girard's place in apocalyptic thought. The respondents, James Alison and Wolfgang Palaver, expressed their appreciation for an outside plenary speaker who had taken his reading of Girard so seriously. Both respondents noted with approval O'Regan's recognition of Girard's "bifocal diagnostic apparatus," that is, his approach and method combing biblical and sociological areas of exploration.[121]

One of the notable papers that were squarely aimed at the conference theme was presented by Tobin Siebers: "In the Name of Pain." He proceeded from the standpoint of how acculturation has produced a certain view of those with disabilities and went on from there to a "converted" perspective that affirms the value and dignity of their existence. (Siebers' two most recent books are *Disability Theory* and *Disability Aesthetics.*) Siebers unveiled how we make assumptions about the painful condition of disabled persons. His intention was to speak against the assumption that a life of pain is not worth living and to reveal that "the fear of pain is one of the most pervasive and insidious justifications of disability oppression."[122] Discrimination takes place in our society and in the courts, and supposedly in the name of doing the best for those who are disabled. Siebers cited some legal cases involving controversial medical interventions, wrongful birth, and euthanasia.

These cases raise in sharpest form the issue of whether a disabled life is worth living, or even whether death is preferable to life for a person who will be disabled from birth. "In a world where pain represents the ultimate measure of quality of life, all disabled people risk to have their existence described as a wrongful life because disability and suffering are thought synonymous."[123] Siebers concluded the paper with the statement, "Everyone will find new reasons to kill disabled people who are thought, like Terri Schiavo, to have no future because they live with pain."

Siebers, a former student of Girard's, is thoroughly familiar with the mimetic theory, as witness some of his scholarly writings earlier in his career. In his paper he does not refer to it at all, although it informs his perspective in everything he studies. His strategy in this paper was to present actual cases and make the paper provocative. One aspect of the mimetic theory appears to loom large in the background of his thinking about disability: disability as a sign of the victim. Another important aspect of the mimetic theory is that culture, like language, is a system of differences, that is, an arrangement or organization of distinctions enabling participants to communicate and make transactions or exchanges in various ways. As we see in ancient myth and symbol (Oedipus being the classical example in Western cultures), the person who is crippled or disabled does not fit conveniently into the system of differences. On could say that this person is "different" in the wrong way. On difference, Siebers says, "To my thinking, disability is a difference prone to representations of inferiority or superiority (subhuman, superhuman, etc.), and these representations thus justify violent behavior and discrimination against the disabled."[124]

The Schwager Memorial Lecturer was introduced by Józef Niewiadomski, who first gave a moving tribute to Raymund Schwager, both to the man and to his contribution to the mimetic theory and Christian theology. The Schwager Lecturer was Susan Mizruchi, whose topic was "The School of Martyrdom: Class and Culture in *The Catcher in the Rye*." Mizruchi, the author of *The Science of Sacrifice,* among many other writings, gave a very interesting talk on Holden Caulfield, J. D. Salinger's memorable adolescent character, as a spiritual rebel. Caulfield's spirituality is radical, a fact often overlooked according to Mizruchi. One of the most striking aspects of the presenter's thesis was the evidence in the novel that Caulfield is obsessed with blood and bloodletting. In spite of his empathy with people he is at the same time alienated from everyone and everything: school, teachers, parents, friends (a teacher, Mr. Antolini, appears at first to be an exception, but it turns out that there is a question about him). The one clear exception is his sister Phoebe. He is prone to tantrums and provocative behavior. At the heart of Mizruchi's argument concerning his martyr complex is the insight that Caulfield seeks a foundational wound comparable to Jesus, the person who died for others, and to the lunatic of Gerasa, who wounded himself continually and whose demons Jesus cast out. With such a wound Caulfield could overcome the grief and guilt he feels as he continues to mourn for the brother who died three years before. He could fulfill his fantasy of being a "catcher in the rye," a savior figure rescuing children before they fall over the cliff at the end of the rye field.[125]

Mizruchi's interesting work could be furthered greatly by taking on the insights of the mimetic theory. My own take is this: given that we human beings are "interdividuals" who relate to the world not by instinct but through imitation of models or mediators of desire, the best way to construe the demoniac's demon possession is that he has internalized the voices of the "others," those in the community to whom he is unusually sensitive and vulnerable for whatever reason. These are the voices of mimetic rivalry that are persecutory toward those who don't "fit in." The striking thing about the passage in Mark 5:1–20 is that in contrast to Matthew and Luke, only Mark mentions the self-wounding. I understand it as preemptive mimesis, that is, doing the persecutory work of the others, the mob, before they do it themselves. The demoniac has internalized the crowd, the others, the mob. From there on I think Mizruchi interprets the Gospel story well. Jesus enacts a catharsis which is sacrificial (the pigs sent into the deep water).[126] As I reflect on her reading of the Caulfield character, I think all of this is very relevant to understanding him. He has internalized all the competing rivalrous voices, which he is trying to expel. Except he cannot on his own.

In his response to Mizruchi, William Johnsen did a brilliant job of reviewing in summary form Mizruchi's body of work and suggesting how the themes and questions she highlights would be extended and fulfilled in the context of Girard's mimetic theory. Many of his sentences were gems. For example, "A scapegoat hypothesis is superior intellectually, scientifically, to sacrifice, because it comprehends both the sacrifice and the sacrificer, tale and teller: we know that they know not what they do."[127] He suggested in conclusion, "It would be most fruitful to integrate her work into our emerging evolutionary history of sacrifice, bringing it under the influence of the untranslatable imperative "achever": *finish it, finish the line of the romantique/romanesque, finish the line which begins in the proto-human and ends in the apocalypse*."[128]

Of the many other good papers given during the conference, Joel Hodge's presentation in a parallel session is particularly worthy of notice. He showed how collective prayer was crucial in ending Indonesian occupation of East Timor. His paper revolved around the concept of transcendence. He defined transcendence as "the human disposition toward the Other" and the ability "to move beyond oneself toward the Other for identity and ontological satisfaction."[129] He reflected on two forms of transcendence, mob violence and Christian solidarity in prayer, which confronted one another in East Timor.

East Timor held an independence referendum in 1999 and voted for independence from Indonesia, whose occupation had been brutal. The Indonesian military then began a campaign of violence resulting in 1,500 deaths. It was a situation illustrating what William Cavanaugh has described as the modern nation-state's assertion of itself as the arbiter of violence and the guarantor of social order.[130] Hodge's examination of the persecution and violence and a prayerful response to it offers an instructive analysis of mimetic desire, scandal, and conversion.

The incident that he highlights as a breakthrough event that symbolized the totality of the Timorese resistance and victory occurred on a beach in 1999. The Indonesian military and militias had herded a group of male Timorese to the beach in order to execute them. As the executioners were about to fire, a Roman Catholic priest arrived and intervened. He asked the militia to allow him to lead the Timorese in prayer before they died. Surprisingly, the military permitted this. "The group then knelt, praying together to God through Christ and Mary. Following this, the militia decided not to kill the group."[131]

Hodge points out three things in connection with the approach stemming from prayer. First, it broke the mimetic cycle by giving the mob and victims space to *remember* themselves as human beings in relation to one another. Scandal was thus overcome. Second, the link of prayer to the pacific transcendence of Christ had a powerful mimetic appeal. Some members of the militia were Christians themselves, and the ones praying sought not vengeance but peace. Third, the solidarity founded in the pacific transcendence of Christ countered the violent transcendence of the mob. The Timorese "did not face the mob as frightened and self-assertive individuals but as persons in relationship with the crucified and risen victim, and so, with each other."[132]

The concluding banquet was an event of good food, fellowship, and a delightful program arranged by Professors Astell and Pfeil. Henry Weinfeld of the University of Notre Dame gave a poetry reading, and Kathy Schuth and Sheila McCarthy, who had graced the beginning of every plenary session with a musical prelude, played for us, McCarthy on the violin and Schuth on the hammer dulcimer. They also led the group in a rousing rendition of "How Can I Keep from Singing?" Ann Astell then recognized the three founders of COV&R—Robert Hamerton-Kelly, Charles Mabee, and James Williams—and asked them to reminisce a bit about the beginnings of COV&R. The "old-timers" were happy to do so, and they managed to reflect on that time without getting long-winded. May our banquets continue.

Brief Biographies of COV&R Leaders

Ann Astell

Ann W. Astell, a member of the Secular Institute of the Schoenstatt Sisters of Mary, was professor of English at Purdue University prior to her appointment as professor of theology at the University of Notre Dame in 2007. The recipient of an NEH Fellowship and of a John Simon Guggenheim Memorial Fellowship, she is the author of six books: *The Song of Songs in the Middle Ages* (1990), *Job, Boethius, and Epic Truth* (1994), *Chaucer and the Universe of Learning* (1996), *Political Allegory in Late Medieval England* (1999), *Joan of Arc and Sacrificial Authorship* (2003), and *Eating Beauty: The Eucharist and the Spiritual Arts of the Middle Ages* (2006). She is also the editor of four essay collections.

A board member for the Society for the Study of Christian Spirituality, she also has served as an advisory board member of COV&R and at this writing is its executive secretary. She was the organizer of the 2005 conference in Koblenz and the co-organizer of the 2010 annual meeting at Notre Dame. Her excellent scholarship in literature, theology, and history, her devotion to COV&R, and warm and smiling personality have been of inestimable value to the Colloquium.

William A. Johnsen

William A. Johnsen is a professor of English at Michigan State University in East Lansing. Since 1979 he has written widely and published articles in journals and book collections on the intersection of mimetic theory with European literature and international modernism. His book, *Violence and Modernism: Ibsen, Joyce and Woolf*, was published in 2003. Johnsen joined COV&R in 1995 and served on the advisory board of COV&R beginning in 2002. He became editor of *Contagion* in 2006. *Contagion* is now published by the Michigan State University Press, and is included in Project Muse, an online database that provides full text and subscription access to scholarly journals in the humanities and social sciences. He edits as well a book series at MSU Press: Violence, Mimesis, and Culture. In his work as editor of *Contagion* and the book series he has been meticulous in helping authors to achieve greater accuracy and clarity in their language.

Since its formation Johnsen has been publications chair of Imitatio, and is a member of the board of directors. As a scholar and a dependable, supportive colleague he has made a significant contribution to both COV&R and Imitatio.

Martha Reineke

Reineke, who obtained her Ph.D. from Vanderbilt University, is professor of religion in the Department of Philosophy and Religion at the University of Northern Iowa. She is the author of *Sacrificed Lives: Kristeva on Women and Violence*, which is an important contribution to women's studies and the mimetic theory. Active in COV&R since the early 1990s, she was asked to become the COV&R coordinator with the American Academy of Religion in 2006, and she has taken the role very seriously, recognizing the need not only for good programs but also the need of graduate students to "go shopping" for jobs, to meet faculty of the various institutions, and so on. By 2009 she succeeded in getting COV&R listed as a Related Scholarly Organization. This was an important accomplishment to the benefit of COV&R.

Reineke and Suzanne Ross held a session at AAR 2009 on curriculum development for college teachers, a program of outreach on behalf of COV&R and the mimetic theory. Through the resources of Raven, which is headed by Suzanne and Keith Ross, they are working also on making contact with high schools to use curricula informed by the mimetic theory. Reineke's scholarship and clear-sighted practical reasoning and administrative ability have been significant in the work of COV&R.

Julie Shinnick

Shinnick first attended COV&R when it held its yearly meeting with AAR/SBL in Chicago in 1994. During a process of looking for enlightening sources on scapegoating, she had been having little success in finding a satisfactory explanation or theory when she happened to come across a notice on René Girard, *The Scapegoat* in a Johns Hopkins Press book catalogue. She ordered the book and when it arrived she read it in twenty-four hours. From then on, she read everything by Girard that she could find. She knew nothing about COV&R until she attended the Medieval Institute in Medieval Latin and Paleography at Notre Dame University in the summer of 1994. At table during one of the meals she asked whether anyone there had heard of Girard. It so happened that Father Ed Ondrako was at Notre Dame that summer, and was also eating at that table. He and I were friends at Syracuse University, and he was my spiritual advisor and catechist as I went through the process of becoming a Roman Catholic in 1992 and 1993. He and Shinnick struck up a conversation, and soon she wrote to me. The rest is history.

Shinnick is a specialist in medieval music history and a member of the faculty of the School of Music at the University of Louisville. She obtained her Ph.D. in musicology from the University of Texas. An interesting aspect of her work is some creative ideas she holds about the relation of music and violence in thirteenth-century Europe. Within COV&R she accepted the office of treasurer in 1998 and served for ten years. In addition, she continued to handle the North American mailing list for an additional two years. Her warm collegiality and long-term commitment of time and energy to the benefit of the organization have been of inestimable value to us.

CHAPTER SIX

Diversity in Community: Concluding Perspective

To compose this brief final chapter I have not only reviewed the entire history as previously presented, but I have also taken note of the statements of perspective in chapters 2, 3, and 4. I have selected those themes and issues that stand out for me as especially important in the work and interactions of those involved in COV&R and that come into play within a "diversity in community," which is actual to some extent and yet always a hopeful vision to an even greater extent. The discussion of these themes and issues includes my own recommendations for the welfare of the Colloquium on Violence and Religion, which I offer for whatever value they may hold.

Cultural or Countercultural?

By "cultural" I mean academic culture in particular, or the academic strand in the dominant Western cultural forms. There are two interrelated questions to pose: Is it desirable that COV&R become a much larger academic society like some of the large, even huge academic societies that have thousands of members? And should we develop a description of the mimetic theory that is basically secular, which does not deal with religion methodologically except as a purely historical phenomenon? The underlying concern in both questions is a matter of cultural acceptance, not only in the academy but also in the general environing culture. Gaining a great influx of members would reflect acceptance and popularity, and both reflect and facilitate greater influence over still more people. A secular description of the mimetic theory would presumably not only attract more people who are not religious but also make it easier for graduate students and others who wish to do research informed by the mimetic theory to get degrees, academic positions, and promotions. On the other hand, is there an advantage to thinking and working counter to cultural trends, especially now and for the foreseeable future?

On the matter of growing and gaining influence, it is obvious that there is some sort of critical mass that must be reached for the survival of an organization like COV&R. In terms of survival, however, the Colloquium is doing well and at this time its prospects as a scholarly society look good. The participation in annual conferences is stable, in meetings at the annual convention of the American Academy of Religion it is increasing, and our financial situation has improved considerably, thanks particularly to support from the Raven Foundation and Imitatio. Yet the motor of COV&R, its dynamic inner character, derives from the intellectual power and ethical and spiritual ramifications of the mimetic theory, whose current moves against the waves of culture in some decisive ways. Our environing cultural forms contain tendencies of the archaic, or something pointing toward the archaic, as Cesáreo Bandera would put it, and these tendencies move people to fall back onto expressions of the scapegoat mechanism and tribal and pagan polarization of conflicts that can rush people into enmity and mob violence. Our cultural forms romanticize and idealize people as models mediating objects of desire who are economically successful. Secular dogmas are apotheosized, such as the enemy twins socialism and capitalism, which have been imagined by their extremist exponents as a kind of secular divinization of historical destiny. Religion has been privatized, so that a large segment of the populaces see it as irrelevant to public affairs or larger communities of human beings, while many of those who understand it as relevant to public life are among those who seek to impose a demonic fundamentalism in the public sphere. It is not a pretty picture, and COV&R stands athwart it in certain fundamental ways.

Now as to a secular description of the mimetic theory, there is no doubt that can be done, but should it be?[1] In Imitatio Robert Hamerton-Kelly and other leading voices favor a methodological orientation to scientific research that is conceptually separate from faith or religious commitment of any kind. However, a question must be posed about that position. Girard's source of inspiration for the mimetic theory is the Christian revelation and his Christian faith. Indeed, he avers, "Mimetic theory is essentially Christian."[2] Would or could it have come about without a great mind informed by a Christian perspective? That's a historical question that is impossible to answer conclusively. The theory had certainly never appeared prior to his work.

In the second place, it is a historical fact that Jesus was crucified as the leader of a movement considered dangerous to law and order both by the Roman government and by the Jewish authorities. However, the preservation of his words and the interpretive witness to the meaning of his life and death would not have occurred without the resurrection faith and commitment of the earliest followers. So on two counts, the specific origination of the mimetic theory and the origin of Christianity, separating faith and mimetic theory is on slippery ground from a historical standpoint.

Of course, it is possible to bracket the anthropological body of the theory from faith itself, garner insights, apply it and refine it in many fields of research. However, the loss of the *beginning* and the *end,* that is, the human predicament and salvation in some form, will make a tremendous difference. Concerning the human predicament, the mimetic theory as developed by Girard certainly holds that there is a predicament. Even if one does not accept a doctrine of "original sin," it is still incumbent to make sense of the mimetism that generates the rivalry and violence that are endemic to human culture.

And if one surmounted that problem with a credible theory of human origins and/or development, the big question would remain: What good is it? What role do research, knowledge, and understanding have in moving toward peace and spiritual health? They could be a necessary condition for many people, but there is no evidence of which I know that knowledge and understanding are a sufficient condition of moral and spiritual healing. The mimetic condition of being human can quickly and easily turn knowledge and understanding into satanic uses. Is there anything short of real *conversion,* whether at an individual or societal level, that would produce salvation or enlightenment of a spiritual sort or peaceful fulfillment? What good would COV&R and Imitatio contribute to being human? When one presses the question that way, one is moving into the realm of faith and religion.

There is another aspect of this, which is a serious issue for many of those involved in Imitatio and COV&R who are concerned with ethics and moral theory. This is the more general meta-question of how one grounds moral theory apart from religion. Without the predication of origins and ends in God, how does one deal with the ethical impulse of mimetic theory? That is the limiting question.[3] Without that ethical impulse coupled with its explanatory power, Girard's mimetic theory would not have attracted most of its passionate adherents. Now we know it is possible to hold a pragmatic position on social consensus in which people agree not to violate one another's rights, and so forth, but what power over the heart and mind does such pragmatism hold? What is it that binds people together if they need to know not simply what is morally right and morally wrong, *but why be moral at all?* Doesn't our moral experience presuppose a basic confidence that all is well and all manner of things are well, as Julian of Norwich said? And doesn't our moral experience presuppose that this confidence is not just in our minds, but grounded in reality itself? As Schubert Ogden pointed out many years ago, "The characteristic deficiency of all nontheistic moral theories is that they leave the final depth of morality itself utterly unillumined. Although they may well focus our moral action and the immanent standards by which it is governed, they fail to render at all intelligible the underlying confidence and its transcendent ground in which our moral activity, as our life generally, actually has its roots."[4]

From my vantage point, therefore, conversation and cooperation with those who wish to keep religion out of mimetic theory are desirable. However, to turn the mimetic theory into a secular (nonreligious) methodology and form of hermeneutics would be a serious error for the identity of COV&R, and I believe for Imitatio as well.

The Tension between Theory and Practice

The tension between theory and practice has come up several times in this history, including a fairly lengthy discussion in the concluding perspective segment of chapter 4. I have also mentioned the ethical impulse of the mimetic theory at more than one point, and there is no doubt that at least a fair number of our active COV&R participants, the author included, are concerned with what used to be called the "social gospel" in twentieth-century America, that is, concerned with the establishment of structures of justice and mutual aid, which are mandated by the love of God revealed in Christ. However, as I regard our history, the personal tendencies of our leaders, and of course the vocation of René Girard in conceiving and clarifying the mimetic theory, I have to conclude that COV&R, though not inhospitable to social activists, will continue to be a professional society primarily concerned with theory.

That is my evaluation of COV&R in its collective identity. However, individuals will continue to work as participants and consultants in various projects of practical application of the insights of mimetic theory, both among churches and a variety of religious groups and in various social and educational organizations. Moreover, the close relationship that COV&R enjoys with organizations such as Imitatio, Theology and Peace, and the Raven Foundation should ensure the connection of COV&R and individual members thereof in projects of ethical and educational outreach.

Yet when all is said and done, the real strength of COV&R lies in its orientation to theory. The dynamic of COV&R is its facilitation of interdisciplinary investigation and conversation centered in the concepts of the mimetic theory and the research implications and many faceted research programs it opens up.

Christianity and the Great Religious Traditions

If COV&R is to continue to grow and sharpen its theoretical vocation of spelling out the ramifications of the mimetic theory for the twenty-first century, its challenge will be to pay more and more careful attention to the great religious traditions of the world.[5] In spite of the importance of the Christian faith of many of its leaders and members, among whom there is a considerable number of Catholics, COV&R cannot let itself be identified as a Christian or Roman Catholic organization.

But the role of religion in its founding and central concerns is beyond doubt and should so remain. The object of COV&R, its raison d'être, is to "explore, criticize, and develop the mimetic model of the relationship between violence and religion in the genesis and maintenance of culture," as stated on the masthead of every issue of *The Bulletin of the Colloquium on Violence and Religion*. Whether or not we might want to revise the wording after twenty years, I have never heard anyone raise a serious question about that definition of what we are about. Indeed, the only questions posed are those that ask why we don't expand our range of concern and investigation. Tentative steps have been taken in that direction, as recounted particularly in our survey of annual conferences in 2000 at Boston College, 2002 at Purdue University, 2007 in Amsterdam, and 2009 in London.

The most immediately pressing issue is that of Islam and its role in the apocalyptic movement of history. However, the close relation of Christianity to Judaism in light of their biblical origins, the influence of the Jewish people in Western culture, and the role of Israel in the modern world, means that we must and will, willy-nilly, take the Jewish heritage into account. Beyond that, it's likely that we can learn from other traditions, such as Buddhism, Hinduism, Sikhism, and Taoism, and at the same time, through conversation and interactive scholarship, not only enrich the mimetic theory and our own religious commitments, but also extend the influence of the mimetic theory.

One question, of course, is how this "dialogue," this interactive discourse, should take place. We can, of course learn much from Westerners, Jewish or

Christian, who practice sensitive scholarship in their investigation of non-Western traditions. However, there is no doubt that we need access to those who actually practice other faiths and come from their milieus. It is simple to conceive what should be done, though the implementation may be difficult. We should invite carefully selected scholars from other traditions who really want to converse with us, to learn from us as we from them. That means that all parties in the dialogue will be open to change—not conversion to another religion (although from the standpoint of my own theology, that could not be absolutely excluded), but revision of thinking and developing new collegial friendships.

Concerning Islam specifically, I think Girard is right in pointing to a reversion to elements of archaic mentality in some forms of Islam, especially modern fundamentalist or "Islamist" movements, which cannot tolerate a sphere of social and political existence not controlled by their religion and whose sanctions against those who transgress its boundaries (prohibitions) are brutal. However, Islam is complex, as are its adherents. There are certainly Muslims who reject that sort of archaism and want to throw their lot in with the Abrahamic revolution.[6]

Mimetic Desire in the Economy and the Media

Mimetic desire in the economy and the communications media was the theme of only one conference, at the University of Innsbruck in 2003. As noted in chapter 4, however, it overlapped the themes of two other conferences, at Wiesbaden in 1994 and at Graz in 1997. The reader will have seen that I was extremely impressed with Józef Niewiadomski's presentation at the Innsbruck conference. Western culture is undergoing an upheaval, which now has spread throughout the world, and this chaotic transition is both reflected in and partially caused by the media of communications.[7] The Internet is the most prominent and dangerous of these means of communication, but others, such as television and film, are not far behind and the technology of all of them is interrelated.

Niewiadomski has pointed to the media, and especially the Internet, as a kind of substitute for the church. There is no doubt that the indifferent consummation of "interchangeable empty forms," as Michael Haneke characterized the modern loss of reality (see chapter 3), is now taking the form of the supposed intimacies of Internet communications that are usually virtual. One can easily be carried away there in a flood of desire issuing in mimetic rivalry without boundaries where individuals assert their autonomy, becoming like gods (or satans) to one another.

The financial markets both feed into this media frenzy and participate in it. Jean-Pierre Dupuy has acutely analyzed the myth of the autonomously operating market and pointed out that as an instance of mass behavior, it is mimetic to the core. One of his important conclusions is that contrary to the mimetic victimage in archaic and traditional societies, economic victimage is now third-person victimage. The prevalent attitude toward these economic victims is *indifference*. One of the functions of the Internet is to serve as an outlet for their rage and resentment, which seeps into politics and all areas of social life.

It would be a boon to COV&R and a service to our respective societies, COV&R and Imitatio, to extend research and discussion of economics and the media, and to produce some more people who can become public commentators on these intertwined subjects. It has been argued that the days of the "public intellectual" are over.[8] Times have changed since there were such well-known public commentators, but could COV&R (and Imitatio) produce or encourage a new breed of public voices?

Violence and Mimesis

There are and have been several points of view on mimetic desire, both from the standpoint of social science and the possibility of its function in the improvement of social, political, and economic conditions and from the standpoint of religion and the possibility of its function in attaining to inner peace, human reconciliation, and ultimate salvation. Some participants in COV&R have taken to the mimetic theory for the sake of pacifist aims, others have hoped it would be a key to conflict resolution. Some colleagues have argued for the possibility of positive mimesis, which from their standpoint Girard has neglected in his own articulation of the mimetic theory. A few of our thinkers have insisted on the inevitable connection of mimesis and violence within the context of historical existence apart from the imitation of Christ and the ultimate realization of the kingdom of God. It appears that René Girard, at least in the last decade, has himself tended toward the latter position and perspective.

There should be no doubt that René Girard's body of work will always serve as the point of departure and continual reference for understanding, applying, and criticizing the mimetic theory. But a dogmatic adherence to it, or an imperative to know what he thought or how he understood it at every turn, should not be incumbent upon any individual or group who may be mimetic theorists. For the Colloquium as an organization, the key will be *balance,* balance in thought and balance in collegial relations.

Balance in thought will be achieved by remaining aware of our history, and especially the insights and spiritual example of our founding thinker. At the same time, it behooves us to remain open to the new problems and challenges that historical existence is made of, in concert with the emerging insights and interpretations of colleagues, of whom many are brilliant and creative.

Balance in collegial relations will be achieved by affirming community, our common purpose and humanity, even though there is great diversity in background, temperament, and points of view in the membership. "Diversity in community" should be the watchword.

Diversity in Community

As I have already indicated in chapter 4, I am not using the word "community" in a colloquial sense, but I think some kind of community, some sort of unity with one another, should be possibility for a professional society such as ours. It is not, of course, the unity of those living together in a common sharing of beliefs and moral values and mutual exchange of speech and services and goods. Nor do I use the word in the spiritual sense of church as community, that is, those in union with one another through faith in Christ and access to the sacraments. However, the idea of community in this ecclesial sense has certainly influenced my own thinking about what our academic society or any body politic should be. In fact, Paul's depiction of the church as one body, the "body of Christ," in which all the members of the body have their respective gifts and functions (1 Corinthians 12 and 14), is one I take as a helpful guide, mutatis mutandis, to understand our own enterprise.

We have a common object, as reiterated in this history, and most of us who make a significant commitment of time and energy to participate in COV&R come into it with passion, with a deep, deep desire to find out more about ourselves, about human relations, about our proclivity for conflict and violence. Probably most of us associate this passionate quest with our religious identity, which is usually Christian, although those who are secularist in orientation or disavow any religious affiliation may still be deeply interested in the interplay of religion and culture.

So this quest is not merely intellectual; it is simultaneously personal and typically spiritual. It characteristically includes the desire to find an association, a "fellowship," or a "friendship" if you will, of those caught up in a common quest. This friendship of the COV&R community should be strong enough to encompass diverse opinions and positions on issues of all sorts.

It is important to have a structure—a policy and a tradition of programming—for airing issues and disagreements. That will work to the benefit of the organization and the enrichment of individuals. The collegial environment of friendship should be strong enough to encompass rivalries that emerge and improve the chances of channeling them into the rivalry of positive emulation, to which Wolfgang Palaver has referred in another context.

Changes will occur, of course. If COV&R, as I hope, is still thriving twenty or thirty years from now, I cannot imagine what it will be like as it responds to its own historical experiences in the context of the larger history of humanity. But to keep its *balance,* it must remember and refer to these formative years and take into account, in a nondogmatic manner, the powerful insights, spiritual model, and inspiring research program bequeathed to it by René Girard, along with the work of all the colleagues who have moved COV&R through its first twenty years.

May the God of Peace bless the Colloquium on Violence and Religion and you, dear reader, and may he make his face to shine upon you, be gracious unto you, and grant you peace! Amen.

APPENDIX 1

A Brief Statement about Scientific Research and the Mimetic Theory

The mimetic theory has many insights and implications for scientific research. At the present time this is most obvious in the social sciences. Here we can point to the work of Scott Garrels and others in the understanding of mirror neurons. They are doing important work in delineating the bioneural basis of mimetic desire. We are familiar with the philosophical sociology of Jean-Pierre Dupuy, who conceptualizes how mimesis drives the stock market and social phenomena such as panic, as well as the function of mimesis in complex systems that interact in nonlinear ways. There is also the social scientific approach of Paul Dumouchel in analyzing emotions and the mimetic element of politics. Finally, the potential contribution of the mimetic theory to understanding human evolution, particularly the development of culture, should be great. As Pierpaolo Antonello and Paul Gifford have stated, mimetic theory "is an interpretative tool, and a basic explanatory principle. It offers to account for the emergence of culture for endogenous reasons: reasons not purely and simply relating to the physical evolution of specific individuals within a given species, but rather to the emergence of systemic group behaviour, which eventually and gradually shape the co-evolution of both the physical and the socio-cultural potentials of this given species "[1] These and other social scientists show that at the very least mimetic theory is not a mode of thought that must be restricted to religion and literature in the humanities.[2]

Britton Johnston's recent anthropological investigations of the phenomenon of faith or ritual healing and his reflections on science and faith are among the promising avenues for applying and extending the mimetic theory. His studies could well lead to a fruitful extension of the kind of analysis found in Girard's essay on the mimetic basis of anorexia and bulimia.[3] The thought and case studies of Jean-Michel Oughourlian have also been very important for Johnston.[4] The influence of Oughourlian can be seen in Johnston's thesis that internalized rivalries get somaticized, provoking an attack on the bodily systems that are particularly vulnerable to stress. Johnston's hypothesis is that mimetic rivalry is a primary factor in autoimmune disorders. From a Christian standpoint, the antidote to this mimetically influenced illness is to trust in a loving mediator who is an internal mediator without rivalry, and who gives himself to the subject who would imitate him.

With the research involved in studying mirror neurons it is obvious that a mimetic methodology dissolves the borders between the social sciences of psychology and sociology, on the one hand, and physical sciences, in this instance neurology and studies of the brain, on the other. This multidisciplinary approach is also important for the work of Pablo Bandera, a physicist. He has presented papers at COV&R conferences in which he argues that any scientist who engages in observation (identifying an object of study, measuring it, manipulating it, etc.) is affected by mimetic relations. He points out that an observer not only observes an object but is also always *observed*. That is, everyone lives and moves in a mimetic mode, within a mimetic triangle. If there is not a mimetic model or mediator immediately looking on and judging what the observer does, the observer nonetheless, as human being, has internalized a model or group of models (an "audience") who are interested spectators. Human subjectivity is the primary factor in all forms of knowledge. If this were recognized, argues Bandera, the argument over probability in quantum theory could be settled, with the objectivity of natural law reinstated and human subjectivity properly acknowledged.[5]

The methodological perspective of Bandera and Johnston does include the usual kind of protocol for scientific studies: the thought processes have to be pragmatic (concerned with what works in practice), with an investigator willing to engage in testing and experimentation that produces evidence or testimony that is not predetermined. The results of the research must be public, that is, they must be subject to examination by others and can be discussed by qualified persons. *To these aspects of scientific research must be added*, as fundamentally important, that any research must take into account mimetic relations. To this extent, the great physicist Niels Bohr was correct: the observer is part of the experiment. In contrast to classical physics, the observer as human subject matters in quantum physics. As Pablo Bandera says, "This opens the door to mimetic theory."[6] However, this does not necessarily mean that Einstein was wrong to affirm a reality independent of the observer, a reality including an environing nature that operates by an ordering causality.[7] The faith of the observers can be provisionally bracketed; however, from the standpoint of the mimetic theory it cannot finally be excluded because the theory has its origin in biblical faith and revelation, which passes the appropriate test of experimentation or experience ("trying out" or "testing") discussed in chapter 1.[8]

However, there is an ongoing argument among Girardians. Jean-Pierre Dupuy, Mark Anspach, Paul Dumouchel, and Robert Hamerton-Kelly, for example, believe that faith (Christian faith or any such religious commitment) is not necessary for research and in fact should not enter at all into scientific investigation.[9] But there is no discernible disagreement among Girardians that the mimetic theory in some form is relevant to both social and physical sciences. Girardians would hold, of course, that all sciences, as forms of knowledge, are fundamentally social because they are the expression of being human. The human being is *the* mimetic creature.

APPENDIX 2

Original and Present Constitutions of the Colloquium on Violence and Religion

Original Constitution as Adopted at the Annual Meeting, May 16–18, 1991

Constitution and By-Laws of the Colloquium on Violence and Religion

Article I: Name

This organization shall be called the Colloquium on Violence and Religion.

Article II: Object

Exploring, criticizing, and extending the theoretical model of René Girard concerning the relationship between violence and religion in the genesis and maintenance of culture. The Colloquium will be concerned both with research and questions of social implementation of research. Scholars from various fields will be encouraged to participate both in the conferences and publications sponsored by the Colloquium, but the focus of activity will be the relevance of Girard's thought for the revitalization of religious studies and theology.

Article III: Officers

1. The officers of the Colloquium shall be a President, an Executive Secretary, and the Editor of the newsletter.
2. The President shall be elected for a two-year term and may succeed himself or herself only once during any period of continuous tenure. The Executive Secretary shall be elected for a three-year term and may succeed himself or herself only once in any period of continuous tenure. The Editor of the newsletter shall be elected for one three-year term and may succeed himself or herself only once during any period of continuous period.
3. The Colloquium may add to the number of officers as situations require and change the terms of office as reflection on experience leads the officers and members to deem appropriate. See Article VIII: Amendment. (E.g., if we have a journal or annual of some sort, the editor would be an office, presumably for the same term as the Editor of the newsletter.)

Article IV: Advisory Board

1. Members of the Advisory Board shall be the President, the Executive Secretary, the Editor of the Newsletter, [Editor of the journal or annual if we sponsor such a publication.], and eight other members. [Note: This is an arbitrary number which could readily be changed.]
2. The additional eight members shall be elected for a term of three years. These members may succeed themselves only once in any period of continuous tenure.
3. René Girard shall be the lifetime honorary chairperson and member of the Advisory Board. A limited number of other lifetime honorary members may be elected.

Article V: Standing Committees

1. A nominating committee with three members shall be proposed by the President and approved by the Advisory Board. The members shall serve a three-year term and may not succeed themselves.
2. Other standing committees may be formed and distinguished from the Advisory Board as deemed necessary by the Board.

Article VI: Membership

1. Any person approved by the Advisory Board shall become an active member of the Colloquium, with full voting privileges. Students at

recognized institutions of learning may apply for membership at a reduced rate.

2. Membership dues shall be fixed by the Colloquium, upon recommendation of the Advisory Board.

Article VII: Meeting

The Colloquium shall meet at least once a year for the communication of research and the transaction of business, at such time and place as the Advisory Board may determine.

Article VIII: Amendment

This Constitution may be amended by a majority vote of the members of the Colloquium present and voting at its annual meeting, on recommendation of the Advisory Board, such amendment having been proposed at a previous meeting of the Colloquium and circulated in writing at least three months prior to the meeting at which final action is taken.

Article IX: By-Laws

The Colloquium shall establish such By-Laws as will, in its judgment, promote its effective operation. A change in the By-Laws may be made at any annual meeting, upon recommendation of the Advisory Board, by a two-thirds vote of the members present and voting.

By-Laws

1. President

The President shall be the presiding officer of the Colloquium. It shall be his duty to make an annual report to the Colloquium, to propose the membership of the nominating committee, and to propose to the Advisory Board any other committees for the administrative work of the Colloquium.

2. Executive Secretary

The Executive Secretary shall be the principal executive officer of the Colloquium. It shall be his duty to conduct the activities of the Colloquium in consultation with the President and the Advisory Board; to conduct the correspondence of the Colloquium; to notify the members of each annual meeting and other meetings; to transmit to them the program of the meetings at least two weeks in advance; to preserve an accurate roll of the members; to present nominations for membership in the Colloquium to the Advisory Board; to make an annual report on the condition of the Colloquium; and to perform such other duties as the Board may direct.

3. Advisory Board

1. It shall be the duty of the Advisory Board to approve active members; to receive nominations for lifetime honorary members; to recommend to the Colloquium the Editors; to establish editorial policy for publications of the Colloquium; to fix the times and places for meeting; and generally to supervise the activities of the Colloquium. All policy touching the conduct of the activities of the Colloquium shall be subject to the review and approval of the Advisory Board.
2. The Advisory Board shall meet in conjunction with the annual meeting of the Colloquium, and at other times as the President and Executive Secretary deem necessary.

4. Editors

The Editors shall receive manuscripts and consult concerning their publication with members of the Board as the Editors consider appropriate or necessary. The Editors shall edit and prepare for printing all manuscripts selected for publication. If it seems useful or necessary, editorial boards may eventually be established upon recommendation of the Editors and with the approval of the Advisory Board.

5. Nominating Committee

It shall be the duty of the Nominating Committee to propose to the Advisory Board candidates for all elective offices in the Colloquium, with the exception of the Nominating Committee itself, which shall be proposed by the President and approved by the Advisory Board.

6. Membership Dues

1. Each active member shall pay annual dues of $30.00. It is understood the dues may be raised by recommendation of the Advisory Board and approval of the Colloquium.
2. A rate of $15 for students at recognized institutions of learning shall be in effect.
3. No payment shall be required of honorary lifetime members.
4. Members one year in arrears shall be dropped from the roster of the Colloquium.

7. Publications

1. A copy of each issue of the newsletter shall be sent to each member of the Colloquium.
2. A copy of each issue of a periodical or any other publication shall be sent to each member of the Colloquium if these other publications are covered by the membership dues, as recommended by the Advisory Board and approved by members of the Colloquium.

Revised form of the Constitution[1]

Constitution and By-Laws of the Colloquium on Violence and Religion

Articles of Constitution

I: Name

This organization shall be called the Colloquium on Violence and Religion at Stanford. The acronym of the Colloquium shall be COV&R.

II: Object

To explore, criticize, and develop the mimetic model of the relationship between violence and religion in the genesis and maintenance of culture. The Colloquium will be concerned with questions of both research and application. Scholars from various fields and diverse theoretical orientations will be encouraged to participate both in the conferences and the publications sponsored by the Colloquium, but the focus of activity will be the relevance of the mimetic model for the study of religion.

III: Officers

1. The officers of the Colloquium shall be a President, an Executive Secretary, the Editor of the newsletter, and a Treasurer.
2. The President shall be elected for a two-year term and may succeed himself or herself only once during any period of continuous tenure. The Executive Secretary shall be elected for one three-year term and may succeed himself or herself only once in any period of continuous tenure. The Editor of the newsletter shall be elected for one three-year term and may succeed himself or herself only once during any period of continuous tenure. The Treasurer shall be elected for one three-year term and may succeed himself or herself only once during any period of continuous tenure.

3. The Colloquium may add to the number of officers as situations require and change the terms of offices as reflection on experience leads the officers and members to deem appropriate. See Article VIII: Amendment.

IV: Advisory Board

1. The members of the Advisory Board shall be the President, the Executive Secretary, any Editors of Colloquium publications, a Treasurer, and eleven other members.
2. The additional eleven members shall be elected for a term of three years. These members may succeed themselves only once in any period of continuous tenure.
3. A limited number of other lifetime honorary members may be elected.

V: Standing Committees

Standing committees may be formed and distinguished from the Advisory Board as deemed necessary by the Board.

VI: Membership

1. Any person approved by the Advisory Board shall become an active member of the Colloquium, with full voting privileges. Students at recognized institutions of learning may apply for membership at a reduced rate.
2. Membership dues shall be fixed by the Colloquium, upon recommendation of the Advisory Board.

VII: Meeting

The Colloquium shall meet at least once a year for the communication of research and the transaction of business, at such time and place as the Advisory Board may determine.

VIII: Amendment

This Constitution may be amended by a majority vote of the members of the Colloquium present and voting at its annual meeting, on recommendation of the Advisory Board.

IX: By-Laws

The Colloquium shall establish such By-Laws as will, in its judgment, promote its effective operation. A change in the By-Laws may be made at any annual meeting, upon recommendation of the Advisory Board, by a two-thirds vote of the members present and voting.

By-Laws

I. President

The President shall be the presiding officer of the Colloquium. It shall be his duty to make an annual report to the Colloquium and to propose to the Advisory Board any other committees for the administrative of the work of the Colloquium.

II. Executive Secretary

The Executive Secretary shall be the principal executive officer of the Colloquium. It shall be his duty to conduct the activities of the Colloquium in consultation with the President and Advisory Board; to conduct the correspondence of the Colloquium; to notify the members of each annual meeting and other meetings; to transmit to them the program of the meetings at least two weeks in advance; to preserve an accurate roll of the members; to present nominations for membership in the Colloquium to the Advisory Board; to make an annual report on the condition of the Colloquium; and to perform such other duties as the Board may direct.

III. Advisory Board

1. It shall be the duty of the Advisory Board to approve active members; to receive nominations for lifetime honorary members; to recommend to the Colloquium the Editors; to establish editorial policy for publications of the Colloquium; to fix the times and places for meeting; and generally to supervise the activities of the Colloquium. All policy touching the conduct of the activities of the Colloquium shall be subject to the review and approval of the Advisory Board.
2. The Advisory Board shall meet in conjunction with the annual meeting of the Colloquium, and at other times as the President and Executive Secretary deem necessary.

IV. Editors

The Editors shall receive manuscripts and consult concerning their publication with members of the Board as the Editors consider appropriate or necessary. The Editors shall edit and prepare for printing all manuscripts selected for publication. If it seems useful or necessary, editorial boards may eventually be established upon recommendation of the Editors and with the approval of the Advisory Board.

V. Treasurer

It shall be the duty of the Treasurer to receive membership dues and other monies paid into the Colloquium, to work with the Executive Secretary in preserving an accurate membership roll, and to report on the Colloquium's financial state at the annual meeting.

VI. Membership Dues

1. Each active member shall pay annual dues of $30.00. It is understood that the dues may be raised by recommendation of the Advisory Board and approval of the Colloquium. There shall be special rates for those from soft currency areas.
2. A rate of $15.00 for students at recognized institutions of learning shall be in effect.
3. The annual dues for member institutions shall be $100.00.
4. No payment shall be required of honorary lifetime members.
5. Members one year in arrears shall be dropped from the roster of the Colloquium.

VII. Publications

1. A copy of each issue of the newsletter shall be sent to each member of the Colloquium.
2. A copy of each issue of a periodical or any other publication shall be sent to each member of the Colloquium if these other publications are covered by the membership dues, as recommended by the Advisory Board and approved by members of the Colloquium.

As amended and approved April 24, 1993, and published in: *The Bulletin of COV&R* 6 (March 1994).

Amendment to Constitution of COV&R

The president explained that the Advisory Board was concerned about finding officers in a relatively small organization like COV&R who were not only willing and able to serve, but who enjoyed the kind of institutional or other support which would enable them to do their jobs properly. Therefore the Advisory Board proposed this amendment to the Constitution: "At the discretion of the Advisory Board, the three-year term of the following officers may be renewed beyond the two-term limit: executive secretary, editor of the

Bulletin, editor of Contagion, and treasurer." This amendment was approved by all but one member present.

As amended and approved May 30, 1998, and published in *The Bulletin of COV&R* 15 (October 1998).

Therefore Article III.2 shall read:

2. The President shall be elected for a two-year term and may succeed himself or herself only once during any period of continuous tenure. The Executive Secretary shall be elected for one three-year term and may succeed himself or herself only once in any period of continuous tenure. The Editor of the newsletter shall be elected for one three-year term and may succeed himself or herself only once during any period of continuous tenure. The Treasurer shall be elected for one three-year term and may succeed himself or herself only once during any period of continuous tenure. At the discretion of the Advisory Board, the three-year term of the following officers may be renewed beyond the two-term limit: executive secretary, editor of the Bulletin, editor of Contagion, and treasurer.

APPENDIX 3

Officers and Board Members of COV&R, 1991–2010

COV&R Pro Tem Advisory Board (1991, Stanford)

Raymund Schwager, President
Wolfgang Palaver, Editor of Newsletter[1]
James Williams, Executive Secretary (from 1990)
René Girard, Honorary Chair
Mark Anspach
Judith Arias
Gil Bailie
Cesáreo Bandera
Diana Culbertson
Robert G. Hamerton-Kelly
Jørgen Jørgensen
Roel Kaptein
Charles Mabee
Thee Smith
Mark Wallace
Walter Wink

Advisory Board (1992, Stanford)

Raymund Schwager, President
Wolfgang Palaver, Editor of Newsletter[2]
James Williams, Executive Secretary
Gil Bailie, Treasurer
René Girard, Honorary Chair
Mark Anspach
Judith Arias
Cesáreo Bandera
Diana Culbertson
Robert G. Hamerton-Kelly
Jørgen Jørgensen
Roel Kaptein
Charles Mabee
Thee Smith
Mark Wallace
Walter Wink

Advisory Board (1993, University of North Carolina)

Raymund Schwager, President
Wolfgang Palaver, Editor of Newsletter[3]
James G. Williams, Executive Secretary
Gil Bailie, Treasurer
René Girard, Honorary Chair
Mark Anspach
Judith Arias
Cesáreo Bandera
Diana Culbertson
Robert G. Hamerton-Kelly
Jørgen Jørgensen
Roel Kaptein
Charles Mabee
Thee Smith
Mark Wallace
Walter Wink

ADVISORY BOARD (1994, WIESBADEN-NAUROD)

Raymund Schwager, President
James Williams, Executive Secretary
Gil Bailie, Treasurer
Wolfgang Palaver, Editor of COV&R *Bulletin*[4]
Judith Arias, Editor of *Contagion*
René Girard, Honorary Chair
Mark Anspach
Cesáreo Bandera
Diana Culbertson
Robert G. Hamerton-Kelly
Jørgen Jørgensen
Roel Kaptein
Charles Mabee
Andrew McKenna
Thee Smith
Mark Wallace
Walter Wink

ADVISORY BOARD (1995, LOYOLA UNIVERSITY CHICAGO)

Cesáreo Bandera, President
James Williams, Executive Secretary
Gil Bailie, Treasurer
Wolfgang Palaver, Editor of *Bulletin*[5]
Judith Arias, Editor of *Contagion*
René Girard, Honorary Chair
Mark Anspach
Diana Culbertson
Sandor Goodhart
Robert G. Hamerton-Kelly
Jørgen Jørgensen
Roel Kaptein
Cheryl Kirk-Duggan
Charles Mabee
Andrew McKenna
Raymund Schwager

Thee Smith
Walter Wink

Advisory Board (1996, Stanford)

Cesáreo Bandera, President
James Williams, Executive Secretary
Gil Bailie, Treasurer
Wolfgang Palaver, Editor of *Bulletin*[6]
Andrew McKenna, Editor of *Contagion*
René Girard, Honorary Chair
Judith Arias
Louis Burkhart
Diana Culbertson
Johan Elsen
Sandor Goodhart
Robert G. Hamerton-Kelly
Cheryl Kirk-Duggan
Gerhard Larcher
Charles Mabee
Marie-Louise Martinez
Raymund Schwager
Thee Smith

Advisory Board (1997, University of Graz, Austria)

Cesáreo Bandera, President
James Williams, Executive Secretary
Gil Bailie, Treasurer, North America
Dietmar Regensburger, Treasurer (Europe)
Wolfgang Palaver, Editor of *Bulletin*
Andrew McKenna, Editor of *Contagion*
René Girard, Honorary Chair
Louis Burkhart
Diana Culbertson
Johan Elsen
Sandor Goodhart

Hans Jørgen Jensen
Cheryl Kirk-Duggan
Gerhard Larcher
Marie-Louise Martinez
Raymund Schwager
Julie Shinnick
Tobin Siebers

Advisory Board (1998, St. Denis, France)

Cesáreo Bandera, President
Diana Culbertson, Executive Secretary
Julie Shinnick, Treasurer (North America)
Dietmar Regensburger, Treasurer (Europe)
Wolfgang Palaver, Editor of *Bulletin*
Andrew McKenna, Editor of *Contagion*
René Girard, Honorary Chair
Louis Burkhart
Robert Daly
Johann Elsen
Giuseppe Fornari
Sandor Goodhart
Hans Jørgen Jensen
Cheryl Kirk-Duggan
Gerhard Larcher
Marie-Louise Martinez
Tobin Siebers
James Williams

Advisory Board (1999, Emory University)

Diana Culbertson, President
Sandor Goodhart, Executive Secretary
Julie Shinnick, Treasurer (North America)
Dietmar Regensburger, Treasurer (Europe)
Johann Elsen, Editor of *Bulletin*
Andrew McKenna, Editor of *Contagion*

René Girard, Honorary Chair
Raymund Schwager, Honorary Member
James Williams, Honorary Member
Gil Bailie
Cesáreo Bandera
Robert Daly
Giuseppe Fornari
Eric Gans
Hans Jørgen Jensen
Cheryl Kirk-Duggan
Marie-Louise Martinez
Józef Niewiadomski
Wolfgang Palaver
Tobin Siebers

Advisory Board (2000, Boston College)

Diana Culbertson, President
Sandor Goodhart, Executive Secretary
Julie Shinnick, Treasurer (North America)
Dietmar Regensburger, Treasurer (Europe)
Johann Elsen, Editor of *Bulletin*
Andrew McKenna, Editor of *Contagion*
René Girard, Honorary Chair
Raymund Schwager, Honorary Member
James Williams, Honorary Member
Gil Bailie
Cesáreo Bandera
Robert Daly
Giuseppe Fornari
Eric Gans
Hans Jørgen Jensen
Cheryl Kirk-Duggan
Józef Niewiadomski
Wolfgang Palaver
Tobin Siebers

Advisory Board (2001, Antwerp)

Diana Culbertson, President
Sandor Goodhart, Executive Secretary
Julie Shinnick, Treasurer (North America)
Dietmar Regensburger, Treasurer (Europe)
Paul Bellan Boyer, Editor of *Bulletin*
Andrew McKenna, Editor of *Contagion*
René Girard, Honorary Chair
Raymund Schwager, Honorary Member
James Williams, Honorary Member
Gil Bailie
Cesáreo Bandera
Robert Daly
Giuseppe Fornari
Eric Gans
William A. Johnsen
Cheryl Kirk-Duggan
Marie-Louise Martinez
William Mishler
Józef Niewiadomski
Wolfgang Palaver

Advisory Board (2002, Purdue University)

Diana Culbertson, President
Sandor Goodhart, Executive Secretary
Julie Shinnick, Treasurer (North America)
Dietmar Regensburger, Treasurer (Europe)
Paul Bellan Boyer, Editor of *Bulletin*
Andrew McKenna, Editor of *Contagion*
René Girard, Honorary Chair
Eric Gans, Honorary Member
Raymund Schwager, Honorary Member
James Williams, Honorary Member
Gil Bailie
Cesáreo Bandera

Robert Daly
Giuseppe Fornari
Per Bjørnar Grande
William A. Johnsen
Marie-Louise Martinez
Williams Mishler
Józef Niewiadomski
Wolfgang Palaver

Advisory Board (2003, University of Innsbruck)

Sandor Goodhart, President
Wolfgang Palaver, Executive Secretary
Julie Shinnick, Treasurer (North America)
Dietmar Regensburger, Treasurer (Europe)
Paul Bellan Boyer, Editor of *Bulletin*
Andrew McKenna, Editor of *Contagion*
René Girard, Honorary Chair
Eric Gans, Honorary Member
Raymund Schwager, Honorary Member
James Williams, Honorary Member
James Alison
Gil Bailie
Cesáreo Bandera
Maria Stella Barberi
Robert Daly
Giuseppe Fornari
Per Bjørnar Grande
William A. Johnsen
Paul Nuechterlein
Józef Niewiadomski
Rusty Palmer

Advisory Board (2004, Ghost Ranch in New Mexico)

Sandor Goodhart, President
Wolfgang Palaver, Executive Secretary

Julie Shinnick, Treasurer (North America)
Dietmar Regensburger, Treasurer (Europe)
Nikolaus Wandinger, Editor of *Bulletin*
Andrew McKenna, Editor of *Contagion*
René Girard, Honorary Chair
Eric Gans, Honorary Member
†Raymund Schwager, Honorary Member
James Williams, Honorary Member
James Alison
Ann W. Astell
Gil Bailie
Cesáreo Bandera
Maria Stella Barberi
Giuseppe Fornari
Per Bjørnar Grande
William A. Johnsen
Paul Nuechterlein
Józef Niewiadomski
Rusty Palmer

Board of Directors (2005, Koblenz. The new title was approved for purposes of eventual incorporation at the COV&R Business Meeting at Koblenz, July 9, 2005)

Sandor Goodhart, President
Wolfgang Palaver, Executive Secretary
Julie Shinnick, Treasurer (North America)
Dietmar Regensburger, Treasurer (Europe)
Nikolaus Wandinger, Editor of *Bulletin*
Andrew McKenna, Editor of *Contagion*
René Girard, Honorary Chair
Eric Gans, Honorary Member
†Raymund Schwager, Honorary Member
James Williams, Honorary Member
James Alison
Ann W. Astell
Maria Stella Barberi
Sonja Bardelang

Benoît Chantre
Per Bjørnar Grande
Michael Kirwan
Paul Nuechterlein
Rusty Palmer
Simon Simonse

Board of Directors (2006, St. Paul's University, Ottawa)

Sandor Goodhart, President
Wolfgang Palaver, Executive Secretary
Julie Shinnick, Treasurer (North America)
Dietmar Regensburger, Treasurer (Europe)
Nikolaus Wandinger, Editor of *Bulletin*
William A. Johnsen, Editor of *Contagion*
René Girard, Honorary Chair
Cesáreo Bandera, Honorary Member
Eric Gans, Honorary Member
†Raymund Schwager, Honorary Member
James Williams, Honorary Member
James Alison
Ann W. Astell
Maria Stella Barberi
Sonja Bardelang
Benoît Chantre
Giuseppe Fornari
Per Bjørnar Grande
Michael Kirwan
Paul Nuechterlein
Rusty Palmer
Simon Simonse

Board of Directors (2007, Amsterdam)

COV&R Officers

Wolfgang Palaver, President

Ann W. Astell, Executive Secretary
Julie Shinnick, Treasurer (North America)
Dietmar Regensburger, Treasurer (Europe)
William A. Johnsen, Editor of *Contagion*
Nikolaus Wandinger, Editor of *Bulletin*
Sandor Goodhart, Fundraising Coordinator
Martha J. Reineke, Coordinator of COV&R Session at the AAR/SBL Annual Meeting
René Girard, Honorary Chair
Cesáreo Bandera, Honorary Member
Eric Gans, Honorary Member
†Raymund Schwager, Honorary Member
James Williams, Honorary Member
James Alison
Maria Stella Barberi
Sonja Bardelang
Benoît Chantre
Stephen Gardner
Michael Kirwan
Paul Nuechterlein
Thérèse Onderdenwijngaard
Rusty Palmer
Simon Simonse
Bruce Ward

Board of Directors (2008, University of California, Riverside)

COV&R Officers

Wolfgang Palaver, President
Ann W. Astell, Executive Secretary
Keith Ross, Treasurer (North America)
Dietmar Regensburger, Treasurer (Europe)
Nikolaus Wandinger, Editor of *Bulletin*
William A. Johnsen, Editor of *Contagion*
Sandor Goodhart, Fundraising Coordinator
Martha J. Reineke, Coordinator of COV&R Session at the AAR/SBL Annual Meeting

René Girard, Honorary Chair
Cesáreo Bandera, Honorary Member
Eric Gans, Honorary Member
†Raymund Schwager, Honorary Member
James Williams, Honorary Member
Jeremiah Alberg
Maria Stella Barberi
Simon de Keukelaere
Stephen Gardner
Michael Kirwan
Thérèse Onderdenwijngaard
Simon Simonse
Susan Srigley
Bruce Ward
Dorothy Whiston

Board of Directors (2009, St. Mary's University College, Twickenham, England)

Wolfgang Palaver, President
Ann W. Astell, Executive Secretary
Keith Ross, Treasurer (North America)
Dietmar Regensburger, Treasurer (Europe)
Nikolaus Wandinger, Editor of *Bulletin*
William A. Johnsen, Editor of *Contagion*
Sandor Goodhart, Fundraising Coordinator
Martha Reineke, Coordinator of COV&R Session at the AAR/SBL Annual Meeting
René Girard, Honorary Chair
Cesáreo Bandera, Honorary Member
Eric Gans, Honorary Member
Robert Hamerton-Kelly, Honorary Member
Charles Mabee, Honorary Member
†Raymund Schwager, Honorary Member
James Williams, Honorary Member
Jeremiah Alberg
Maria Stella Barberi
Simon de Keukelaere

Stephen Gardner
Michael Kirwan
Thérèse Onderdenwijngaard
Martha J. Reineke
Simon Simonse
Susan Srigley
Bruce Ward
Dorothy Whiston

Board of Directors (2010, Notre Dame University)

Wolfgang Palaver, President
Ann W. Astell, Executive Secretary
Keith Ross, Treasurer (North America)
Dietmar Regensburger, Treasurer (Europe)
Nikolaus Wandinger, Editor of *Bulletin*
William A. Johnsen, Editor of *Contagion*
Sandor Goodhart, Fundraising Coordinator
Martha Reineke, Coordinator of COV&R Session at the AAR/SBL Annual Meeting
René Girard, Honorary Chair
Cesáreo Bandera, Honorary Member
Eric Gans, Honorary Member
Robert Hamerton-Kelly, Honorary Member
Charles Mabee, Honorary Member
†Raymund Schwager, Honorary Member
James Williams, Honorary Member
Jeremiah Alberg
Maria Stella Barberi
Simon de Keukelaere
Giuseppe Fornari
Stephen Gardner
Michel Kirwan
Thérèse Onderdenwijngaard
Simon Simonse
Susan Srigley
Bruce Ward
Dorothy Whiston

Notes

Preface

1. Dietmar Regensburger and Michael Elias are in the process of recovering the websites. They are able to do this by mounting "mirrored" copies.

Chapter One. In the Beginning

1. Girard points out that "Monkeys cannot reach [the level of symbolicity], because one needs a catastrophic moment in the evolutionary process, which isn't solely tied to encephalization. This catastrophe is the mimetic crisis. . . . The scapegoat resolution, which saves the proto-communities from this crisis of mimetic violence, is disciplined into a ritual system of norms and prohibitions" (*Evolution and Conversion,* 110.)
2. Since Jesus spoke Aramaic and we have texts only in Greek, we could not have his precise words anyway. The fact is that the New Testament in Greek already reflects a period of time between Jesus and the earliest Palestinian community and the movement out into the Greek-speaking Graeco-Roman world. Thus we have to reckon with transmission, the development of tradition, and translation into Greek. No doubt much of the Gospel texts reflect the thought and work of authors and editors writing in Greek.
3. Charles Mabee remembers the departure from Funk's vision as a "coup." It was certainly that in terms of leadership, for Mabee was not the leader Funk had in mind initially. The person whom Funk asked to chair the formation of the group, Werner Kelber, withdrew from participation, presumably because the seminar was not constituted as he had expected. My description of the beginning of BINAC is partly reconstructed from telephone conversations with Mabee on March 6 and 12, 2009.
4. Girard taught at Johns Hopkins for two periods, 1957–1968 and 1975–1980, and was on the faculty of the State University of New York at Buffalo in the intervening years.

5. This was when BINAC participants first became acquainted with Gil Bailie, who provided a place for meeting with Girard in his Sonoma office. See Bailie's account in "On Paper and in Person," in Goodhart et al., *For René Girard,* 180–183.
6. Girard would also go to meet with BINAC for the third time. That meeting in March 1990 was indeed the last time BINAC met.
7. Robert Hamerton-Kelly was the exception to the limits of our state of knowledge, as he had already known Girard and had many conversations and discussions with him for at least seven years before Girard first met with BINAC.
8. The title of the French original, *Mensonge romantique, vérité romanesque* (Romantic Lie, Novelistic Truth), more accurately represented his thesis.
9. He says that as he wrote the last chapter of the book, "I was particularly attracted to the Christian elements [in the novels], for example, Stepan Verkhovensky's final journey and turn to the Gospel before his death," in Dostoevsky's *Demons. The Girard Reader*, 285.
10. See *The Girard Reader,* 283–286.
11. Girard, *Deceit,* 14.
12. Girard, *Deceit,* 187; full footnote on 186–187.
13. *In Battling to the End,* Girard refers to this book as the "key to my work" (61).
14. See Girard, *Violence and the Sacred*, 104–110, and Simon Simonse, *Kings of Disaster.*
15. Girard, *Violence and the Sacred*, 12, my translation.
16. The original work in French, *Les choses cachées depuis la fondation du monde*, was published in 1978. The English translation came out in 1987.
17. In this discussion of *Things Hidden since the Foundation of the World* I am following the lead of Girard's own introduction to *De la violence à la Divinité.* This volume gathers his first four major works in one book.
18. See also the beginning of the interview with Girard in *The Girard Reader,* 262.
19. Girard, *De la violence à la Divinité*, 23.
20. *De la violence à la Divinité*, 24.
21. *De la violence à la Divinité*, 25–26.
22. *De la Violence à la Divinité*, 26.
23. Girard says that it is synonymous with Satan. The distinction between the two lies in the fact that scandal is the initial process of contagion that multiplies and leads to accusation, persecution, and violence. Accusation, persecution, and violence become personified and symbolized in the figure of Satan, the Adversary and Accuser. See Matthew 16:23 where Jesus says to Peter, "Get behind me Satan! You are a hindrance (*skandalon*) to me." Girard, *Evolution and Conversion*, 223–225.
24. Girard, *Things Hidden*, 431.
25. Girard, *The Scapegoat*, 206, my translation.
26. See *parakletos* in Arndt and Gingrich, *Greek-English Lexicon of the New Testament and Other Early Christian*, 623–624. The early Latin translators of New Testament occurrences usually rendered it as *advocatus*.

27. Girard devotes several pages to Hölderlin in *Violence and the Sacred*, 155–158, but I either ignored or suppressed that fact. I had heard a lot about Hölderlin from a couple of Syracuse University colleagues, but they were enamored of the Greek-pagan side of his poetry, and due to this I formed a prejudice in my mind about him.

28. Girard, *Battling to the End*, 124.

29. Girard, *Battling to the End*, 125. On "the god is near" see the poet's "Patmos."

30. Girard, *Evolution and Conversion*, 177–178. These conversations with Pierpaolo Antonello and Joåo Cezar de Castro Rocha were translated from the French original, *Les origines de la culture*.

31. Girard, *Evolution and Conversion*, 110. Terrence W. Deacon, *The Symbolic Species*.

32. Girard, *Evolution and Conversion*, 125.

33. Girard, *Things Hidden*, 185–190.

34. *Things Hidden*, 187–188.

35. Girard, *Evolution and Conversion*, 235.

36. Girard, *Battling to the End*, ix.

37. In this period up to 1990 he published also a collection of essays *To Double Business Bound*, an important study of the biblical book of Job, and was well along in writing a volume on Shakespeare.

38. There is now a fourth moment, which will be taken up in chapter 5.

39. Girard, *The Girard Reader*, 262.

40. Fleming, *René Girard*, 153.

41. Williams, *The Bible, Violence, and the Sacred*, 13.

42. *The Bible, Violence, and the Sacred*, 13–14.

43. *The Bible, Violence, and the Sacred*, 14.

44. See Hamerton-Kelly, *Sacred Violence*, 1–4 and 42–44; Michael Kirwan, *Girard and Theology*, chapter 3, especially 28–32.

45. Note the etymology of intuition from the Latin *intuitus*, a past participle of *intueri*, to look at, regard. It is usually associated with immediate, pre-analytical knowledge.

46. Girard, *Evolution and Conversion*, 164.

47. *Evolution and Conversion*, 164.

48. Popper, *Conjectures and Refutations*.

49. Those attending were Ed McMahon, Mark Wallace, Barbara Mabee, Charles Mabee, Diana Culbertson, Theophus Smith, Robert Hamerton-Kelly, Stefano Cochetti, Hans Jensen, Jørgen Jørgensen, Byron Bland, Vernon Robbins, Mark Anspach, Brigitte Cazelles, Richard Keady, René Girard, Charles Ozeck, James Williams, Gil Bailie, Robert Bater, and Bruce Chilton.

50. On Girard's later provisional revision of his hypothesis that human sacrifice always preceded the offering of animal victims, see the section on the 2008 conference of COV&R in Riverside, chapter 5.

51. At that time I had no inkling of the Dutch Girard Circle, which held its first meetings in 1981. More on the Dutch group in chapter 5.

Chapter Two. Early Development of COV&R, 1990–1993

1. At our first meeting at the New Orleans Marriot in November 1990 the bill was $172.96 for coffee in the morning and afternoon, with assorted pastries in the morning. That was for twenty people, and was not too onerous, but the expense per person became astronomically higher at subsequent meetings. I eventually realized that I had been very naïve about the expense required for various aspects of our organizational work.
2. An orientation that Philip Rieff has described in an intriguing and provocative way as "third culture." See Rieff, *My Life among the Deathworks*.
3. Especially if it were "therapeutic" in orientation. See Philip Rieff, *The Triumph of the Therapeutic*.
4. Raymund Schwager, S.J., *Must There Be Scapegoats?* The German original: *Brauchen wir einen Sündenbock?*
5. Jørgen Jørgensen was our contact person with the Innsbruck faculty. On August 19, 1990 he met with Raymund Schwager, Józef Niewiadomski, and Wolfgang Palaver to work out the *Überlegungen*.
6. From a telephone conversation with Bandera on February 3, 2009. These conferences included a symposium "Disorder and Order" at Stanford in 1980, conceived by Jean-Pierre Dupuy and sponsored by Girard's Program of Interdisciplinary Research; the "Colloque de Cerisy-la-Salle" in 1983, organized by Dupuy and Paul Dumouchel; a forum at Brigham Young in early 1982, organized by Terry Butler; and an interdisciplinary discussion at Pajaro Dunes (near Santa Cruz, California) in 1983. These latter conversations among Girard, Walter Burkert, Jonathan Z. Smith, and ten others were transcribed and published in a book, *Violent Origins*, edited by Robert G. Hamerton-Kelly.
7. I no longer have a clear recollection of the discussions among Mabee, Hamerton-Kelly, and me, but it was probably Hamerton-Kelly who first suggested that we ask Schwager to become our president. The important thing was that all concerned were agreed on this choice.
8. Facsimile of May 6, 1990. My fax to him was dated April 30, 1990.
9. COV&R will hold an annual conference in Asia if provisional plans for the 2012 meeting in Japan succeed.
10. Conversation with Józef Niewiadomski, July 7, 2009.
11. This as presented in *Jesus of Nazareth*. The acts are worded differently in *Jesus in the Drama of Salvation*, which appeared first in German in 1990.
12. Published in *Orientierung* 38:4, 41–44.
13. Schwager to Girard, September 16, 1975. In speaking of a meeting in Avignon Schwager seems to refer to a date quite recent. René and Martha Girard believe they met Schwager much earlier, in 1972 or 1973. It is certain that it would have been in August, when René taught there. However, the extant correspondence gives no indication of a meeting earlier than 1975.

14. The prohibition of coveting what belongs to one's neighbor is not simply one commandment (prohibition) among others, it in effect sums up and states the ethical principle that lies behind the previous four of the Ten Commandments. See Williams, *The Bible, Violence, and the Sacred*, 108–113 and Girard, *I See Satan Fall Like Lightning*, 7.

15. Girard in a letter to Schwager, November 2, 1975.

16. It is interesting, however, that they do not *se tutoir*, that is, use the familiar *tu* with one another, until 1984. Girard suggested it in a letter of April 13, 1984: "Est-ce que ça ne te gêne pas si on se dit tu?" ("Would it not bother you if we said *tu* to each other?") He sends a letter dated May 8, 1984, in which he uses the formal *vous*, evidently because he hasn't yet received a reply from his Jesuit friend. In Schwager's next extant letter to Girard, from September 30, 1984, he uses *tu*.

17. See Hebrews 12:33.

18. *Things Hidden*, 447.

19. *The Scapegoat*, 207, Girard's emphasis.

20. Given the importance of the Holy Spirit as Paraclete in the theological dimension of Girard's thinking, it is noteworthy that this Person of the Trinity does not appear to have a significant role in his last two major books, *Evolution and Conversion* and *Battling to the End*. The Holy Spirit is mentioned just one time in each of these last two books. There seems to be a correlation between the disappearance of the Spirit and his growing pessimism concerning Christianity and human history.

21. Girard, "Mimetische Theorie und Theologie," in Józef Niewiadomski and Wolfgang Palaver, *Vom Fluch und Segen der Sündenböcke*, 15–29. Niewiadomski translated the paper from French into German. The original essay in French was later published in Girard, *Celui par qui le scandale arrive* (The One by Whom Scandal Occurs), 63–82.

22. Schwager, *Must There Be Scapegoats*, 210.

23. Girard, "Mimetische Theory und Theologie," 16. My translation.

24. Girard, "Mimetische Theorie und Theologie," 24. My translation.

25. Girard, "Mimetische Theorie und Theologie," 28.

26. "Mimetische Theorie und Theologie," 29. My translation.

27. *De la Violence à la Divinité*, 1001 n. 1.

28. First published in French in 1972. Anecdote from a conversation with Bandera February 3, 2009.

29. Judith Hepler Arias, Cesáreo Bandera, Paul Duff and Joseph Hallman (who presented a paper together), René Girard, Robert Hamerton-Kelly, Michael Hardin, Cheryl Kirk-Duggan, Stuart Lasine, Charles Mabee, Andrew McKenna, Raymund Schwager, Simon Simonse, and Ivan Strenski.

30. Published as an appendix to Richard J. Golsan, *René Girard and Myth*, 151–179, and reproduced in Girard, *The Girard Reader*, 118–141.

31. Hugo Assmann, *Götzenbilder und Opfer: René Girard im Gespräch mit der Befreiungstheologie* (Idols and Sacrificial Victims: René Girard in Dialogue with Liberation Theology). In a letter to me of July 26, 1990, Girard commented on the conference and mentioned a half dozen participants who especially impressed him. One of these was James Alison, who came to the COV&R conference at Stanford in 1991.

32. He remembers another personal experience related to racial or ethnic bias. In their younger days he and his wife Martha were in Mexico City attending a bullfight. Martha noticed some American women sitting nearby who were staring at them. René and Martha sensed that the staring women thought that he was a Mexican because of the olive tint of his skin. The staring indicated either surprise or negative judgment. It was Martha's first time outside the United States, so she may have been much more sensitive to such incidents.

33. Assmann, *Götzenbilder und Opfer*, 264. The relevant sections are pp. 263–265, 284.

34. *Dramatische Erlösungslehre: Ein Symposion.*

35. *Dramatische Erlösungslehre*, 339–384.

36. *Dramatische Erlösungslehre*, 356–360.

37. See chapters 2 and 3 of Schwager, *Banished from Eden.*

38. Those meeting were Robert Hamerton-Kelly, Jørgen Jørgensen, Roel Kaptein, Wolfgang Palaver, Raymund Schwager, and James Williams.

39. Girard, *Des choses caches depuis la fondation du monde*, 296–297. My translation. *Things Hidden*, 203.

40. I would note however, that Girard's perspective on mimesis in his latest work, *Achever Clausewitz* (Finishing [Off] Clausewitz), is hopeful but not optimistic concerning mimesis and mimetic rivalry. More on this in chapter 5.

41. Williams, *The Bible, Violence, and the Sacred* (2007), iii–iv, v.

42. I wrote a critique of the work of Siebers and of two other former students of Girard, Eric Gans and Paisley Livingston, which was published in the online journal that Gans edits: "René Girard without the Cross?". The less positive aspect of my critique of Siebers and Livingson, who are very different in their concerns and approach to literature and culture criticism, is that they think they can use the mimetic scapegoat concept without its beginning and its end, that is, without positing an originary predicament of violence and without affirming the revelation of God, above all in Jesus' death and resurrection, which is salvific. They are left in the postmodern predicament of no "whence?" and no "whereto?" As for Gans, he posits a "whence?" and "whereto," but he holds that culture and language began without violence, although he has to predicate violence as what the origins of culture and language presuppose.

43. For the news release go to news-service.stanford.edu/pr/92/920512Arc2222.html. There were about 9,500 in attendance.

44. One could argue that a violent zeal for the Law, as exemplified by Phineas in the Old Testament, informed Paul's persecutory zeal prior to his conversion. (See Numbers 25:6–15; Psalms 106:28–31; Sirach 45:23–34; 1 Maccabees 2:26, 54). Hamerton-Kelly discusses this zealotry in *Sacred Violence*, 72–77. However, there is not a good basis for arguing that the Phineas model, perpetuated in the Maccabean tradition, exhausts the meaning of Torah in the Jewish tradition. Perhaps it was one strain in the Pharisaic thought and practice of Maccabean and post-Maccabean Judaism; it would appear that Paul embraced it before his conversion to Christ. On the other hand, Hamerton-Kelly construed Goodhart's reference to the Holocaust as unfair, in that it could be used as a weapon against any criticism of Jewish Scripture or tradition.

45. See Hamerton-Kelly, *Sacred Violence*, 68.

46. For abstracts of the papers and responses, see *Bulletin of COV&R* 4 (March 1993): 9–10.

47. Williams, "Sacrifice and the Beginning of Kingship"; Krondorfer, "Response to James G. Williams."

48. Krondorfer, "Response to James G. Williams," 106.

49. Krondorfer, "Response to James G. Williams," 106.

50. Three posthumous volumes on *Sacred Order / Social Order* by Rieff have been published. The first of these, *My Life among the Deathworks*, has already been cited above.

51. *The Girard Reader*, 64–65. The original record of the interview with Adams was published as "Violence, Difference, Sacrifice."

52. I first encountered an allusion to this in Girard's book, *The Scapegoat*, 92, where he credits Michel Serres for translating *in turba* as "in the crowd" from Livy's account of Romulus's slaying of Remus. The Latin *turba*, fracas, crowd, chaos, is the root of the English "turbulence." See also Girard's essay, "The Plague in Literature and Myth," in *"To Double Business Bound,"* 138–154. He speaks of "a reciprocal affinity" between plague and social disorder without pursuing the question as to which is prior. The father of modern sociology, Emile Durkheim, held that the categories of reason underlying the thinking process in human beings were first of all collective representations whose empirical reference is the mental state of groups. Time, for example, is "the rhythm of social life." Durkheim, *Elementary Forms of Social Life*, 32 n. 23; see pp. 13–33.

53. Published that year in *Biblical Interpretation* 1, no. 3 (1993), 339–352; most of the article is reprinted in *The Girard Reader*, 211–221.

54. See the biographical sketch of Bandera at the end of chapter 3.

55. Bandera, "Separating the Human from the Divine," 76.

56. Bandera, "Separating the Human from the Divine," 83.

57. "Separating the Human from the Divine," 83.

58. Bandera, "Separating the Human from the Divine," 84.

59. Durkheim, *The Elementary Forms of Religious Life*, 54, as quoted in Bandera, "Separating the Human from the Divine," 85.

60. Bandera, "Separating the Human from the Divine," 85.

61. On this Bandera cites Jean Delumeau, *Sin and Fear.*

62. "Separating the Human from the Divine," 88.

63. "Separating the Human from the Divine," 89.

64. Bandera's statement in an email message of January 14, 2010.

65. Literally, "I go forth masked." The Christian dynamic is still "masked" in the sense that it goes forth undetected, unrecognized, because human beings cannot face up to its luminous truth.

66. The source of this paragraph, including the quotes, is the message from Bandera on January 14, 2010. The Quixote book by Bandera is *The Humble Story of Don Quixote*.

67. Susan Nowak's paper was published in the first volume of *Contagion*. In the interactions that occurred at a subsequent conference Nowak became disenchanted with COV&R and the mimetic theory.

68. Nowak, "The Girardian Theory and Feminisim," 29. Girard holds, of course, that human culture began in mimetic rivalry, acquisitive desire, and violence. On the other hand, he assumes that conflict and violence are not absolutely necessary in a world that is good according to the Jewish and Christian doctrine of creation. Reinhold Niebuhr's formula, "not necessary but inevitable" with respect to human sin, is relevant here. Mimetic desire that spins out of control into violence is not necessary but inevitable in human existence. It should be added, however, that in Girard's later thought the inevitability of violence practically overwhelms the possibility of avoiding it short of the kingdom of God.

69. Personally I know of just a few, though perhaps there were others of which I am unaware. One was Krondorfer's reaction to our meeting in conjunction with AAR/SBL in San Francisco. Another was the reaction of a New Testament scholar to the approach of one of the papers at the 1991 conference at Stanford, and a third was the angry reaction of a presenter in 1991 who thought that an important person in attendance did not take his paper seriously. Also, there was a group of two or three at one of the meetings who made an issue of androcentric language used by some of the speakers. Most COV&R members have reacted negatively to political correctness and the "policing" of the speech of others. There are, however, admittedly complex issues in the use of images and pronouns that are exclusively masculine in gender.

Chapter Three. International Meetings and Growth of Membership, 1994–1998

1. Germany had developed a civic governance system whereby larger cities were connected in a kind of satellite relationship with surrounding towns and villages.

2. See the excellent report on the symposium by Raymund Schwager in *Bulletin of COV&R* 7 (October 1994): 6–7.

3. The theme of "containing" violence came up again in Wolfgang Palaver's treatment of Thomas Hobbes's interpretation of the *katechon* in 2 Thessalonians 2:6. See below. The powers of the *katechon* have the same structure as the market as analyzed by Dupuy. See also the following note below, on Satan.

4. This dynamic structure is basically the same as that of "Satan," which at the anthropological level is a projection of the total mimetic mechanism. Satan is both the ruler of human structures of order (the "prince of this world") and the source of disorder (the accuser, the adversary). See also Girard, *I See Satan Fall*, 33 and *Evolution and Conversion*, 223–225. This seemingly paradoxical dynamic of the mimetic mechanism is why Girard holds that Satan casts out Satan.

5. See chapter 10 of Jean-Pierre Dupuy, *Le Sacrifice et L'Envie*; and "Totalization and Misrecognition."

6. Milbank, *Theology and Social Theory*, 392–398.

7. See his essay, "Hobbes and Secularization."

8. "Hobbes and Secularization," 55.

9. See William T. Cavanaugh, *Torture and Eucharist*.

10. Palaver, "Hobbes and the KATECHON."

11. Summary reports on the three workshops prepared by Andrew McKenna, Anthony Bartlett, and James Williams, and Jacques-Jude Lépine may be found in *Bulletin of COV&R* 7 (October 1994): 7–8.

12. Willard M. Swartley, *Violence Renounced*. The other COV&R members contributing were Diana Culbertson, Charles Mabee, and Willard Swartley, with a response to the essays by René Girard. Other contributors to the anthology included Marlin E. Miller, Ted Grimsrud, Gordon H. Matties, Loren L. Johns, Paul Keim, and Jim Fodor.

13. Swartley, *Violence Renounced*, 24–26.

14. See my preface to the 2007 reprinted edition of *The Bible, Violence, and the Sacred*, iii–vi.

15. "Loving Mimesis and Girard's 'Scapegoat of the Text.'"

16. "Loving Mimesis," 280.

17. *Things Hidden*, 430–431.

18. Adams, "Loving Mimesis," 281.

19. Adams, "Loving Mimesis," 289.

20. "Loving Mimesis," 289.

21. "Loving Mimesis," 290.

22. "Loving Mimesis," 291–293.

23. She puts "proto" in the concept to indicate that the subject's "subjectivity is unformed prior to the imitation represented in the paradigm." "Loving Mimesis," 306 n. 28.

24. "Loving Mimesis," 294.

25. Reineke, "Transforming Space."

26. Reineke, "Transforming Space," 91.

27. Astell, "Maternal Compassion in the Thought of René Girard, Emil Fackenheim, and Emmanuel Levinas," *Contagion* 11, 15.

28. Petra Steinmair-Pösel also makes a significant contribution to a theology of divine grace as the basis of positive mimesis. Her contribution will be noted in chapter four in the section on the 2006 annual conference at St. Paul University in Ottawa

29. For a more complete explication, see Daly, *Sacrifice Unveiled*.

30. A few of us interested in biblical and Jewish studies did have a kind of "rump session" at Chapel Hill that was not part of the formal program.

31. As found in the archives of Girard-Dokumentation at the University of Innsbruck and published in *The Bulletin of the Colloquium on Violence and Religion*.

32. See *The Girard Reader*, 302–303.

33. Other contributors were Susan Nowak, Andrew J. McKenna, Jacques-Jude Lépine, Raymund Schwager, Cesáreo Bandera, James G. Williams, Charles D. Orzech, William Mishler, Richard J. Prystowsky, Chistopher G. Flood, and Richard J. Golsan. Judith Hepler Arias wrote the editor's introduction and Robert G. Hamerton-Kelly offered a statement of tribute to Girard.

34. Judith Arias, "Editor's Introduction," vii.

35. Robert Hamerton-Kelly, "Tribute to René Girard on His 70th Birthday," xii.

36. Girard's paper was published in *Contagion*: "Eating Disorders and Mimetic Desire."

37. I did attempt reconciliation on behalf of COV&R with the two persons named. With one it was partially successful, with the other it was to no avail. One thing to ponder is whether in the course of such incidents there is an inevitable "screening" or "filtering" of people whose interests, goals, and personalities are not right for a given kind of group. William Johnsen has commented that many of those who come and go in the Colloquium see the mimetic theory as fitting into some aspect of their own projects, but they are not committed to the theory as the dominant vision and way of going about their work.

38. Arias was the editor from 1993 to 1995, but she edited the issues of *Contagion* that appeared in 1994, 1995, and 1996, the first three issues.

39. "Report on 'Violence Conversion,'" 8.

40. "Report on 'Violence Conversion,'" 8.

41. See Girard, *Evolution and Conversion*, 109–110.

42. In an email of September 2, 2009, Elgee wrote to me that his recollection is not completely clear, but he thinks that a mutual friend, Sam Keen, a well-known writer on religion, psychology, and culture, introduced him to Bailie.

43. The Syracuse University Department of Religion and Hendricks Chapel at Syracuse University also cosponsored a Girard-Becker conference in October 1996.

44. Robert Hamerton-Kelly, "Report from the COV&R Conference held at Stanford, June 27–29, 1996," 10.

45. Bland, "Marching and Rising."

46. "Marching and Rising," 108.

47. "Marching and Rising," 118.

48. http://www.corrymeelaorg/sitepage/aboutus.aspx.

49. "Roel Kaptein," 8.

50. From the report by Thee Smith, "Advisory Board Self-Review," 2–3.

51. I later learned from Julie Shinnick that she laid claim to that distinction.

52. Girard told me in a conversation on September 29, 2009, that he did not give the event a second thought, perhaps in part because he was so preoccupied with his writing. When I mentioned that several colleagues and close friends had advised against including the "Blue Moon" event in this history, he did not hesitate in his response: "Go ahead and include it."

53. An instance of illustrative skits is recounted in chapter 4, in the section on the conference at Ottawa in 2006.

54. Walter Ong describes the professor-student relationship in the beginning of universities in medieval Europe as that of rivalry, an *agon* or contest. See Ong, *Fighting for Life*.

55. Duff, "Whoever is Not with Me Is Against Me," *BCOV&R* 12, 11..

56. Culbertson, "Reply to Paul Duff," *BCOV&R* 12, 11.

57. Williams, "Reply to Paul Duff," *BCOV&R* 12, 11.

58. Kirk-Duggan, "What's Violence Got to Do with It," *BCOV&R* 12, **12.**

59. Shinnick, "Reply to Kirk-Duggan, *BCOV&R* 12, *12.*

60. "The Tragic Instability of the Akedah (Binding of Isaac) in Ibsen's *Brand*," 12.

61. Hamerton-Kelly, "Ethnic Conflict and Historical Identity in South East Europe," 37.

62. Hamerton-Kelly, "Ethnic Conflict," 37.

63. "Ethnic Conflict," 38.

64. Larcher, "Report from the COV&R Conference held at Graz, June 23–27, 1997," 7.

65. Michael Haneke, "Media and Violence." The passage quoted is present in the paper distributed at the conference, but not in the published form.

66. Girard, *Things Hidden*, 216.

67. Girard, unpublished paper, quoted in James G. Williams, "Report from the COV&R Meeting in San Francisco, November 22, 1997," 5.

68. Martinez, "For a Non-Violent Accord."

69. Ricoeur, "Religion and Symbolic Violence," 11.

70. Kirwan, *Girard and Theology*, 106.

Chapter Four. Stability and Transition, 1999–2006

1. Smith, "Report from the Annual Meeting of COV&R," 3. My comments on the conference follow Smith's report as printed in the *Bulletin*. His concerns are related to my own, not only for the balance of theory and practice—engaged theory and theoretically grounded practice—but also public accountability.

2. Girard, *Evolution and Conversion*, 235.

3. *Evolution and Conversion*, 262.

4. *Evolution and Conversion*, 262.

5. Eric Gans, "Reflections on the Atlanta COV&R Conference," 4. Originally published in Gans's *Chronicles of Love and Resentment*, an Internet column, June 12, 1999.

6. Anthony Bartlett, "Abstract of Boston American Academy of Religion COV&R Paper," 2.

7. Quoted from an email message from Robert Daly dated May 10, 2009.

8. The record of this conference was unusually complete because an entire issue of *Contagion* (volume 9, Spring 2002) was given over to it. This was a labor of love by Robert Daly. It includes the five major papers with the respondents' responses, plus a summary of the discussion in each plenary session, a wrap-up summary, and an epilogue in which Daly offers his reflections on the conference. Daly spent many hours listening to audio recordings of the sessions in order to summarize the discussions.

9. Daly indicated that he understood institution in the general sense of "any significant or established practice, relationship, structure, system, or organization in a society or culture." Daly, "Papers of the COV&R Conference 2000 in Boston," 4.

10. Robert Daly, "Violence and Institution in Christianity," 30–31.
11. Francis X. Clooney, "Violence and Non-violence in Hindu Religious Traditions," 128–137.
12. "Violence and Non-violence," 128.
13. Christopher Ives, "Dharma and Destruction," 170.
14. Leo Lefebure, "A Response to Christopher Ives," 177.
15. *Contagion* 9 (2002): 186, 188, respectively.
16. *Contagion* 9 (2002): 191.
17. *Contagion* 9 (2002): 196.
18. *Contagion* 9 (2002): 196.
19. *Contagion* 9 (2002): 186.
20. Subsequent publications by Girard and discussions of his thought have raised the question whether he now conceives of positive mimetic desire. Girard and his commentators all agree, however, that for positive mimesis it is necessary to have a good model. One could even postulate that for liberation from negative mimesis it would be necessary to have a perfect, i.e., divine, model.
21. *Contagion* 9 (2002): 188–189.
22. This paragraph incorporates most of Daly's final reflections on the conference, *Contagion* 9 (2002): 195–196. In the final paragraph of his "Epilogue" to the *Contagion* volume Daly says, "Perhaps it is now time for COV&R members to come together for some constructive navel-gazing, to take stock of what we have been accomplishing, and . . . to be reflecting on what issues we might possibly want to prioritize or single out for special attention" (*Contagion* 9 (2002): 196).
23. *I See Satan Fall Like Lightning*, 125.
24. Goodhart, "We will cling fast to your Torah."
25. For this overview I draw upon the "Report from Antwerp Meeting" by William Mishler and Vanheeswijk's paper as later published: "The Place of René Girard in Contemporary Philosophy."
26. Vanheeswijk, "The Place of René Girard," 105. In a conversation with Girard on September 28, 2009, I read this paragraph to him. He commented, "Maybe this statement goes too far. There is something true in Heidegger's concept of the Logos. I am reserving judgment on that." But he went on to say that he follows the Christian Logos of the Gospel of John, and that it is incorrect to view the Christian logos and the Greek logos as identical. "They cannot be put on the same level."
27. See Girard, "Nietzsche versus the Crucified" 260–261.
28. McKenna, *Violence and Difference*, 24.
29. Depoortere, *Christ in Postmodern Philosophy*, 25–26.
30. Depoortere, *Christ in Postmodern Philosophy*, 25. Depoortere mentions Altizer and Dietrich Bonhoeffer.
31. See *The Girard Reader*, 283–286.

32. Vanheeswijk, "The Place of René Girard," 106–107.
33. Mishler, "Report from the Antwerp Meeting," 6.
34. Taylor, *A Secular Age*, 821 n. 64. See also pp. 639, 648, 686, 708, and 842 n. 16.
35. Mishler, "Report from the Antwerp Meeting," 7.
36. Led by Tom Michael, this involved interpreting the dreams of a group as a clue to their psychosocial dynamics.
37. Hamerton-Kelly, *Violent Origins*, 141.
38. See Walter Brueggemann on the "embrace of pain" in "A Shape for Old Testament Theology."
39. Raymond Schwager narrates this vividly and profoundly in his *Jesus of Nazareth*.
40. http://www.uibk.ac.at/platform-wrg/hintergrund.
41. Anthony (Tony) Bartlett's review of my work is "The Work of James Williams."
42. But on the Servant Song in Isaiah 52:13–53:12 as a full disclosure of the innocent victim, see William Mishler's report on Sandor Goodhart's paper at the Antwerp conference: "Report on the Antwerp Meeting," 7.
43. Girard, *I See Satan Fall*, 26.
44. *I See Satan Fall*, 145.
45. Girard, chapter 1 of *The Scapegoat*.
46. For the discussion of the papers of Fishbane and Chilton I am drawing on my notes. "Sites and Scenes of Sacrifice."
47. The disciples are addressed collectively: the second-person plural is used throughout, which means that the community, the church, not the individual is presupposed as immediate locus of prayer and conduct.
48. I had also got an initial clue of this in the late 1990s or early in the next decade when he mentioned to me how he was engrossed in reading Terrence Deacon, *The Symbolic Species: The Co-Evolution of Language and Brain*, to which he refers in *Evolution and Conversion*, 109–110, 125.
49. Grande, "Key Impressions of the Innsbruck Conference," 4.
50. Girard, "The Passionate Oxymoron in *Romeo and Juliet*," 25.
51. "The Passionate Oxymoron," 26.
52. "The Passionate Oxymoron,"30.
53. Dupuy, "Panic and the Paradoxes of the Social Order," 230. Dupuy refers to Keynes's book, *The General Theory of Employment, Interest and Money*.
54. Dupuy, "Panic and Paradoxes," 231.
55. Keynes, *General Theory of Employment*, 157–158, as quoted in Dupuy, "Panic and Paradoxes," 231.
56. As quoted in Petra Steinmair-Pösel, "Economy and Mimetic Theory," 81–82. See also Jørgen Jørgensen, "Report from the Innsbruck Conference," 2–3. Eric Gans makes a similar point in "The Market and Resentment," 101.

57. Palaver, "Envy or Emulation," 156.

58. Palaver, "Envy or Emulation," 156.

59. "Envy or Emulation," 157.

60. Niewiadomski, "Extra Media Nulla Salus?" 497. Niewiadomski's use of the word "passion" is worthy of comment. When speaking of God's passion he wants to remove it from the realm of mimetic desire. For him it is a kind of participatory intention and way of relating. Most of those accepting the mimetic theory who believe in God agree that there is a real sense, based on the biblical testimony and the Augustinian heritage, that God "desires" or is "passionate." (Cf. Abraham Heschel, *The Prophets*.) I remember the argument that many of us had with Roel Kaptein in the 1992 annual conference. Roel held that the redeemed condition of men and women moved them beyond mimesis, beyond desire. The problem is clearly due both to the ambiguity of mimetic desire and to the difficulty of characterizing another, higher state of being that is still informed by desire or passion in some sense of the words. Rebecca Adams's proposal concerning a theological improvement of the mimetic theory is also related to this topic. Moreover, many passages in Girard and Chântre, *Battling to the End*, suggest that Girard, at least in his later years, has come to agree with Kaptein.

61. Niewiadomski, "Extra Media," 489.

62. "Extra Media," 498.

63. Niewiadomski, "Extra Media," 499.

64. "Extra Media," 500.

65. "Extra Media," 500.

66. Niewiadomski, "Extra Media," 505.

67. See my comparison of Niewiadomski's critique of contemporary social media to Tony Bartlett's more positive perspective in my review of Bartlett's book, *Virtually Christian*.

68. Steinmair-Pösel, "Key Impressions of the COV&R 2004 Conference in New Mexico," 2.

69. Serres, "EGO CREDO," 10.

70. Steinmair-Pösel, "Key Impressions of the COV&R 2004 Conference in New Mexico," 2.

71. Of course, the idea of the divine origin of forms goes back to Plato, and the Bible speaks of God as a sort of craftsman in Genesis 2 inasmuch as he forms or shapes Adam from the soil (the Hebrew verb *yatsar*, which is utilized for the act of a potter, is used in Genesis 2:7). However, the biblical perspectives on human being tend toward the dynamic; human beings are created and informed by the divine speaking (the word of command in Genesis 1) and the divine breath (the *nefesh* or "soul" in Genesis 2).

72. Emphasis mine. Quote from Schiemann, "Nanotechnology and Nature," cited from his conclusion. Schiemann is the author of *Natur, Technik, Geist*.

73. "Kings and Gods as Ecological Agents," 39.

74. "Kings and Gods as Ecological Agents," 45. It is true that human being according to Genesis is not mandated to manage cosmic order, but *'adam*, man and woman, are to rule the earth. Are we now on the verge of extending human dominion into nonearthly areas of the cosmos?

75. Private communication, spring of 2009.

76. This is not to say that Bartlett's position raises no questions of its own. He seems to be saying that theologians think and speak directly out of revelation without the mediation of the "world" in a human sense (body, significant others, cultural institutions, etc.). Even the first witnesses in the Apostolic Age could not function in a completely immediate sense in relation to God. See further below on "mediated immediacy," chapter 4. Furthermore, theologians need institutions; however weak their institutional connections may be, they still depend on them for personal formation or reaction to that formation.

77. Michel Serres, "Receiving René Girard into l'Académie Francaise," 17.

78. From the discourse as published on the website of L'Académie Francaise: http://www.academie-francaise.fr/immortels/discours_reponses/serres_2005.html.

79. My translation.

80. "For René Girard," 15.

81. "Letter from the President," 4.

82. "Koblenz: Site of the COV&R Conference," 2.

83. Sr. M. Kornelia Fischer in the Press Office and Dick Graf, technical assistant, were also members of the committee.

84. According to Wilhelm Guggenberger's report in "Report on the COV&R Conference, Schönstatt-Koblenz," 4, there were 180 participants. Here I am following Ann Astell's unpublished notes in putting the figure at 160.

85. "Symbols of the (Other) Self," 1.

86. "Symbols of the (Other) Self," 5.

87. "Symbols of the (Other) Self," 5.

88. "Symbols of the (Other) Self," 7.

89. "Symbols of the (Other) Self," 8.

90. "Symbols of the (Other) Self," 10–11.

91. "Symbols of the (Other) Self," 12.

92. Schwager's early exploration of discipleship was published in the monograph *Jesus-Nachfolge. Woraus lebt der Glaube* (Imitation of Jesus: How Faith Lives).

93. Józef Niewiadomski, "Following Jesus,"

94. "Following Jesus."

95. Summarized by Michael Hardin, "COV&R at the AAR in Philadelphia." See the note on Norbert Lohfink's paper on Deuteronomy at COV&R 1994 in chapter 3.

96. See Hardin, "COV&R at the AAR in Philadelphia."

97. COV&R members and anyone committed to a Girardian perspective on atonement will be especially interested in "Sacrifice and Girardian Mimetic Theory: The End of Sacrifice?" in Daly, *Sacrifice Unveiled*.

98. *Sacrifice Unveiled*, 220.

99. For a report on the event see Nikolaus Wandinger, "Celebrating Raymund Schwager's 70th Birthday."

100. Keukelaere, "Constitution of the First Official French Girard-Association Voted in the French Institute," 5.

101. "Mimesis, Creativity, and Reconciliation," 7.

102. "Transforming Space."

103. "Transforming Space," 82.

104. "Transforming Space," 84.

105. "Transforming Space," 83. Linus with his "sacred" blanket in the Peanuts cartoons, which Ulanov uses to illustrate another point, is a good example of this.

106. "Transforming Space," 85.

107. "Transforming Space," 86.

108. For me, this raises once more the question of the "evil imagination" of which the Bible speaks (Genesis 6:5 and 8:21) and which many sages in the rabbinic tradition counted as good because they held it was part of God's creation, which is "very good." Some of the rabbis held that the evil imagination, the *yetser ha-ra,* results in sexual intercourse, fertility, commercial exchange, and rivalry, all of which are needed for the world to operate. Is this simply an acceptance of the world operating by means of the scapegoat mechanism, or is it an insight into the way things are and should be in God's world? Michael Elias's paper given at the 2009 conference of COV&R in London deals with this subject: "Evil Impulse (*yetzer ha-ra*) and Mimetic Desire."

109. Reineke, "Transforming Space," 89.

110. *I See Satan Fall Like Lightning*, 16. Quoted by Steinmair-Pösel, "Original Sin," 4.

111. Sloterdijk, "Erwachen im Reich der Eifersucht," 250. Quoted by Steinmair-Pösel, "Originial Sin," 6.

112. "Original Sin," 11. The three conclusions are stated on pp. 10–11.

113. Found on p. 189 of *I See Satan Falling.* Quoted by Steinmair-Pösel, "Original Sin," 11.

114. "Love vs. Resentment."

115. Gans, *Signs of Paradox*, 23. Quoted in Bandera, "Love vs. Resentment," 15.

116. *Signs of Paradox*, 119 and "Paradoxes of Love and Resentment," 20–21.

117. "Love vs. Resentment," 22. I will take up Hamerton-Kelly's challenge to the emphasis on loving or positive mimesis in chapter 5.

118. See my review of Swartley's book. In my opinion it is an outstanding resource at many points and different levels for those working in New Testament studies, peacemaking and conflict resolution, and the mimetic theory.

119. My review of Swartley's book, 20.

120. "Letter from the President," 2.

121. Hamerton-Kelly's position on violence and mimesis and Gil Bailie's perception of an Islamic threat to Western culture stand as a challenge to the assumptions driving comparative theological study and dialogue with others traditions. See the discussion in the next chapter.

122. Bartlett, "The Work of James Williams," 6.

123. See also Bartlett, *Virtually Christian*, for a concept of the Christian potential of the Internet and film.

124. Oughourlian, *The Puppet of Desire*, 2.

125. In the year 1960, as I recall, while I was a ministerial student at Perkins School of Theology (Southern Methodist University), I read a book by John Baillie in which he described the relationship with God not as an immediate one in the ordinary sense, but as a "mediated immediacy." That book was *Our Knowledge of God*. I think that Baillie's insight holds also to some extent for personal relationships and everything we call "knowledge." We speak of certain kinds of knowing as "immediate," but I surmise that this kind of primal existential knowing is also in the mode of mediated immediacy. It is a different level and quality of knowing, but it is wrong to assume that it is not mediated.

126. This paragraph and other sections of the book dealing with the mimetic theory and philosophy owe much to private conversations with Stephen Gardner, although his knowledge and insights concerning the interstices of philosophy, politics, and sociology are much greater and more sophisticated than I am able to articulate.

127. *The Elementary Forms of Social Life*, 31–32.

128. From a theological standpoint the relevant concept would be "creation," although "creation" and "redemption" become overlapping terms in many biblical contexts.

Chapter Five. New Outreach and Possibilities, 2007–2010

1. Nikolaus Wandinger, "Network Meeting," 10.
2. I was also consulted and gave my support to the formation of a new organization. I attended the initial meeting in Akron, PA.
3. See "Mission and Vision" on the Theology and Peace website, www.theologyandpeace.org. A related website is that of Preaching Peace at www.preachingpeace.org.
4. "Memento," 3.
5. See Scott Garrels's article "Imitation, Mimetic Theory, and Religious & Cultural Evolution."
6. For other writings and dissertations see the website at www.bezinnungscentrum.nl/links/special_links3/dissertaties.shtml.
7. To see Buruma's abstract go to the website of COV&R, www.uibk.ac.at/theol/cover/, select "Past Events," then select "Past COV&R Conferences," where you will find the 2007 conference in Amsterdam. Buruma's moderate and pragmatic version of faith in "Enlightenment values" is on display in the third chapter of his book *Taming the Gods*, published in 2010.
8. For Palaver's response paper go to "Commentary from Mimetic Theory to Ian Buruma's 'Enlightenment Wars.'"
9. Joel Hodge, "Vulnerability, Imagination, and Christ's Body."
10. Hodge, "Vulnerability, Imagination, and Christ's Body."
11. Beunders, "Fortuyn, Van Gogh, Hirsi Ali," 213.

12. See in this regard the *Catechism of the Catholic Church*, no. 1805: Justice is the cardinal moral virtue "that consists in the constant and firm will to give their due to God and neighbor." According to paragraph 1807, it entails treating all alike, poor or great, without partiality, and judging one's neighbor with righteousness (Leviticus 19:15).

13. Duyndam, "Girard and Levinas, Cain and Abel, and the Face," 246–247. It should be noted that according to Deuteronomy 17:7, it is the actual witnesses of an outlawed deed who are to be the first to cast stones. Whether or not this is the presupposition of Jesus in John 8:7, the basic point about personal responsibility and scapegoating is still valid.

14. Cavanaugh is the author of *Torture and Eucharist*, *Being Consumed*, *Theopolitical Imagination*, and *The Myth of Religious Violence*. His books raise a powerful voice and perspective on religion, violence, and the state. In my view, his work in ecclesiology and Eucharistic theology and that of COV&R's own Robert Daly on the Eucharist and sacrifice complement and supplement each other. See Daly, *Sacrifice Unveiled*.

15. Hodge, "Vulnerability, Imagination, and Christ's Body." It appears that Hodge's critical view of the state claiming the role of savior goes beyond even Thomas Hobbes's concept of the state in *Leviathan*. See the report on papers presented by Paul Dumouchel and Wolfgang Palaver, in chapter 3.

16. From Borgman's "The Weak Presence of Grace."

17. Keukelaere, "Modesty Has Settled upon the Organ of Conviction."

18. See Bailie's article, "The Vine and the Branches Discourse," 143.

19. *NRC Handelsblad*, July 18, 2007.

20. "COV&R 2007 in Amsterdam—My First-Time Impressions," 8.

21. For papers and other information about the 2007 conference go to www.bezinningscentrum.nl/links/special_links3/covr2007.shtml. A postconference page with comments and reflections may be found at www.bezinnungscentrum.nl/teksten/girard/c/covr2007 post conference.htm.

22. Johnston, "COV&R at the AAR/SBL in San Diego 2007," 8.

23. See Nikolaus Wandinger's review of the book.

24. Johnston, "Mimetic Theory and Neuroscience, UCLA, January 2008," 10.

25. "Mimetic Theory and Neuroscience," 9.

26. Thiel received degrees in philosophy and law at Stanford University and is the coauthor, with David Sacks, of *The Diversity Myth: Multiculturalism and the Politics of Intolerance at Stanford*. He is the founder and CEO of Clarium Capital. He was a cofounder of PayPal, which he sold to eBay in 2002, and he sits on the board of directors of FaceBook.

27. Subsequently Lindy Fishburne was appointed to the position of executive director. Hamerton-Kelly retired in May 2010.

28. Imitatio's website is www.imitatio.com. Hamerton-Kelly's report on the meeting may be found at benfold.lunarbreeze.com/~imita0/fileadmin/user_upload/The FoundingForty.pdf.

29. Wiel Eggen, "Workshop at Florence," 12–13.

30. See the Raven website at www.ravenfoundation.org.

31. McKenna, review of *The Wicked Truth*. Suzanne Ross is also the author of *The Wicked Truth About Love*.
32. "COV&R Meeting June 18–22 in Riverside, CA 2008," 8.
33. Keukelaere, "COV&R Meeting . . . in Riverside, CA 2008."
34. Keukelaere, "COV&R Meeting . . . in Riverside, CA 2008," 8.
35. Dupuy, "Detour and Sacrifice." Most of this essay was previously published in French: "Le detour et le sacrifice: Ivan Illich et René Girard," *Esprit*, May 2001, 26–46.
36. See Dumouchel and Dupuy, *L'enfer des choses: René Girard et la logique de l'économie* (The Hell of Things: René Girard and the Logic of Economy).
37. Dupuy, "Detour and Sacrifice," 70.
38. "Detour and Sacrifice," 71. See in chapter 4 the report on Dupuy's remarks at the 2003 conference in Innsbruck.
39. "Detour and Sacrifice," 75. It should be noted, however, that Girard's apocalyptic thinking is rooted in a Christian eschatology that is not tied to a realization of the kingdom of God within the course of history in a this-worldly sense.
40. The description of his position that I present here owes much to the hours of conversation with Hamerton-Kelly in Palo Alto on September 30, 2009. I would like to thank him, Lindy Fishburne, and Imitatio for supporting my travel there to have extended conversations with René Girard and him over a period of four days. This discussion of Hamerton-Kelly's thought was the basis of a plenary session at the 2010 conference at Notre Dame.
41. On mind, brain, and social networks Hamerton-Kelly's thinking has been reinforced and extended through his reading of Nicholas A. Christakis and James H. Fowler, *Connected* and Douglas Hofstadter, *I Am A Strange Loop*. These ways of understanding mind and human being as biosocial are also pertinent to his concept of the Holy Spirit as the Mind of God. Although he did not mention him in our lengthy conversation, Paul Dumouchel's analysis in *Emotions: Essai sur le corps et le social* is very relevant both to Hamerton-Kelly's position and to mimetic theory generally. An essay-length summary of his argument in English titled "Social Emotions" is available at www.mimetic theory.net/bios/dumouchel.html. Dumouchel's thesis is that emotions are fundamentally social because they make us sensitive to each other and enable us to coordinate our relations to one another. They are the matter that social codes and organizations influence but do not construct, and the affective actions stemming from emotions require a relationship with the other.
42. Cesáreo Bandera says, "It is not just one topic among many. In my view, it was at the beginning—and apparently still is today—one of the two fundamental (founding) topics. The other one being the historical function and the Christian meaning of sacrifice" (from an email message of December 3, 2009).
43. Gardner did not have a text of the presentation that he could give me for review, but I have drawn on a number of essays he has written about Rieff, particularly "Charisma and the Case of Philip Rieff" and "The Eros and Ambitions of Psychological Man." The books of Rieff that I have in mind for this report are his two early ones, *Freud: The Mind of the Moralist*, 3rd ed., and *The Triumph of the Therapeutic*, plus two of the posthumous works: *My Life among the Deathworks* and *Charisma*. Stephen Gardner and I have also had several long discussions of Rieff's thought and its relevance to the mimetic theory.
44. *My Life among the Deathworks*, 64.

45. *My Life among the Deathworks*, 66.

46. These last two quotations are from Gardner's "Charisma and the Case of Philipp Rieff."

47. For a video recording of Girard's presentation, go to www.imitatio.org/mimetic-theory-audio-selections/selections-from-covr-conference-2008-html.

48. See Burkert, *Homo Necans* and his contribution to Robert G. Hamerton-Kelly, *Violent Origins:* "The Problem of Ritual Killing"; his comments in the discussions are found throughout the volume.

49. René Girard, *Achever Clausewitz* (Finishing [Off] Clausewitz). The English translation, *Battling to the End,* was published by the Michigan State University Press in 2009.

50. The German edition of Clausewitz's work that the authors used was *Vom Kriege,* published in 1973. The English edition was *On War,* ed. and tr. Michael Howard and Peter Paret, published in 1984.

51. *Battling to the End,* ix.

52. *Battling to the End,* 19.

53. *Battling to the End,* 46.

54. *Battling to the End,* 46.

55. *Battling to the End,* 48.

56. *Battling to the End,* 48.

57. *Battling to the End,* 119.

58. *Battling to the End,* 120.

59. *Battling to the End,* 53, 54.

60. *Battling to the End,* 57.

61. *Battling to the End,* 57.

62. *Battling to the End,* 137. Clausewitz looks to Frederick the Great as a mythical model, but this "ploy was doomed to failure at the outset" (*Battling to the End,* 137).

63. *Battling to the End,* 27–28 and 222 n. 1.

64. *Battling to the End,* 144.

65. Quoted in *Battling to the End,* 121.

66. *Battling to the End,* 122.

67. *Battling to the End,* 162.

68. *Battling to the End,* 169.

69. *Battling to the End,* 171. I question whether the translation of *dérapage* as "blunder" is accurate; "blunder" is a word that appears to trivialize the Holocaust, which is certainly not Girard's intention, as clearly seen in the context. It frequently has the meaning of skidding out of control, as an automobile or bicycle. It thus seems very close to the sense of the term that Girard frequently uses, "rising (escalating) to extremes."

70. *Battling to the End,* 201.

71. *Battling to the End,* 201.

72. *Battling to the End,* 35.

73. *Battling to the End,* 35.

74. *Battling to the End,* 63.

75. *Battling to the End,* 80. See also 79, 125–126, 215.

76. *Battling to the End,* xi.

77. *Battling to the End,* 215.

78. The translation into English, *Battling to the End,* did not come out until late in 2009.

79. Surah 5:30–31. See Palaver, "Abrahamitische Revolution, politische Gewalt und positive Mimesis: Der Islam aus der Sicht der mimetische Theorie" (Abrahamic Revolution, Political Violence, and Positive Mimesis: Islam from the Viewpoint of the Mimetic Theory); on Cain and Abel in Surah 5, p. 50. The translation and numeration of *ayat* (in Western languages we say verses, but in Arabic *ayah* means sign or miracle) is different from Palaver's in the edition of the Quran that I have: *The Holy Qur-an: Text, Translation and Commentary,* by A. Yusuf Ali.

80. Palaver, "Abrahamitische Revolution," 64.

81. Quoted in "Abrahamitische Revolution," 64. My translation.

82. *Battling to the End,* 118: "This [the escalation of violence with more and more victims] is the terrifying future of the world for which Christians carry the responsibility. Christ will have tried to bring humanity into adulthood, but humanity will have refused. I am using the future perfect because there is a deep failure in all this." (*Achever Clausewitz,* 212). The French text has "insane (*affolé*) future of the world."

83. Astell, "Musings from the Executive Secretary," 7.

84. Wandinger, "COV&R Meeting at the AAR in Chicago, November 1, 2008," 9.

85. See also pp. 185–188 of *The Bible, Violence, and the Sacred* for a statement of the thesis of the book.

86. "COV&R Meeting at the AAR," 9.

87. "COV&R Meeting at the AAR," 9.

88. "COV&R Meeting at the AAR," 10.

89. Robert Doran, "MLA Lifetime Achievement Award for René Girard," 7–8.

90. "'Fearful Symmetries," 10.

91. The quotation is part of a message to me from Professor Rowland, January 24, 2010.

92. In *Radical Reform,* 139, Ramadan states that "Islam means entering (giving oneself wholly away to) God's peace."

93. *Radical Reform,* 276.

94. Girard, *I See Satan Fall Like Lightning,* 158.

95. The version of the Quran that I possess, Ali, *The Holy Qur-an,* places this ayah at 5:51.

96. Palaver, "Letter from the President," 6; full comment on Ramadan's lecture: 5–6. I have drawn on Palaver's "Letter from the President" and his unpublished notes, "Tariq Ramadan," as well as Nikolaus Wandinger's report on the conference, "Fearful Symmetries,'" 8–9.

97. I have not had the time to look into an extensive array of sources, but it is quite clear that he has a very ambiguous reputation. I have read Buruma, *Taming the Gods,* and I have sampled various sources on the Internet, including Sandro Magister, "Tariq Ramadan's Two-Faced Islam"; Carool Keister, "Tariq Ramadan fired by Rotterdam City Council"; Allan Nadler, "Tariq Ramadan Gets a Hero's Welcome, and Cold Shoulders, at Religion Scholars' Confab." The "Religion Scholars' Confab" of the title was the American Academy of Religion in November 2009.

98. Nadler, "Tariq Ramadan Gets A Hero's Welcome." But see Buruma, *Taming the Gods,* 120–121. Buruma says, "What makes Ramadan such a tricky figure is the apparent discrepancy between his religious orthodoxy and his neo-Marxist politics" (*Taming the Gods,* 117). He notes however, that "Ramadan's position, however ambiguous, does not make him a terrorist" (*Taming the Gods,* 121).

99. A streaming video of his talk may be found on Bailie's website at cornerstone-forum.org/streaming.aspx.

100. Most COV&R participants would probably agree that there should be a different format from the one arranged for Ramadan. There must be an opportunity to hold real discussion, perhaps debate. Also, the matter of how many outside speakers to invite is a related but distinct issue already mentioned in this history.

101. Alison says that "they are the same protagonism as the creator." He evidently means they are persons or agents sharing the same being as the Creator.

102. *Catechism of the Catholic Church,* subheadings 2357 and 2358.

103. The contributors to the homage volume for Girard were Gil Bailie, Cesáreo Bandera, Anthony Bartlett, Chris Allen Carter, Robert J. Daly, Paul Dumouchel, Jean-Pierre Dupuy, Giuseppe Fornari, Eric Gans, Richard J. Golsan, Sandor Goodhart, Tyler Graham, Robert Hamerton-Kelly, Michael E. Hardin, William A. Johnsen, Jacques-Jude Lépine, Charles Mabee, Andrew J. McKenna, Józef Niewiadomski, Jean-Michel Oughourlian, Wolfgang Palaver, Sonja Pos, Martha Reineke, Michel Serres, Eugene Webb, and James G. Williams.

104. In this section I am following Nikolaus Wandinger's report, "Report from COV&R Activities at the AAR Meeting 2009 in Montreal" - except for a brief word about the Teaching Religion Section, which he was unable to attend, and a more extensive account of the panel discussion of Girard's book, *Achever Clausewitz,* to which I added commentary based on Stephen Gardner's extension of his critique subsequent to the panel event.

105. Wandinger, "Report from COV&R Activities," 8.

106. Gardner, "Deepening Impasse of Modernity" and "René Girard's Apocalyptic Critique of Historical Reason." The works by Aron that Gardner presupposes are *Clausewitz, Philosopher of War* and *The Century of Total War.*

107. Gardner does not deal directly with current U.S. politics, but this clash is happening now in American political life, a phenomenon rooted in religious-cultural polarities.

108. Both quotations from Gardner, "Rene Girard's Apocalyptic Critique of Historical Reason."

109. On the polarity of the archaic and the modern in modern Western culture, cf. the related article of Cesáreo Bandera, "Separating the Human from the Divine." Bandera's thinking about this, which amounts to both a literary theory and cultural critique informed by the mimetic theory, is presented in chapter 2.

110. But note Martha Reineke's comment contradicting Gardner's observation that Girard never speaks of good mimetic desire. See in this chapter, and below, note 116. It is possible, of course, that Girard's view has changed, or perhaps become more ambivalent, in the last decade.

111. As stated in an email message from Martha Reineke, May 5, 2010. The description of the presentations by Reineke and Ross is based on information in an email message from Reineke, April 26, 2010.

112. Email message from Suzanne Ross, May 18, 2010.

113. I have scanned some sources indicating that the earlier White dispossession of Native Americans from their lands, primarily the Potawatami people, is a story similar to other examples of violent dispossession and unjust treaties in the history of European settlement in the New World. Such topics are not the subject of this history except as constant reminders of the truth of the account of cultural origins that stems from the mimetic theory: human civilizations, meaning complex organizations of society, which typically feature concomitant exploitation of technological advances, are universally founded on acts of violence. In archaic culture these founding acts of violence were accepted as sacred deeds. Traces of the ancient sacred are still easily identifiable in the European settlement in America.

114. Here I am thinking of concern for the poor and the unjustly persecuted, the need for hospitals open to all, and the end of witch trials and the beginning of science.

115. Reineke, unpublished response paper presented at COV&R, June 30, 2010. Reineke credits Stephen Gardner for the insight concerning Protestantism in his essay review of *Battling to the End.*

116. However, as Reineke notes, Girard acknowledges the existence of good mimetic desire in the interview with Rebecca Adams, and in *I See Satan* he even calls it "intrinsically good." See Adams' interview of Girard (1993) an excerpt of which is printed in *The Girard Reader,* 62–65 (the relevant page is 65), and Girard, *I See Satan Fall Like Lightning,* 15.

117. Reineke, response paper and email message of July 17, 2010.

118. Email message from Reineke, July 17, 2010. The relevant text by Kristeva is *Strangers to Ourselves.*

119. Although his recent oral and written statements on this subject seemed to say or imply the contrary.

120. When the floor was opened for discussion, Hamerton-Kelly asserted that Girard had little knowledge or interest in the work of Levinas. Whether or not that is the case, it still does not speak to the point that there may be an affinity of the one for the other in their understanding of ethics and history.

121. Or more properly, biblical and anthropological areas. To hear the full responses of Alison and Palaver, which were excellent, go to the website of Chicago Amplified. The Raven Foundation arranged for all the plenary sessions to be recorded.

122. Siebers, "In the Name of Pain."

123. Siebers, "In the Name of Pain." The legal cases mentioned are those pertaining to Ashley X, the "pillow angel" in Seattle; Nicholas Perruche in France; and Terry Schiavo, whose life was terminated by withdrawing food and water for thirteen days.

124. Email message from Siebers, July 21, 2010.

125. Holden Caulfield hears a boy singing Robert Burns's verse; the boy evidently misunderstands a word, singing "catch a body" instead of "kiss a body."

126. See Girard, *The Scapegoat,* chapter 13 and Williams, *The Bible, Violence, and the Sacred,* 219–220. On internalization of rivalry with mediators to the point of wounding oneself as preemptive action, see Girard's essay on anorexia and bulimia in "Eating Disorders and Mimetic Desire."

127. Johnsen, "The Treacherous Years."

128. Johnsen, "The Treacherous Years."

129. Hodge, "The Transcendence of State-Sanctioned Violence and Christian Prayer:."

130. See Cavanaugh, *Theopolitical Imagination* and *The Myth of Religious Violence.*

131. Hodge, "Transcendence."

132. Hodge, "Transcendence."

Chapter Six. "Diversity in Community:" Concluding Perspective

1. The paragraphs addressing the question of a secular mimetic theory are adapted from my comments in the Epistemological Forum of Imitatio.

2. *Battling to the End,* 113.

3. On the "limiting question," see Schubert M. Ogden, *The Reality of God and Other Essays,* 29–37. An important reference for Ogden is Stephen Toulmin, *An Examination of the Place of Reason in Ethics.*

4. Ogden, *The Reality of God,* 40.

5. In emphasizing the great religious traditions I don't mean to exclude various other religious movements and phenomena in the contemporary world. As a matter of fact, the modern nation-state as the primary mediator of secularism may arguably be construed as a "religious" phenomenon that should be set among the forefront of our concerns. But my point is that we cannot ignore those religious traditions that still hold sway over so many of the world's inhabitants.

6. Wolfgang Palaver argues cogently that Islam certainly belongs to the Abrahamic revolution, and that its authenticity in regard to a fundamental recognition of victimage and the necessity of siding with the victim goes back to the prophet Muhammad himself. See his interview for *Die Zeit:* Wolfgang Palaver and Thomas Assheuer. "Blut, Schwerter, Barmherzigkeit. Ist der Islam eine gewalttätige Religion? Ein Gespräch mit dem Theologen Wolfgang Palaver über die Botschaft des Korans" (Blood, Swords, Compassion. Is Islam a Violent Religion? A Conversation with the Theologian Wolfgang Palaver on the Message of the Quran). See also Palaver, "Letter from the President, and an Essay on Islam and the Return to the Archaic."

7. The power and designs of the modern secular nation-state is another great factor in this upheaval, which seems to be leading men and women to violent extremes of behavior.

8. Russell Jacoby, in *The Last Intellectuals,* argues that public intellectuals have disappeared because thinkers have resorted to the universities for the sake of professional and economic security. Thomas Bender, in *Intellect and Public Life,* holds that a thesis like Jacoby's does not do justice to the complex development of historical circumstances, although he does agree that intellectuals are now too comfortably ensconced within the boundaries of the academy.

Appendix 1. A Brief Statement about Scientific Research and the Mimetic Theory

My thanks to Britton Johnston and Pablo Bandera for conversations by email and in person about science and the mimetic theory.

1. Antonello and Gifford, "From Animal to Human: "What Mimetic Theory Brings to the Understanding of Cultural Evolution," featured paper on the Imitatio website, 3. Raymund Schwager's *Banished from Eden* should be acknowledged as a pioneering attempt to bring evolutionary theory and the Christian doctrine of original sin into a critical and fruitful juxtaposition. In it he calls into question the modern dogma of the separation of nature and freedom and draws upon the mimetic theory to sketch a Christian view of human evolution.

2. See in the Bibliography Garrels, "Imitation, Mimetic Theory, and Cultural and Religious Evolution"; Dupuy, *L'enfer des choses* (with Paul Dumouchel), *La panique,* and *Le sacrifice et l'envie;* Dumouchel, *L'enfer des choses* (with Jean-Pierre Dupuy), "Hobbes and Secularization," and *Emotions.*

3. Johnston, "Breaching the Sacred Walls of Illness: A Girardian Model of Forgiveness as Healing," *Journal of Spirituality in Mental Health,* 12: 2, 118—149; "How Girard's Mimetic Theory Can Help Us Understand the Relationship between Science and Religion," *Metanexus Anthropos* Oct. 25, 2004 (go to website of the global spiral, find in articles under Anthropos); Girard, René, "Eating Disorders and Mimetic Desire," *Contagion* 3, 1–20. In an email message to me of August 10, 2010, Johnston has proposed that the mimetic theory has an even deeper and long term effect on scientific experiment in general. He says, "A scientific experiment is like this [in providing a model or mediator to deal with the crowd], but it follows on the discovery of the guilt of the crowd. The rational/scientific crowd has repented of its desire for self-congratulation. Because the gospel has taught science not to trust its own motivations, science has developed a new kind of external mediator that is independent of the old poetics - is a poesis of seeking uninterested sources of external mediation. Physical nature is one of these. Probably the original such external mediator was the God of Israel, whom Israel learned to glorify even at the cost of their own shame. The New Testament represents a genuinely new development, perhaps, in that Jesus is not really an external mediator; instead, he is an internal mediator without rivalry. He achieves this by first surrendering himself to those who would imitate him."

4. See Oughourlian, *The Puppet of Desire* and *The Genesis of Desire.*

5. See in the Bibliography Pablo Bandera, "The Anthropology of Observation (Bandera has a forthcoming monograph on this topic) and "The Physics of a Miracle."

6. Email message from Pablo Bandera, July 13, 2010.

7. See Kumar, *Quantum*, 244; 262; 317; 359–360.
8. Cf. also Williams, *The Bible, Violence, and the Sacred*, 187.
9. See the discussion in the Epistemological Forum of Imitatio.

Appendix 2. Original and Present Constitutions of the Colloquium on Violence and Religion

1. This revised form of the Constitution approved in 1993, and as amended in 1998, is the one in effect.

Appendix 3. Officers and Board Members of COV&R, 1991–2010

1. Not a Board Member: Józef Niewiadomski: Assoc. Editor of Newsletter
2. Not a Board Member: Józef Niewiadomski: Assoc. Editor of Newsletter
3. Not Board Members: Józef Niewiadomski and Dietmar Regensburger, Assoc. Editors of Newsletter
4. Not Board Members: Józef Niewiadomski and Dietmar Regensburger, Associate Editors of Bulletin
5. Not Board Members: Józef Niewiadomski and Dietmar Regensburger, Associate Editors of Bulletin
6. Not Board Members: Józef Niewiadomski and Dietmar Regensburger, Associate Editors of Bulletin

Bibliography

Aron, Raymond. *The Century of Total War,* 1st ed. Garden City, NY: Doubleday, 1954.

———. *Clausewitz, Philosopher of War.* New York: Simon and Schuster, 1986.

Adams, Rebecca. "Loving Mimesis and Girard's 'Scapegoat of the Text': A Creative Reassessment of Mimetic Desire." In *Violence Renounced,* ed. by W. M. Swartley. Telford, PA: Pandora Press, 2000: 277–307.

———. "Violence, Difference, Sacrifice: A Conversation with René Girard." *Religion and Literature* 25, no. 2 (1993): 9–33.

Ali, A. Yusuf. *The Holy Qur-an: Text, Translation and Commentary.* Beirut: Dar al-Arabia, 1968.

Alison, James. "Brokeheart Mountain: Reflections on Monotheism, Idolatry, and the Kingdom." Paper presented at the Annual Conference of COV&R, London, 2009. www.jamesalison.co.uk/texts/eng58.html.

———. *The Joy of Being Wrong: Original Sin through Easter Eyes.* New York: Crossroad, 1998.

Arias, Judith. "Editor's Introduction." *Contagion* 1 (1994): vii–viii.

Arndt, William F., and F. Wilbur Gingrich, eds. *A Greek-English Lexicon of the New Testament and Other Early Christian Literature.* Cambridge: Cambridge University Press, 1957.

Assmann, Hugo, ed. *Götzenbilder und Opfer: René Girard im Gespräch mit der Befreiungstheologie.* Thaur: Druck- und Verlagshaus Thaur, LIT Verlag, 1991.

Astell, Ann W. *Chaucer and the Universe of Learning.* Ithaca, NY: Cornell University Press, 1996.

———. *Eating Beauty: The Eucharist and the Spiritual Arts of the Middle Ages.* Ithaca, NY: Cornell University Press, 2006.

———. *Job, Boethius, and Epic Truth.* Ithaca, NY: Cornell University Press, 1994.

———. "Maternal Compassion in the Thought of René Girard, Emil Fackenheim, and Emmanuel Levinas." *Contagion* 11 (2004): 15–24.

———. "Musings from the Executive Secretary." *Bulletin of COV&R* 33 (October 2008): 7.

———. *Political Allegory in Late Medieval England.* Ithaca, NY: Cornell University Press, 1999.

———. *The Song of Songs in the Middle Ages.* Ithaca, NY: Cornell University Press, 1990.

———. "Symbols of the (Other) Self." Paper presented at the Annual Conference of COV&R, Schönstatt, 2005.

Astell, Ann W., with Bonnie Wheeler, eds. *Joan of Arc and Sacrificial Authorship.* Notre Dame, IN: University of Notre Dame Press, 2003.

Bailie, Gil. "Christian Virtues Gone Mad." Paper presented at the Annual Conference of COV&R, London, 2009. Cornerstone-forum.org/streaming.aspx.

———. "The Vine and the Branches Discourse: The Gospel's Psychological Discourse." *Contagion* 4 (1997): 129–145.

———. *Violence Unveiled: Humanity at the Crossroads.* New York: Crossroad, 1996.

———, Letter to the editor of *NRC Handelsblad,* July 18, 2007.

Baillie, John. *Our Knowledge of God*. New York: Charles Scribner's Sons, 1959.

Bandera, Cesáreo. *The Humble Story of Don Quixote: Reflections on the Birth of the Modern Novel*. Washington, DC: Catholic University of America Press, 2006.

———. *Mímesis conflictiva: Ficción literaria y violencia en Cervantes y Calderón*. Madrid: Editorial Gredos, 1975.

———. *El Poema de Mio Cid: Poesía, historia, mito*. Madrid: Gredos, 1969.

———. *The Sacred Game: The Role of the Sacred in the Genesis of Modern Literary Fiction*. University Park: Pennsylvania State University Press, 1994.

———. "Separating the Human from the Divine." *Contagion* 1 (1994): 73–90.

Bandera, Pablo. "The Anthropology of Observation: The Conceptual Framework for the Understanding of Quantum Theory." Paper presented at the Annual Conference of COV&R, London, 2009.

———. "Love vs. Resentment: The Absence of Positive Mimesis in Generative Anthropology." *Contagion* 14 (2007): 13–26.

———. "The Physics of a Miracle: The Resurrection Body of Jesus from the Standpoint of Quantum Theory." Paper presented at the Annual Conference of COV&R, Notre Dame, 2010.

Bartlett, Anthony. "Abstract of Boston American Academy of Religion COV&R Paper." *Bulletin of COV&R* 18 (April 2000): 2.

———. *Virtually Christian: How Christ Changes Human Meaning and Makes Creation New*. Washington, DC: O Books, 2011.

———. "The Work of James Williams." *Bulletin of COV&R* 21 (September 2002): 6–9.

Bartlett, Anthony, with James G. Williams. "Workshop on Mimetic Theory and Biblical Literature (Chair: James G. Williams)." *Bulletin of COV&R* 7 (October 1994): 8.

Becker, Ernest. *The Birth and Death of Meaning*. Boston: Free Press, 1971.

———. *The Denial of Death*. New York: Free Press, 1973.

———. *Escape from Evil*. Boston: Free Press, 1975.

Bender, Thomas. *Intellect and Public Life*. Baltimore: Johns Hopkins University Press, 1993.

Beunders, Henri. "Fortuyn, Van Gogh, Hirsi Ali: Why the Unholy Trinity Was Driven Out of the Netherlands." *Contagion* 15–16 (2008–2009): 201–219.

Blake, William. *Songs of Innocence and Experience*. Minneapolis: Filiquarian, 2007.

Bland, Byron. "Marching and Rising: The Rituals of Small Differences and Great Violence." *Contagion* 4 (1997): 101–119.

Borgman, Eric. "The Weak Presence of Grace: A Theological Plea for the Return to the Ambivalences of Modernity." Paper presented at the Annual Conference of COV&R, Amsterdam, 2007. www.bezinningscentrum.nl/links/special_links3/abstracts.shtml.

Brueggemann, Walter. "A Shape for Old Testament Theology, II." *Catholic Biblical Quarterly* 47 (1985): 395–415.

Burkert, Walter. *Homo Necans: The Anthropology of Ancient Greek Sacrificial Ritual and Myth*, tr. by Peter Bing. Berkeley: University of California Press, 1983.

———. "The Problem of Ritual Killing." In *Violent Origins: Ritual Killing and Cultural Formation*, ed. by Robert G. Hamerton-Kelly. Stanford, CA: Stanford University Press, 1987.

Buruma, Ian. "Enlightenment Wars." Paper presented at the Annual Conference of COV&R, Amsterdam, 2007. www.bezinningscentrum.nl/links/special_links3/abstracts.shtml.

———. *Murder in Amsterdam: Theo van Gogh and the Limits of Tolerance*. London: Penguin, 2006.

———. *Taming the Gods: Religion and Democracy on Three Continents*. Princeton: Princeton University Press, 2010.

Buruma, Ian, and Avishai Margalit. *Occidentalism: The West in the Eyes of Its Enemies*. London: Penguin, 2004.

Catechism of the Catholic Church. New York: Doubleday, 1997.

Cavanaugh, William T. *Being Consumed: Economics and Christian Desire*. Grand Rapids, MI: Eerdmans, 2008.

———. *The Myth of Religious Violence*. New York: Oxford University Press, 2009.

———. *Theopolitical Imagination*. London: T & T Clark, 2002.

———. *Torture and Eucharist: Theology, Politics, and the Body of Christ*. Oxford: Blackwell, 1998.

Chilton, Bruce. *Abraham's Curse: The Roots of Violence in Judaism, Christianity, and Islam*. New York: Doubleday, 2008.

———. *The Temple of Jesus: His Sacrificial Program within a Cultural History of Sacrifice*. College Station: Pennsylvania State University Press, 1992.

Christakis, Nicholas A., and James H. Fowler. *Connected: The Surprising Power of Our Social Networks and How They Shape Our Lives*. New York, Little, Brown, 2009.

Clausewitz, Carl von. *On War*, ed. and tr. by Michael Howard and Peter Paret. Princeton: Princeton University Press, 1984.

———. *Vom Kriege*. Bonn: Dummler, 1973.

Clooney, Francis X. "Violence and Nonviolence in Hindu Religious Traditions." *Contagion* 9 (2002): 109–139.

Cochrane, Charles Norris. *Christianity and Classical Culture*. New York: Oxford University Press, 1957.

Culbertson, Diana. *God in a World of Violence*. Rocky Ridge, OH: Center for Learning, 2003.

———, ed. *Invisible Light: Poems about God*. New York: Columbia University Press, 2000.

———, "Letter from the President." *Bulletin of COV&R* 21 (September 2002): 2–3

———. *The Poetics of Revelation: Recognition and the Narrative Tradition*. Macon, GA: Mercer University Press, 1989.

———. "Reply to Paul Duff, '"Whoever Is Not with Me Is against Me": Witchcraft Accusations and the *Revelation of John*, '" *Bulletin of COV&R* 12 (March 1997): 11.

———, ed. *Rose Hawthorne Lathrop: Selected Writings*. New York: Paulist Press, 1993.

Daly, Robert. *Christian Sacrifice: The Judeo-Christian Background before Origen*. Washington, DC: Catholic University of America Press, 1978.

———, ed. *The Eucharist in the West: History and Theology*, by Edward J. Kilmartin. Collegeville, MN: Liturgical Press, 1999.

———, ed. "Papers of the COV&R Conference 2000 in Boston: Violence and Institution in Christianity, Judaism, Hinduism, Buddhism, and Islam." *Contagion* 9 (2002).

———. *Sacrifice Unveiled: The True Meaning of Christian Sacrifice*. New York: T & T Clark, 2009.

———. "Violence and Institution in Christianity." *Contagion* 9 (2002): 4–33.

Deacon, Terrence W. *The Symbolic Species: The Co-evolution of Language and the Brain*. New York: Norton, 1997.

Delumeau, Jean. *Sin and Fear: The Emergence of a Western Guilt Culture 13th–18th Centuries*, tr. by Eric Nicholson. New York: St. Martin's Press, 1990.

Delval, Quentin. "COV&R 2007 in Amsterdam—My First-Time Impressions." *Bulletin of COV&R* 31 (October 2007): 7–8.

Depoortere, Frederiek. *Christ in Postmodern Philosophy: Gianni Vattimo, René Girard and Slavoj Žižek*. New York: T & T Clark, 2008.

Derrida, Jacques. "Plato's Pharmacy." In Derrida, *Dissemination*, tr. by Barbara Johnson. Chicago: University of Chicago Press, 1981.

Doran, Robert. "MLA Lifetime Achievement Award for René Girard." *Bulletin of COV&R* 34 (May 2009): 7–8.

Dostoevsky, Fyodor. *Demons*, tr. by Richard Pevear and Larissa Volokhonsky. New York: Knopf, 1994.

——— "The Double," tr. by George Bird. In *Great Short Works of Dostoevsky*. New York: Harper and Row, 1968.

Duff, Paul, "'Whoever Is Not with Me Is against Me': Witchcraft Accusations and the *Revelation of John*, "*Bulletin of COV&R* 12 (March 1997): 11.

Dumouchel, Paul. *Emotions: Essai sur le corps et le social*. Paris: Editions du Seuil, 1995.

———. "Hobbes and Secularization: Christianity and the Political Problem of Religion." *Contagion* 2 (1995): 39–56.

———. "Social Emotions." www.mimetic theory.net/bios/dumouchel.html.

———. *Violence and Truth: On the Work of René Girard*. Stanford, CA: Stanford University Press, 1988.

Dumouchel, Paul, and Jean-Pierre Dupuy. *L'enfer des choses: René Girard et la logique de l'économie*. Paris: Seuil, 1979.

Dupuy, Jean-Pierre. "Detour and Sacrifice: Illich and Girard." In *For René Girard: Essays in Friendship and in Truth*, ed. by Sandor Goodhart, Jørgen Jørgensen, Tom Ryba, and James G. Williams. East Lansing: Michigan State University Press, 2009.

———. "Panic and the Paradoxes of the Social Order." In *Passions in Economy, Politics, and the Media—In Discussion with Christian Theology*, ed. by Wolfgang Palaver and Petra Steinmair-Pösel. Vienna: LIT, 2005.

———. *La panique*. Collection Les Empêcheurs de Penser en Rond, Paris: Laboratoires Delagrange, 1991.

———. *Pour un catastrophisme éclairé*. Paris: Les Editions de Seuil, 2004.

———. *Le Sacrifice et L'Envie: Le libéralisme aux prises avec la justice sociale*. Paris: Calmann-Lévy, 1992.

———. "Totalization and Misrecognition." In *Violence and Truth: On the Work of René Girard*, ed. by Paul Dumouchel. Stanford, CA: Stanford University Press, 1988.

Durkheim, Emile. *Elementary Forms of Social Life*, tr. by Joseph Ward. New York: Macmillan, 1915.

Duyndam, Joachim. "Girard and Levinas, Cain and Abel, and the Face." *Contagion* 15–16 (2008–2009): 237–248.

Eggen, Wiel. "Workshop at Florence." *Bulletin of COV&R* 33 (October 2008): 12–13.

Elias, Michael. "Evil Impulse (*yetzer ha-ra*) and Mimetic Desire." Paper presented at the Annual Conference of COV&R, London, 2009.

Euripides. *The Bacchae*. In *Three Plays of Euripides*, tr. by Paul Roche. New York: Norton, 1974.

Fleming, Chris. *René Girard: Violence and Mimesis*. Cambridge: Polity Press, 2004.

Frankfurter, David. *Evil Incarnate: Rumors of Demonic Conspiracy and Ritual Abuse in History*. Princeton: Princeton University Press, 2006.

Freud, Sigmund. *Standard Edition of the Complete Psychological Works*, tr. and ed. by James Strachey et al., 24 vols. London: Hogarth, 1953–1974.

Gans, Eric. "The Market and Resentment." In *Passions in Economy, Politics, and Media—In Discussion with Christian Theology*, ed. by Wolfgang Palaver and Petra Steinmair-Pösel. Vienna: LIT, 2005.

———. "Paradoxes of Love and Resentment." In *Chronicles of Love and Resentment* 9 (September 9, 1995). www.anthropoetics.ucla.edu/views/VIEWS9/HTM.

———. "Reflections on the Atlanta COV&R Conference." *Bulletin of COV&R* 17 (October 1999): 4.

———. *Signs of Paradox: Irony, Resentment, and Other Mimetic Structures*. Stanford, CA: Stanford University Press, 1997.

Gardner, Stephen L. "Charisma and the Case of Philip Rieff." Paper presented to a conference of the International Society for the Study of European Ideas, Helsinki, 2008.

———. "The Deepening Impasse of Modernity." *Society* 47 (2010): 452–460.

———. "The Eros and Ambitions of Psychological Man." In *The Triumph of the Therapeutic: Uses of Faith after Freud*, by Philip Rieff. Fortieth Anniversary Edition. Wilmington, DE: ISI Books, 2006.

———. "René Girard's Apocalyptic Critique of Historical Reason." *Contagion* 18 (2011): 1–22.

Garrels, Scott, "Imitation, Mimetic Theory, and Religious & Cultural Evolution." *Bulletin of COV&R* 31 (October 2007): 10.

———. "Imitation, Mirror Neurons and Mimetic Desire: Convergence between the Mimetic Theory of René Girard and Empirical Research on Imitation," *Contagion* 12–13 (2006), 47–86.

Girard, Martha, and René Girard. "Memento: Elizabeth Bailie." *Bulletin of COV&R* 30 (May 2007): 3.

Girard, René. "American Opinion of France, 1940–1943." Ph.D. diss., Indiana University, 1950.

———. *Le bouc émissaire*. Paris: Grasset, 1982.

———. *Celui par qui le scandale arrive*. Paris: Desclée de Brouwer, 2001.

———. *Deceit, Desire, and the Novel*. Baltimore and London: Johns Hopkins University Press, 1966.

———. *De la violence à la Divinité*. Paris: Bernard Grasset, 2007.

———. *Dostoievski: Du double à l'unité*. Paris: Plon, 1963.

———. "Eating Disorders and Mimetic Desire." *Contagion* 3 (1996): 1–20.

———. *Les feux de l'envie*, tr. by Bernard Vincent. Paris: Grasset, 1990.

———. *The Girard Reader*, ed. by James G. Williams. New York: Crossroad, 1996.

———. *I See Satan Fall Like Lightning*, tr. by James G. Williams. Maryknoll, NY: Orbis Books, 2001.

———. *Mensonge romantique, vérité romanesque*. Paris: Bernard Grasset, 1961.

———. "Mimetische Theorie und Theologie." In *Vom Fluch und Segen der Sündenböcke*, ed. by Józef Niewiadomski and Wolfgang Palaver. Innsbruck: Kulturverlag, 1995.

———. "Nietzsche versus the Crucified." In *The Girard Reader*, ed. by James G. Williams. New York: Crossroad, 1996.

———. "The Passionate Oxymoron in *Romeo and Juliet*." In *Passions in Economy, Politics, and the Media: In Discussion with Christian Theology*, ed. by Wolfgang Palaver and Petra Steinmair-Pösel. Vienna: LIT, 2005.

———. "Python and His Two Wives: An Exemplary Scapegoat Myth." In *The Girard Reader*, ed. by James G. Williams. New York: Crossroad, 1996.

———. *Resurrection from the Underground: Feodor Dostoevsky*, tr. by James G. Williams. New York: Crossroad, 1997.

———. "Roel Kaptein." *Bulletin of COV&R* 11 (October 1996): 8.

———. *The Scapegoat*. Baltimore: Johns Hopkins University Press, 1986.

———. *A Theater of Envy*. New York: Oxford University Press, 1991.

———. *"To Double Business Bound": Essays on Literature, Mimesis, and Anthropology*. Baltimore: Johns Hopkins University Press, 1978.

———. "A Venda Myth Analyzed." In R. J. Golsan, *René Girard and Myth: An Introduction*. New York: Garland, 1993.

———. "La vie privée à Avignon dans la seconde moitié du XVe siècle." License thesis at l'Ecole des Chartres, 1947.

———. *Violence and the Sacred*. Baltimore: Johns Hopkins University Press, 1977.

———. *La violence et le sacré*. Paris: Editions Bernard Grasset, 1972.

———. *Je vois Satan tomber comme l'éclair*. Paris: Grasset & Fasquelle, 1999.

Girard, René, with Pierpaolo Antonello and João Cezar de Castro Rocha. *Evolution and Conversion: Dialogues on the Origin of Culture*. New York: Continuum International, 2007.

———. *Les origines de la culture*. Paris: Desclé de Brouwer, 2004.

Girard, René, with Benoît Chantre. *Achever Clausewitz: Entretiens avec Benoît Chantre*. Paris: Carnets Nord, 2007.

———. *Battling to the End: Conversations with Benoît Chantre*, tr. by Mary Baker. East Lansing: Michigan State University Press, 2010.

Girard, René, with Jean-Michel Oughourlian and Guy LeFort. *Des choses cachées depuis la fondation du monde*. Paris: Grasset, 1978.

———. *Things Hidden since the Foundation of the World*, tr. by S. Bann and M. Metteer. Stanford, CA: Stanford University Press, 1987.

Goodhart, Sandor. "Letter from the President." *Bulletin of COV&R* 28 (March 2006): 3–4.
———. "Reading the Ram: Abraham, Isaac, and the Text of Sacrifice." *Bulletin of COV&R* 5 (1993): 8–9.
———, ed. *Reading Stephen Sondheim: A Collection of Critical Essays*. New York: Routledge, 1999.
———. *Sacrificing Commentary: Reading the End of Literature*. Baltimore: Johns Hopkins University Press, 1996.
———. "We will cling fast to your Torah. . . ." *Bulletin of COV&R* 19 (November 2000): 14–17.
Goodhart, Sandor, Jørgen Jørgensen, Tom Ryba, and James G. Williams, eds. *For René Girard: Essays in Friendship and in Truth*. East Lansing: Michigan State University Press, 2009.
Grande, Per Bjørnar. "Key Impressions of the Innsbruck Conference." *Bulletin of COV&R* 23 (November 2003): 4–6.
Guggenberger, Wilhelm. "Report on the COV&R Conference, Schönstatt-Koblenz July 2005." *Bulletin of COV&R* 27 (November 2005): 4–5.
Guillaume de Machaut. *Oeuvres*, vol. 1, *Le Jugement du Roi de Navarre*. Paris: Ernest Hoeppfner, 1908.
Hamerton-Kelly, Robert G. "Ethnic Conflict and Historical Identity in South East Europe." In *Visible Violence: Sichtbare und verschleierte Gewalt im Film*, ed. by Gerhard Larcher. Münster: LIT, 1998: 25–40.
———. *The Gospel and the Sacred: Poetics of Violence in Mark*. Minneapolis: Fortress Press, 1994.
———. "Heraclitus Hierophant." Paper presented at the Annual Conference of COV&R, Riverside, CA, June 18–22, 2008.
———, ed. *Politics and Apocalypse*. East Lansing: Michigan State University Press, 2007.
———. "Report from the COV&R Conference held at Stanford, June 27–29, 1996." *Bulletin of COV&R* 11 (October 1996): 10.
———. Report on the founding conference of Imitatio: benfold.lunarbreeze.com/~imita0/fileadmin/user_upload/The FoundingForty.pdf.
———. *Sacred Violence: Paul's Hermeneutic of the Cross*. Minneapolis: Fortress Press, 1992.
———. "Tribute to René Girard on His 70th Birthday." *Contagion* 1 (1994): ix–xii.
———, ed. *Violent Origins: Ritual Killing and Cultural Formation*. Stanford, CA: Stanford University Press, 1987.
Haneke, Michael. "Media and Violence." In *Visible Violence: Sichtbare und verschleierte Gewalt im Film*, ed. by Gerhard Larcher. Münster: LIT, 1998: 93–97.
Hardin, Michael. "COV&R at the AAR in Philadelphia." *Bulletin of COV&R* 28 (March 2006): 6.
Hardin, Michael, and Brad Jersak, eds. *Stricken by God? Nonviolent Identification and the Victory of Christ*. Grand Rapids, MI: Eerdmans, 2007.
Heim, Mark. *Saved from Sacrifice: A Theology of the Cross*. Grand Rapids, MI: Eerdmans, 2006.
Heschel, Abraham. *The Prophets*. New York: Harper and Row, 1962.
Hodge, Joel. "The Transcendence of State-Sanctioned Violence and Christian Prayer: East Timor and the End of the Indonesian Occupation." Paper presented at the annual conference at Annual Conference of COV&R, University of Notre Dame, 2010.
———. "Vulnerability, Imagination, and Christ's Body." Paper presented at the Annual Conference of COV&R, Amsterdam, 2007. www.bezinningscentrum.nl/links/special_links3/abstracts.shtml.
Hofstadter, Douglas. *I Am A Strange Loop*. New York: Basic Books, 2007.
Ives, Christopher. "Dharma and Destruction: Buddhist Institutions and Violence." *Contagion* 9 (2002): 151–174.
Jacoby, Russell. *The Last Intellectuals: American Culture in the Age of Academe*. New York: Basic Books, 1987.
Johnsen, William. "The Treacherous Years: Salinger, Mizruchi, and Girard." Paper presented at the Annual Conference of COV&R, University of Notre Dame, 2010.

———. *Violence and Modernism: Ibsen, Joyce, and Woolf.* Gainesville: University Press of Florida, 2003.

Johnson, Luke Timothy. *The Gospel of Luke.* Collegeville, MN: Liturgical Press, 1991.

Johnston, Britton. "Breaching the Sacred Walls of Illness: A Girardian Model of Forgiveness as Healing." *Journal of Spirituality in Mental Health* 12, no. 2 (2010): 118–149

———. "COV&R at the AAR/SBL in San Diego 2007." *Bulletin of COV&R* 32 (April 2008): 8–9.

———. "How Girard's Mimetic Theory Can Help Us Understand the Relationship between Science and Religion." *Metanexus Anthropos*, October 25, 2004.

———. "Mimetic Theory and Neuroscience, UCLA, January 2008." *Bulletin of COV&R* 32 (April 2008): 10.

Jones, Joe R. *A Grammar of Faith: Systematic Explorations in Christian Life and Doctrine,* 2 vols. Lanham, MD: Rowman & Littlefield, 2002.

Jørgensen, Jørgen. "Report from the Innsbruck Conference: Polarity." *Bulletin of COV&R* 23 (November 2003): 2–4.

Kearnes, Cleo. *The Virgin Mary, Monotheism, and Scripture.* Cambridge: Cambridge University Press, 2008.

Kersten, Carool. "Tariq Ramadan Fired by Rotterdam City Council." http://caroolkersten.blogspot.com.

Keukelaere, Simon de. "Constitution of the First Official French Girard-Association Voted in the French Institute." *Bulletin of COV&R* 28 (March 2006): 5.

———. "COV&R Meeting June 18–24 in Riverside, CA 2008." *Bulletin of COV&R* 33 (October 2008): 8–10.

———. "Modesty Has Settled upon the Organ of Conviction." Paper presented at the Annual Conference of COV&R, Amsterdam, 2007. www.bezinningscentrum.nl/teksten/girard//c/c2007_Keukelaere_Simon_post_conference1.htm.

Keynes, J. M. *The General Theory of Employment, Interest and Money.* London: Macmillan, 1936.

Kirk-Duggan, Cheryl A., "What's Violence Got to Do with It?: Inflamers, and the Lizzie Bordens of Ancient Israel: Women Who Slay and/or Cause Wrongful Deaths," *Bulletin of COV&R* 12 (March 1997): 11–12.

Kirwan, Michael. *Discovering Girard.* London: Darton, Longman and Todd, 2004.

———. *Girard and Theology.* New York: T & T Clark, 2009.

Kristeva, Julia. *Strangers to Ourselves*, tr. by Leon S. Roudiez. New York: Columbia University Press, 1994.

Krondorfer, Björn. "Response to James G. Williams: Re-mythologizing Scriptural Authority: On Reading 'Sacrifice and the Beginning of Kingship.'" *Semeia* 67 (1994): 93–107.

Kumar, Manjit. *Quantum: Einstein, Bohr, and the Great Debate about the Nature of Reality.* New York: Norton, 2008.

Kuntzmann, Raymond. *Le symbolisme des jumeaux au Proche Orient ancien.* Paris: Beauchesne Editeur, 1983.

Larcher, Gerhard. "Report from the COV&R Conference held at Graz, June 23–27, 1997." *Bulletin of COV&R* 13 (October 1997): 6–7.

———, ed. *Visible Violence: Sichtbare und verschleierte Gewalt im Film.* Münster: LIT, 1998.

Lefebure, Leo D. "Buddhism and Mimetic Theory: A Response to Christopher Ives." *Contagion* 9 (2002): 175–184.

Lépine, Jacques-Jude. "Workshop on Mimetic Theory and Literature (Sandor Goodhart & Jacques-Jude Lépine, co-chairs)." *Bulletin of COV&R* 7 (October 1994): 8.

Lonergan, Bernard. *Insight: A Study of Human Understanding.* Toronto: University of Toronto Press, 1957.

———. *Method in Theology.* New York: Herder and Herder, 1972.

Mabee, Charles. *Reading Sacred Texts through American Eyes: Biblical Interpretation as Cultural Critique.* Macon, GA: Mercer University Press, 1991.

———. *Reimagining America*. Macon, GA: Mercer University Press, 1985.

Magister, Sandro. "Tariq Ramadan's Two-Faced Islam." www.chiesa.espresso.repubblica.it.

Martinez, Marie-Louise. "For a Non-Violent Accord: Educating the Person." *Contagion* 6 (1999): 55–76.

McClymond, Kathryn. *Beyond Sacred Violence: A Comparative Study of Sacrifice*. Baltimore: Johns Hopkins University Press, 2008.

McKenna, Andrew. Review of *The Wicked Truth: When Good People Do Bad Things*. *Bulletin of COV&R* 32 (April 2008): 18–19.

———. *Violence and Difference*. Urbana: University of Illinois Press, 1992.

———. "Workshop on the Mimetic Model and Psychotherapy (Chair: Roel Kaptein)." *Bulletin of COV&R* 7 (October 1994): 7.

Milbank, John. *Theology and Social Theory: Beyond Secular Reason*. Oxford: Blackwell, 1990.

Mishler, William, "Report from the Antwerp Meeting," *Bulletin of COV&R* 20 (April 2002), 5–7.

———. "The Tragic Instability of the Akedah (Binding of Isaac) in Ibsen's *Brand, Bulletin of COV&R* 12 (March 1997), 12.

Mishnah Aboth (Sayings of the Fathers). In *The Mishnah*, tr. by Herbert Danby. Vol. 1. London: Oxford University Press, 1938.

Nadler, Allan. "Tariq Ramadan Gets A Hero's Welcome, and Cold Shoulders, at Religion Scholars' Confab." www.forward.com.

Niewiadomski, Józef. "Extra Media Nulla Salus?" In *Passions in Economy, Politics, and the Media—In Discussion with Christian Theology*, ed. by Wolfgang Palaver and Petra Steinmair-Pösel. Vienna: LIT, 2005: 489–508.

———. "Following Jesus: Dietrich Bohoeffer and Raymund Schwager's Theology of 'Imitatio Christi.'" Paper presented at the Annual Conference of COV&R, Schönstatt, 2005.

———. *Herbergsuche: Auf dem Weg zu einer christlichen Identität in der modernen Kultur*. Münster: LIT-Verlag, 1999.

Niewiadomski, Józef, and Wolfgang Palaver, eds. *Dramatische Erlösungslehre: Ein Symposion*. Innsbruck: Tyrolia-Verlag, 1992.

———, eds. *Vom Fluch und Segen der Sündenböcke*. Innsbruck: Kulturverlag, 1995.

Niewiadomski, Józef, with M. Scharer. *Faszinierendes Geheimnis: Neue Zugänge zur Eucharistie in Familie, Schule und Gemeinde*. Mainz: Matthias-Grünwald-Verlag, 1999.

Nowak, Susan. "The Girardian Theory and Feminism: Critique and Appropriation." *Contagion* 1 (1994): 19–29.

Ogden, Schubert M. *The Reality of God and Other Essays*. New York: Harper, 1966.

Ong, Walter. *Fighting for Life*. Ithaca, NY: Cornell University Press, 1981.

O'Regan, Cyril. *Theology in the Spaces of Apocalyptic*. Milwaukee: Marquette University Press, 2009.

Oughourlian, Jean-Michel. *Un mime nommé désir: Hystérie, transe, possession, adorcisme*. Paris: Grasset et Fasquelle, 1982.

———. *The Puppet of Desire: The Psychology of Hysteria, Possession, and Hypnosis*, tr. by Eugene Webb. Stanford, CA: Stanford University Press, 1991.

Palaver, Wolfgang. "Abrahamitische Revolution, politische Gewalt und positive Mimesis: Der Islam aus der Sicht der mimetische Theorie." In W. Guggenberger and W. Palaver, *Wettstreit um das Gute. Annäherungen an den Islam aus der Sicht der mimetischen Theorie*. Münster: LIT Verlag, 2009.

———. "Collective Security in Europe and Austrian Neutrality: An Ethical Reflection from the Point of View of Catholic Social Teaching." In *European Collective Security: The Policy of Neutrality*. Brussels: Pax Christi International, 1992.

———. "A Commentary from Mimetic Theory to Ian Buruma's 'Enlightenment Wars.'" Paper presented at the Annual Conference of COV&R, Amsterdam, 2007. www.bezinningscentrum.nl/links/special_links3/abstracts.shtml.

———. "Envy or Emulation." In *Passions in Economy, Politics, and the Media—In Discussion with Christian Theology*, ed. by Wolfgang Palaver and Petra Steinmair-Pösel. Vienna: LIT, 2005.

———. "Hobbes and the katechon: The Secularization of Sacrificial Christianity." *Contagion* 2 (1995): 57–74.

———. "Letter from the President." *Bulletin of COV&R* 35 (October 2009): 5–7.

———. "Letter from the President, and an Essay on Islam and the Return to the Archaic." *Bulletin of COV&R* 37 (October 2010): 5–10.

———. *Die mythischen Quellen des Politischen*. Stuttgart: Kohlhammer, 1998.

———. *Politik und Religion bei Thomas Hobbes. Eine Kritik aus der Sicht der Theorie René Girards*. Innsbruck: Tyrolia-Verlag, 1991.

———. *René Girards mimetische Theorie*. Münster: LIT Verlag, 2003.

———. "Tariq Ramadan: 'Islam, Justice, Penal Code and Mercy.'" Presentation notes for the Annual Conference of COV&R, London, 2009.

Palaver, Wolfgang, and Thomas Assheuer. "Blut, Schwerter, Barmherzigkeit. Ist der Islam eine gewalttätige Religion? Ein Gespräch mit dem Theologen Wolfgang Palaver über die Botschaft des Korans." *Die Zeit*, October 14, 2010, 64.

Palaver, Wolfgang and Petra Steinmair-Pösel, eds. *Passions in Economy, Politics, and the Media—In Discussion with Christian Theology*. Vienna: LIT Verlag, 2005.

Popper, Karl. *Conjectures and Refutations*. London: Routledge, 1963.

Ramadan, Tariq. *Radical Reform: Islamic Ethics and Liberation*. Oxford: Oxford University Press, 2009.

Reineke, Martha. *Sacrificed Lives: Kristeva on Women and Violence*. Bloomington: Indiana University Press, 1997.

———. "Transforming Space: Creativity, Destruction, and Mimesis in Winnicott and Girard." *Contagion* 14 (2007).

Ricoeur, Paul. "Religion and Symbolic Violence." *Contagion* 6 (1999): 1–11.

Rieff, Philip. *Charisma: The Gift of Grace and How It Has Been Taken Away from Us*. New York: Pantheon, 2007.

———. *Freud: The Mind of the Moralist*, 3rd. ed. Chicago: University of Chicago Press, 1979.

———. *My Life among the Deathworks*, vol. 1 of *Sacred Order*, general editor Kenneth S. Piver. Charlottesville: University of Virginia Press, 2006.

———. *The Triumph of the Therapeutic: Uses of Faith after Freud*. Fortieth Anniversary Edition. Wilmington, DE: ISI Books, 2006.

Ross, Suzanne. *The Wicked Truth: When Good People Do Bad Things*. Glenview, IL: Raven Foundation, 2007.

———. *The Wicked Truth about Love*. Glenview, IL: Doers, 2009.

Schiemann, Gregor. *Natur, Technik, Geist*. New York: Gruyter, 2005.

———. "Nanotechnology and Nature: Two Criteria for Defining Their Relationship." In *HYLE* 11, no. 1 (2005): 77–96. www.hyle.org/journal/issues/11–1/schiemann.htm.

Schwager, Raymund. *Banished from Eden: Original Sin and Evolutionary Theory in the Drama of Salvation*, tr. by James G. Williams. Leominster: Gracewing, 2006.

———. *Brauchen wir einen Sündenbock?* Munich: Koesel-Verlag, 1978.

———. *Dem Netz des Jägers entronnen—Das Jesusdrama nacherzählt*. Munich: Koesel-Verlag, 1991.

———. *Erbsünde und Heilsdrama. Im Kontext von Evolution, Gentechnologie und Apokalyptik*. Münster: LIT Verlag, 2004.

———. *Für Gerechtigkeit and Frieden. Der Glaube als Antwort auf die Anliegen der Gegenwart*. Innsbruck: Tyrolia Verlag, 1986.

———. *Jesus im Heilsdrama. Entwurf einer biblischen Erlösungs Lehre*. Innsbruck: Tyrolia Verlag, 1990.

———. *Jesus in the Drama of Salvation: Toward a Biblical Doctrine of Redemption*, tr. by James G. Williams and Paul Haddon. New York: Crossroad, 1999.

———. *Jesus of Nazareth: How He Understood His Life*, tr. by James G. Williams. New York: Crossroad, 1998.
———. *Jesus-Nachfolge. Woraus lebt der Glaube*. Basel: Herder, 1973.
———. *Must There Be Scapegoats? Violence and Redemption in the Bible*. New York: Harper and Row, 1987.
———. Review of Girard, *La violence et le sacré*. *Orientierung* 38:4 (1974): 41–44.
———. "September 11, 2001 and a Theology of the Signs of the Times."
———. *Der wunderbare Tausch: Zur Geschichte und Deutung der Erlösungslehre*. Munich, 1986.
Serres, Michel. "Discours Prononcé dans la Séance Publique." Talk at reception of René Girard into the French Academy. www.academie-francaise.fr/immortels/discours_reponses/serres_2005.html.
———. "EGO CREDO." *Contagion* 12–13 (2006): 1–12.
———. "One God or a Trinity?" *Contagion* 1 (1994): 1–17.
———. "Receiving René Girard into l'Académie Francaise." In *For René Girard: Essays in Friendship and in Truth*, ed. by Sandor Goodhart, Jørgen Jørgensen, Tom Ryba, and James G. Williams. East Lansing: Michigan State University Press, 2009.
Siebers, Tobin. *Disability Aesthetics*. Ann Arbor: University of Michigan Press, 2010.
———. *Disability Theory*. Ann Arbor: University of Michigan Press, 2008.
———. *The Ethics of Criticism*. Ithaca, NY: Cornell University Press, 1988.
———. "In the Name of Pain." Paper presented at the Annual Conference of COV&R, University of Notre Dame, 2010.
Simonse, Simon. "Kings and Gods as Ecological Agents: From Reciprocity to Unilateralism in the Management of Natural Resources." *Contagion* 12–13 (2006): 31–46.
———. *Kings of Disaster*. Leiden: Brill Academic, 1992.
Sloterdijk, Peter. "Erwachen im Reich der Eifersucht: Notiz zu René Girards anthropologischer Sendung." Epilogue to Girard's *Ich sah den Satan vom Himmel fallen wie einen Blitz: Ene kritische Apologie des Christentums*. Munich: Carl Hanser Verlag, 2002.
Smith, Thee. "Advisory Board Self-Review." *Bulletin of COV&R* 11 (October 1996): 2–3.
———. *Conjuring Culture: Biblical Formations of Black America*. New York: Oxford University Press, 1994.
———. "Report from the Annual Meeting of COV&R." *Bulletin of COV&R* 17 (October 1999): 3.
———. "Report on 'Violence Conversion: Towards a Theory and Practice of Benign Force.'" *Bulletin of COV&R* 10 (March 1996): 8.
Smith, Thee, ed. with Mark Wallace. *Curing Violence*. Sonoma, CA: Polebridge Press, 1994.
Sophocles. *The Oedipus Cycle*, tr. by D. Fitts and R. Fitzgerald. New York: Harcourt, Brace & World, 1949.
Stein, Edith. *Studie über Johannes a Cruce: Kreuzeswissenschaft*. Freiburg: Herder, 1983.
Steinmair-Pösel, Petra. "Economy and Mimetic Theory." In *Passions in Economy, Politics, and the Media—In Discussion with Christian Theology*, ed. by Wolfgang Palaver and Petra Steinmair-Pösel. Vienna: LIT, 2005.
———. "Key Impressions of the COV&R 2004 Conference in New Mexico." *Bulletin of COV&R* 24–25 (November 2004): 2–3.
———. "Original Sin, Grace, and Positive Mimesis." *Contagion* 14 (2007): 1–12.
Swartley, Willard M.. *Covenant of Peace: The Missing Peace in New Testament Theology and Ethics*. Grand Rapids, MI: Eerdmans, 2006.
———, ed. *Violence Renounced*. Telford, PA: Pandora Press, 2000.
Taylor, Charles. *A Secular Age*. Cambridge, MA: Harvard University Press, 2007.
Thiel, Peter, and David Sacks. *The Diversity Myth: "Multiculturalism" and the Politics of Intolerance at Stanford*. Oakland, CA: Independent Institute, 1996.

Tillich, Paul. *Systematic Theology,* vol. 2. Chicago: University of Chicago Press, 1957.
Toulmin, Stephen. *An Examination of the Place of Reason in Ethics*. Cambridge: Cambridge University Press, 1950.
Ulanov, Ann Bedford. *Finding Space: Winnicott, God, and Psychic Reality*. Louisville, KY: Westminster John Knox Press, 2001.
Vanheeswijk, Guido. "The Place of René Girard in Contemporary Philosophy." *Contagion* 10 (2003): 95–110.
Vattimo, Gianni. *Belief*, tr. by Luca D'Isanto and David Webb. Stanford, CA: Stanford University Press, 1999.
———. *Credere di credere*. Milan: Garzanti Editore, 1996.
Wallace, Mark and Theophus Smith, eds. *Curing Violence*. Sonoma, CA: Polebridge Press, 1994.
Wandinger, Nikolaus. "Koblenz: Site of the COV&R Conference, July 6–10, 2005." *Bulletin of COV&R* 26 (April 2005): 1–2.
———. "Celebrating Raymund Schwager's 70th Birthday." *Bulletin of COV&R* 28 (March 2006): 6–8.
———. "COV&R Meeting at the AAR in Chicago, November 1, 2008." *Bulletin of COV&R* 34 (May 2009): 9–10.
———. "'Fearful Symmetries': Report from the COV&R Conference in London." *Bulletin of COV&R* 35 (October 2009): 8–11.
———. "'Mimesis, Creativity and Reconciliation': Report on the 2006 COV&R Meeting in Ottawa." *Bulletin of COV&R* 29 (October 2006): 6–8.
———. "Network Meeting: Lonergan-Dramatic Theology in Innsbruck." *Bulletin of COV&R* 30 (May 2007): 10.
———. "Report from COV&R Activities at the AAR Meeting 2009 in Montreal." *Bulletin of COV&R* 36 (April 2010): 7–9.
———. Review of Michael Hardin and Brad Jersak, eds., *Stricken by God? Bulletin of COV&R* 32 (April 2008): 16–18.
Webb, Eugene. *Philosophers of Consciousness*. Seattle: University of Washington Press, 1988.
Williams, James G. *The Bible, Violence, and the Sacred: Liberation from the Myth of Sanctioned Violence*. San Francisco: Harper San Francisco, 1991.
———. *Gospel Against Parable: Mark's Language of Mystery*. Sheffield: Almond Press, 1985.
———. "René Girard without the Cross? Religion and Mimetic Theory." *Anthropoetics* 2, no. 1 (1996). http://www.anthropoetics.ucla.edu/ap0201/girardw.htm.
———, "Reply to Paul Duff, '"Whoever Is Not with Me Is against Me": Witchcraft Accusations and the *Revelation of John*,'" *Bulletin of COV&R* 12 (March 1997): 11.
———. "Report from the COV&R Meeting in San Francisco, November 22, 1997." *Bulletin of COV&R* 14 (March 1998): 5.
———. Review of Anthony Bartlett, *Virtually Christian*. *Bulletin of COV&R* 38 (May 2011): 12–17.
———. Review of Willard M. Swartley, *Covenant of Peace*. *Bulletin of COV&R* 29 (October 2006): 18–20.
———. "Sacrifice and the Beginning of Kingship." *Semeia* 67 (1994): 73–92.
———. "Sites and Scenes of Sacrifice: James Williams' Reflections on Purdue." *Bulletin of COV&R* 21 (September 2002): 3–5.
———. *Those Who Ponder Proverbs: Aphoristic Thinking and Biblical Literature*. Sheffield: Almond Press, 1981.
———. *Women Recounted: Narrative Thinking and the God of Israel*. Sheffield: Almond Press, 1982.
Williams, James G., with Anthony Bartlett. "Workshop on Mimetic Theory and Biblical Literature (Chair: James G. Williams)." *Bulletin of COV&R* 7 (October 1994): 8.
Wink, Walter. *Engaging the Powers*. Minneapolis: Fortress Press, 1992.

Index

Karin Peter

Apokalyptische Schrifttexte: Gewalt schürend oder transformierend?

Ein Beitrag zu einer dramatisch-kritischen Lesart der Offenbarung des Johannes

Sind es nicht die von – gerade den monotheistischen – Religionen als verbindlich betrachteten Hl. Schriften, die Gewalt legitimieren und schüren? Und apokalyptische Schriften dabei im Besonderen?/absatz Dieser gesellschaftlich durchaus propagierte Vorwurf wird in dieser Studie aufgegriffen. Es erfolgt eine nähere Auseinandersetzung mit der Offenbarung des Johannes, dem einzigen Buch des Neuen Testaments, das im Umkreis der Apokalyptik angesiedelt wird.

In der Perspektive Dramatischer Hermeneutik beschreiben apokalyptische Schrifttexte und deren vermeintliche Gewaltpassagen – auch die Offenbarung des Johannes – nicht Gottes Gewalttätigkeit, sondern legen die Konsequenzen der Gewalttaten von Menschen offen. Innerhalb der Offenbarung des Johannes entpuppt sich die Figur des Lammes als entscheidende Christusfigur und Leseschlüssel für das letzte Buch der Bibel.

Bd. 29, 2011, 528 S., 49,90 €, br., ISBN 978-3-643-50269-8

LIT Verlag Berlin – Münster – Wien – Zürich – London

Auslieferung Deutschland / Österreich / Schweiz: siehe Impressumsseite

Hüseyin I. Cicek

Martyrium zwischen Gewalt und Gewaltfreiheit

Eine Kriteriologie im Blick auf Christentum, Islam und Politik

Die Diskussionen über das Martyrium nehmen kontinuierlich zu. Dies hängt natürlich auch damit zusammen, dass sich radikale muslimische Gruppierungen durch ihren gewaltsamen Tod selbst den Status des Märtyrers verleihen. Sowohl im christlichen als auch im islamischen Sprachgebrauch wird das Martyrium inflationär verwendet. Das vorliegende Buch stellt sich die Aufgabe, die unterschiedlichen Kriteriologien der Martyriumsauffassung in Christentum, Islam und Politik herauszuarbeiten und in weiterer Folge Analogien und Differenzen aufzuzeigen.

Bd. 31, 2011, 224 S., 19,90 €, br., ISBN 978-3-643-50318-3

LIT Verlag Berlin – Münster – Wien – Zürich – London

Auslieferung Deutschland / Österreich / Schweiz: siehe Impressumsseite